A·N·N·U·A·L E·D·I·T·I·O·N·S

Criminal Justice

Twenty-Third Edition

99/00

EDITOR

Joseph L. Victor
Mercy College, Dobbs Ferry

Joseph L. Victor is professor and chairman of the Department of Law, Criminal Justice, and Safety Administration at Mercy College. Professor Victor has extensive field experience in criminal justice agencies, counseling, and administering human service programs. He earned his B.A. and M.A. at Seton Hall University, and his Doctorate of Education at Fairleigh Dickinson University.

D1278030

Dushkin/McGraw-Hill
Sluice Dock, Guilford, Connecticut 06437

Visit us on the Internet
http://www.dushkin.com/annualeditions/

Credits

1. Crime and Justice in America
Facing overview—Dushkin/McGraw-Hill photo.
2. Victimology
Facing overview—Dushkin/McGraw-Hill photo by Pamela Carley.
3. The Police
Facing overview—Photograph © Daemmrich/Stock Boston.
4. Judicial System
Facing overview—EPA/Documerica photo.
5. Juvenile Justice
Facing overview—© 1999 by Cleo Freelance Photography.
6. Punishment and Corrections
Facing overview—Criminal Justice Publications, New York. 181–185—Photos by Alex Von Kleydorff.

Copyright

Cataloging in Publication Data
Main entry under title: Annual Editions: Criminal justice. 1999/2000.
    1. Criminal Justice, Administration of—United States—Periodicals. I. Victor, Joseph L., *comp.* II. Title: Criminal justice.
HV 8138.A67   364.973.05   77–640116
ISBN 0–07–033007–7   ISSN 0272–3816

Twenty-Third Edition

Cover image © 1999 PhotoDisc, Inc.

Printed in the United States of America   1234567890BAHBAH5432109   Printed on Recycled Paper iii

To the Reader

In publishing ANNUAL EDITIONS we recognize the enormous role played by the magazines, newspapers, and journals of the public press in providing current, first-rate educational information in a broad spectrum of interest areas. Many of these articles are appropriate for students, researchers, and professionals seeking accurate, current material to help bridge the gap between principles and theories and the real world. These articles, however, become more useful for study when those of lasting value are carefully collected, organized, indexed, and reproduced in a low-cost format, which provides easy and permanent access when the material is needed. That is the role played by ANNUAL EDITIONS.

New to ANNUAL EDITIONS is the inclusion of related World Wide Web sites. These sites have been selected by our editorial staff to represent some of the best resources found on the World Wide Web today. Through our carefully developed topic guide, we have linked these Web resources to the articles covered in this ANNUAL EDITIONS reader. We think that you will find this volume useful, and we hope that you will take a moment to visit us on the Web at *http://www.dushkin.com* to tell us what you think.

During the 1970s, criminal justice emerged as an appealing, vital, and unique academic discipline. It emphasizes the professional development of students who plan careers in the field and attracts those who want to know more about a complex social problem and how this country deals with it. Criminal justice incorporates a vast range of knowledge from a number of specialties, including law, history, and the behavioral and social sciences. Each specialty contributes to our fuller understanding of criminal behavior and of society's attitudes toward deviance.

In view of the fact that the criminal justice system is in a constant state of flux, and because the study of criminal justice covers such a broad spectrum, today's students must be aware of a variety of subjects and topics. Standard textbooks and traditional anthologies cannot keep pace with the changes as quickly as they occur. In fact, many such sources are already out of date the day they are published. *Annual Editions: Criminal Justice 99/00* strives to maintain currency in matters of concern by providing up-to-date commentaries, articles, reports, and statistics from the most recent literature in the criminal justice field.

This volume contains units concerning crime and justice in America, victimology, the police, the judicial system, juvenile justice, and punishment and corrections. The articles in these units were selected because they are informative as well as provocative. The selections are timely and useful in their treatment of ethics, punishment, juveniles, courts, and other related topics.

Included in this volume are a number of features designed to be useful to students, researchers, and professionals in the criminal justice field. These include a *topic guide* for locating articles on specific subjects; the *table of contents abstracts*, which summarize each article and feature key concepts in bold italics; and a comprehensive section on *crime statistics*, a *glossary*, and an *index*. In addition, each unit is preceded by an *overview* that provides a background for informed reading of the articles, emphasizes critical issues, and presents challenge questions.

This edition also includes *World Wide Web* sites that can be used to further explore the topics. These sites are cross-referenced by number in the topic guide.

We would like to know what you think of the selections contained in this edition. Please fill out the postage-paid *article rating form* on the last page and let us know your opinions. We change or retain many of the articles based on the comments we receive from you, the reader. Help us to improve this anthology—annually.

Joseph L. Victor
Editor

Contents

To the Reader iv
Charts and Graphs 1
Topic Guide 2
◎ Selected World Wide Web Sites 4

Overview 6

UNIT 1

Crime and Justice in America

Six selections focus on the overall structure of the criminal justice system in the United States. The current scope of crime in America is reviewed, and topics such as criminal behavior, race issues, and policing practices are discussed.

1. **What Is the Sequence of Events in the Criminal Justice System?** *Report to the Nation on Crime and Justice, Bureau of Justice Statistics,* January 1998. 8
   This report reveals that the response to ***crime*** is a complex process, involving citizens as well as many agencies, levels, and branches of government.

2. **Looking Backward to Look Forward: The 1967 Crime Commission Report in Retrospect,** Mark H. Moore, *National Institute of Justice Journal,* December 1997. 14
   This article is an abridgement of an address that the author presented at the symposium on the 30th anniversary of the ***President's Commission on Law Enforcement and Administration of Justice.*** It presents a synthesis of symposium proceedings.

3. **A Thinker Attuned to Doing: James Q. Wilson Has Insights, Like Those on Cutting Crime, That Tend to Prove Out,** Richard Bernstein, *New York Times,* August 22, 1998. 19
   Insight is offered into what makes ***James Q. Wilson*** "tick." Beginning with his ***"broken window theory,"*** dating back to 1982, Wilson has frequently written on crime prevention. He has been given credit for an important concept in the much-publicized reduction of crime in American cities.

4. **African American Males in the Criminal Justice System,** Jerome G. Miller, *Phi Delta Kappan,* June 1997. 22
   Many are aware of the fact that ***African American males*** are disproportionately involved in the criminal justice system. Jerome Miller contends that this phenomenon can be attributed to the system's attempt to criminalize a race. He presents to the reader unstated assumptions that, he says, underlie policies and practices of the ***criminal justice system.***

5. **Is the U.S. Morally in Trouble?** George Roche, *USA Today Magazine (Society for the Advancement of Education),* January 1997. 31
   According to this report by George Roche, ***America in the 1990s*** is suffering from loss of values, truth, moral literacy, trust, empathy, independence, confidence, family, and faith. However, for more than 200 years, we have found ways of overcoming adversity and succeeding against all odds.

6. **Why America's Murder Rate Is So High,** Fox Butterfield, *New York Times,* July 26, 1998. 34
   The high ***murder rate*** in the South is a key factor behind America's disproportionately high homicide rate compared with other democratic, industrialized nations.

The concepts in bold italics are developed in the article. For further expansion please refer to the Topic Guide, the Glossary, and the Index.

UNIT 2

Victimology

Four articles discuss the impact of crime on the victim. Topics include the rights of crime victims and the consequences of family violence.

Overview   **38**

7. Victimization and the Victim Industry, Joel Best, **40**
Society, *May/June* 1997.
During the 1960s, Americans became sensitized to victims and victimization; by the 1970s, there was a widespread *ideology of victimization.* As this ideology gained acceptance in key institutions, it created a *victim industry* that now supports the identification of large numbers of victims.

8. Researchers Unravel the Motives of Stalkers, Jane **47**
E. Brody, *New York Times,* August 25, 1998.
Citing studies that examined the psychology of *stalking.* Jane Brody found that the underlying problems of stalkers run the gamut of psychiatric and personality disorders.

9. Battered Women Face Pit Bulls and Cobras, Jane **50**
E. Brody, *New York Times,* March 17, 1998.
After a decade of research, two psychology professors have found that abusive men tend to fall into one of two categories, *"cobras"* or *"pit bulls,"* each with distinct characteristics.

10. Child Victims: In Search of Opportunities for **53**
Breaking the Cycle of Violence, Cathy Spatz Widom, *National Institute of Justice Reports,* November 1997.
The three goals of this in-depth report are to describe how *childhood victimization* and violent criminal behavior are related, to illustrate promising strategies and opportunities for intervention, and to suggest some important principles of intervention prior to formulating or proposing new policy.

UNIT 3

The Police

Six selections examine the role of the police officer. Some of the topics discussed include the stress of police work, multicultural changes, and ethical policing.

Overview   **64**

11. Disrespect as Catalyst for Brutality, Deborah Sontag **66**
and Dan Barry, *New York Times,* November 19, 1997.
This article maintains that many *police officers* on the streets of New York City see disrespect as a threat, not just to their job performance but sometimes to their lives.

12. Advocacy and Law Enforcement: Partners **71**
against Domestic Violence, Marie P. Defina and Leonard Wetherbee, *FBI Law Enforcement Bulletin,* October 1997.
Taking advantage of the expertise and insight of both *civilian domestic violence counselors* and police personnel, two Massachusetts communities forge a partnership to fight *family violence.*

The concepts in bold italics are developed in the article. For further expansion please refer to the Topic Guide, the Glossary, and the Index.

13. **Incorporating Diversity: Police Response to Multicultural Changes in Their Communities,** Brad R. Bennett, *FBI Law Enforcement Bulletin*, December 1995.   75

Brad Bennett discusses the findings of a study undertaken to determine how four California law enforcement agencies responded to ***demographic*** changes in their communities. Bennett notes that the country is being called on to open its arms to people from many different ***ethnic*** backgrounds. He says police departments must do their parts to respond to ***multicultural*** changes.

14. **Afterburn: The Victimization of Police Families,** Andrew H. Ryan, *The Police Chief,* October 1997.   79

The impact of "doing the police job" can have debilitating, long-lasting effects on both ***law enforcement officers*** and their families.

15. **Marketing Community Policing: What Can We Expect?** Michael E. Clark, *Community Policing Exchange,* May/June 1998.   82

Over the past decade, hundreds of the police departments across the country have embraced the ***community policing philosophy.*** In spite of this, much of the public, media, and even the police themselves remain unclear about what it is and what to expect from it.

16. **A LEN Interview with Police Chief Randall Aragon of Whiteville, N.C.,** Peter C. Dodenhoff, *Law Enforcement News,* April 30, 1998.   84

A strong proponent of Total Quality Management (TQM), Chief Randall Aragon maintains that it takes time to implement an effective ***community-oriented policing*** effort.

Overview   94

17. **Adversarial Justice,** Franklin Strier, *The World & I,* August 1995.   96

Franklin Strier reveals what he sees as the flaws in America's ***adversary trial system,*** including its "weakness in exposing the truth." He calls on judges to use their authority to reform the "failing" system.

18. **How to Improve the Jury System,** Thomas F. Hogan, Gregory E. Mize, and Kathleen Clark, *The World & I,* July 1998.   104

The ***jury trial*** is revered as the most democratic institution in our own society; yet, it is not without blemish. Changes recommended by the authors include allowing jurors to take notes and to submit written questions for witnesses.

Judicial System

Five selections discuss the process by which the accused are moved through the judicial system. Prosecutors, courts, the jury process, and judicial ethics are reviewed.

19. Jury Nullification: A Perversion of Justice? 108
Andrew D. Leipold, *USA Today Magazine (Society for the Advancement of Education)*, September 1997.
There has been a lot of discussion lately about *jury nullification.* Andrew Leipold explores the nullification decision, which occurs when jurors in a criminal case acquit the defendant despite their belief that he or she was guilty of the crime charged.

20. Confronting the Breakdown of Law and Order, 112
Bruce Wiseman, *USA Today Magazine (Society for the Advancement of Education)*, January 1997.
The courts and psychiatry have bent over backwards in their interpretations of sanity and responsibility, thus perverting the idea of *justice.*

21. A Little Learning, James Q. Wilson, *National Review,* 115
June 2, 1997.
Professor James Wilson asserts that when judges allow *expert witnesses* to present their private theories in court, justice is the victim.

Overview 118

22. Restoring the Balance: Juvenile and Community 120
Justice, Gordon Bazemore and Susan E. Day, *Juvenile Justice,* December 1996.
Alternatively referred to as *restorative justice,* the balanced approach, and balanced and restorative justice, this alternative approach to addressing juvenile crime focuses on the interests of multiple justice clients.

23. Juvenile Offenders: Should They Be Tried in 129
Adult Courts? Michael P. Brown, *USA Today Magazine (Society for the Advancement of Education)*, January 1998.
The *"get tough" approach* of dealing with young law violators that is seen throughout the criminal justice system is society's reaction to violent, uncaring youths.

24. A Decline in Crime? Timothy W. Maier and Michael 132
Rust, *Insight,* April 27, 1998.
Killings by children have horrified Americans and spurred lawmakers to push what some call "feel good" legislation that is aimed at curbing criminal violence.

25. Kids and Guns: From Playgrounds to Battlegrounds, 136
Stuart Greenbaum, *Juvenile Justice,* September 1997.
Guns are now the weapon of choice for youth. The lethal mix of children and guns has reached a crisis in the United States.

26. With Juvenile Courts in Chaos, Critics Propose 142
Their Demise, Fox Butterfield, *New York Times,* July 21, 1997.
The nation's *juvenile courts* have been so overwhelmed by the increase in *violent teenage crime* and the breakdown of the family that judges and politicians are debating a solution that was once unthinkable: abolishing the system and trying most minors as adults.

UNIT 5

Juvenile Justice

Eight selections review the juvenile justice system. The topics include effective ways to respond to violent juvenile crime, juvenile detention, and youths in gangs.

The concepts in bold italics are developed in the article. For further expansion please refer to the Topic Guide, the Glossary, and the Index.

27. Now, Justice Is Served by Youths, for Youths, 147
Regina Marcazzo, *New York Times,* July 26, 1998.
The **Youth Court** is a judicial innovation in which minors who choose to plead guilty to misdemeanors are given the option of being sentenced by their peers.

28. Preventing Crime, Saving Children: Sticking to 149
the Basics, John J. Dilulio Jr., *Perspectives,* Spring 1998.
This article argues that the key to **preventing youth crime** and **substance abuse** among our country's expanding juvenile population is to improve the real, live, day-to-day connection between responsible adults and young people.

29. Pairing Juvenile Offenders with Volunteer Advocates, 155
Kim G. Frentz, *Perspectives,* Fall 1997.
Detroit's **Partners Against Crime** (PAG) one-to-one mentoring program reports impressive results. Kids are improving in school, enhancing coping skills, and staying out of trouble.

Overview 158

30. Probation in the United States: Practices and 160
Challenges, Joan Petersilia, *National Institute of Justice Journal,* September 1997.
No one advocates the abolition of **probation,** but many call for its reform. How should that be done? Joan Petersilia, a professor at the University of California, gives her recommendations.

31. Probation and Parole Supervision: Time for a 166
New Narrative, Edward E. Rhine, *Perspectives,* Winter 1998.
The past 20 years have witnessed a marked devaluation of traditional **probation and parole** supervision in favor of surveillance-oriented, control-based strategies of supervision.

32. Education as Crime Prevention: Providing Educa- 169
tion to Prisoners, *Research Brief (The Center on Crime, Communities & Culture),* September 1997.
This research brief presents recent data on the impact of **education** on crime and crime prevention, and examines the debate on providing higher education to inmates.

33. Ethical Considerations in Probation Practice, 175
Marylouise E. Jones and Arthur J. Lurigio, *Perspectives,* Summer 1997.
Probation officers frequently face decisions that place the needs of offenders in direct conflict with the welfare of society. In making such decisions, they can benefit from a firm foundation in **ethics.**

UNIT 6

Punishment and Corrections

Ten selections focus on the current state of America's penal system and the effects of sentencing, probation, overcrowding, and capital punishment on criminals.

The concepts in bold italics are developed in the article. For further expansion please refer to the Topic Guide, the Glossary, and the Index.

ix

34. The Other Women of Bedford Hills, Stephanie **181**
Gertler, *Spotlight,* April 1998.
Some **women** in this affluent Westchester community live behind
white picket fences and sprawling estates. Others live behind
barbed wire. Writer Stephanie Gertler enters **Bedford Hills Correctional Facility** to learn about life on the inside.

35. Prison Population Growing although Crime Rate **186**
Drops, Fox Butterfield, *New York Times,* August 9, 1998.
Experts say the **imprisonment boom** has developed a built-in
growth dynamic independent of the crime rate.

36. The Color of Justice, John H. Trumbo, *Death Row,* **187**
1995.
There are more nonwhite men on **death row** than their Caucasian
counterparts, a fact supported by the numbers. The real question
is this: Is the disparity due to **racial discrimination** or other
not-so-black-and-white issues?

37. Restorative Justice and Offender Rehabilitation: **192**
A Meeting of the Minds, Ann H. Crowe, *Perspectives,*
Summer 1998.
This article examines the potential for integrating and implementing
both **restorative justice** and **offender rehabilitation** perspectives, in order to achieve justice more effectively.

38. Death County, Arlene Levinson, *The Post-Star,* August 30, **205**
1998.
A hawkish district attorney, an army of prosecutors, and a weak
system of court-appointed defense lawyers, are some of the reasons
why one Texas county is leading states in **executions.**

39. U.S. Prisons: Gulags or Country Clubs? Alfred N. **208**
Himelson, *The World & I,* October 1997.
Whether to make **U.S. prison life** harder or softer is basically
a political and philosophical question regarding notions of **retribution and justice.**

Crime Statistics **212**
Glossary **221**
Index **225**
Article Review Form **228**
Article Rating Form **229**

The concepts in bold italics are developed in the article. For further expansion please refer to the Topic Guide, the Glossary, and the Index.

Charts and Graphs

Sequence of Events in the Criminal Justice System	10–11
Top 10 Offenses, Duval County, Florida, 1989–94	25
Southern States Still Have the Highest Murder Rates	36–37
Homicide Rate in 1996, State by State	37
Profiles of Abuse	50–51
Ethnic Changes in Total Population	78
Response to Juror Summonses in D.C.	106
Participants in a Balanced and Restorative Juvenile Justice System	124
What's New about the Balanced Approach?	125
Outcome Measures and Priorities for Practice in the Balanced Approach	126
New Roles in the Balanced and Restorative Justice Model	127
Youth Violence Arrests Are Down	132
Murder News Up	133
Juvenile Gun Homicides	137
Juvenile Caseload: A Closer Look	144
Five Pillars of Mentoring	157
Origin and Evolution of Probation	161
Who Is on Probation?	162
Literacy Levels for U.S. Adults	170
Recidivism Rates for Degree Holders Leaving the Texas Department of Criminal Justice, 1990–1991	171
Cost of Incarceration vs. Higher Education in Correctional Facilities, per Year, per Inmate	171
American Probation and Parole Association's Code of Ethics	178
Federal Probation Officers' Association Code of Ethics	179
Regional Disparity—States with the Highest and Lowest Rates of Federal and State Prisoners in 1997	186
Race of Death Row Inmates	189
Race of Defendants Executed	189
Race of Victims	189
Executions by Race—By State (1977–1994)	191
Traditional Justice	194
Offender Rehabilitation	195
Restorative Justice	195
Comparison of Restorative Justice, Offender Rehabilitation, and Criminal Justice Models	196
Priorities of Present Criminal Justice System	199
Fundamental Concepts of Restorative Justice	200
Foundations for a Restorative Justice System	201
Community Justice Model	201
Restorative Justice and Offender Rehabilitation Principles in Educational Settings	202
Life in the Lockup	209
Crime Clock, 1997	212
Crime in the United States, 1987–1997 Index	213
Crime Index Offenses Reported:	
Murder	214
Forcible Rape	215
Robbery	216
Aggravated Assault	217
Burglary	218
Larceny-Theft	218
Motor Vehicle Theft	219

Topic Guide

This topic guide suggests how the selections and World Wide Web sites found in the next section of this book relate to topics of traditional concern to criminal justice students and professionals. It is useful for locating interrelated articles and Web sites for reading and research. The guide is arranged alphabetically according to topic.

The relevant Web sites, which are numbered and annotated on pages 4 and 5, are easily identified by the Web icon (◎) under the topic articles. By linking the articles and the Web sites by topic, this ANNUAL EDITIONS reader becomes a powerful learning and research tool.

TOPIC AREA	TREATED IN	TOPIC AREA	TREATED IN
Attorneys	17. Adversarial Justice ◎ *9, 16, 21, 33*	**Crime Victims** **Criminal Justice**	*See* Victimology 1. What Is the Sequence of Events in the Criminal Justice System? 2. Looking Backward to Look Forward 4. African American Males 37. Restorative Justice and Offender Rehabilitation ◎ *3, 10, 14, 16, 18, 22, 25*
Battered Families	9. Battered Women Face Pit Bulls and Cobras 10. Child Victims 12. Advocacy and Law Enforcement ◎ *11, 12, 13, 26, 27*		
Bias	4. African American Males 19. Jury Nullification 36. Color of Justice ◎ *3, 4, 5, 6, 10, 27*	**Death Penalty**	36. Color of Justice 38. Death County ◎ *30, 33*
Brutality	11. Disrespect as Catalyst for Brutality	**Delinquency**	*See* Juvenile Justice
Children	*See* Juveniles	**Education**	32. Education as Crime Prevention ◎ *26*
Community Policing	13. Incorporating Diversity 15. Marketing Community Policing 16. LEN Interview with Police Chief Randall Aragon ◎ *7, 8, 17, 18*	**Ethics**	5. Is the U.S. Morally in Trouble? 17. Adversarial Justice 33. Ethical Considerations in Probation Practice ◎ *14, 21, 28, 33*
Corrections	30. Probation in the United States 31. Probation and Parole Supervision 32. Education as Crime Prevention 33. Ethical Considerations in Probation Practice 34. Other Women of Bedford Hills 35. Prison Population Growing 36. Color of Justice 37. Restorative Justice and Offender Rehabilitation 38. Death County 39. U.S. Prisons ◎ *28, 29, 30, 31, 32, 33, 34*	**Expert Witnesses**	20. Confronting the Breakdown of Law and Order 24. Little Learning
		Family Violence **Gender**	*See* Battered Families 34. Other Women of Bedford Hills ◎ *11, 34*
		Guns	25. Kids and Guns ◎ *24*
		Jury	18. How to Improve the Jury System 19. Jury Nullification ◎ *1, 16, 19, 20, 21, 22, 23, 25*
Courts	17. Adversarial Justice 19. Jury Nullification 20. Confronting the Breakdown of Law and Order 21. Little Learning 23. Juvenile Offenders 26. With Juvenile Courts in Chaos 27. Now, Justice Is Served by Youths, for Youths ◎ *19, 20, 21, 22, 23, 25*	**Juveniles**	*See* Juvenile Justice
		Juvenile Justice	10. Child Victims 22. Restoring the Balance 23. Juvenile Offenders 24. Decline in Crime? 25. Kids and Guns 26. With Juvenile Courts in Chaos 27. Now, Justice Is Served by Youths, for Youths 28. Preventing Crime, Saving Children 29. Pairing Juvenile Offenders ◎ *1, 6, 17, 23, 24, 25, 26, 27*
Crime	1. What Is the Sequence of Events in the Criminal Justice System? 2. Looking Backward to Look Forward 3. Thinker Attuned to Doing: James Q. Wilson 6. Why America's Murder Rate Is So High ◎ *1, 3, 5, 8, 9, 10, 15, 16, 24, 34*	**Multicultural**	13. Incorporating Diversity ◎ *1, 3, 4, 6, 10, 14, 16, 25*
		Parole	31. Probation and Parole Supervision ◎ *28*

2

TOPIC AREA	TREATED IN	TOPIC AREA	TREATED IN

Police	11. Disrespect as Catalyst for Brutality
	12. Advocacy and Law Enforcement
	13. Incorporating Diversity
	14. Afterburn
	15. Marketing Community Policing
	16. LEN Interview with Police Chief Randall Aragon
	  ○ *14, 15, 16, 17, 18, 19, 20*
		Sentencing	27. Now, Justice Is Served by Youths, for Youths
			37. Restorative Justice and Offender Rehabilitation
			  ○ *19, 23, 25, 27*

Prevention	27. Now, Justice Is Served by Youths, for Youths
	28. Preventing Crime, Saving Children
	32. Education as Crime Prevention
	  ○ *1, 4, 7, 15, 16*
		Stalkers	8. Researchers Unravel the Motives of Stalkers
			  ○ *11, 12, 13*

Prisons	34. Other Women of Bedford Hills
	35. Prison Population Growing
	39. U.S. Prisons
	  ○ *28, 29, 30, 31, 32, 33, 34*
		Stress	14. Afterburn
			  ○ *31*

Probation	30. Probation in the United States
	31. Probation and Parole Supervision
	33. Ethical Considerations in Probation Practice
	  ○ *28*
		Victimology	7. Victimization and the Victim Industry
			8. Researchers Unravel the Motives of Stalkers
			9. Battered Women Face Pit Bulls and Cobras
			10. Child Victims
			  ○ *11, 12, 13*

Prosecution	17. Adversarial Justice
	  ○ *19, 20, 21, 22, 23*
		Violence	9. Battered Women Face Pit Bulls and Cobras
			10. Child Victims
			12. Advocacy and Law Enforcement
			14. Afterburn
			24. Decline in Crime
			26. With Juvenile Courts in Chaos
			  ○ *4, 11, 12, 13, 15, 24, 27*

Psychiatry	20. Confronting the Breakdown of Law and Order ○ *31*	**Volunteer Advocate**	29. Pairing Juvenile Offenders
Punishment	*See* Corrections	**Women**	9. Battered Women Face Pit Bulls and Cobras 12. Advocacy and Law Enforcement 34. Other Women of Bedford Hills ○ *11, 12, 13, 29*

Race	4. African American Males
	13. Incorporating Diversity
	19. Jury Nullification
	36. Color of Justice
	38. Death County
	  ○ *6, 7, 8, 10, 14, 26, 27*
		Youth Court	27. Now, Justice Is Served by Youths, for Youths
			  ○ *19, 23, 25, 27*

Restorative Justice	22. Restoring the Balance 37. Restorative Justice and Offender Rehabilitation ○ *6, 23, 25, 27, 28, 31*		

● AE: Criminal Justice

The following World Wide Web sites have been carefully researched and selected to support the articles found in this reader. If you are interested in learning more about specific topics found in this book, these Web sites are a good place to start. The sites are cross-referenced by number and appear in the topic guide on the previous two pages. Also, you can link to these Web sites through our DUSHKIN ONLINE support site at *http://www.dushkin.com/online/*.

The following sites were available at the time of publication. Visit our Web site—we update DUSHKIN ONLINE regularly to reflect any changes.

General Sources

1. American Society of Criminology
http://www.bsos.umd.edu/asc/four.html
This is an excellent starting place for study of all aspects of criminology and criminal justice, with links to international criminal justice, juvenile justice, court information, police, governments, and so on.

2. Federal Bureau of Investigation
http://www.fbi.gov
The main page of the FBI Web site leads to lists of the most wanted criminals, uniform crime reports, FBI case reports, major investigations, and more.

3. National Archive of Criminal Justice Data
http://www.icpsr.umich.edu/NACJD/index.html
NACJD holds more than 500 data collections relating to criminal justice; this site provides browsing and downloading access to most of these data and documentation. NACJD's central mission is to facilitate and encourage research in the field of criminal justice.

4. Social Science Information Gateway
http://sosig.esrc.bris.ac.uk
This is an online catalog of thousands of Internet resources relevant to social science education and research. Every resource is selected and described by a librarian or subject specialist. Enter "criminal justice" under Search Sosig for an excellent annotated list of sources.

5. University of Pennsylvania Library: Criminology
http://www.library.upenn.edu/resources/subject/ social/criminology/criminology.html
This site provides an excellent list of criminology and criminal justice resources.

Crime and Justice in America

6. Campaign for Equity-Restorative Justice
http://www.cerj.org
This is the home page of CERJ, which sees monumental problems in justice systems and the need for reform. Examine this site and its links for information about the restorative justice movement.

7. Crime-Free America
http://www.announce.com/cfa/
Crime-Free America is a grassroots, nonprofit group dedicated to ending the crime epidemic that it feels has gripped the United States over the last four decades. This site has links to the Bureau of Justice Statistics, forums, and crime watch profiles.

8. Crime Times
http://www.crime-times.org/titles.htm
This interesting site listing research reviews and other information regarding biological causes of criminal, violent, and psychopathic behavior consists of many articles, listed by title. It is provided by the Wacker Foundation.

9. Ray Jones
http://blue.temple.edu/~eastern/jones.html
In this article, subtitled "A Review of Empirical Research in Corporate Crime," Ray Jones explores what happens when business violates the law. An extensive interpretive section and a bibliography are provided.

10. Sourcebook of Criminal Justice Statistics Online
http://www.albany.edu/sourcebook/
Data about all aspects of criminal justice in the United States are available at this site, which includes more than 600 tables from dozens of sources. The site also has a search mechanism.

Victimology

11. Connecticut Sexual Assault Crisis Services, Inc.
http://www.connsacs.org
This site has links that provide information about women's responses to sexual assault and related issues. It includes extensive links to sexual violence–related Web pages.

12. National Crime Victim's Research and Treatment Center
http://www.musc.edu/cvc/
At this site, find out about the work of NCVC at the Medical University of South Carolina, and click on Related Resources for an excellent listing of additional Web sources.

13. Office for Victims of Crime
http://www.ojp.usdoj.gov/ovc/
Established by the 1984 Victims of Crime Act, the OVC oversees diverse programs that benefit the victims of crime. This is its Web site from which you can download a great deal of pertinent information.

The Police

14. ACLU Criminal Justice Home Page
http://aclu.org/issues/criminal/hmcj.html
This "Criminal Justice" page of the American Civil Liberties Union Web site highlights recent events in criminal justice, addresses police issues, lists important resources, and contains a search mechanism.

15. FBI Violent Criminal Apprehension Program
http://www.fbi.gov/vicap/vicap.htm
VICAP's mission is to facilitate cooperation, communication, and coordination among law enforcement agencies and provide support in their efforts to investigate, identify, track, apprehend, and prosecute violent serial offenders. This site gives you access to VICAP's data information center resources.

16. Introduction to American Justice
http://www.uaa.alaska.edu/just/just110/home.html
Open this site to find an excellent outline of the causes of crime, including major theories, prepared by Professor Darryl Wood of the Justice Center at the University of Alaska at Anchorage. It provides an introduction to crime, law, and the criminal justice system; police and policing; the court system; corrections; and more.

17. Law Enforcement Guide to the WWW

http://leolinks.com

This page is dedicated to excellence in law enforcement. It contains links to every possible related category: community policing, computer crime, forensics, gangs, and wanted persons are just a few.

18. National Institute of Justice

http://www.ojp.usdoj.gov/nij/lawedocs.htm

The NIJ sponsors projects and conveys research findings to practitioners in the field of criminal justice. Through this site, you can access the initiatives of the 1994 Violent Crime Control and Law Enforcement Act, apply for grants, monitor international criminal activity, learn the latest about policing techniques and issues, and more.

Judicial System

19. Center for Rational Correctional Policy

http://pierce.simplenet.com

This is an excellent site on courts and sentencing, with many additional links to a variety of criminal justice sources.

20. Justice Information Center

http://www.ncjrs.org

Provided by the National Criminal Justice Reference Service, this JIC site connects to information about corrections, courts, crime prevention, criminal justice, statistics, drugs and crime, law enforcement, and victims—among other topics—and presents news and current highlights.

21. National Center for Policy Analysis

http://www.public-policy.org/~ncpa/pd/law/index3.html

Through the NCPA's "Idea House" you can click onto links to read discussions on an array of topics that are of major interest in the study of the American judicial system. There are sections on the courts, judges, lawyers, and other aspects of the legal system.

22. U.S. Department of Justice

http://www.usdoj.gov

The DOJ represents the American people in enforcing the law in the public interest. Open its main page to find information about the U.S. judicial system. This site provides links to federal government Web servers, topics of interest related to the justice system, documents and resources, and a topical index.

Juvenile Justice

23. Crime Connections on the Web!

http://www.appstate.edu/~robinsnmb/crime.htm

Dr. Matt Robinson offers a thorough Web list of resources that includes an excellent section on Juvenile Justice. The list is updated weekly. Try also *http://www.ncjrs.org/ jjhome.htm* for links provided by the Justice Information Center.

24. Gang Land: The Jerry Capeci Page

http://www.ganglandnews.com

Although this site particularly addresses organized-crime gangs, its insights into the gang lifestyle—including gang families and their influence—are useful for those interested in exploring issues related to juvenile justice.

25. Institute for Intergovernmental Research

http://www.iir.com

The IIR is a research organization that specializes in law enforcement, juvenile justice, and criminal justice issues. Explore the pro-jects, links, and search engines from this home page. Topics addressed include youth gangs and white-collar crime.

26. National Network for Family Resiliency

http://www.nnfr.org

This organization's main Web page will lead you to a number of resource areas of interest in learning about resiliency, including General Family Resiliency, Violence Prevention, and Family Economics.

27. Partnership against Violence Network

http://www.pavnet.org

The Partnership against Violence Network is a virtual library of information about violence and youths at risk, representing data from seven different federal agencies—a one-stop searchable information resource.

Punishment and Corrections

28. American Probation and Parole Association

http://www.csg.org/appa/

Open this APPA site to find information and resources related to probation and parole issues, position papers, the APPA code of ethics, and research and training programs and opportunities.

29. The Corrections Connection

http://www.corrections.com

This site is an online network for corrections professionals.

30. Critical Criminology Division of the ASC

http://sun.soci.niu.edu/~critcrim

Here you will find basic criminology resources and related government resources, provided by the American Society of Criminology, as well as other useful links. The death penalty is also discussed.

31. David Willshire's Forensic Psychology & Psychiatry Links

http://www.ozemail.com.au/~dwillsh/

This site offers an enormous number of links to professional journals and associations. It is a valuable resource for study into possible connections between violence and mental disorders. Topics include serial killers, sex offenders, and trauma.

32. Oregon Department of Corrections

http://www.doc.state.or.us/links/welcome.htm

Open this site for resources in such areas as crime and law enforcement and for links to U.S. state corrections departments.

33. Prison Law Page

http://www.wco.com/~aerick/prison.htm

This site contains resources on prisons and on the death penalty debate.

34. Stop Prisoner Rape, Inc.

http://www.spr.org/spr.html

For a change of pace, open some of the materials available through this site to gain understanding into the social relationships that may develop in incarceration facilities.

We highly recommend that you review our Web site for expanded information and our other product lines. We are continually updating and adding links to our Web site in order to offer you the most usable and useful information that will support and expand the value of your Annual Editions. You can reach us at: *http://www.dushkin. com/annualeditions/*.

www.dushkin.com/online/

Unit Selections

1. **What Is the Sequence of Events in the Criminal Justice System?**
   Report to the Nation on Crime and Justice, Bureau of Justice Statistics
2. **Looking Backward to Look Forward: The 1967 Crime Commission Report in Retrospect,** Mark H. Moore
3. **A Thinker Attuned to Doing: James Q. Wilson Has Insights, Like Those on Cutting Crime, That Tend to Prove Out,** Richard Bernstein
4. **African American Males in the Criminal Justice System,** Jerome G. Miller
5. **Is the U.S. Morally in Trouble?** George Roche
6. **Why America's Murder Rate Is So High,** Fox Butterfield

Key Points to Consider

❖ In your view, what is behind the dramatic drop in crime?

❖ What factors contribute to the involvement of a disproportionate number of African American males in the criminal justice system?

❖ Why is the murder rate high in the South?

 **Links**   **www.dushkin.com/online/**

6. **Campaign for Equity-Restorative Justice**
   http://www.cerj.org
7. **Crime-Free America**
   http://www.announce.com/cfa/
8. **Crime Times**
   http://www.crime-times.org/titles.htm
9. **Ray Jones**
   http://blue.temple.edu/~eastern/jones.html
10. **Sourcebook of Criminal Justice Statistics Online**
    http://www.albany.edu/sourcebook/

These sites are annotated on pages 4 and 5.

Crime continues to be a major problem in the United States. Court dockets are full, our prisons are overcrowded, probation and parole caseloads are overwhelming, and our police are being urged to do more. The bulging prison population places a heavy strain on the economy of the country. Clearly crime is a complex problem that defies simple explanations or solutions. While the more familiar crimes of murder, rape, and assault are still with us, drugs are an ever-increasing scourge. The debate continues about how best to handle juvenile offenders, sex offenders, and those who commit acts of domestic violence. Crime committed using computers and the Internet is already an issue to be dealt with.

Annual Editions: Criminal Justice 99/00 focuses directly upon crime in America and the three traditional components of the criminal justice system: police, courts, and corrections. It also gives special attention to crime victims in the victimology unit and to juveniles in the juvenile justice unit. The articles presented in this section are intended to serve as a foundation for the materials presented in subsequent sections.

The unit begins with "What Is the Sequence of Events in the Criminal Justice System?" which outlines the process in the administration of justice. The response to crime is a very complex process that involves citizens as well as many agencies, levels, and branches of government. Then, in "Looking Backward to Look Forward," Mark Moore presents a synthesis of symposium proceedings held to mark the thirtieth anniversary of the 1967 Crime Report issued by the President's Commission on Law Enforcement and Administration of Justice. The next essay, "A Thinker Attuned to Doing: James Q. Wilson Has Insights, Like Those on Cutting Crime, That Tend to Prove Out," focuses on a prominent figure who has frequently written on crime prevention. Are African American males disproportionately involved in the criminal justice system? Jerome Miller's article contends that they are. America in the 1990s is suffering from loss of values, yet historically we have found ways of overcoming adversity, according to "Is the U.S. Morally in Trouble?" The South appears to fuel the high murder rate in America, asserts Fox Butterfield in "Why America's Murder Rate Is So High."

What is the sequence of events in the criminal justice system?

The private sector initiates the response to crime

This first response may come from individuals, families, neighborhood associations, business, industry, agriculture, educational institutions, the news media, or any other private service to the public.

It involves crime prevention as well as participation in the criminal justice process once a crime has been committed. Private crime prevention is more than providing private security or burglar alarms or participating in neighborhood watch. It also includes a commitment to stop criminal behavior by not engaging in it or condoning it when it is committed by others.

Citizens take part directly in the criminal justice process by reporting crime to the police, by being a reliable participant (for example, a witness or a juror) in a criminal proceeding and by accepting the disposition of the system as just or reasonable. As voters and taxpayers, citizens also participate in criminal justice through the policymaking process that affects how the criminal justice process operates, the resources available to it, and its goals and objectives. At every stage of the process from the original formulation of objectives to the decision about where to locate jails and prisons to the reintegration of inmates into society, the private sector has a role to play. Without such involvement, the criminal justice process cannot serve the citizens it is intended to protect.

The response to crime and public safety involves many agencies and services

Many of the services needed to prevent crime and make neighborhoods safe are supplied by noncriminal justice agencies, including agencies with primary concern for public health, education, welfare, public works, and housing. Individual citizens as well as public and private sector organizations have joined with criminal justice agencies to prevent crime and make neighborhoods safe.

Criminal cases are brought by the government through the criminal justice system

We apprehend, try, and punish offenders by means of a loose confederation of agencies at all levels of government. Our American system of justice has evolved from the English common law into a complex series of procedures and decisions. Founded on the concept that crimes against an individual are crimes against the State, our justice system prosecutes individuals as though they victimized all of society. However, crime victims are involved throughout the process and many justice agencies have programs which focus on helping victims.

There is no single criminal justice system in this country. We have many similar systems that are individually unique. Criminal cases may be handled differently in different jurisdictions, but court decisions based on the due process guarantees of the U.S. Constitution require that specific steps be taken in the administration of criminal justice so that the individual will be protected from undue intervention from the State.

The description of the criminal and juvenile justice systems that follows portrays the most common sequence of events in response to serious criminal behavior.

Entry into the system

The justice system does not respond to most crime because so much crime is not discovered or reported to the police. Law enforcement agencies learn about crime from the reports of victims or other citizens, from discovery by a police officer in the field, from informants, or from investigative and intelligence work.

Once a law enforcement agency has established that a crime has been committed, a suspect must be identified and apprehended for the case to proceed through the system. Sometimes, a suspect is apprehended at the scene; however, identification of a suspect sometimes requires an extensive investigation. Often, no one is identified or apprehended. In some instances, a suspect is arrested and later the police determine that no crime was committed and the suspect is released.

Prosecution and pretrial services

After an arrest, law enforcement agencies present information about the case and about the accused to the prosecutor, who will decide if formal charges will be filed with the court. If no charges are filed, the accused must be released. The prosecutor can also drop charges after making efforts to prosecute (*nolle prosequi*).

A suspect charged with a crime must be taken before a judge or magistrate without unnecessary delay. At the initial appearance, the judge or magistrate informs the accused of the charges and decides whether there is probable cause to detain the accused person. If the offense is not very serious, the determination of guilt and assessment of a penalty may also occur at this stage.

Often, the defense counsel is also assigned at the initial appearance. All suspects prosecuted for serious crimes have a right to be represented by an attorney. If the court determines the suspect is indigent and cannot afford such representation, the court will assign counsel at the public's expense.

A pretrial-release decision may be made at the initial appearance, but may occur at other hearings or may be changed at another time during the process. Pretrial release and bail were traditionally intended to ensure appearance at trial. However, many jurisdictions permit pretrial detention of defendants accused of serious offenses and deemed to be dangerous to prevent them from committing crimes prior to trial.

The court often bases its pretrial decision on information about the defendant's drug use, as well as residence, employment, and family ties. The court may decide to release the accused on his/her own recognizance or into the custody of a third party after the posting of a financial bond or on the promise of satisfying certain conditions such as taking periodic drug tests to ensure drug abstinence.

In many jurisdictions, the initial appearance may be followed by a preliminary hearing. The main function of this hearing is to discover if there is probable cause to believe that the accused committed a known crime within the jurisdiction of the court. If the judge does not find probable cause, the case is dismissed; however,

if the judge or magistrate finds probable cause for such a belief, or the accused waives his or her right to a preliminary hearing, the case may be bound over to a grand jury.

A grand jury hears evidence against the accused presented by the prosecutor and decides if there is sufficient evidence to cause the accused to be brought to trial. If the grand jury finds sufficient evidence, it submits to the court an indictment, a written statement of the essential facts of the offense charged against the accused.

Where the grand jury system is used, the grand jury may also investigate criminal activity generally and issue indictments called grand jury originals that initiate criminal cases. These investigations and indictments are often used in drug and conspiracy cases that involve complex organizations. After such an indictment, law enforcement tries to apprehend and arrest the suspects named in the indictment.

Misdemeanor cases and some felony cases proceed by the issuance of an information, a formal, written accusation submitted to the court by a prosecutor. In some jurisdictions, indictments may be required in felony cases. However, the accused may choose to waive a grand jury indictment and, instead, accept service of an information for the crime.

In some jurisdictions, defendants, often those without prior criminal records, may be eligible for diversion from prosecution subject to the completion of specific conditions such as drug treatment. Successful completion of the conditions may result in the dropping of charges or the expunging of the criminal record where the defendant is required to plead guilty prior to the diversion.

Adjudication

Once an indictment or information has been filed with the trial court, the accused is scheduled for arraignment. At the arraignment, the accused is informed of the charges, advised of the rights of criminal defendants, and

asked to enter a plea to the charges. Sometimes, a plea of guilty is the result of negotiations between the prosecutor and the defendant.

If the accused pleads guilty or pleads *nolo contendere* (accepts penalty without admitting guilt), the judge may accept or reject the plea. If the plea is accepted, no trial is held and the offender is sentenced at this proceeding or at a later date. The plea may be rejected and proceed to trial if, for example, the judge believes that the accused may have been coerced.

If the accused pleads not guilty or not guilty by reason of insanity, a date is set for the trial. A person accused of a serious crime is guaranteed a trial by jury. However, the accused may ask for a bench trial where the judge, rather than a jury, serves as the finder of fact. In both instances the prosecution and defense present evidence by questioning witnesses while the judge decides on issues of law. The trial results in acquittal or conviction on the original charges or on lesser included offenses.

After the trial a defendant may request appellate review of the conviction or sentence. In some cases, appeals of convictions are a matter of right; all States with the death penalty provide for automatic appeal of cases involving a death sentence. Appeals may be subject to the discretion of the appelate court and may be granted only on acceptance of a defendant's petition for a *writ of certiorari*. Prisoners may also appeal their sentences through civil rights petitions and *writs of habeas corpus* where they claim unlawful detention.

Sentencing and sanctions

After a conviction, sentence is imposed. In most cases the judge decides on the sentence, but in some jurisdictions the sentence is decided by the jury, particularly for capital offenses.

In arriving at an appropriate sentence, a sentencing hearing may be held at which evidence of aggravating

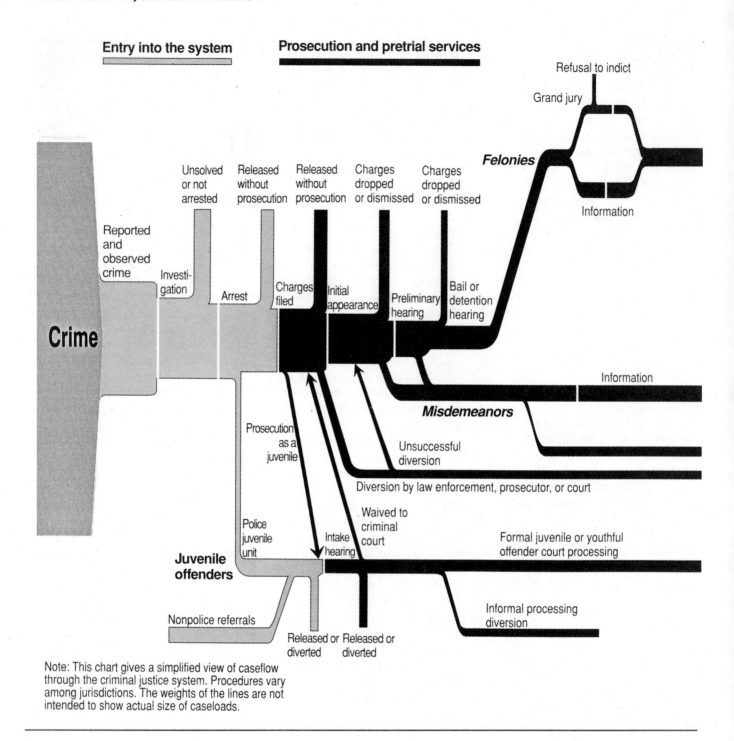

Entry into the system

Prosecution and pretrial services

Refusal to indict

Grand jury

Felonies

Information

Unsolved or not arrested

Released without prosecution

Released without prosecution

Charges dropped or dismissed

Charges dropped or dismissed

Reported and observed crime

Investigation

Arrest

Charges filed

Initial appearance

Preliminary hearing

Bail or detention hearing

Crime

Information

Misdemeanors

Prosecution as a juvenile

Unsuccessful diversion

Diversion by law enforcement, prosecutor, or court

Police juvenile unit

Intake hearing

Waived to criminal court

Formal juvenile or youthful offender court processing

Juvenile offenders

Nonpolice referrals

Informal processing diversion

Released or diverted

Released or diverted

Note: This chart gives a simplified view of caseflow through the criminal justice system. Procedures vary among jurisdictions. The weights of the lines are not intended to show actual size of caseloads.

or mitigating circumstances is considered. In assessing the circumstances surrounding a convicted person's criminal behavior, courts often rely on presentence investigations by probation agencies or other designated authorities. Courts may also consider victim impact statements.

The sentencing choices that may be available to judges and juries include one or more of the following:

• the death penalty
• incarceration in a prison, jail, or other confinement facility
• probation—allowing the convicted person to remain at liberty but subject to certain conditions and restrictions such as drug testing or drug restrictions such as drug testing or drug treatment
• fines—primarily applied as penalties in minor offenses

• restitution—requiring the offender to pay compensation to the victim. In some jurisdictions, offenders may be sentenced to alternatives to incarceration that are considered more severe than straight probation but less severe than a prison term. Examples of such sanctions include boot camps, intense supervision often with drug treatment and testing, house arrest and electronic

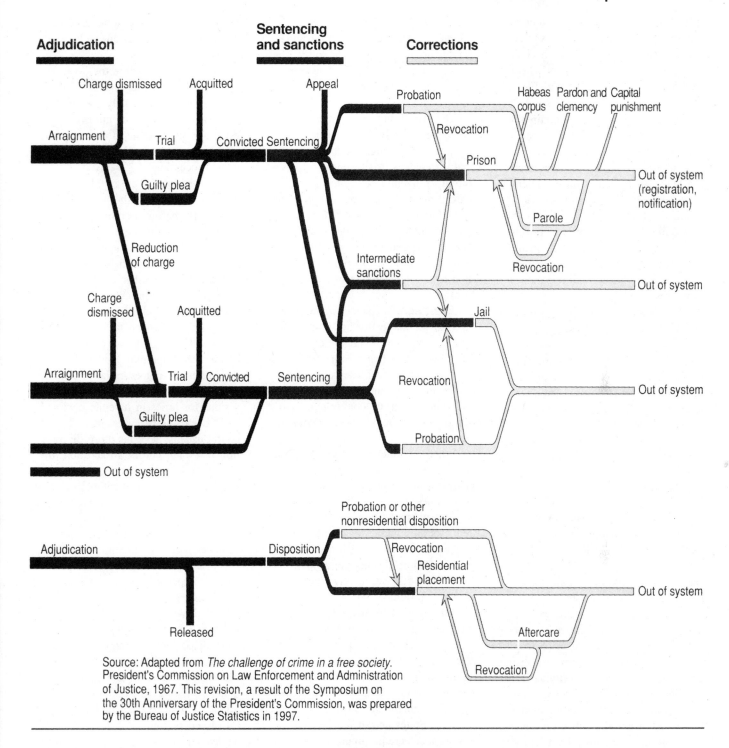

Adjudication

Charge dismissed   Acquitted

Arraignment   Trial   Convicted

Guilty plea

Reduction of charge

Charge dismissed   Acquitted

Arraignment   Trial   Convicted

Guilty plea

Out of system

Sentencing and sanctions

Appeal

Sentencing

Intermediate sanctions

Sentencing

Corrections

Probation   Habeas corpus   Pardon and clemency   Capital punishment

Revocation

Prison

Out of system (registration, notification)

Parole

Revocation

Out of system

Jail

Revocation

Out of system

Probation

Adjudication   Disposition   Probation or other nonresidential disposition

Revocation

Residential placement

Out of system

Aftercare

Released   Revocation

Source: Adapted from *The challenge of crime in a free society.* President's Commission on Law Enforcement and Administration of Justice, 1967. This revision, a result of the Symposium on the 30th Anniversary of the President's Commission, was prepared by the Bureau of Justice Statistics in 1997.

monitoring, denial of Federal benefits, and community service.

In many jurisdictions, the law mandates that persons convicted of certain types of offenses serve a prison term. Most jurisdictions permit the judge to set the sentence length within certain limits, but some have determinate sentencing laws that stipulate a specific sentence length that must be served

and cannot be altered by a parole board.

Corrections

Offenders sentenced to incarceration usually serve time in a local jail or a State prison. Offenders sentenced to less than 1 year generally go to jail; those sentenced to more than 1

year go to prison. Persons admitted to the Federal system or a State prison system may be held in prison with varying levels of custody or in a community correctional facility.

A prisoner may become eligible for parole after serving a specific part of his or her sentence. Parole is the conditional release of a prisoner before the prisoner's full sentence has been served. The decision to grant parole is made by an authority such as a parole board, which has power to grant or revoke parole or to discharge a parolee altogether. The way parole decisions are made varies widely among jurisdictions.

Offenders may also be required to serve out their full sentences prior to release (expiration of term). Those sentenced under determinate sentencing laws can be released only after they have served their full sentence (mandatory release) less any "goodtime" received while in prison. Inmates get goodtime credits against their sentences automatically or by earning them through participation in programs.

If released by a parole board decision or by mandatory release, the releasee will be under the supervision of a parole officer in the community for the balance of his or her unexpired sentence. This supervision is governed by specific conditions of release, and the releasee may be returned to prison for violations of such conditions.

Recidivism

Once the suspects, defendants, or offenders are released from the jurisdiction of a criminal justice agency, they may be processed through the criminal justice system again for a new crime. Long term studies show that many suspects who are arrested have prior criminal histories and those with a greater number of prior arrests were more likely to be arrested again. As the courts take prior criminal history into account at sentencing, most prison inmates have a prior criminal history and many have been incarcerated before. Nationally, about half the inmates released from State prison will return to prison.

The juvenile justice system

Juvenile courts usually have jurisdiction over matters concerning children, including delinquency, neglect, and adoption. They also handle "status offenses" such as truancy and running away, which are not applicable to adults. State statutes define which persons are under the original jurisdiction of the juvenile court. The upper age of juvenile court jurisdiction in delinquency matters is 17 in most States.

The processing of juvenile offenders is not entirely dissimilar to adult criminal processing, but there are crucial differences. Many juveniles are referred to juvenile courts by law enforcement officers, but many others are referred by school officials, social services agencies, neighbors, and even parents, for behavior or conditions that are determined to require intervention by the formal system for social control.

At arrest, a decision is made either to send the matter further into the justice system or to divert the case out of the system, often to alternative programs. Examples of alternative programs include drug treatment, individual or group counseling, or referral to educational and recreational programs.

When juveniles are referred to the juvenile courts, the court's intake department or the prosecuting attorney determines whether sufficient grounds exist to warrant filing a petition that requests an adjudicatory hearing or a request to transfer jurisdiction to criminal court. At this point, many juveniles are released or diverted to alternative programs.

All States allow juveniles to be tried as adults in criminal court under certain circumstances. In many States, the legislature *statutorily excludes* certain (usually serious) offenses from the jurisdiction of the juvenile court regardless of the age of the accused. In some States and at the Federal level under certain circumstances, prosecutors have the *discretion* to either file criminal charges against juveniles directly in criminal courts or proceed through the juvenile justice process. The juvenile court's intake department or the prosecutor may petition the juvenile court to *waive* jurisdiction to criminal court. The juvenile court also may order *referral* to criminal court for trial as adults. In some jurisdictions, juveniles pro-

cessed as adults may upon conviction be sentenced to either an adult or a juvenile facility.

In those cases where the juvenile court retains jurisdiction, the case may be handled formally by filing a delinquency petition or informally by diverting the juvenile to other agencies or programs in lieu of further court processing.

If a petition for an adjudicatory hearing is accepted, the juvenile may be brought before a court quite unlike the court with jurisdiction over adult offenders. Despite the considerable discretion associated with juvenile court proceedings, juveniles are afforded many of the due-process safeguards associated with adult criminal trials. Several States permit the use of juries in juvenile courts; however, in light of the U.S. Supreme Court holding that juries are not essential to juvenile hearings, most States do not make provisions for juries in juvenile courts.

In disposing of cases, juvenile courts usually have far more discretion that adult courts. In addition to such options as probation, commitment to a residential facility, restitution, or fines, State laws grant juvenile courts the power to order removal of children from their homes to foster homes or treatment facilities. Juvenile courts also may order participation in special programs aimed at shoplifting prevention, drug counseling, or driver education.

Once a juvenile is under juvenile court disposition, the court may retain jurisdiction until the juvenile legally becomes an adult (at age 21 in most States). In some jurisdictions, juvenile offenders may be classified as youthful offenders which can lead to extended sentences.

Following release from an institution, juveniles are often ordered to a period of aftercare which is similar to parole supervision for adult offenders. Juvenile offenders who violate the conditions of aftercare may have their aftercare revoked, resulting in being recommitted to a facility. Juveniles who are classified as youthful offenders and violate the conditions of aftercare may be subject to adult sanctions.

The governmental response to crime is founded in the intergovernmental structure of the United States

Under our form of government, each State and the Federal Government has its own criminal justice system. All systems must respect the rights of individuals set forth in court interpretation of the U.S. Constitution and defined in case law.

State constitutions and laws define the criminal justice system within each State and delegate the authority and responsibility for criminal justice to various jurisdictions, officials, and institutions. State laws also define criminal behavior and groups of children or acts under jurisdiction of the juvenile courts.

Municipalities and counties further define their criminal justice systems through local ordinances that proscribe the local agencies responsible for criminal justice processing that were not established by the State.

Congress has also established a criminal justice system at the Federal level to respond to Federal crimes such as bank robbery, kidnaping, and transporting stolen goods across State lines.

The response to crime is mainly a State and local function

Very few crimes are under exclusive Federal jurisdiction. The responsibility to respond to most crime rests with State and local governments. Police protection is primarily a function of cities and towns. Corrections is primarily a function of State governments. Most justice personnel are employed at the local level.

Discretion is exercised throughout the criminal justice system

Discretion is "an authority conferred by law to act in certain conditions or situations in accordance with an official's or an official agency's own considered judgment and conscience."[1] Discretion is exercised throughout the government. It is a part of decisionmaking in all government systems from mental health to education, as well as criminal justice. The limits of discretion vary from jurisdiction to jurisdiction.

Concerning crime and justice, legislative bodies have recognized that they cannot anticipate the range of circumstances surrounding each crime, anticipate local mores, and enact laws that clearly encompass all conduct that is criminal and all that is not.[2]

Who exercises discretion? These criminal justice officials . . .	..must often decide whether or not or how to—
Police	Enforce specific laws Investigate specific crimes Search people
Prosecutors	File charges or petitions for adjudication Seek indictments Drop cases Reduce charges
Judges or magistrates	Set bail or conditions for release Accept pleas Determine delinquency Dismiss charges Impose sentence Revoke probation
Correctional officials	Assign to type of correctional facility Award privileges Punish for disciplinary infractions
Paroling authorities	Determine date and conditions of parole Revoke parole

Therefore, persons charged with the day-to-day response to crime are expected to exercise their own judgment within limits set by law. Basically, they must decide—
• whether to take action
• where the situation fits in the scheme of law, rules, and precedent
• which official response is appropriate.[3]

To ensure that discretion is exercised responsibly, government authority is often delegated to professionals. Professionalism requires a minimum level of training and orientation, which guide officials in making decisions. The professionalism of policing is due largely to the desire to ensure the proper exercise of police discretion.

The limits of discretion vary from State to State and locality to locality. For example, some State judges have wide discretion in the type of sentence they may impose. In recent years, other states have sought to limit the judge's discretion in sentencing by passing mandatory sentencing laws that require prison sentences for certain offenses.

Notes

[1] Roscoe Pound, "Discretion, dispensation and mitigation: The problem of the individual special case," *New York University Law Review* (1960) 35:925, 926.
[2] Wayne R. LaFave, *Arrest: The decision to take a suspect into custody* (Boston: Little, Brown & Co., 1964), p. 63–184.
[3] Memorandum of June 21, 1977, from Mark Moore to James Vorenberg, "Some abstract notes on the issue of discretion."

Bureau of Justice Statistics (*www.ojp.us-doj.gov/bjs/*). January 1998. NCJ 167894. To order: 1-800-732-3277.

Looking Backward to Look Forward: The 1967 Crime Commission Report in Retrospect

The Challenge of Crime in a Free Society: Looking Back Looking Forward

by Mark Moore*

Thirty years ago, the report of the President's Commission on Law Enforcement and Administration of Justice was released. Entitled "The Challenge of Crime in a Free Society," the report reflected the Commission's leadership in setting forth a vision that was appropriate and powerful for its time. In this symposium, held to commemorate publication of the report, we have an opportunity to recommit ourselves to a new set of purposes by drawing on the Commission's insights and reshaping them from the perspectives of the changes that have occurred in the intervening years.

Max Weber thought the crucial defining characteristic of a statesman or a politician was passion—not the feckless variety characteristic of some intellectuals, but the kind he described as including a "sense of matter-of-fact," an ability to let the cold realities of a situation operate on one's mind with inner calmness and concentration. What distinguished the Commission was this kind of passion, "a passion for justice and knowledge." It should animate us as well today.

The Commission's vision: better criminal justice in the context of a commitment to social justice

The Crime Commission delivered two major messages. The first was an operational theory of what society would have to do to produce an effective and decent criminal justice system. The second was a larger idea about what society would have to do to deal with crime. The two are not the same. The Commission judged that the criminal justice system had to be constructed, reformed, and developed in ways that would enable it to deliver justice reliably and well. But in their view, this was not the only requirement for controlling crime. To meet the "challenge of crime in a free society," we had to work at producing *social* justice as well as producing *criminal* justice.

Aside from this substantive vision of the Commission was the managerial or implementation vision of how the processes and institutions of the criminal justice system needed

*Mark H. Moore, Ph.D., is Guggenheim Professor of Criminal Justice Policy and Management at Harvard University's Kennedy School of Government. This article is an abridgment of the address he presented at the closing of the symposium on the 30th anniversary of the President's Commission on Law Enforcement and Administration of Justice, sponsored by the Office of Justice Programs and the Office of Community Oriented Policing Services, U.S. Department of Justice. The address was a synthesis of the symposium proceedings.

to be developed. These serve either to implement whatever strategy is decided upon, or are a way of developing and adopting a new idea if the old idea turns out to be inappropriate. I want to first discuss the Commission's vision of the operational theory of crime control through the justice system, and second to discuss the managerial or process theory of what is needed to reform the criminal justice system if not the social justice system.

Controlling crime, preserving liberty, ensuring fairness. The Commission understood there were two important values to be preserved in criminal justice system operations that might be in opposition to each other. On the one hand is the goal of controlling crime, which could be achieved, perhaps, if we were willing to expend a great deal of State authority and reduce individual freedom. But the Commission was dead set against that because they thought another important societal goal should be to minimize the use of State authority. The Commission conceptualized the value question as: How could we reduce crime while preserving freedom? They understood that the goal of the system was to control crime *with justice,* not simply control crime. Freedom and justice also meant a sustained effort to expunge race and class bias from criminal justice system operations. Because the Commission's goal was to see that authority was invoked only when justified, the operations of the criminal justice system had to be reformed and reshaped. That meant being willing to take a loss in crime control effectiveness. They then, I think, hoped to replace some of the potentially lost effectiveness through greater efficiency in the operations of the criminal justice system, through the application of scientific management, and through more effective cooperation among the various elements of the system.

The complementary role of social justice. In its report, the Commission went on to say that although reform of the criminal justice system could produce criminal justice, it would not necessarily control crime. The real solution to the crime problem lay in the creation of *social justice.* The Commission discussed the importance of providing education, recreation, jobs, and strong families for kids as the way of controlling crime. Today, we could go further in thinking about social justice, recognizing the needs of adults as well as children. That might mean thinking about what to do with adjudicated offenders, and it might also mean a special obligation to concentrate on reducing racial disparities and the perception and reality of racial discrimination. In short, in the Commission's view, it was important to do *social* justice as well as *criminal* justice not only because social justice is a good in itself, but also because it would strengthen the performance of the criminal justice system.

In sum, the substantive vision of the Commission was to offer the Nation a way to deal with its crime problem in a just and fair way that would preserve liberty and realize the promise of democracy. In that vision, we had to repair the criminal justice system and make it operate justly and fairly, but we also had to repair the social system through a social justice policy that would create the conditions under which the criminal justice system could be both effective and fair.

A contemporary critique of the Crime Commission vision

Although in many respects the Commission's vision has stood the test of time, from today's perspective it may perhaps be a too narrow or austere view of criminal justice.

Criminal justice and just relationships. What we might want to consider is that the institutions of the criminal justice system ought to be trying to produce justice, not simply crime control within a context of restricting civil liberties. That would mean, among other things, paying attention to the rights of the defendant, and this was the part of justice on which the Crime Commission focused our attention. It would also mean paying attention to the rights—and the interests, and the feelings—of *victims.*

But there's an even more ambitious vision of justice. The idea of justice isn't simply that we balance the defendant's rights against the victim's rights in deciding what is a proportionate sentence. It is, instead, that the courts do the work of restructuring relationships that have come apart. The purpose of the many specialized courts—drug courts, family courts, juvenile courts, the restorative justice processes—is to construct just relationships. The aim is to do so not only among strangers (offenders and victims), but also among more intimate groups—husbands and wives, neighborhood merchants and the kids who victimized them, parents who become estranged from their kids—to construct a whole set of social relationships that ought to be guided and shaped by justice and mutual responsibility and even love.

Government can't create love, but it can create the occasions in which love—or tolerance, or obligation, or duty—might be rediscovered. It may be that this is the important idea of justice that we would try to build into a justice system—a "thicker," more substantial concept of justice than the guarantee of due process rights of victims and offenders.

It's easiest to imagine that the relationship the criminal justice system is trying to construct is best described in due process terms when we're talking about relationships between offenders and victims who don't know one another. But I would argue that even this is too abstract and attenuated a view of these relationships, let alone of relationships between victims and offenders who are intimates. We need to be reminded that all offenders—or most of them—come back to the community. In other words, our relationship with them will be ongoing.

People with the type of passion Weber recommended might recognize this, but it flies in the face of two common fantasies about the criminal justice system, which I'll call the Right Fantasy and the Left Fantasy. In the Right Fantasy, when people commit crime, we can end our relationship with them either by locking them up and throwing

---

"THE CHALLENGE OF CRIME IN A FREE SOCIETY"—30 YEARS LATER

Impelled by the high level of public concern about crime in the 1960s, President Lyndon Baines Johnson ordered the establishment of the President's Commission on Law Enforcement and Administration of Justice, whose mission was to examine "every facet of crime and law enforcement in America." The results of that examination, which covered the nature and amount of crime and crime trends in America, were published in 1967 as "The Challenge of Crime in a Free Society." The Commission's work laid the foundation for the current Federal role in assisting State and local law enforcement and justice administration. The Justice Department's Office of Justice Programs evolved from predecessor organizations created as a result of the Commission.

In a retrospective held in June 1997, prominent criminologists; professionals and practitioners from law enforcement, the courts, and corrections; Federal and State officials; and members of the Commission staff convened in a symposium to commemorate the landmark report. They assessed the reach of change that has occurred in the intervening years, focusing on the outcome of the Commission's recommendations. The symposium, whose theme was "looking backward, looking forward," was sponsored by the Office of Justice Programs (OJP), its constituent bureaus, and the Justice Department's Office of Community Oriented Policing Services. Participants examined changes in the nature of crime and the criminal justice system, in the use of research and statistics, and in the societal response to crime and the criminal justice system.

A publication based on the symposium papers, including the full address by Mark Moore, who synthesized the proceedings, is now being prepared by OJP.

A Gallery of Symposium Participants
Looking Backward to Look Forward

James Vorenberg (center) was Executive Director of the Crime Commission from 1965 to 1967. He is now Roscoe Pound Professor of Law at Harvard. John McCausland (left), one of his assistants on the Commission, became an attorney and is now an Episcopal priest, serving parishes in New Hampshire. Sheila Ann Mulvihill, also a member of the Commission staff, is now an editor for the National Academy of Sciences and other organizations.

Attorney General Janet Reno (right) and Assistant Attorney General (Office of Justice Programs) Laurie Robinson (left) at the symposium.

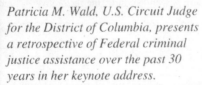

Patricia M. Wald, U.S. Circuit Judge for the District of Columbia, presents a retrospective of Federal criminal justice assistance over the past 30 years in her keynote address.

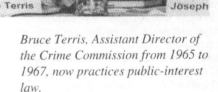

Bruce Terris, Assistant Director of the Crime Commission from 1965 to 1967, now practices public-interest law.

Joseph Vining was a member of James Vorenberg's staff on the Commission and is now Hutchins Professor of Law at the University of Michigan.

David Burnham (left), Assistant Director of the Commission in 1965, is now a professor at Syracuse University and codirector of the Transactional Records Access Clearinghouse; Thomas Cahill (right) served on the Commission from 1965 to 1967 and is now retired from the San Francisco Police Department, remaining active as a past president of the International Association of Chiefs of Police.

Photos by Twin Lens Photo

away the key or by executing them. In the Left Fantasy, when people commit crime, it gives us an opportunity to supply them with enough services to turn them into the person they always wanted to be.

In some sense, both those fantasies are deeply flawed. The reality is that we are going to be locked into a long-term relationship with offenders. So we might want to ask, "What kind of a relationship do we want to have?" That is a very different way of asking the question, "What are we trying to do with criminal justice dispositions?" We are asking what would be a just relationship for us to have, as well as what relationship would achieve some practical goals in controlling crime.

Partnerships across boundaries. The Commission held the view that it was important for each institution to get outside its boundaries and see itself as interacting with other institutions in broader systems. That was an important idea. But the interactions that the Commission highlighted were those of the agencies within the criminal justice system. Thus, police had to interact with prosecutors, prosecutors had to interact with courts, courts had to interact with correctional institutions, and so forth.

The key relationships missing from the Commission's view were those with other governmental units—child welfare, parks and recreation, the public education system—and those with the *communities* that would be necessary to animate and give weight and power to an emerging conception of a justice system that wanted to produce "thick" justice rather than the austere sort.

In working with victims and offenders, and particularly with children, we need to foster naturally occurring systems of support outside the justice system. For example, in criminal justice institutions like drug courts, we need to bring in parents, coworkers, and supervisors and engage them in the process of controlling the behavior of the offender and helping him or her stay off drugs. We are reaching into *informal* systems of control, support, and assistance, using the apparatus of the criminal justice system to mobilize and shape that particular kind of control.

The criminal justice system as a support to social justice. My third point about the Crime Commission's substantive vision is that it did not include the idea that criminal justice system operations might support the construction of conditions that could lead to social justice. Of course, it would be easy to overestimate the extent to which the institutions of the criminal justice system could do this. But it would also be a mistake, I think, not to recognize the contribution these institutions could make.

To understand this, we need to think not only of crime as the result of social injustice, but also of crime control as a means to the end of producing social justice. Some might object to this on grounds that we would be attempting to execute social policy by creating new criminal liability and thus a new responsibility for the criminal justice system.

The Crime Commission defined the forms of professionalism we have today and established the basis for the development of talented professionals in the criminal justice field.

An example is the prospect of criminalizing attacks of parents against children in the same way we have criminalized attacks of men against women in the context of domestic violence. To criminalize such acts could be perceived as wrong because it is an inappropriate use of State power or it is an imprudent use of State power. But the fact is we do not know whether it would be wrong. If it were wrong in either respect, then that might create an opportunity for the criminal justice system to support what had previously been considered an important goal of social policy: to produce safe families. In the Commission report, there was no suggestion that the criminal justice system as a whole could support and help further the goals of the social justice system beyond providing a tolerably just and effective response to those who had committed offenses.

Crime prevention. It is significant, I think, that the first chapter of the Crime Commission's report was about prevention. But what I think is quite interesting is that we have a very broad juxtaposition of different systems of prevention. According to the prevention theory associated with criminal justice operations, we can prevent crime (if not the first, at least many subsequent crimes) through deterrence, incapacitation, and rehabilitation. We might even prevent an offender's first offense if general deterrence works.

At the other extreme is a social justice theory of prevention. It holds that if we extended great opportunities to both children and adults to live profitably and well and if we lived up to the promise of equality of opportunity, fewer people would wish to become offenders, would choose to become offenders, or would feel motivated to become offenders. So we have criminal justice prevention on the one hand (reactive, with extensive use of State authority) and the social justice theory of prevention on the other (anticipatory, hopeful, accepting of our broader responsibilities to society at large, holding open the possibility of realizing a society

we'd all like to be part of). Those are the two ideas of prevention presented in the Commission report.

How much space is there between those different ideas of prevention and how much of that space have we explored at this stage to find effective crime prevention techniques? By way of an answer, let me start from the Right end, with the "spare" deterrence—incapacitation and rehabilitation—of professional criminal justice agencies. To find another kind of prevention, you could take one step over and discover that a great deal of what is celebrated as important preventive techniques I would describe as "thick" deterrence. It functions the way mentors function. You behave when your mentor is sitting next to you, partly because he or she is sitting next to you. You may have impulses to break loose, but with your mentor next to you, you know where your duty lies. There's a concept of support in that closeness, but there's also control.

Let me explain how "thick" deterrence might be applied to handling persistent minor offenders. They are a very difficult problem in the criminal justice system; their persistence makes it hard to ignore the fact that they're leaving behind a string of victims. On the other hand, their offenses aren't very serious, so it doesn't seem appropriate to sever our relationship to them by either life imprisonment or execution. I recall watching James Vorenberg, a member of the Crime Commission (who is here today), on television shortly after publication of the Commission report, talking about this type of offender. He said, "There are just some people who need a leash." That is the picture of "thick" deterrence: prevention different from probation and also different from incapacitation.

Another idea of prevention, much discussed recently, is "situational crime prevention": reducing the opportunities to commit offenses. Some portion of that idea lies in making less property available to be stolen. But another part is trying to reduce the number of occasions in which people will be provoked into committing crime. Once again, we begin thinking about relationships—as potentially criminogenic and needing to be fixed as a way to block the opportunity for future offending. Those relationships are in domestic violence, child abuse and neglect, crimes committed among gangs, and even hate crimes. All acquire their meaning and motivation through *relationships,* not through the acquisition of property. If the courts and other parts of the criminal justice system are in the business of reconstructing relationships, they may be able to reduce these crimes.

Notice what I'm doing is edging over to the categories of prevention that eventually reach the "root causes of crime" approach to prevention. The one step remaining before I get there is the concept of prevention most popular in our symposium discussion: as an interruption of the trajectories of children headed toward future criminal offending. A number of researchers have demonstrated the possibility of intervening early in children's development to deflect them from careers of criminal offending.

In sum, the point I wish to make is that there is a general concept of prevention, widely and enthusiastically embraced for a long time. In order for that concept to become operational, we have to have a much more differentiated and clear picture of prevention; more specifically, which notions of prevention I've talked about are included in the general idea. In the recent crime control debate, one of the sadder aspects is the loss of an argument about crime prevention. A truly distinctive aspect of the Clinton administration's approach to crime was its willingness to emphasize prevention of a particular type and to include it in Federal crime legislation. The constraints subsequently placed on this idea have been disappointing. The argument that the Crime Commission set us up to be able to make was recently lost, and I think we need to reclaim some of that terrain.

Institutions and processes

Some of the Crime Commission's views of criminal justice processes and institutions might also be altered in our contemporary view.

Effective policymaking. In our symposium discussions, we spent a lot of time talking about effective policymaking. We espoused an idea of policymaking guided by data and knowledge rather than ideology and base passion—guided by a sort of Weberian approach to passion. And yet today in a panel of policymakers, the dominant theme was the importance of righteous anger, "craziness," "the glint in the eye." The panel supported my belief that it is wrong to imagine effective policymaking as devoid of passion, anger, craziness. Passions are going to be there inevitably, so you might as well understand that we could use them, not just deplore them and try to expunge them.

What excites people's passions, I think, are their values—the images of justice that they'd like to see translated into action. The anger that comes from indignation, from being badly treated, from the sense of being part of an unjust system turns out to be enormously useful in mobilizing oneself and others to take a particular action. Values associated with conceptions of justice are important in driving reforms. As a purely logical matter, one cannot decide what to do simply on the basis of fact. You have to have the fact attached to a value. From there the question becomes a political matter, when we determine what are the values that we care about, in the operation of the criminal justice system or in the organization of society.

In much of its work, the Commission focused on empirical questions of what works. But I think a lot of what animated enthusiasm for the Commission's vision of social justice (and criminal justice) was an idea about justice and about what society wanted and expected as justice. The Commission's view was based on a normative appeal to an ideal. I think today we have a different normative idea of what constitutes justice in this country than we had earlier. I do not believe this idea will be rooted out only by additional facts but by a different argument about values, about the kind of society we want to be, and about the kind of justice we want.

The central research and development model. I want to say one word about what I describe as the central R&D model. I think for a long time our picture of the way knowledge enters criminal justice decisionmaking/policymaking was a picture of academics working hand in glove with the Federal Government to develop ideas, to test them, and, once they were proven to work, to disseminate them. A lot of our justice institutions were set up with that kind of understanding, and for a long time I believed in this model.

The difficulty is I have never seen it work. What I've learned in 20 to 30 years of trying to interact with the world and make what contributions I can is that I am usually behind the best practitioners. The practitioners who are facing the problems are often doing what I haven't thought of. Often my job as an academic is to scurry around behind them and explain to everybody else why what they're doing is interesting.

The Crime Commission's contribution to leadership. I do believe the Crime Commission defined the forms of professionalism we have today and established the basis for the development of talented professionals in the criminal justice field. A lot of the imagination and brains, the glints in the eye, and the creativity and "craziness" necessary to find solutions to today's problems are now within the practice field, not just in academia. That is an enormous asset.

All of us who benefited from the educational programs created by the Commission (myself included) grew up with the legacy of the Commission—the spirit of authorization, the pursuit of justice, the quest for knowledge. All of us felt we had the opportunity to imagine and to work out for ourselves what it meant to produce justice. There are at least three concepts of professionalization—technically competent people, people committed to the right values, and people who feel authorized to imagine and act in their particular location to deal with the problems they see right in front of them. What we heard in our discussions today is recognition of the decentralization and spread of leadership in criminal justice. Leadership now comes not just from national commissions but also from those in the field in all the Nation's communities. The authorization to experiment, to do the work, has spread very widely, and it is due largely to the impetus provided by the Commission.

Building on the Commission's work

The Commission reminded us of some important values to guide us in reforming the criminal justice system, controlling crime, and reconstructing society. Those values included respect for individual rights; the determination to protect liberty and to use State authority sparingly; the ambition to ensure that when we use State authority we do so fairly; and the necessity of acting outside the criminal justice system to produce social justice as well as a certain kind of criminal justice. That was the course the Commission set us on, and it was the right course.

Today's course involves producing justice and constructing relationships, in addition to protecting freedoms. It includes engaging communities and government agencies as well as ensuring fairness by operating across the criminal justice system. It means using the criminal justice system to strengthen the institutions that supply social justice as well as using it to control crime. And it means a more intense and differentiated focus on prevention as well as on control.

The final legacy of the Crime Commission, and the one that has made us feel the saddest, involves social justice. As I've stated, part of the Commission's teaching was the importance of producing *social* justice as well as *criminal* justice. I think a lot of the pain we have felt during this symposium comes from our awareness of society's retreat from its commitment to producing social justice. Part of the pain comes from the fact that as society has retreated from this commitment, criminal justice institutions are given more rather than fewer resources. Thus, those of us who work in the criminal justice system find our lives enriched while the rest of society and its other institutions are shrinking. This violates what we think is true and important about how society ought to be constructed. I am here, energized, animated, excited about the prospects of using criminal justice institutions to contribute to society, at precisely the same time as the other institutions key to achieving what we want to achieve as a society are being cut back deeply.

So I come out of this symposium with the excitement and enthusiasm that come from working on institutions I care about deeply and that I think are socially important and valuable. At the same time, I end this meeting with a profound sense of shame and regret about the failure of society to attend to the other important teaching of the Crime Commission report: Without *social justice,* ultimately, there can be no criminal justice.

A Thinker Attuned to Doing

James Q. Wilson Has Insights, Like Those on Cutting Crime, That Tend to Prove Out

By RICHARD BERNSTEIN

MALIBU, Calif.—If the ultimate reward for a man of ideas is to see an idea make a difference in the real world, then James Q. Wilson should feel rewarded indeed. No less a figure than William J. Bratton, the former New York City Police Commissioner, has given him credit for an important concept in the much-publicized reduction of crime in American cities, especially in New York.

The idea is known as the "broken window" theory, and it dates back to an essay Mr. Wilson wrote in The Atlantic Monthly in 1982 with George Kelling. The authors argued that paying attention to the small things—drug dealing on street corners, street walkers, petty vandalism, fare beating—could have a disproportionate effect on the big things as well. Over the years, Mr. Wilson, a political and social scientist who has written frequently on crime prevention, continued to make that argument, and Mr. Bratton and others who know Mr. Wilson's work report a direct link to initiatives like Mayor Rudolph W. Giuliani's quality-of-life campaign and the widespread practice of community policing.

"I'm glad that it's had some influence," Mr. Wilson, interviewed here at his home an hour's drive north of Los Angeles, said of the broken-windows concept. "It was important that the police pay attention to orderliness as well as to crime. But 'Broken Windows' is the title of one essay I wrote among many. I don't see it as a great literary moment in my life."

Mr. Wilson has in fact had quite a few ideas in his many years of writing about public policy, bureaucratic behavior and human values. Jim Wilson, as he is known to his friends, has over the years been among the most influential thinkers in the country, an academic who has combined scholarship with widely read public commentaries on issues ranging from drugs to morals. He is known as a conservative, a label he does not repudiate. He has, for example, been on the boards of conservative organizations like the Smith-Richardson Foundation, the Randolph Foundation and the American Enterprise Institute. He is also on the publication committee of The Public Interest Quarterly.

But what many of his colleagues and friends believe sets Mr. Wilson apart has been the way in which the data have driven his ideas, not some pre-existing ideological commitment. Writing on such subjects as the social bases of Reaganism, the behavior of bureaucracies and the police, crime prevention, and, most recently, the role of morality in hu-

man affairs, Mr. Wilson has focused on the empirical, on practical consequences: in a word, on the facts.

"He's very empirically grounded," said Neal Kozodoy, the editor of Commentary magazine and the publisher of numerous Wilson articles. "He engages the big questions of human existence, like morality and character, but he does so not from a religious position or on the basis of immutable first principles, but from what the evidence allows us to say. The interesting thing is how consistently the evidence confirms those immutable first principles."

Ester Fuchs, a professor of political science at Barnard College and Columbia University, said she saw Mr. Wilson "as one of the most important political scientists of the past 40 years." She continued: "His perceptions about city politics remain paradigmatic in that field. People hold him up as a conservative thinker, but he's first and foremost a social scientist. There's nothing, for example, inherently conservative about the broken-windows idea."

Mr. Wilson put it this way: "I know my political ideas affect what I write, but I've tried hard to follow the facts wherever they land. Every topic I've written about begins as a question. How do police departments behave? Why do bureaucracies function the way they do? What moral intuitions do people have? How do courts make their decisions? What do blacks want from the political system? I can honestly say that I didn't know the answers to those questions when I began looking into them."

Mr. Wilson was born in Denver but grew up in Long Beach, Calif. He graduated from the nearby University of Redmond and, after three years in the Navy, went on to finish graduate studies in political science at the University of Chicago. He arrived at Harvard in 1961, teaching there until 1983, when he moved back "home" to U.C.L.A. He now lives north of Malibu, in a home that he and his wife, Roberta, built a decade or so ago. It is an airy, open place and has sweeping views of the Pacific, but it is also unpretentious, like Mr. Wilson himself.

Mr. Wilson, a trim and youthful 67, was in the midst of planning a scuba diving expedition to Truk Island that he and his wife are to go on later this summer, and he was not working on a book. He still participates in cattle roundups in Colorado and likes to drive fast cars, occasionally on a racetrack. ("Once," he said, "my driver's license was suspended in three states.") He has a quiet, unobtrusive style, more West Coast than East Coast, even though most of his career was spent in Cambridge, Mass., where for three years he was director of the Joint Institute for Urban Studies of M.I.T. and Harvard.

One of his notable early essays was called "A Guide to Reagan Country: The Political Culture of Southern California," which was published in Commentary when Ronald Reagan was only beginning to be seen as a strong possible contender for the Presidency. Not a Reagan backer himself, Mr. Wilson presciently observed that Mr. Reagan's support rested on a bedrock of values and preferences that, while perhaps strongest in Southern California, were widespread elsewhere. "We must, I think, take Reaganism seriously," he

wrote. "It will be with us for a long time under one guise or another."

"I was in Cambridge, Massachusetts," Mr. Wilson recalled, "and that essay very literally grew out of a desire to explain the West to my Eastern friends." (Mr. Wilson sardonically noted in his Commentary essay that even if he liked Mr. Reagan, he wouldn't admit it anyplace where his Harvard colleagues were likely to see it.)

A logical progression of interests from the political to the moral.

Asked whether there is a single thematic strand running through his work, Mr. Wilson hesitated for a moment and then said no. And yet it is tempting to see in his hundreds of articles and books (with the exception of the scuba diver's guide to viewing fish that he wrote with Mrs. Wilson) if not exactly a single thread, then at least a logical progression of interests, moving from the narrowly political to the broadly moral.

What seems to bind together much of Mr. Wilson's work is the combination of empirical research for which he is known and what are generally taken to be conservative social values. To Mr. Wilson, "Southern California had become an outpost of Middle Western civility." It is clear that he identifies with that civility and with what he believes are its characteristics, among them "a strong socially reinforced commitment to property."

"It has to do with growing up in an era when there was no such thing as moral ambiguity," Mr. Wilson said. "Individualism and personal effort were highly rewarded. It was a white Anglo-Saxon culture, and it had all of the defects of that culture, especially its racism, but it also had all of the advantages."

Mr. Wilson studied urban politics under his mentor, Edward Banfield

at the University of Chicago, one of whose interests was discovering the informal rules and incentives by which organizations worked. Under Mr. Banfield, Mr. Wilson was one of the first political sociologists to look closely at the role of blacks in urban politics. Early in his career at Harvard, he was teaching a course in public administration, part of which involved a study of police departments. The result was a book, "The Varieties of Police Behavior," and after that, an invitation to serve on the Commission on Crime and the Administration of Justice created by Lyndon B. Johnson in 1966.

"There seemed to be a shortage of criminologists with an interest in public policy," Mr. Wilson recalled. "I had to learn about crime, a subject in which I had no professional training, in order to function on that task force."

But that interest led Mr. Wilson to frame a common question in an uncommon way. "The standard question was why did people commit crimes," he recalled. "I wanted to ask why people don't commit them. And that led me eventually to my book 'The Moral Sense.'"

Mr. Wilson's argument in that book is complicated, and the goal is ambitious: to reassert the validity of morality in an age that lacks religious conviction and is dominated by moral relativism. It asserted the neglected notion that moral rules are part of human nature and spring from the ordinary experiences of life. The dominant relativism portrays morality as nothing more than a social convention, an arbitrary set of rules that differ from one society to the next. What Mr. Wilson found was that while specific rules certainly do vary from culture to culture, every culture has what he calls a moral disposition.

"There is to be found," he wrote in one article in Commentary on this subject, "a desire not only for praise but for praiseworthiness, for fair dealings as well as for good deals, for honor as well as for advantage." Mr. Wilson argued further that the moral sense stemmed from everyday experience. "A good character," he wrote, "arises from the repetition of many small acts, and begins early in youth. That habituation operates on a human nature innately prepared to respond to training."

The same, of course, could be said about Mr. Wilson's broken-windows theory of crime prevention. In his view, just as society can disintegrate when it ceases to pay attention to small violations, to an overall orderliness, so, too, individuals can disintegrate when they fail to perform the "small acts" that construct the moral sense.

The idea that the moral sense is innate but that the practice of morality is learned seems to be at the heart of many of Mr. Wilson's positions and of his conservative conviction that the liberal culture has eroded the practice of morality.

"Take an adult cautioning the young people about something they've done wrong, like telling a kid not to litter or not to shout in a crowded subway car," he said. "It's almost unheard of now, but when I was growing up it was common for an adult to say to a child, 'You shouldn't do that.' We've passed that point because of fear and because we think it improper, that we don't have the right to interfere in somebody else's behavior."

Mr. Wilson's lament may sound to some people like nostalgia, a yearning for the lost wholeness of small-town America, and perhaps there is something of that in there. But his work is too firmly oriented toward practical consequences, the data of everyday life, for nostalgia to play a big role.

Long ago, in an essay in Commentary, Mr. Wilson provided what could be a credo about the social necessity of enforcing the habit of good behavior:

"If morality is thought to be nothing but convention or artifice, then it will occur to those persons who are weakly attached to society and its rules that they are free to act as they wish provided they can get away with it. And if they would have broken the rules anyway, the relativism of our age makes it easier for them to justify their action by the claim that the rules are arbitrary enactments."

AFRICAN AMERICAN MALES

IN THE CRIMINAL JUSTICE SYSTEM

BY JEROME G. MILLER

I N THE MIDST of two decades of social neglect, the white majority in America presented its inner cities with an expensive gift—a new and improved criminal justice system. It would, the government promised, bring domestic tranquillity—particularly with regard to African Americans. No expense was spared in crafting it and delivering it inside the city gates. It was, in fact, a Trojan Horse.

While neoconservative commentators such as Charles Murray argued that payments through the Aid to Families with Dependent Children (AFDC) program had undermined family

JEROME G. MILLER is the author of Search and Destroy: African-American Males in the Criminal Justice System *(Cambridge University Press, 1996). He is co-founder of the National Center on Institutions and Alternatives, a nonprofit center dedicated to issues in juvenile justice and located in Washington, D.C. He is now general receiver in charge of the child welfare system for the District of Columbia.*

stability and sabotaged work incentives, the real value of AFDC and food stamp payments to the poor had been steadily declining.[1] Meanwhile, urban schools had deteriorated and fallen into disrepair. Not so with criminal justice. In a society obsessed with single mothers on welfare, more money ($31 billion) was being spent annually at the local, state, and federal levels on a failed drug war alone than on that symbol of vaunted liberal largesse, AFDC ($22 billion).[2]

As government investment in social and employment programs in the inner cities was held stable or cut back during the 1980s, the criminal justice system was ratcheted up to fill the void. Federal, state, and local expenditures for police grew 416%; for courts, 585%; for prosecution and legal services, 1,019%; for public defense, 1,255%; and for corrections, 989.5%. Federal spending for justice grew 668%; county spending increased 710.9%; state spending surged 848%. By 1990 the country was spending $75 billion annually to catch and lock up offenders.[3] For the white majority, it was a popular way to go—particularly as it became clear that these draconian measures would fall

heaviest on minorities in general and African American males in particular. The rationale for all this criminal justice activity lay in the putatively exploding crime rates—particularly the rate of violent crime. As it turned out, even this premise was questionable.[4]

In the late 1980s and early 1990s, crime as a social problem and political issue took on the character of a national

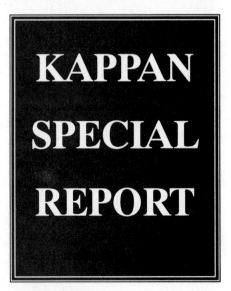

KAPPAN

SPECIAL

REPORT

From *Phi Delta Kappan,* June 1997, pp. K1-K5, K9-K12. © 1997 by Jerome G. Miller. Reprinted by permission.

game of "bait and switch" that meshed with the interests of an aggressive law enforcement establishment. The bait was "violent crime," usually seen as involving inner-city African American youths. The "switch" occurred when law enforcement armamentaria were brought to bear. Since relatively few violent offenders could be found among the millions of citizens of color in the so-called underclass who were being dragged into the justice system, the labels and definitions as to who was dangerous were broadened to include as many as possible as often as possible.

The FBI *Uniform Crime Reports,* on which the media routinely base official estimates of crime, inflated both the numbers and the seriousness of the types of incidents reported. Whereas most European nations report their crime statistics on the basis of convictions, *UCR* statistics are based on complaints or arrests. However, about 43 of every 100 individuals arrested for a felony either were not prosecuted or had their cases dismissed outright at the first court appearance. These dismissals had nothing to do with plea bargains; usually there was not sufficient reason to proceed with the case.[5]

For example, of the 399,277 arrests for "aggravated assault" reported by the FBI in 1990 (a grossly disproportionate percentage of them involving African Americans), only 53,861 (13.4%) resulted in felony convictions.[6] Though figures like this are usually taken by conservative commentators as demonstrating the permissiveness of the justice system, in fact there is quite another phenomenon at work. Police were charging arrestees with violent crimes that they didn't, in fact, commit.

A survey of the "adjudication outcome" for felony defendants in the 75 largest counties in the country revealed that half of the cases of defendants charged with an assault were dismissed outright; half of the remaining charges were reduced to misdemeanors.[7] All of this "overcharging" of defendants comes with a distinctly racial message.

A 1993 California study revealed that, while 64% of the drug arrests of whites were not sustainable, 92% of the black men arrested by police on drug charges were subsequently released for lack of evidence or for inadmissible evidence.[8] These figures are entirely consistent with the thesis that individuals were being routinely overcharged in racially biased ways. Very little of this police activity had to do with serious or violent crime.

By the early 1990s, an absolute majority of young minority males were being arrested—most for minor crimes and misdemeanors. In addition to the approximately three million arrests for "in-

> ## By the early 1990s, an absolute majority of young minority males were being arrested—most for minor things.

dex" (violent or serious) crimes, there were 11 million arrests for lesser crimes and misdemeanors (excluding traffic offenses). Grossly disproportionate percentages of the arrestees were young African American men. The negative effects of this situation on the black community have been largely ignored.

DIFFERENT WORLDS

It is perhaps not so ironic that the incident that plunged South Central Los Angeles into civil disorder involved the acquittal of police officers in the beating of a convicted felon. Dubbed a "gorilla in the mist" on a police radio, a drunken Rodney King had led the police on a high-speed chase. Though a white suburban jury might buy the crisp difference between the "criminal" and the law-abiding citizen, such neat distinctions had limited force in communities where almost everyone has seen a father, son, brother, or close friend given the same "criminal" label.

When Los Angeles city prosecutors ran background checks on the first 1,000 rioters who were arrested and charged with misdemeanors (most having to do with curfew violations), they found that 40% had criminal records and that nearly one-third were on probation or parole. From this important bit of information, the deputy city attorney drew the kind of flawed conclusion that has shaped justice policy in the inner city for most of the past two decades: "This was not an instantaneous 'good guy rage' kind of thing," he said. "This was a 'bad guy' taking advantage of a situation out of control."[9]

The city attorney's statement was disingenuous at best. He seemed not to realize that, had the police stopped any 1,000 young African American men in the inner city, at least 400 would be found to have criminal records. Moreover, the matter of what kinds of criminal records these LA offenders had was not pursued. The deputy public defender for Los Angeles County cited the case of one of his clients, a 50-year-old man whose criminal record consisted of a single drunk driving arrest 20 years before.[10]

In the year preceding the riots, one-third of all the young black men (between the ages of 20 and 29) living in Los Angeles County had been jailed at least once.[11] At this point, "good guy" versus "bad guy" analyses begin to break down.

The markers for the social disaster that was overtaking African American males had been present for a long time. In a 1967 article, Alfred Blumstein had estimated that, if current patterns continued, the chances of a black male city resident's being arrested at some time in his life for a nontraffic offense were as high as 90%.[12] Later, Blumstein and Elizabeth Graddy looked at arrest statistics gathered from the country's 56 largest cities. They concluded that, whereas one of every four males living in a large city would be arrested for a felony in his lifetime, the majority of nonwhite males could anticipate being arrested for a felony at some time during their lifetime.[13]

Misdemeanors weren't included in these calculations. Had they been, the percentage of nonwhite males who could anticipate being arrested—and at least briefly jailed—would have reached Blumstein's original 90% prediction. As appalling as these numbers seemed at the time, they were confirmed by others over the ensuing two decades.

In 1987 a California criminologist found a similar pattern in his study of arrests (including misdemeanors) not over a lifetime but in the short 12-year span between ages 18 and 30. Drawing on a statewide sample of males of all races who had been 18 years old in 1974, Robert Tillman traced their arrest records between 1974 and 1986, when they turned 30. Two-thirds of the non-white adult males had been arrested and jailed before completing their 29th year (41% for a felony).[14] Tillman included neither juvenile arrests nor arrests after age 30 in his study. Had he done so, the lifetime risk of arrest would easily have reached 90%.

A 1990 RAND Corporation study of the District of Columbia found that one-third of all 18- to 21-year-old African American males who lived there had been arrested and charged with a criminal offense during those three years of their lives. Similarly, the National Center on Institutions and Alternatives found that, on any given day in 1992, 42% of all the 18- to 35-year-old African American males who lived in the District of Columbia were in jail, in prison, on probation/parole, out on bond, or being sought on arrest warrants.[15]

A survey in Baltimore proved to be even more disturbing. Of 60,715 African American males aged 18 to 35 living in Baltimore, 34,025 (56%) were under justice supervision of some sort. The rationale given for the high arrest rates among young black men was fear of violence. However, fewer than one in 10 arrests in Baltimore were for violent crimes. Most young black men who were arrested and jailed were accused of lesser felonies and misdemeanors. The racial disparities were most alarming when drug arrests were singled out. African Americans were being arrested at *six times* the rate of whites, and more than 90% of these arrests were for simple possession.

A 1994 study by the California Commission on the Status of African American Males revealed that one-sixth of California's 625,000 black men 16 years of age and older were being arrested each year, "thereby creating police records which hinder later job prospects." Black men, who make up only 3% of California's population, accounted for 40% of the state's prison inmates.

All these findings challenged what Tillman referred to as the two assumptions that underlie most popular discussion of crime:

• that the world is made up of two types of people—those who commit crimes and those who don't—and

> # One-fourth of young African American males (aged 18 to 34) in Duval County were being jailed each year.

• that criminals form a very small portion of the total population.

As Tillman put it, "The problem appears to be rooted in 'social-structural' conditions, i.e., political, economic, and social institutions that adversely affect large numbers of young adult males, particularly those within certain strata of society. Unless these conditions are recognized and steps taken to alter them, little change can be expected in the frequency with which young men become the subjects of the criminal justice system."[16]

The practice of assaulting social problems through our various wars on crime has succeeded in identifying an unusually large number of enemies. By 1994 the number of criminal records in the U.S. approached 50 million—with nearly 60% of the increase occurring in the last decade. With more than 90% of these cases being males and with only about 130 million males residing in the country (including children and the aged), one can only conclude that a larger number of one's young and middle-aged male friends and relatives have a "criminal history" than most would care to acknowledge.[17] Among minority families, the numbers of young men with criminal records would prove to be devastating.

A COUNTY JAIL EXPERIENCE

From 1989 to 1994, I was appointed by the federal court to monitor jail overcrowding in Jacksonville, Florida (Duval County). African American males were being jailed in grossly disproportionate numbers. While African Ameri-

cans made up about 12% of the county's population, half of the men being brought into the jail each day were African American. Because they were less likely to be able to make even the most modest bail, they tended to stay in jail longer—accounting for 65% to 70% of the population on any given day.

One-fourth of young African American males (aged 18 to 34) in Duval County were being jailed each year.[18] Three-fourths of 18-year-old black youths living in the county would be jailed at least once before reaching age 35. A quarter of all African Americans between the ages of 15 and 17 were arrested during the last four months of 1991 alone.

Very little of this pandemic jailing had to do with serious or violent crime. It was mostly directed at those accused of offenses against "public order" and other lesser offenses. The 10 charges for which individuals were being arrested and jailed most frequently are shown in Table 1.

These figures for Duval County were consistent with national trends. For example, there were an estimated 14,211,900 arrests in the U.S. in 1991. Of these, 2,971,400 were listed as being for index crimes. The remaining 11,240,500 arrests were for nonindex offenses, including everything from forgery (103,700) to public drunkenness (881,100) to curfew and loitering offenses (93,400) to "runaways." The largest single category was the all-inclusive "other." Arrests classified as "other" made up 21% of all reported arrests nationally in 1991. By definition, these arrests were for minor offenses that could not be classified under the "index" categories set forth by the nomenclature of the FBI *Uniform Crime Reports.*[19]

Fewer than 5% of the thousands of young men run through the Duval County Jail ultimately received a state prison sentence. Why? The routine response to this question has been the "commonsense" conclusion that someone is letting the criminals off easy and that slick attorneys are part of the problem. But that conclusion doesn't seem to work in Duval County, which has a statewide reputation as being among the harshest jurisdictions in dealing with offenders.

Most inmates pled guilty to minor charges in order to be released from jail with "time served." Their actual guilt or innocence was beside the point. Because they were poor and could not come up with bail, maintaining their innocence and requesting a trial simply guaranteed that they would sit in jail for weeks or months awaiting a hearing date—a longer wait than many sentences that might later be imposed should they be found guilty of the charges for which they were being held. As for slick lawyers, most inmates were lucky to meet their court-appointed attorneys on the way into the courtroom.

RABBLE MANAGEMENT

At its worst, the experience of the poor and minorities who have overpopulated this one large local corrections system lends validity to California sociologist John Irwin's unhappy characterization of jails as institutions for "rabble management." Here are just a few examples.

• A young African American man suffering from asthma and pneumonia had been held in the jail for 22 days on $1,500 bond. He had been jailed on a warrant for not paying $35 in court costs on a four-month-old shoplifting charge. While in jail he lost his job as a truck driver.

• An unemployed 25-year-old African American male had been jailed for "petty theft" and was being held for want of $353 bond. The police arrest report stated, "Investigation revealed that suspect walked into Woolworths, then suspect went to the candy isle [sic] and

picked up two Snickers valued at $1.58. Suspect was observed by store security placing the items in bag without paying for the merchandise. Suspect had to be physical [sic] restrained by store security since suspect was uncooperative."

• A frail 81-year-old African American man was arrested for "gambling" (i.e., playing cards for money with friends).

• A 30-year-old man was being held after having been released two weeks earlier from a Florida state prison where he had served six years. He was out three days and, as per the conditions of his release, had reported to the local police station. He was arrested on the spot on an outstanding traffic fine that was four years old. He was in the state prison when the warrant had been issued and was unaware of it.

Among the "guilty," similar patterns emerged.

• An 18-year-old African American was sentenced to 45 days for taking one cigarette out of a pack on a store shelf, smoking it, and returning the pack to the shelf.

• A 31-year-old African American was given four months in jail for taking a pair of sunglasses from a store.

• A 37-year-old unemployed African American man was sentenced to 150 days in jail for nonpayment of child support.

• A 32-year-old African American man was given 60 days for shoplifting a package of lunch meat.

• A 29-year-old African American man was sentenced to 60 days for petty theft from a gas station convenience store, having put food items into his pants pocket.

• An 18-year-old African American was sentenced to 60 days for selling fake "crack" to vice police for $20.

• A clearly psychotic 54-year-old African American male was sentenced to 60 days for "trespassing" and "resisting arrest without violence." He had been harassing customers at a convenience store and had refused to leave.

• A 34-year-old African American was serving 60 days for shoplifting a package of meat from a supermarket. Pending sentencing, he had been at home, having paid the $150 cash bond. He returned to court for his sentencing and jailing.

Absent some unusual condition, in very few of these cases would a white person of moderate means, with adequate legal representation, expect to be jailed.

In those rare cases where black men were allowed an "alternative" to incarceration, similar patterns emerged. In the "home detention" program, for example, an electronic "bracelet" is attached to the person's ankle. He or she is unable to leave home without a signal being sent to a central computer system, thereby incurring an "escape" charge. Here are some of those who were sentenced to this alternative.

• A 72-year-old man was sentenced to one year for "driving under the influence" on his moped. He was allowed into the home detention program because of his age and arthritis. Unable to work, he was placed on 24-hour curfew. He lived alone with his dog.

• A 43-year-old man was given four months for "resisting arrest without violence." He was a first offender and a practicing attorney.

• A 22-year-old had been charged with sale and possession of crack cocaine and placed on home detention. He was placed in the program because of his handicapping condition: he had been shot and was totally blind. He was undergoing eye surgery while in home detention.

• A 25-year-old was sentenced to 30 days for petty theft and "resisting and opposing" a police officer. He was in the advanced stages of Hodgkin's disease and, while on home detention, had to be rushed to a hospital emergency room on

---

TABLE 1.

Top 10 Offenses, Duval County, Florida, 1989–94

Offense	Percentage of All Arrests
Other*	18.4
Traffic (excluding drunk driving)	16.3
Shoplifting	9.1
Driving Under Influence	7.0
Assault (simple)	6.6
Drug Sale/Purchase	6.0
Assault (aggravated)	5.0
Disorderly Intoxication	3.0
Worthless Checks	3.0
Burglary	3.0

*"Other" refers to mostly misdemeanor offenses that did not fit the Uniform Crime Report categories (which include all major felony charges). Among offenses classified as "other" in this case were such charges as feeding alligator or crocodile, resisting without violence, loitering, trespassing, nonsupport, technical violations of probation/parole, feeding unsterilized garbage to animals, impersonating a massage license holder, contempt, and 2,990 other transgressions.

two occasions to be resuscitated. He died one week prior to the expiration of his 30-day sentence.

One could draw the obvious conclusion from these examples that, at best, the justice system was engaged in some kind of "overkill." Studies in jurisdictions as disparate as Rochester, New York, and Los Angeles showed similar patterns.[20]

Despite legitimate concern over violence among inner-city youths, the bulk of young African American men being dragged into the justice system are charged with misdemeanors and lesser nonviolent felonies. All of this suggests that the currently popular "broken window theory" of arresting individuals for petty violations of public order comes with an ingrained racial twist.

Indeed, according to Shirley Ann Vining Brown, many blacks migrated north in the early 1900s because of their resentment of the law-enforcement tactics in southern counties where officials were paid a bounty for every man arrested. "Large numbers of Black men were rounded up for petty infractions of the law such as littering and disorderly conduct. Others were arrested on various charges of suspicion. Heavy fines were often levied for such small violations, and frequently those who could not pay were imprisoned." Black men were arrested "when the labor market was in low supply and workers were needed for road work, ensuring that poor or working-class black males would have to spend time in prison."[21]

As these men came north, arrests there increased dramatically. A U.S. Department of Labor study revealed that, in Cleveland, blacks were routinely being arrested by police and sent to prison on the charge of "suspicion."[22] "It was," as Brown commented, "this type of action by police that accounted for much of the 'Negro Crime' reported during this period (in the 1920s) in the United States."[23]

Continuing into the 1980s and 1990s, this process, so massive in implementation and so racially skewed in outcome, has produced a climate of alienation, hostility, social unrest, and violence in the nation's inner cities.

UNANTICIPATED CONSEQUENCES

On 6 March 1990 an 18-year-old African American man was acquitted of a felony by a black jury in the District of Columbia. That would not have been unusual, but something else was afoot in this courtroom. As the *Washington*

> **Arresting individuals for petty violations of public order comes with an ingrained racial twist.**

Post described the scene: "One young juror was crying when the verdict came. The prosecutor gaped as it was read. The crashing sound in the courtroom was the defendant, whose elation propelled him backward over his chair."[24]

Three weeks later, a letter arrived at D.C. Superior Court. It was from one of the jurors, who wrote that, though most of the jury believed the defendant to be guilty, they had bowed to those who "didn't want to send any more young black men to jail."

The incident was an unsettling example of one of the unanticipated consequences of the national war against crime. It has been repeated in a number of jurisdictions across the nation. In communities in which so many families have seen their sons, brothers, fathers, and friends dragged into the justice system, the idea of galvanizing and organizing the residents against the "criminals"—as though they were outsiders and enemies—is naive. The expectation that the average citizen in an inner-city neighborhood will "inform" on young men in trouble so that they might be arrested and jailed is equally naive. The reality is that the massive intrusion of the criminal justice system into the community is perceived as being as destructive and threatening as the harm done by most offenders.

The great University of Chicago social psychologist George Herbert Mead first posed the central dilemma presented to those who would use the justice system to negotiate what he referred to as the "social settlement"—a di-

lemma that plagues governments run increasingly by lawyers who sometimes seem constitutionally unable to recognize the limitations of their models. Mead wrote:

> We assume that we can detect, pursue, indict, prosecute, and punish the criminal and still retain toward him the attitude of reinstating him in the community as soon as he indicates a change in social attitude himself, that we can at the same time watch for the definite transgression of the statute to catch and overwhelm the offender, and comprehend the situation out of which the offense grows.
>
> *But the two attitudes, that of control of crime by the hostile procedure of the law and that of control through comprehension of social and psychological conditions, cannot be combined.*[25] (Emphasis added.)

Mead hoped that the newly invented juvenile courts would for the first time be able to consider theretofore "irrelevant" factors associated with delinquency and crime—the familiar root causes, such as unemployment, health problems, emotional disturbance, disorganized communities, and so on. Indeed, Mead's vision led Harvard law professor Roscoe Pound to suggest some 30 years later that the founding of the juvenile courts was as significant an event in the history of jurisprudence as the signing of the Magna Carta. But Mead's hopes were never realized, and Pound's assessment has not been borne out.

THE VERY LONG ARM OF THE LAW

Since so many young black men are being brought under the auspices of the justice system, it seems sensible to "train" them for the experience. Thus in Washington, D.C., the county police, local educators, the local chapter of the National Association for the Advancement of Colored People, and the black lawyers association sponsor courses that attempt to teach people how they should handle themselves if stopped by the police.

Here is how a reporter described one of those classes in a majority black high school just outside Washington, D.C.

> With his fingers laced behind his head and the Prince George's County police officer grabbing hard at the pager

clipped to his waistband, the smile disappeared from 17-year-old Carl Colston's face.

Later, Colston described his thoughts as the officer frisked him.

> # Contemporary white society confers a perverse identity on the young African American male postulant.

"You feel uncertain. You don't know what they are going to do."[26]

"I have been pulled over by the police numerous times," said Hardi Jones, president of the county NAACP. To many white people, this seems an odd admission though it is an entirely common experience for a black man.

HOW WIDE A NET?

In 1992 there were more than 12 million bookings into local jails. At least four to five million of those booked were African American males, most accused of minor offenses. Because many of these arrestees were jailed more than once in the same year, it is difficult to know how many individuals were involved. However, there are only about 5.5 million African American men between the ages of 18 and 39 living in the U.S. The percentages mount cumulatively each year as the pool of still unarrested but "arrestable" black men shrinks. Moreover, the process is much more complicated than the simple arrest statistics might suggest, and the implications are more far-reaching than even the most startling statistics indicate.

The scope of the problem was brought home to me in another way in Duval County. I was astonished to find that this one county of approximately 720,000 people maintained more than

330,000 active criminal records. The bulk of them had been gathered over the last 15 years. In addition, there were more than 75,000 outstanding misdemeanor arrest warrants and another 10,000 outstanding felony warrants.

RITE OF PASSAGE?

Adolescent bravado notwithstanding, going to jail is not just another rite of passage for a young male—at least not the first or second time. To suggest otherwise is to engage in the kind of nonsensical thinking we would never tolerate if the subjects were middle-class white teenagers from the suburbs. For many African American youths, the experience soon turns into a psychological struggle over whether to meekly assume or to aggressively reject the identity the ritual demands. From "assuming the position," being handcuffed, and being placed in a police van; being moved from place to place, being shackled to a line of peers and older African American males, and posing for a mug shot; being tagged at the wrist or ankle with an ID bracelet; being confined in crowded "tanks" or holding cells with a common toilet or open hole in the middle; to appearing before a robed judge, having a price set on one's head, being detained for want of bail, and, finally, joining one's peers inside or being reunited with anxious relatives outside—the entire experience is a distorted ceremonial expression of manhood for the black male in contemporary American society.

The American anthropologist Robert Linton notes the crucial fact that the identity given a novice is conferred on him by the larger society. "The child becomes a man not when he is physically mature but when he is formally recognized as a man by society. This recognition is almost always given ceremonial expression in what are technically known as puberty rites."[27] In contemporary America, the official representatives of the majority white society confer a perverse identity on the young African American male postulant. He is labeled a renegade, fit to be treated as trash. As one West Coast urban affairs writer put it:

> The L.A.P.D.'s "Operation Hammer" and other antigang dragnets that arrested kids at random . . . have tended to criminalize black youth without

class distinction. Between 1987 and 1990, the combined sweeps of the L.A.P.D. and the County Sheriff's Office ensnared 50,000 "suspects." Even the children of doctors and lawyers from View Park and Windsor Hills have had to "kiss the pavement" and occasionally endure some of the humiliations that the homeboys in the flats face every day.[28]

SNITCHING

The most vicious and bloody prison riot of this century, which occurred at the New Mexico State Prison in 1980, provides perhaps the best example of the negative outcomes of snitching, a practice that has fed violence in the inner city. In his study of the riot, Roger Morris discussed the practice of using snitches. "When two or more inmates gathered anywhere, Rodriguez would boast during his tenure as warden and afterward, half of them belonged to him. Snitching and informing in exchange for power, for revenge, for survival, for fear, occasionally even for justice . . . was a way of life at the New Mexico pen."[29]

When the lid blows in such societies, it looses violence that is as much directed at peers as at the authorities. The act of killing a "snitch" is elevated to the level of symbol—a public demonstration to others of the hardness of feeling and the ability to inflict pain or death. In prison society, such displays of violence are related to "fronting," described below. Exposed to this distorted world, the youngest inmates emerge aggressively proud of having taken as their own an identity that, when acted out on the street, ensures their alienation from the larger society.

Probably no single tactic of law enforcement has contributed more to inner-city violence than the practice of seeding the streets with informers and offering deals to snitches. The rise of wanton violence in the early 1990s coincides with the development of a national antidrug strategy based in the widespread use of informers in the cities—particularly in black communities. It has become routine for prosecutors to overcharge defendants and threaten them with stiff sentences unless they give information on a wide array of friends, associates, acquaintances, childhood chums, and relatives.

Law enforcement agencies see informers as crucial in breaking criminal organizations. However, arrests have become so pervasive in the inner city that they have affected most families. The practice of relying on informers threatens and eventually cripples much more than the criminal enterprise; it eats away at whatever social organization there is—including families—that might otherwise keep violence within bounds.

FRONTING

I first became aware of "fronting" when, as Commissioner of Children and Youth for the state of Pennsylvania, I headed an effort to remove 400 teenagers from an adult prison in Pennsylvania. In our debriefing of the young inmates we had placed in alternative settings, the term "fronting" came up repeatedly. Here's how one 16-year-old described his experience.

When I first got there this guy threatened me and told me he was going to make me his "girl." I yelled that I would beat his butt if he tried. I didn't know it then, but I'd just "fronted" on him. I had challenged him in front of the others. The other inmates told me that I had only a few days to "set up" a confrontation with the guy or I was fair game to be gang raped or taken as someone's "punk."

The young man waited for the appropriate moment when, in front of others, he could accuse the other inmate (falsely) of trying to steal his toothpaste. He then hit the inmate full in the face, breaking his nose. An all-out fight ensued. Both suffered injuries and were sent to the "hole" for a month. But the "new boy" had publicly demonstrated his willingness to be violent and had thereby established his reputation before his peers. When he emerged from the isolation unit, he would have renewed respect. Though the violence was relatively minor, the point was made. Such confrontations are just as likely to involve stabbings, serious injury, or death.

Fronting is a by-product of jailing. It allows a young man to pretend he is in control of a crazy and violent world. You see it in the pathetic posturing, menacing swagger, and cold stares that have come to define the persona of so many young males on the streets of the nation's inner cities; they tell us to watch out. The dynamic is there for all to see in the gratuitous violence of those

> **Most young black men can anticipate being ushered through a series of hothouses for sociopathy.**

who beat a white truck driver in LA. It is the stuff of public arguments that turn into shootouts and drive-by killings. It betrays the person who has learned never to make an idle threat in front of peers. If you run off at the mouth, you'd best deliver proudly within a relatively short time. It is the royal road to "respect."

It might be well to reexamine here the words of the great American sociologist Gresham Sykes, whose "participant observation" research study, *The Society of Captives,* remains a classic of American criminological literature. Written 30 years ago, it describes the identities conferred by immersion in the criminal justice system.

Imprisonment [is] directed against the very foundations of the prisoner's being. The individual's picture of himself—as a morally acceptable adult male who can present some claim to merit in his material achievements and his inner strength—begins to waver and grow dim.... As one of many, [he] finds two paths open ... to bind himself to his fellow captives with ties of mutual aid, loyalty, affection, and respect, firmly standing in opposition to the officials. [Or] he can enter into a war of all against all.[30]

Indeed, it is now a sad reality that most of the young black men can anticipate being at least briefly ushered through a series of hothouses for sociopathy: prisons, jails, detention centers, and reform schools—all of which nurture those very characteristics that can subsequently be labeled as pathological.

INTERGENERATIONAL CRIME

In an attempt to measure other unanticipated consequences of the system, John Hagan of the University of Toronto and Alberto Palloni of the University of Wisconsin reanalyzed data from the 1960s on working-class boys in London. The original study of 410 boys involved surveys, interviews, and a search of official records. The boys were interviewed at ages 8, 10, 14, 16, 18, 21, and 24. Retrospective data were also collected on the parents. The British researchers had concluded that "a constellation of adverse features of family background (including poverty, too many children, marital disharmony, and inappropriate child-rearing methods), among which parental criminality is likely to be one element, leads to a constellation of antisocial features when sons reach the age of 18, among which criminality is again likely to be one element."[31] These kinds of statements weren't particularly new. They had been made by many over the last century. Hagan and Palloni commented, "This conception of a dangerous, criminal class that is concentrated and reproduced across generations is highly durable."

When Hagan and Palloni reanalyzed the London data, however, they found more important matters at work than "defects in character or behavior." Delinquent careers among inner-city youths—indeed, patterns of intergenerational delinquency in families—were as likely to be due to intervention by the justice system in families' lives as they were to result from variables of culture and character. The better predictor of future delinquency was whether a boy or his father had been effectively labeled as a criminal by the larger society.

In a recent reanalysis of the classic American study of delinquents in Massachusetts by Sheldon Glueck and Eleanor Glueck, sociologists John Laub and Robert Sampson found essentially the same negative effects from criminal and juvenile justice interventions.[32]

There is little reason to believe that the routing of so many African American youths through the justice system would be any less debilitating than it was for white youths in London or Boston. Indeed, when applied to those with little going for them in the larger society, strategies that rely primarily on de-

> **Anticrime policy in the U.S. is highly unlikely to be derived from humane impulse or careful analysis.**

terrence are more likely to exacerbate their situations.

PROBATION

Invented by John Augustus, a Boston shoemaker, over 100 years ago as a way of offering an alternative to jail, probation has deteriorated to the point where the average probation officer is indistinguishable from a policeman. The effects have been only too obvious.

In 1993 almost one-third of the 130,000 inmates in California's state prisons had been put there by their probation officers. These inmates were imprisoned for "technically violating" the conditions of their probation or parole—such things as missing appointments, not attending Alcoholics Anonymous meetings, being unemployed, or moving or marrying without permission. They had not engaged in behavior sufficient to warrant an arrest or criminal charge.

In the world of criminal justice, professional diagnosticians and therapists are expected to deliver one basic commodity, what the late British social anthropologist Sir Edmund Leach called "treatment" when applied to delinquents: "the imposition of discipline by force—the maintenance of the existing order against threats which might arise from its own internal contradictions."[33]

SENTIMENTALIST VERSUS IGNORAMUS

At its best, the criminal justice system affords a democratic society mostly short-term control of and protection from those whose lives are out of control and who represent a threat to others. Such control is obviously necessary in some cases. However, when the justice system becomes the definer of social problems and the foundation of social policy, matters turn dangerous for all concerned. Relying on "experience" emanating from the justice system is dicey even in the best of circumstances. Its rituals and procedures distort social realities and feed stereotypes at virtually every step.

It all harks back to George Herbert Mead's comment regarding those who would attempt to solve social problems through the criminal trial process: "The social worker in the court is the sentimentalist, [but] the legalist in the social settlement, in spite of his learned doctrine, is the ignoramus."[34]

The rigid categories that the justice system stands ready to create in abundance seem particularly precious in a society grown vicious over crime—offering refuge in an artificial world of black-and-white issues that carry the system ever further from the complexity of human narrative. Acknowledging the specific conditions out of which a particular violent offender might have arisen is apparently more threatening to our society now than the violent act itself. Such uncomfortable realities undermine the sense of certainty that feeds the moral indignation and drives the punitive response on which the justice system rests. It is much easier to gear the citizenry up to fight the devil than it is to ask it to consider the devilish details that brought the demon to the door. We would rather immerse ourselves in a massive exercise in selective inattention.

THE LIKELY FUTURE

If we have learned anything over the past two decades, it is that anticrime policy in the U.S. is highly unlikely to be derived from either humane impulse or careful analysis. Rather, it is judged for its potential to be distilled into succinct sound bites and applause-garnering throwaway lines. There is less interest in what is correct or even in what "works" than in what sounds good.

Given the racial patterns now firmly fixed in American criminal justice policy and practice, the idea that the costs saved by undoing welfare and family support programs might be used to institutionalize a substantial percentage of the black male population seems increasingly attractive to the majority. One can anticipate ever more florid justifications of the national embarrassment of a nation that will shortly see that it has incarcerated most of its young black men.

DEALING WITH THE DISPOSABLE

Neoconservative dogma currently shapes our national crime policy. It is all there: the objectification of offenders as different from everyone else, the ever larger proportions of minority citizens filling prisons, the destruction of hope through dismissing the possibility of rehabilitation, the shunting of greater numbers of juveniles into adult prisons, and, most recently, the triage management of the disposable through calls to begin removing nondelinquent inner-city youngsters from largely African American single-parent homes to state institutions, camps, or what Charles Murray calls "lavishly funded orphanages" and James Q. Wilson calls "boarding schools."[35] Joining the call for removing children from single-parent homes to "orphanages" is William Bennett.[36]

The Pandora's box that Wilson and Richard Herrnstein opened in their 1985 book, *Crime & Human Nature,* is likely to lead to that more alluring search that has entranced racially obsessed commentators for the last century: the quest for "criminal man." It will set the country on a new adventure that will avoid the murkiness of "root causes" while providing the white majority with a more comforting analysis. We can then move on from deterrence to more sophisticated preventive strategies. The researchers appropriate to this task are standing in line ready to guide us down the slippery slope toward eugenics.

It was Graham Greene, speaking to a conference in France three years after the fall of Nazism, who observed, "The totalitarian state contrives, by educating its citizens, to suppress all sense of guilt, all indecision of mind."[37] One can hope that, when it comes to the African American male, some "indecision of mind" will linger in America for a while longer. And for readers of the *Kappan,* we can also hope that American educators will become increasingly aware of the unstated assumptions that underlie the policies and practices of the criminal justice system in America. Meanwhile, any "solutions" proposed in our current state are likely to smack of finality.

1. E. J. Dionne, *Why Americans Hate Politics* (New York: Simon & Schuster, 1992), p. 6.
2. Patrick Murphy, *Keeping Score: The Frailties of the Federal Drug Budget* (Santa Monica, Calif.: RAND Drug Policy Research Center, Issue Paper, January 1994), p. 5.
3. *Justice Expenditure and Employment, 1990* (Washington, D.C.: Bureau of Justice Statistics, U.S. Department of Justice, Bulletin NCLJ-135777, August 1992), p. 1.
4. Scott Boggess and John Bound, *Comparison Study of Uniform Crime Report, National Crime Survey and Imprisonment Rates* (Ann Arbor: National Bureau of Economic Research, University of Michigan, 1993). In reanalyzing the major sources of crime statistics, the authors concluded that the rate of serious crime as measured by Uniform Crime Report data actually fell by 2% between 1979 and 1991, while the National Crime Survey registered a 27% drop in crimes against persons and a 31% drop in property crimes during the same period.
5. *The Prosecution of Felony Arrests* (Washington, D.C.: Office of Justice Programs, U.S. Department of Justice, 1987).
6. Patrick Langan and John M. Dawson, *Felony Sentences in State Courts, 1990* (Washington, D.C.: Bureau of Justice Statistics, U.S. Department of Justice, NCJ-140186, March 1993), p. 5.
7. Pheny Z. Smith, *Felony Defendants in Large Urban Counties, 1990* (Washington, D.C.: Bureau of Justice Statistics, U.S. Department of Justice, NCJ-1441872, May 1993), p. 13.
8. Sonia Nazario, "Odds Grim for Black Men in California," *Washington Post,* 12 December 1993, p. A-9.
9. Paul Lieberman, "40% of Riot Suspects Found to Have Criminal Records," *Los Angeles Times,* 19 May 1992, p. B-4. A later *Times* survey of 700 people convicted of riot-related felonies (more than 90% convicted of "looting") found that 60% had previously been arrested. See *Los Angeles Times,* 2 May 1993, p. A-34.
10. Lieberman, p. B-4.
11. James Austin and Donald Irie, *Los Angeles County Sheriff's Department Jail Population Analysis and Policy Simulations: Briefing Report* (San Francisco: National Council on Crime and Delinquency, 21 August 1992).
12. Alfred Blumstein, "Systems Analysis and the Criminal Justice System," *Annals of the American Academy of Political and Social Science,* November 1967, p. 99.
13. Alfred Blumstein and Elizabeth Graddy, "Prevalence and Recidivism in Index Arrests: A Feedback Model," *Law and Society Review,* vol. 16, 1981–82, pp. 279–80.
14. Robert Tillman, "The Size of the 'Criminal Population': The Prevalence and Incidence of Adult Arrests," *Criminology,* Fall 1987, pp. 335–47.
15. Jerome Miller and Barry Holman, *Hobbling a Generation: African American Males in the District of Columbia's Criminal Justice System* (Washington, D.C.: National Center on Institutions and Alternatives, March 1992).
16. Tillman, p. 6.
17. *Proceedings of BJS/SEARCH Conference* (Washington, D.C.: U.S. Department of Justice, January 1992, NCJ-133532).
18. Jerome Miller, *Duval County Jail Report,* submitted to the Honorable Howell W. Melton, U.S. District Judge, Middle District of Florida, Jacksonville, 1 June 1993, pp. 82–83.
19. Federal Bureau of Investigation, *Crime in the United States, 1991* (Washington, D.C.: U.S. Department of Justice, 1992), p. 213.
20. *Justice in Jeopardy,* Report to Monroe County Bar Association Board of Trustees, May 1992; and James Austin, *Los Angeles County Sheriff's Department Jail Population Analysis and Policy Simulations* (San Francisco: National Council on Crime and Delinquency, 21 August 1992).
21. Shirley Ann Vining Brown, "Race as a Factor in the Intra-Prison Outcomes of Youthful First Offenders" (Doctoral dissertation, University of Michigan, 1975).
22. F. D. Tyson, *Negro Migration in 1916–17* (Washington, D.C.: U.S. Department of Labor, 1918), p. 141.
23. Brown, op. cit.
24. Bart Gellman and Sari Horwitz, "Letter Stirs Debate After Acquittal: Writer Says Jurors Bowed to Racial Issue in D.C. Murder Case," *Washington Post,* 29 March 1990, p. A-1.
25. George Herbert Mead, "The Psychology of Punitive Justice," *American Journal of Sociology,* vol. 23, 1917, pp. 577–602.
26. "The Dreaded 'Encounter' with Police," *Washington Post,* 18 January 1994, Metro Section, p. 1.
27. Robert Linton, *The Study of Man* (New York: Appleton-Crofts, 1936).
28. Mike Davis, "In LA, Burning All Illusions," *The Nation,* 1 June 1992, p. 744.
29. Roger Morris, *The Devil's Butcher Shop: The New Mexico Prison Uprising* (New York: Franklin Watts, 1983), p. 87.
30. Gresham Sykes, *The Society of Captives* (Princeton, N.J.: Princeton University Press, 1958), pp. 78–79.
31. John Hagan and Alberto Palloni, "The Social Reproduction of a Criminal Class in Working-Class London Circa 1950–1980," *American Journal of Sociology,* September 1990.
32. John H. Laub and Robert J. Sampson, "The Long-Term Effect of Punitive Discipline," revised version of paper presented at the Life History Research Society Meeting, 6 May 1992, Boston.
33. Edmund Leach, *A Runaway World: The BBC Reith Lectures* (London: British Broadcasting Corporation, 1967).
34. Mead, p. 585.
35. James Q. Wilson, "Redefining Equality: The Liberalism of Mickey Kaus," *Public Interest,* Fall 1992, p. 102.
36. *Washington Times,* 25 January 1994, p. C-3.
37. Graham Greene, *Reflections,* edited by Judith Adamson (London: Reinhardt Books, 1991).

AMERICAN THOUGHT

IS THE U.S. MORALLY IN TROUBLE?

America in the 1990s is suffering from loss of values, truth, moral literacy, trust, empathy, independence and confidence, family, and faith. However, for more than 200 years, we have found ways of overcoming adversity and succeeding against all odds.

by George Roche

I AM an inveterate list maker. I love making lists—of tools and gadgets to buy at the hardware store, grocery staples that need restocking. New Year's resolutions—of little yet vitally important details of living of which I often need to be reminded. Many of the notes I write to myself, especially those on my own shortcomings, begin with the words, "I must remember to. . . ."

So, it is not surprising that, when I was asked to reflect on our present culture and the general state of American society, my immediate response was to pick up a pen and pad. At the top of the first page, I wrote the heading: "America in the 1990s: Why We Are in So Much Trouble." The following list is the result, a compilation of what the nation has lost:

The loss of values. Values are the building blocks and mortar that keep our entire civilization together. Yet, we no longer seem to think our values are worth defending. "Political correctness" dominates the academy and the public square. This doctrine holds that all differences in ideas, values, and lifestyles are equally valid and that any attempt to prefer one over the other is an act of prejudice. Moreover, the differences between people—between blacks and whites, men and women, rich and poor, Westerners and non-Westerners—are more important than the qualities and values they share in common. According to PC advocates, questions of race, gender, class, and power are the only real issues that govern human events.

If you think this kind of thinking is confined to college campuses and our intellectual elites, just consider the Los Angeles riots, the O.J. Simpson murder trial, or any number of recent events that demonstrate how values have been destroyed by political correctness. Philosopher Jacques Barzun had it right when he said that political correctness does not legislate tolerance; it only organizes hatred.

The loss of truth. PC advocates claim that truth really isn't objective at all; it depends on our point of view. One person's truth is supposed to be just as good (or, more to the point, just as unreliable) as another's. What has been passed off as "truth" are merely the collective prejudices of the dominant ruling class and culture. We must be shown how to "deconstruct" what we think is true.

The only truth that political correctness *will* admit is that everything—every poem, book, historical event or person, emotion, attitude, belief, and action—must be viewed

From *USA Today Magazine*, January 1997, pp. 26-27. © 1997 by the Society for the Advancement of Education. Reprinted by permission.

in a political context as an instrument of exclusion, oppression, or liberation.

The loss of moral literacy. Honor and virtue increasingly are rare commodities. Cheating and lying have become acceptable, especially in school, because children believe that, with few exceptions, "everybody's doing it." Sadly for America, they may be right. In a 1995 *Reader's Digest* article, Daniel R. Levine notes that *Who's Who Among American High School Students* polled more than 3,000 juniors and seniors who were at the top of their class. Seventy-eight percent admitted cheating and 89% indicated that cheating was common at their schools.

In Kansas, Levine adds, a survey of the same number of college students led to almost identical results. Emporia State University psychology professor Stephen F. Davis found that 76% had cheated. He commented: "The numbers alone are disturbing, but even more alarming is the attitude. There's no remorse. For students, cheating is a way of life."

Educators are not only doing a poor job of teaching the three Rs, they are failing to teach children the difference between right and wrong. Observers have characterized this as "a hole in the moral ozone," "moral poverty," or "moral illiteracy."

The loss of trust. We live in what may be the most cynical age in history—and the most gullible. Americans are skeptical about many of the things we should believe, while blindly accepting many of the things we should question. On the one hand, we distrust politicians, journalists, and filmmakers because we know that they often have lied to us and deceived us, but, on the other hand, we still look to them as primary sources of information and interpreters of reality.

According to social scientist Francis Fukuyama, author of *Trust: The Social Virtues and the Creation of Prosperity,* we seem to trust our fellow citizens less and less. This "decline of sociability" dramatically weakens our communities, economy, and civil society, which all depend on the "social capital" that is created by shared goodwill, ethical norms, and expectations. He warns that, if we do not revive our trust in others, we will end up cooperating only under a system of coercion and regulation.

The loss of empathy. I am not talking about what Pres. Clinton meant when he said to the nation, "I feel your pain." By empathy, I am referring to the ability to transcend our own immediate concerns to understand other human beings—to see the world from their perspectives without surrendering our own. Former National Endowment for the Humanities chairman Lynne V. Cheney tells of an incident that occurred in 1994 that provides "a chilling vision of life" without empathy:

"That summer, Mohammed Jaberipour, 49, was working a route in south Philadelphia in a Mister Softee ice cream truck when a 16-year-old tried to extort money. Jaberipour refused, and the youth shot him. As the father of three lay dying, neighborhood teenagers laughed and mocked his agony in a rap song they composed on the spot: 'They killed Mr. Softee.'

" 'It wasn't human,' another ice cream truck driver, a friend of Jaberipour who came on the scene shortly after the shooting, told the Philadelphia *Daily News,* 'People were laughing and asking me for ice cream. I was crying. . . . They were acting as though a cat had died, not a human being.' "

Cheney quotes the conclusion of newspaper columnist Bob Greene: "We have increasingly become a nation of citizens who watch anything and everything as if it is all a show." She adds, "But however it has come about, people who laugh at a dying man have no sense that a stranger can suffer as they do."

The loss of independence and confidence. I don't know the statistics, but I am willing to bet that there are more laws and regulations on the books than there are people living in the U.S. The state dictates how we should educate our children, earn our living, guard our health, take care of our communities, and even worship our God. Although there has been a tremendous resurgence of conservatism in this country, too many of us still look to Washington to provide a vast array of services that better would be left to the private sector and to assume responsibilities we once proudly bore.

The fact is that we no longer are independent because we have lost confidence in ourselves. We have grown accustomed to thinking that there are some problems that are just so big and complex that only something else that is big and complex—like government—can tackle them.

The loss of family. The good news is that the vital role of the traditional family at long last is the subject of national attention. The breakdown of the family—rather than poverty, race, or any other factor cited by the liberal establishment—is widely recognized now as the real root cause of rising rates of substance abuse, teen suicide, abortion, academic failure, welfare dependency, and violent crime.

The bad news, though, is that this time bomb isn't ticking—it already has exploded, and we are experiencing the fallout. Nearly one-third of all children are now born to single mothers. If this trend continues, in 20 years, nearly half of all children in our nation will be born out of wedlock. Meanwhile, the national crime rate has tripled in the space of 30 years, and observers like Princeton University sociologist John J. Dilulio, Jr., warn that we

are breeding a whole new group of "super-predators"—youths who commit violent acts with absolutely no sense of remorse or respect for human life and who, according to one prosecutor, "kill or maim on impulse, without any intelligible motive."

It is no wonder that, for the first time in decades, almost all the experts on the right and the left in psychology, sociology, social work, and law enforcement agree: Our children need capable, responsible parents who have made a lifelong commitment to each other within the specific institution of marriage. This is because children need stability and consistency in their lives. They need the thousands of little moral and practical lessons that are taught in the context of daily family life. Above all, they need the love that only a mother and father can give.

The loss of faith. Although millions of us still attend church and profess to believe in a Creator, we hold ourselves aloof from God. He is not, as He should be, the most important, guiding force in our daily lives. In one way, this is more shocking than if we had become atheists. While atheists deny God and His authority, we accept Him, but refuse to take Him seriously. At school, work, social gatherings, and in public, we are too afraid, reluctant, or embarrassed to even mention His name.

We constantly are searching for substitutes just as dieters crave fat-free cookies and ice cream. We want the taste of faith,

but not the substance, and we expect to find it in the trendy new Life Experience Enrichment movement that peddles its secrets at New Age retreats, on motivational cassettes, and in glitzy paperbacks and infomercials.

In terms of sheer numbers, the Judeo-Christian community still is the largest group of any kind in America, but we have embraced a mainly post-Judeo-Christian culture in which traditional forms of any religion are relegated to the "back of the bus."

Yet, after examining this gloomy list, I feel that, despite our troubles, we have many reasons to expect a bright future. There literally are millions of us who, for the most part, do defend our values; tell the truth; live honorably and virtuously; live up to high moral standards; exhibit trust, independence, and empathy; build strong families; and are courageous witnesses to faith.

For more than 200 years, we have found ways of overcoming adversity and succeeding against all odds. Though they may sometimes be threatened, our best qualities—optimism, resilience, moral indignation, ingenuity, charity, compassion, and spiritual strength—have a way of resurfacing when we need them most.

Southern Curse

Why America's Murder Rate Is So High

By FOX BUTTERFIELD

MURDER in the United States has been dropping dramatically for years, to the lowest level since the modern crime wave began in the 1960's. But this encouraging decline has masked a fundamental fact—that there is no such thing as an American murder rate.

In fact, there are sharp regional differences in homicide, with the South having by far the highest murder rate, almost double that of the Northeast, a divergence that has persisted for as long as records have been kept, starting in the 19th century. The former slaveholding states of the old Confederacy all rank in the top 20 states for murder, led by Louisiana, with a rate of 17.5 murders per 100,000 people in 1996. The 10 states with the lowest homicide rates are in New England and the northern Midwest, with South Dakota's the lowest at 1.2 murders per 100,000 people.

It's Personal

Experts note, in addition, that much of the disparity in murder rates between the South and other sections of the country stems from a difference in the character of Southern homicide. In the South, many murders are of a personal and traditional nature: a barroom brawl, a quarrel between acquaintances or a fight between lovers. Elsewhere, homicides usually begin with another crime, like a robbery gone bad, and typically involve strangers.

Most important, the experts say, the high Southern murder rate is a key factor behind America's disproportionately high homicide rate compared with other democratic, industrialized nations. In 1996, the last year for which data are available, the United States murder rate was 7.4 per 100,000 people. The next closest country was Finland, at 3.2 per 100,000 people,

with France at 1.1, Japan at 0.6 and Britain at 0.5.

While the United States has much more murder than comparable countries, it does not necessarily have much more crime. England has a higher rate of burglary. France has a higher rate of auto theft. The Netherlands and Australia have about the same total crime rate.

"The whole American scandalously high homicide rates are Southern in origin," says Roger Lane, a professor of history at Haverford College and author of "Murder in America: A History" (Ohio State University Press, 1997). Until the 1960's, Professor Lane said, America's big cities actually had murder rates lower than the national average, since the national rate had been skewed upward by Southern homicides.

The question of why murder is so prevalent in the South has fascinated observers as far back as Alexis de Tocqueville, who in the early 1830's recorded a remark by a young lawyer he encountered in Alabama. "There is no one here but carries arms under his clothes," the lawyer said. "At the slightest quarrel, knife or pistol comes to hand. These things happen continually; it is a semi-barbarous state of society."

A study of 19th century judicial records completed in 1980 by Michael Hindus, a lawyer, found that from 1800 to 1860 the murder rate in South Carolina, an overwhelmingly rural, agrarian area, was four times higher than that of Massachusetts, then the most urban, industrial state. More than a century later, the difference persists in almost the same magnitude. In 1996, the murder rate in South Carolina was 9 per 100,000 people, according to the Federal Bureau of Investigation; in Massachusetts it was 2.6 per 100,000 people.

High Southern homicide rates challenge a central theory of criminology, which predicts more murder in densely populated urban areas where crowding and poverty break down traditional social ties and values.

Southern homicide was typically rural, and over the years many theories have been advanced to explain it. Frederick Law Olmsted, who traveled through the South in the 1850's and wrote about it in "Journeys and Explorations in the Cotton Kingdom," pointed to the persistence of frontier conditions in the region. Southern plantation agriculture, characterized by widely scattered settlements and a lack of roads and schools, left the region a frontier until after the Civil War, helping to breed lawlessness.

'Primal Honor'

Contemporary historians have suggested other sources of Southern bellicosity. David Hackett Fischer, a professor of history at Brandeis University, says a critical factor was the heavy settlement of the South by immigrants referred to today as Scotch Irish—people from the north of Britain, the lowlands of Scotland and the north of Ireland.

These settlers, whom Benjamin Franklin described as "white savages," brought with them a culture based on centuries of fighting between the kings of England and Scotland over the borderlands they inhabited. They had a penchant for family feuds, a love of whisky and a warrior ethic that demanded vengeance, Professor Fischer said.

The mother of Andrew Jackson, herself an immigrant from the north of Ireland, advised her boy: "Andrew, never tell a lie, nor take what is not your own, nor sue anybody for slander, assault and battery. Always settle them cases yourself." He did, becoming a famous pistol dueler.

Behind such toughness was an ethnic of "primal honor," according to Bertram Wyatt-Brown, a professor of history at the University of Florida. Above all, honor meant reputation. "You identified yourself on the basis of what others think of you, so appearances mattered," Professor Wyatt-Brown said.

Honor was reinforced by slavery. Slavery by its nature dishonors one group and contrives to give all honor to another. In the South, race helped turn the distinction between master and slave into an absolute divide, perpetuating whites' belief that they were people of honor. And since slavery could be maintained only by the daily exercise of brute force, slave owners became very sensitive to the slightest threat to their superiority, a touchiness that expanded from plantation fields to all areas of their lives, Professor Lane said.

Outlaw Legacy

The Reconstruction period after the Civil War, in which white Southerners often resorted to terror or killings to restore their political control, helped perpetuate the high level of violence in the South, a problem that reached its apogee in the 1890's with lynching.

The cult of honor was gradually transmuted into African-American slave society, scholars now believe, as slaves and their emancipated descen-

dants found themselves outside the law in the South, with sheriffs, judges and juries all controlled by whites. "For blacks in the South, there was no alternative to settling disputes personally and physically," said Professor Lane.

The South in the 20th century has become more like the rest of the nation, as it has become more urban and industrial. Waves of whites flocking from the cold North to the Sun Belt states and the great migration of blacks going the other way also have made the regions more similar.

But the concern with honor persists, especially in smaller cities and rural areas, said Richard Nisbett, a professor of psychology at the University of Michigan. In analyzing homicide data for whites, Professor Nisbett found there was no difference in murder rates between white males in the largest cities in the South and the rest of the country. But in medium-sized cities, with populations between 50,000 and 200,000, Southern white males commit murder at a rate twice that of their counterparts in the rest of the nation, he said. In small cities, with populations from 10,000 to 50,000, the ratio is 3 to 1 and in rural areas it is 4 to 1. The excess murder in the South, he said, comes from crimes "where you could plausibly say an insult had been involved."

Professor Nisbett devised a psychological test, administered to students at the University of Michigan, that appears to demonstrate a Southern sensitivity to insult and disposition to violence. In the test, a person unexpectedly bumps into a subject as he walks down a corridor, and calls him a jerk. Out-of-state white male students from the South, even premed students, tend to react with anger and show measurable increases in levels of testosterone and cortisol, hormones that indicate stress. White Northern males typically respond by laughing the incident off and do not show the same hormonal reactions, Professor Nisbett said.

In the view of historians, traditional Southern influences and attitudes help explain Louisiana's

The Southern States Still Have the Highest

ACROSS THE NATION, MURDER RATES HAVE DROPPED ...

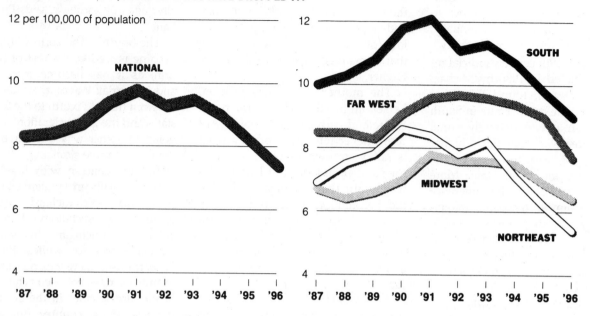

12 per 100,000 of population

NATIONAL

10

8

6

4

'87 '88 '89 '90 '91 '92 '93 '94 '95 '96

12

SOUTH

FAR WEST

10

MIDWEST

8

6

NORTHEAST

4

'87 '88 '89 '90 '91 '92 '93 '94 '95 '96

... BUT ARE STILL HIGHER IN THE SOUTH THAN IN OTHER REGIONS

The FBI divides the nation into four regions: the Northeast, the South, the Midwest and the West. Here are the states in each region and the regional homicide rates in 1996.

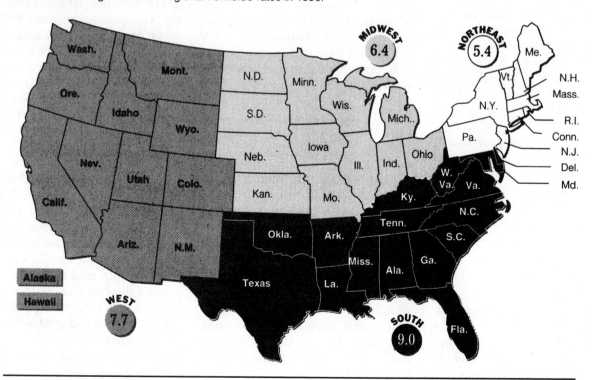

Murder Rates

THE HOMICIDE RATE IN 1996, STATE BY STATE

Twelve of the 20 states with the highest murder rates per 100,000 of population are in the South.

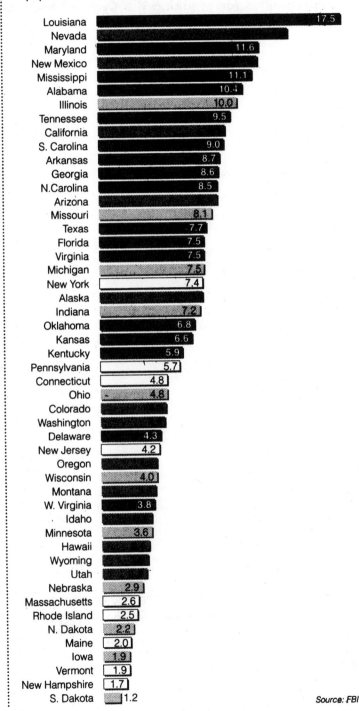

State	Rate
Louisiana	17.5
Nevada	
Maryland	11.6
New Mexico	
Mississippi	11.1
Alabama	10.4
Illinois	10.0
Tennessee	9.5
California	
S. Carolina	9.0
Arkansas	8.7
Georgia	8.6
N. Carolina	8.5
Arizona	
Missouri	8.1
Texas	7.7
Florida	7.5
Virginia	7.5
Michigan	7.5
New York	7.4
Alaska	
Indiana	7.2
Oklahoma	6.8
Kansas	6.6
Kentucky	5.9
Pennsylvania	5.7
Connecticut	4.8
Ohio	4.8
Colorado	
Washington	
Delaware	4.3
New Jersey	4.2
Oregon	
Wisconsin	4.0
Montana	
W. Virginia	3.8
Idaho	
Minnesota	3.6
Hawaii	
Wyoming	
Utah	
Nebraska	2.9
Massachusetts	2.6
Rhode Island	2.5
N. Dakota	2.2
Maine	2.0
Iowa	1.9
Vermont	1.9
New Hampshire	1.7
S. Dakota	1.2

Source: FBI

ranking as the state with by far the highest homicide rate. Before the Civil War, Louisiana had the most brutal conditions for slavery, in large part because it was the one state where sugar cane was grown, and cane production is particularly harsh work.

In addition, said Samuel Hyde Jr., a historian at Southeastern Louisiana University, eastern Louisiana was in a state of near anarchy for most of the 19th century, a result of its pine-woods isolation, lack of political authority and vicious guerrilla fighting during the Civil War. Professor Hyde, the author of "Pistols and Politics," (Louisiana State University Press, 1996), relates how his own great-grandfather, Samuel Hyde, a sawmill owner and postmaster in rural Tangipahoa Parish, survived being shot in the back on two different occasions as a result of a local feud—only to be fatally ambushed in 1897 while on horseback, hit in the back by 36 buckshot, with another rifle slug in the back of his head.

Professor Hyde remembers his father and uncles passing on the story to him when he was 13. His grandfather, the slain man's son, eventually avenged the killing by shooting the assassins' ringleader. "I have felt like I dishonored my family," Professor Hyde said, "because I am the only one who never killed anyone."

Unit Selections

7. **Victimization and the Victim Industry,** Joel Best
8. **Researchers Unravel the Motives of Stalkers,** Jane E. Brody
9. **Battered Women Face Pit Bulls and Cobras,** Jane E. Brody
10. **Child Victims: In Search of Opportunities for Breaking the Cycle of Violence,** Cathy Spatz Widom

Key Points to Consider

❖ What lifestyle changes might you consider to avoid becoming victimized?

❖ How successful are crime victims when they fight their assailants?

❖ Does marital status influence victimization risk? Defend your answer.

 **Links**   **www.dushkin.com/online/**

11. **Connecticut Sexual Assault Crisis Services, Inc.**
    http://www.connsacs.org
12. **National Crime Victim's Research and Treatment Center**
    http://www.musc.edu/cvc/
13. **Office for Victims of Crime**
    http://www.ojp.usdoj.gov/ovc/

These sites are annotated on pages 4 and 5.

For many years, crime victims were not considered an important topic for criminological study. Now, however, criminologists consider focusing on victims and victimization to be essential in understanding the phenomenon of crime. The popularity of this area of study can be attributed to the early work of Hans von Hentig and the later work of Stephen Schafer. These writers were the first to assert that crime victims play an integral role in the criminal event, that their actions may actually precipitate crime, and that unless the victim's role is considered, the study of crime is not complete.

In recent years a growing number of criminologists have devoted increasing attention to the victim's role in the criminal justice process. Generally, areas of particular interest include calculating costs of crime to victims, taking surveys of victims to measure the nature and extent of criminal behavior, establishing probabilities of victimization risks, studying victim precipitation of crime and culpability, and designing services expressly for victims of crime. As more criminologists focus their attention on the victim's role in the criminal process, victimology will take on even greater importance.

This unit provides sharp focus on key issues. In the lead article, "Victimization and the Victim Industry," Joel Best discusses how a widespread ideology of victimization created a victim industry, which now supports the identification of large numbers of victims.

Psychiatric and personality disorders were found to underlie the problems of stalkers, according to Jane Brody in "Researchers Unravel the Motives of Stalkers." The next essay, "Battered Women Face Pit Bulls and Cobras," places batterers into two categories, each with distinct characteristics. The unit closes with an article by Cathy Spatz Widom. "Child Victims: In Search of Opportunities for Breaking the Cycle of Violence" is aimed at describing how childhood victimization and violent criminal behavior are related.

Victimization and the Victim Industry

Joel Best

Victimization has become fashionable, the focus of talk shows, political speeches, and concerned commentaries as diverse as Alan Dershowitz's *The Abuse Excuse* (1994), Robert Hughes's *Culture of Complaint* (1993), Wendy Kaminer's *I'm Dysfunctional, You're Dysfunctional* (1992), and Charles Sykes's *A Nation of Victims* (1992). Though these critics approach the topic from different directions, they agree that claims of victimization are spreading, and they worry that this threatens basic assumptions about personal responsibility that are fundamental to the social order. Yet focusing on the moral consequences of claims about victims causes most critics to overlook the social arrangements that foster these claims.

The announcement of new forms of victimization has become commonplace during the last twenty-five years. Journalists, activists, academics, and talk show hosts have called attention to the neglected or unnoticed victims of marital rape, acquaintance rape, date rape, elder abuse, sibling abuse, peer abuse, emotional abuse, telephone abuse, clergy abuse, Satanic ritual abuse, sexual abuse, sexual harassment, sexual addiction, love addiction, food addiction, eating disorders, post-traumatic stress disorder, multiple-personality disorder, chronic fatigue syndrome, false memory syndrome, credit-card dependency, codependency, dysfunctional families, hate crimes, battering, stalking, drunk driving, and UFO abductions. Some of these claims gained wide acceptance, whereas others met with considerable skepticism. But debating the merits of particular claims ignores underlying patterns in the way contemporary Americans interpret victimization. During the 1960s, Americans became sensitized to victims and victimization; by the 1970s, there was a widespread ideology of victimization. As this ideology gained acceptance in key institutions, it created a victim industry—a set of social arrangements that now supports the identification of large numbers of victims.

Discovering Victims in the 1960s

Whether human actions and experiences are best understood as products of individuals' choices or as shaped by social arrangements is a central issue in social theory. Focusing on victims discounts individuals' ability to control their own lives and emphasizes the power of social forces because victims cannot control what happens to them. Contemporary discussions of victimization have their roots in the 1960s and early 1970s, when several developments drew attention to—and reshaped attitudes toward—the social arrangements that produced victims and victimization. During this period, a broad array of activists, conservatives, liberals, therapists, lawyers, and victimologists spoke out about victims and their problems.

The civil rights movement's successes during the early 1960s inspired other social movements demanding equal rights for women, homosexuals, the disabled, the elderly, children, and others. Later movements borrowed tactics, rhetoric, and sometimes personnel from their predecessors. Typically, movement activists identified large segments of the population as victims of prejudice and discrimination (or, in more politicized language, by oppression and exploitation), described the processes of their victimization, and advocated reforms to correct the inequities.

The rhetoric of equal rights also inspired slogans about victims' rights. Many political conservatives deplored the Supreme Court decisions under Chief Justice Earl Warren extending the rights of criminal suspects and restricting police powers; the courts, they argued, protected the rights of criminals but ignored the rights of the criminals' victims. Republican political candidates began advocating victims' rights, and this rhetoric eventually spawned a victims' rights movement that demanded such reforms as victims compensation, victim impact statements, and victim allocution at sentencing and parole hearings.

The Left also adopted victim imagery. In 1971, William Ryan, a psychologist and civil rights activist, published a well-received book *Blaming the Victim,* which focused on the problems of what would later be called the black underclass. Ryan argued that the underclass were victims of racial and class oppression and that criticizing street crime or welfare dependency amounted to blaming powerless people for their own victimization. The expression "blaming the victim" quickly took on a life of its own; Ryan's original focus on the underclass was lost, and the phrase became a rhetorical trump card, play-

From *Society,* May/June 1997, pp. 9–17.

able in almost any political contest. The notion was not new—earlier generations of psychiatrists and social workers had argued that delinquents were "victims of society"—but Ryan's rephrasing caught on. Part of its appeal may have been its ambiguity; it let one identify victims without necessarily specifying who was doing the victimizing.

Furthermore, since 1960 the ranks of mental health professionals has grown more rapidly than has the general population. Public and private medical insurance plans spread and their coverage for mental health services (for example, substance-abuse programs and personal counseling) expanded. These benefits fostered a growing number of therapeutic professionals—clinical psychologists, licensed clinical social workers, family counselors, and so on—whose eligibility to receive compensation from insurers was established in new state and federal legislation. These professionals medicalized family dynamics and other aspects of their patients' lives, often helping them interpret their experiences as forms of victimization. These therapists could apply a growing number of diagnoses; the American Psychiatric Association's *Diagnostic and Statistical Manual* (the official catalog of diagnostic categories) has grown with each revision.

Parallel developments occurred within the law, as reforms made it easier to litigate cases of alleged harms and risks. Following the U.S. Surgeon General's 1964 report on tobacco use, warnings proliferated about risks associated with a wide range of products, foods, and activities. Emerging health and consumer movements focused on those victimized by dangerous technologies, unsafe products, and inadequate regulation. Increasingly, government agencies sought to regulate risks, while hazard victims turned to the civil courts, demanding compensation for their suffering. These regulations and court cases attracted news coverage, contributing to the awareness of risk and victimization.

Increasingly, critical social scientists defined their task as exposing powerful institutions and defending society's most vulnerable members. Within criminology, a growing interest in victimization led to the emergence of victimology as a subspecialty, with its own professional societies, textbooks, and journals. Academics melded activists' calls for equal rights and victims' rights, warn-

ings against blaming victims, therapeutic interpretations of family dynamics, and legal theories of liability into a general study of victims.

The net effect of these developments was to sensitize Americans to the plight of victims and the processes of victimization. Victim advocates argued that victims had long been neglected, even ignored. But by the mid-1970s, victims had become familiar figures on the social landscape.

The Ideology of Victimization

This familiarity coalesced in an ideology of victimization, a set of widely accepted propositions about the nature of victimization. These propositions tend to be invoked piecemeal, that is, in individual campaigns by advocates drawing attention to particular kinds of victims rather than in a general theory of victimization. However, this ideology's seven central tenets underpin most contemporary claims about victims. Each proposition seems unexceptional by itself, but in combination they form a powerful ideology that makes it easy to identify large numbers of victims.

1. Victimization is widespread. Attempts to draw attention to social problems often emphasize the large numbers of people affected, and claims about victims routinely argue that victimization is widespread, sometimes almost ubiquitous. Thus, for example, we are told that 96 percent of families are dysfunctional or that 96 percent of the population is codependent. Even forms of victimization that might seem rare are alleged to be surprisingly common: A national survey suggested that 1 in 50 adults shows signs of having been abducted by UFOs.

Claims that victimization is common often depend upon broad definitions. Horror stories—especially severe and clear-cut examples—serve to focus attention on a category of victims, but the problem is defined in much broader terms. The problem's domain often expands once the initial claims gain widespread acceptance. Thus, for example, the contemporary campaign against child abuse first addressed the "battered-child syndrome" (typified by severe beatings of very young children); the acceptance of child abuse as a social problem then laid a foundation for expanding its domain to include neglect, sexual abuse, emotional abuse, and so on. Similarly, post-traumatic stress disorder (PTSD) originated as a diagnosis for

combat-related psychiatric problems of Vietnam veterans; but the notion of "traumatic stress" proved remarkably flexible, and the PTSD label is now applied to victims whose experiences range from battering and incest to receiving contaminated fast food. Broad definitions, of course, help justify large estimates for the extent of victimization. If the domain of sexual violence includes flashing and "touching assaults by relatively young boys," then the proportion of females who have been victims of sexual violence will be far greater than if some narrower definition is applied.

2. Victimization is consequential. Even a single, brief incident can have consequences that extend throughout the victim's life. One analysis of sexual abuse, for instance, warns that one childhood experience of being flashed or fondled "can have profound and long-term consequences." Victimization's consequences are fundamentally psychological: The victim experiences anxiety, doubt, fear, or other psychological reactions. While victims may have impaired social relationships, the root cause of these problems is not social forces but lasting psychological damage. This characterization invites the medicalization of victimization, since therapists presumably have the appropriate knowledge and skills for treating psychological problems. The theme of lasting consequences is central to the claims of intergenerational victimization—cycles of abuse in which abused children become abusive parents—that have inspired movements of adult children (and grandchildren) of alcoholics, abusive parents, and divorced couples. These reverberating effects further support claims that victimization is widespread. If apparently minor incidents can be consequential, then victimization should be defined broadly.

3. Relationships between victims and their victimizers are relatively straightforward and unambiguous. Most claims about victims describe victimization as exploitative encounters between a victimizer who takes advantage and a victim who suffers. Usually, the perpetrator is portrayed as more powerful than the victim, more aware of the exploitative nature of their relationship, and more responsible for the victimization. In this view, victimization is morally unambiguous: The victimizer is exploitative, the victim innocent.

In practice, people identified as victimizers may dispute that characterization, and even people labeled victims may be unsure whether an offense "really" occurred (as suggested by the title of an influential book on date rape, *I Never Called It Rape*). Victim advocates define these denials and uncertainty as part of the pattern of victimization. Where those involved may see ambiguity, advocates perceive clear-cut, unambiguous exploitation. They make few distinctions among forms of victimization, emphasizing the similarities between, say, forcible rape and date rape rather than exploring any differences.

4. Victimization often goes unrecognized. If victimization is common, consequential, and clear-cut, it should be a visible, prominent part of social life. But victim advocates argue that victimization often goes unrecognized and unacknowledged, not only by the larger society but even by the victims themselves.

Society may simply be unaware of victimization. New ways of thinking about some form of victimization or new evidence or a new willingness of victims to speak up can make a neglected social problem visible. In this view, identifying new types of victims reflects social progress, as a more enlightened society gives victimization the attention it deserves. According to more critical advocates, language, culture, and institutional arrangements obscure victims' suffering. For example, feminists argue that the patriarchy discounts the significance of women's victimization and activists denounce police failures to treat hate crimes seriously.

Victimization also may be deliberately concealed. Some claims describe victimization concealed by numerous or powerful actors, such as a million-member Satanic blood-cult conducting undetected human sacrifices or highly advanced aliens in UFOs experimenting on abducted victims. But secrecy does not require great conspiracies. Offenders may convince individual victims, for example, sexually abused children, to keep the experience secret; if such secrets are widespread, then their sum may be collective invisibility.

Beyond society's failure to acknowledge victims, victims themselves may not recognize victimization for what it is. They may define victimization too narrowly, or they may be ashamed, afraid, or otherwise unwilling to reveal their victimization to others. Some therapists argue that many victims cannot remember their experiences, that a common response to the trauma of victimization is to repress memories of the experience (see Richard Ofshe and Ethan Watters, "Making Monsters," *Society*, March 1993). These victims cannot recall or acknowledge being victimized; they are "in denial." Here again, victimization is portrayed as a psychological problem requiring medical treatment.

5. Individuals must be taught to recognize others' and their own victimization. Because victimization often goes unrecognized by both victims and the larger society, people must be educated. Potential victims may need preventive education, such as "stranger, danger" and "good touch, bad touch" programs designed to warn preschoolers about abduction and sexual abuse or campus campaigns to make college students aware of—and help them avoid—date rape. Other educational efforts seek to inform the larger society about particular forms of victimization. Newsmagazine feature stories, talk shows, made-for-TV movies, and other press and entertainment genres regularly present information about victims; these treatments routinely adopt the views promoted by victim advocates.

In addition to educational programs aimed at potential victims or the general public, advocates seek to teach victims to recognize, acknowledge, and address their victimization. Therapy and support groups offer ways to deal with one's victimization—once the individual acknowledges that victimization has occurred. But what of those victims said to be in denial, unaware that some prior, now-forgotten victimization continues to trouble them? Though these individuals cannot recall their victimization, they are often aware that something is amiss.

Those unaware of their own victimization must be helped to recognize and identify the root of their problems. Victim advocates offer checklists of symptoms to help diagnose prior victimization. Thus, for example, adult children of alcoholics may "have difficulty following a project through from beginning to end," "feel they are different from other people," and "are either super responsible or super irresponsible"; codependents may "feel angry, victimized, unappreciated, and used," "blame themselves for everything," "come from trou-

bled, repressed, or dysfunctional families," or "deny their family was troubled, repressed, or dysfunctional"; while child victims of ritual abuse may be preoccupied with urine, feces, and flatulation, be clingy, resist authority, destroy toys, or have nightmares. These inventories of symptoms may be lengthy; Melody Beattie's best-selling book *Codependent No More* lists more than 230 characteristics of codependents. Sometimes advocates' lists specify contradictory symptoms. For instance, a review of various guidelines for identifying sexually abused children notes: "Some believe . . . that a reluctance to disclose is characteristic of a true allegation, while others look for spontaneity in the child's disclosure as an index of veracity."

Of course, many—probably more—people display several symptoms on these lists yet deny having been victimized. To victim advocates, a denial of prior victimization may be just another symptom. Regarding her recently recovered memories of childhood sexual abuse, comedienne Roseanne declared: "When someone asks you, 'Were you sexually abused as a child,' there's only two answers. One of them is, 'Yes,' and one of them is, 'I don't know.' You can't say no." Similarly, a failure to display symptoms need not be significant; the review of guidelines for identifying sexual abuse warns: "The absence of positive indicators does not mean the child hasn't been sexually abused." Within such diagnostic frameworks, claims of victimization are easily made but difficult to dismiss. Coupled with the claim that victimization is widespread, these frameworks justify a suspicion that virtually anyone might be victim.

Such checklists of symptoms merely raise the possibility that someone is a victim; confirming this possibility requires additional investigation. Sometimes, the therapist's task is defined as helping the victim "recover the memories" of victimization. Critics note that transcripts of therapists' conversations with patients sometimes reveal leading questions and other tactics that encourage patients to acknowledge their victimization. Or therapists may adopt special techniques to elicit memories of victimization, including hypnosis, play with dolls or puppets, massage, and fantasizing. These methods are often successful. As *The Courage to Heal,* a popular guidebook for survivors of child sexual abuse, notes: "Assume your feelings are valid. So far, no one we've talked to thought she might have been abused, and then later discovered that she hadn't been. The progression always goes the other way, from suspicion to confirmation. If you think you were abused and your life shows the symptoms, then you were." The belief that victimization is widespread but largely hidden justifies extraordinary measures to identify individuals who have been victimized and to encourage them to acknowledge and address their victimization.

6. Claims of victimization must be respected. Once individuals learn, via education or therapeutic intervention, to recognize their victimization, their claims to be victims must not be challenged. Victim advocates insist that it takes great courage to step forward and acknowledge one's victimization, that such individuals take a precarious stand against the institutional forces that promote and conceal widespread victimization. Injunctions against challenging claims of victimization often warn against "blaming the victim"; victims have already suffered, and calling their claims into question can only constitute further victimization.

Advocates often argue that skepticism is unwarranted, asserting that some victims' claims should be seen as true by definition (for example, early activists sometimes insisted that children never lie about being sexually abused) or at least that there is no reason for individuals to make false claims about being victimized. Or advocates may suggest that similarities in the stories of many victims (for example, accounts of Satanic ritual abuse or UFO abduction) constitute strong evidence for the stories' truth. Memories of victimization that have been recovered through hypnosis or other therapeutic techniques receive validation from therapists who insist that these techniques elicit reliable information, that challenges are unwarranted and unfair, and that society should support the claims of vulnerable, innocent victims.

7. The term "victim" has undesirable connotations. Some advocates reject the very term "victim" on the grounds that it carries negative connotations of being damaged, passive, and powerless. They prefer more positive, "empowering" terms, such as "survivor," "adult child," "recovering," or even "persons" (for example, "persons with AIDS"). This renaming affirms that victimization occurred, while possibly serving to reduce individuals'

reluctance to define themselves or others as victims. In addition, to the degree that these category names derive from therapeutic discourse, they offer further medical or scientific legitimacy to claims of victim status.

These seven ideological propositions appear routinely in contemporary discussions of victimization. Combined, they form an extremely powerful ideology, one that encourages identifying and labeling victims: It defines victimization as common, serious, morally unambiguous, yet largely unrecognized; it justifies methods to identify individuals (and help those individuals recognize themselves) as victims; it delegitimizes doubts about victims' claims; and it provides new, nonstigmatizing labels for those who have suffered.

Again, there is no overarching "victims movement"; rather, advocates address particular forms of victimization. Typically, these campaigns begin modestly, with the initial claims addressing clear-cut, outrageous instances of exploitation. Then, after these initial claims gain acceptance, the problem's domain expands to incorporate other cases. Thus, for example, early claims about sexual harassment focused on instances in which female workers' jobs were overtly threatened unless they complied with their male supervisors' sexual demands. Once sexual harassment gained recognition as a social problem, advocates began expanding its domain to include a broader range of behaviors and conditions, including "conduct that creates an intimidating, hostile, or offensive environment." Such domain expansion is self-reinforcing: Expanded definitions support claims of larger problems; larger problems justify increased attention; and increased attention in turn encourages further expanding the problem's domain.

Institutional Responses to Victimization

Ideologies exist within institutional contexts, receiving more or less ratification and support from different institutions. Campaigns drawing attention to new forms of victimization seek recognition in several institutional arenas. Typically, advocates' initial appeals are sensitizing: They seek to draw an institution's attention to victims whose plights have been neglected. Once an institution acknowledges these victims, advocates call for accommodations to

integrate victims' needs within the existing institutional structure. When such accommodation is deemed insufficient, advocates may call for institutional changes—significant alterations to meet the victims' needs.

Typically, the responses to sensitization—accommodation and change—have seemed modest; advocates sought particular reforms to protect particular victims from particular abuses. Thus, a state might pass a law to extend the period within which victims of sexual abuse can file charges or sue for damages, so that adults who recover memories of abuse can bring cases against their abusers, or a university might require all faculty to attend workshops on sexual harassment. Though each reform is limited, taken together they represent considerable institutional support for the ideology of victimization. This support extends across several major institutions, including law, the medical and therapeutic professions, academia, the mass media, and the recovery movement.

Law. Because much of the law concerns protecting individuals against exploitation, it becomes an important institutional arena for claims about victimization. The contemporary ideology of victimization has influenced the law's various facets, including legislation, the criminal justice and court systems, and legal scholarship.

Advocates often call for new laws prohibiting the exploitation of victims or requiring reporting of victimization. For example, following actress Rebecca Schaeffer's well-publicized murder by a fan, claims that stalking was widespread led to California's passing of an antistalking law in 1990. Within two years, forty-seven other states and the District of Columbia had similar laws, and Congress had ordered the National Institute of Justice to devise a model antistalking code and was considering proposals to make stalking a federal crime. Similarly, several states have added a "victims' bill of rights" to their constitutions; state and federal law enforcement agencies have been ordered to collect data on hate crimes; and state laws requiring reporting of various forms of child abuse continue to expand.

In addition to calling for new laws, victim advocates criticize the legal system's failure to protect individuals from victimization, as well as its further failure to treat victims appropriately once they complain to legal authorities. Thus, the criminal justice system's insensitive treatment of victims of rape and child sexual abuse (for example, not responding to all complaints, investigating some allegations with skepticism, and subjecting complainants to humiliating courtroom interrogations) represent a "second rape" or a "second form of child abuse." In this view, the law discourages victims, blames them for their suffering, forces them to humiliate themselves, and then fails to deliver justice. Such claims have inspired reforms to make the legal system more accessible to and protective of victims, ranging from relatively minor accommodations (such as letting child victims testify while seated in child-size chairs) to more substantial institutional changes (such as prohibiting or limiting the cross-examination of child victims giving testimony). The criminal justice system's relatively elaborate arrangements for preserving the rights of defendants (viewed as victimizers by victim advocates) have inspired growing interest in victims using the less restrictive civil courts to bring suits.

Many of these legislative and procedural reforms find support in law schools and law reviews. New claims about victimization often receive sympathetic treatment, as legal scholars recommend ways to modify the law to redress victims' grievances. Though scholars do not agree on all issues (there has, for example, been considerable debate over how to balance the rights of complainants and defendants in sexual abuse trials), many members of law school faculties—and legislatures and courts—accept elements of the ideology of victimization.

The Medical and Therapeutic Professions. Many advocates medicalize victimization, defining treatment as the appropriate response and assigning therapeutic professionals ownership of these social problems. Medicalization carries scientific authority; claims couched in medical language seem almost beyond questioning or criticism. A diverse set of professionals receive this scientific imprimatur, as the medical model—usually associated with physicians, psychiatrists, and perhaps clinical psychologists—has spread throughout the "helping professions." Those who treat victims may have been trained in various disciplines, including social work, family counseling, education, and health science, and their treatment practices

may be guided by various other ideologies, ranging from fundamentalist Christianity to feminism. Some therapists are "professional ex's," individuals with little formal training who, having recovered from victimization, have now begun careers helping others into recovery. Some specialize in identifying and helping particular types of victims (such as helping victims of Satanic ritual abuse to recover those memories), while others address a broad range of problems.

Many of the medical experts who work with victims argue that their principal responsibility is to their patients rather than to abstract principles of inquiry. This rationale justifies therapeutic practices which some critics argue are inconsistent with scientific objectivity or criminal investigations. For example, therapists interviewing children thought to have been sexually abused may use leading questions to elicit acknowledgment of abuse and justify this practice as a necessary therapeutic step, or therapists may urge patients to ignore doubts and ambiguity when acknowledging their victimization. Such practices, justified as therapeutically necessary, distinguish much treatment of victims from traditional medical or scientific inquiry.

Medicalized discussions often focus on the harms experienced by the victims while largely ignoring the victimizers. Whereas earlier psychiatric claims medicalized deviants (such as sexual psychopaths), contemporary claims medicalize victims (such as survivors of sexual abuse). When deviance is deemed extraordinary, we search for explanations in the peculiarities of offenders, but when victimization is seen as commonplace, victimizers seem less remarkable, simply part of an oppressive social system.

Academia. The ideology of victimization also has made significant inroads into education. The need to educate victims, potential victims, and society at large is central to the ideology. Because victimization often occurs during childhood, teachers are encouraged to attend workshops to learn how to teach students to recognize victimization. Within higher education, enthusiasm for the ideology of victimization seems greatest in the helping professions, such as social work, health education, educational counseling, family relations, criminal justice, and child development programs. Students trained in these fields learn to identify and respond

to a range of human problems, and claims about victimization are presented as up-to-date knowledge with useful applications. Victims become the subjects of lectures, classes, term papers, theses, and dissertations. Researchers may find foundations and government agencies eager to fund research on victimization, conferences and professional associations emerge as forums for inquiry, and the proliferation of scholarly publishing has produced specialized journals devoted to studying victims (for example, *Dissociation* publishes studies of multiple-personality disorder). Of course, the audience for these conferences and journals largely endorses victimization claims. Concern with victims also appears in more scholarly disciplines, especially in feminist writings, and women's studies programs often provide leadership for on-campus advocacy. Many campuses develop programs to educate or protect students from victimization. Like medicalization, academics' support gives authority to claims about victims.

Mass Media. Most advocates depend upon the mass media to disseminate their claims to the public. In general, claims about victims receive sympathetic coverage in the press, in popular culture, and, most especially, in the talk shows, made-for-TV movies, and other genres that combine news and entertainment. Claims about victims tend to fit the media's template for social problems coverage: They can be typified in dramatic terms (an innocent victim beset by an exploitative villain); they seem relevant (if victimization is widespread, then many people are, might become, or at least have ties to victims); they offer hope (via the intervention of authority figures from law, medicine, or academia); and they lack unacceptable political overtones (so long as the claims focus on the individual victimizer rather than on the social system—for example, patriarchy or the class system—as producing the victimization). Moreover, because most advocates depict victimization as straightforward exploitation and because most claims arouse little organized opposition, the media typically feel no obligation to "balance" their coverage by presenting "both sides" of the issue. Changing media structures also have worked to the advocates' advantage. Cable and satellite delivery have caused television channels to proliferate; broadcasters need relatively inexpensive, relatively popular offerings to fill these channels, and talk shows and "reality shows" (like *America's Most Wanted*) meet these requirements. These genres frequently cover claims about victimization.

The Recovery Movement. U.S. culture has a long fascination with self-help. In recent years, the self-help movement—and Alcoholics Anonymous in particular—has inspired numerous campaigns to help victims recover. This recovery movement has many facets: twelve-step groups, weekend workshops and conferences, lecture tours, and publishers who generate books, pamphlets, magazines, and audio- and videotapes filled with inspirational advice. During the 1980s, most bookstores opened substantial sections devoted to "Recovery." By 1990, nearly three hundred bookstores sold nothing but recovery movement literature, featuring separate sections devoted to alcoholism, adult children of alcoholics, codependency, and so on. The popularity of recovery movement literature seems to transcend otherwise important ideological divisions: Recovery sections can be found in both women's bookstores and Christian book shops. The recovery movement often provides a grassroots embodiment of claims about victims; it offers continual socialization for both neophytes and experienced members, links victims to experts, and often inspires media coverage.

Other institutional supports for victims' claims include policies promoted by government agencies, religious bodies, and private industry. Again, these involve many parallel movements, each promoting recognition of a particular type of victim, each seeking particular reforms within particular institutions. Some campaigns have been more successful than others; issues such as sexual abuse, stalking, and sexual harassment have received widespread institutional validation, whereas, aside from the well-publicized claims of Harvard professor John Mack, victims of UFO abductions have found relatively few visible supporters in law, medicine, and academia. But the overall pattern is clear: Several major institutions respond sympathetically to the ideology of victimization.

The Victim Industry

The ideology of victimization, when coupled with institutional support for that ideology, makes it possible to label large numbers of victims. Studies of witchhunts and political purges speak of social control as an "industry," engaged in the "manufacturing" or the "mass production" of deviants. Analogously, we may speak of a contemporary victim industry mass producing victims. According to Elliott Currie, the great European witchhunt had three key organizational characteristics that fostered the discovery of many thousands of witches: (1) The witchhunters faced few restraints from other social institutions; (2) They had few internal restraints on their powers; and (3) They had a vested interest in identifying witches. Analogous arrangements support the victim industry's campaign to identify large numbers of victims.

Absence of External Restraints. Because the contemporary ideology of victimization has been accepted and incorporated by key institutions, victims advocates face little external opposition. For instance, individuals being treated for some form of victimization may find that their claims—and the claims of their therapists—are protected by sympathetic laws, ratified by academics, depicted favorably in the mass media, and endorsed by the recovery movement. The ideological prohibition against challenging victims' claims further discourages skepticism. Moreover, because identifying victims is defined as beneficial, both to the individual being identified and to the society at large, there is no obvious source of resistance.

It is significant that advocates often demand support for victims while largely ignoring victimizers. Some victimizers cannot be identified: the stranger-rapist who was never apprehended; the unfamiliar adult Satanists who abused the victim as a child; or even extraterrestrial aliens. But for many forms of victimization rooted in family dynamics, the victimizers' identities are presumably known. Yet so long as advocates do not identify and denounce particular people as victimizers, few people have cause to oppose claims about victimization. Thus, for example, claims about recovered memories of Satanic ritual abuse faced little opposition until victims began bringing suits against their relatives for childhood abuse. At that point, a countermovement, the False Memory Syndrome Foundation, emerged. But this is an exception: Relatively few victims' movements generate well-organized opposition because relatively few specify their opponents. Most movements face few external restraints.

Absence of Internal Restraints. The contemporary ideology of victimization offers many alternative ways of identifying victims: long lists of symptoms indicative of victimization, rationales for doubting individuals' denials of victimization, and so on. Moreover, this ideology is endorsed by people with impressive credentials: therapists, lawyers, academics, and professional ex's. Defined as experts, they can influence discussions of putative victimization. Because victimization is often hidden and because these experts have the means to discover and reveal it, their assessments become authoritative. Moreover, under their ideology, these individuals have a right—even an obligation—to label individuals as victims and guide them into accepting that label. Since advocates see themselves as helping both the victim and the larger society understand the truth, they have little reason to question their own actions. The knowledge and techniques needed to detect otherwise hidden victimization give these advocates extraordinary powers to label others as victims, even when those individuals deny that the labels fit. At the same time, the ideology of victimization offers few internal restraints on such labeling.

Vested Interests. Participants in the victim industry often have a stake in the identification of victims. Advocates' vested interests include enhanced prestige and influence for themselves and their professions, supportive validation from important social institutions, and, at least among those therapists who label on a fee-for-service basis, increased income. In addition, some people benefit from being identified as victims: They become professional ex's, write books, travel on the lecture circuit, appear on talk shows, receive praise and favorable attention, and even get treated as experts in their own right. They may become victim-celebrities (known for their experiences as victims)—some, of course, are also celebrity victims (that is, established celebrities who reveal their victimization, such as Roseanne). In short, both those doing the labeling and those being labeled often benefit from the process.

Obviously, the contemporary concern for victims is not a witchhunt. Yet the organizational features that supported large-scale witchhunting also make the victim industry productive. Problems that psychiatrists considered relatively rare twenty or thirty years ago (such as incest or multiple-personality disorder) have been redefined as relatively common conditions, and those labels are often applied. The net effect of the victim industry has been the identification of many thousands of victims.

Why Victims?

No doubt many of the similarities among contemporary victim movements reflect advocates' awareness of one another; rhetoric and methods proven effective in one campaign are borrowed and used to draw attention to other forms of victimization. But this begs a larger question: Why do claims about victims strike a responsive chord in contemporary society? Why are so many kinds of victims being identified at this time and in this society?

The contemporary concern for victims began during the 1960s, when established status hierarchies weakened. Challenges from below—from blacks, women, students, homosexuals, and so on—questioned the legitimacy of existing status arrangements. Talking about victims was often an effective way of pressing these claims. Victimization dramatized the illegitimacy of social arrangements that allowed the exploitation of the vulnerable. Advocates used the ideology of victimization not only to draw attention to specific social problems but also to challenge existing hierarchies. What sort of society fostered and then ignored widespread victimization? Calls to protect victims were also bids to raise the status of those vulnerable to victimization, and victim advocacy was often tied to broader social

movements, such as the women's movement.

In addition, victim movements offer a contemporary answer to fundamental, primal issues that every culture must address—issues of justice and evil. Social order is society's most basic accomplishment. But in every society, order sometimes breaks down. Some people do the right thing, but they do not get their just rewards. Other people break the rules. Social control attempts to right these wrongs and restore order to the social system.

In most societies during most of recorded history, punishment has been central to social control. Society roots out the rule breakers, the deviants, and the evildoers and dispenses justice by punishing them. But during the twentieth century, we have become increasingly suspicious of these traditional practices. We favor a rational, scientific point of view, and we suspect that evil is a superstitious notion and that punishment is a barbaric method of achieving justice.

The social sciences bear a good deal of responsibility here. They are in the business of explaining social patterns, of identifying causes and their effects, and they have diligently tried to understand the causes of deviance. But the social scientific perspective on deviance doesn't translate terribly well into social policy. The sticking point, of course, is the notion—fundamental to law—of responsibility. If we can point to the causes of deviant behavior, how can we hold the deviant responsible? Is it just to blame deviants for rule breaking when we believe that their deviance is caused by social conditions? Note the term "blame"—it is central to much social control but largely foreign to social science.

This reveals the attractions of talking about victims. Talking about victims can avoid many of the conflicts between the social scientific and social policy perspectives raised in debates over deviants. To social scientists, victims can be understood as the effects of causal processes. But, as advocates continually warn, social policy must sympathize with—support—victims, not blame them. This helps explain why victims movements tend to gloss over the victimizers. Once advocates start identifying victimizers, they're back in the messy, divisive business of trying to both understand and blame deviants. So long as they stay focused on the victims, advocates can hope to win consensus.

This explanation suggests that victim movements may have more than organizational features in common with witchhunting. The victim plays a symbolic role in our society, not unlike the role played by witches during the witch craze. Both allow society to identify evil and injustice. In societies that interpret events in religious terms, witches consorting with the demonic can explain all sorts of problems. Similarly, our contemporary society, which seeks to understand the world in rational, scientific terms, finds processes of victimization useful explanations for all sorts of contemporary ills. In this way, new victims answer old questions.

Joel Best is professor and chair of the Department of Sociology at Southern Illinois University at Carbondale. He is the editor of the journal Social Problems. *His books include* Threatened Children *and the collection* Images of Issues.

Researchers Unravel The Motives of Stalkers

By JANE E. BRODY

STALKERS are wreaking havoc in the lives of millions of Americans. Every year, a recent national study by the Justice Department disclosed, an estimated one million women and 400,000 men are plagued by unrelenting pursuers who harass, terrorize and in some cases kill the victims or anyone else deemed to be in the way of a stalker's desired goal.

Studies show stalkers do not fit a single behavior pattern.

One in 20 women in the United States will be stalked at some point in their lives, various studies have suggested. In a survey last year among college students in West Virginia, 34 percent of the women and 17 percent of the men said they had been stalked. The ability of stalkers to find and harass their victims has been aided in recent years by computers, E-mail and the Internet, which has spawned a new psychiatric legal term: cyberstalking.

The extent of the stalking problem and its potential for growth through cyberstalking has astonished even the most astute researchers in the field

and prompted a call for stronger laws and stricter enforcement of existing statutes to better protect the victims of stalkers, even when there is no direct threat to their physical safety.

"Stalkers simply do not fade away," said Rhonda Saunders, Deputy District Attorney in Los Angeles and head of the Stalking and Threat Assessment Team. Stronger state laws, she said, would "enable law enforcement to intervene before serious bodily injury is inflicted on the victim or those surrounding the victim."

Though stalking is centuries old, it is a relatively new crime, first rendered illegal in this country by a 1990 California statute and later by laws in every state and the District of Columbia. The legal definitions and the arrests they precipitated opened the way to detailed scientific research, which is summarized for the first time in "The Psychology of Stalking: Clinical and Forensic Perspectives," edited by Dr. J. Reid Meloy and published this summer by Academic Press.

Although only 2 percent of stalkers commit homicide, half of them threaten their victims with violence or say they are going to damage property or injure pets, according to studies. Even when no physical harm results, the repeated harassment commonly results in acute emotional dis-

tress and can seriously disrupt the way victims live. Some lose their jobs when stalkers plague them at work, and some are forced to move and change their identity and appearance.

Dr. Paul E. Mullen, professor of psychiatry at Monash University in Australia, who runs a clinic that treats both stalkers and their victims, said that 70 percent of the victims suffered from a form of post-traumatic stress disorder, marked by chronic anxiety, depression and sleep disturbances. Nearly one in four victims has considered suicide, he said.

About half of stalking victims never report the crime.

Yet only about half the stalking victims ever report their problem to the police, studies indicate. Even when they do, the police may not take action until and unless the victim is physically injured or threatened with a weapon.

Movies like "The Graduate," in which the stalking man eventually wins the resistant woman, "Fatal Attraction," in which an unhinged woman stalks her married one-night stand, and dramatic cases like John Hinckley Jr.'s attempt to woo the actress Jodie Foster by shooting President Ronald Reagan, have created many mistaken impressions about stalkers, their motives, their usual victims and how successful they are. In most cases, a man who stalks a former lover succeeds only in torturing his victim, not winning her back.

The new collection of studies reports that in addition to former boyfriends and husbands, stalkers include casual acquaintances, disgruntled employees and business associates, vengeful neighbors and total strangers, as well as former girlfriends and wives.

The studies described in the book, the first in-depth look at the psychology of stalkers, found that the underlying problems of stalkers run the gamut of psychiatric and personality disorders.

And virtually anyone can become a victim. Although celebrities like Madonna and David Letterman who are stalked by crazed strangers are most likely to make the news, the vast majority of victims are ordinary people who knew their stalkers, usually as lovers or spouses.

Stalking after the break-up of a physically abusive relationship has received considerable public attention in recent years, but experts on the subject report that women are more commonly stalked by men they once dated or married who were not abusive before the relationship ended.

Dr. Doris M. Hall, a specialist in criminal justice at California State University at Bakersfield, tells of a California woman who was stalked by her former husband for 31 years. Though the woman had a hard time persuading the police to take the matter seriously, her stalker was finally arrested after being found on her block with a loaded gun.

Sometimes stalkers seem to pick their victims at random, prompted, perhaps, by the end of a relationship with someone else, by some real or imagined slight or, out of paranoia,

for a reason that has no apparent connection to reality.

Dr. Kristine K. Kienlen, a psychologist in St. Peter, Minn., who evaluates criminals and patients who are mentally ill and dangerous, tells of a 31-year-old man who, after his divorce, began stalking a young teenage girl he knew. At first he merely attended her athletic events and wrote of his desire to date her. But after four years of failing to achieve his goal, he began breaking into her home and stealing items from her bedroom, including her photo album, the contents of which he returned to her one picture at a time.

A Minnesota woman said in an interview that she has been tormented for nearly two years by a man she had dismissed from his job for repeatedly calling her and another woman at home and at work, accusing them of "wanting his body and stealing from his home." When the man began showing up at his former boss's home with a shotgun, she got a restraining order and a gun of her own. But he has yet to be imprisoned. And only after she dismissed him did the woman learn that the "glowing recommendation" he had received from a previous employer had failed to mention that he was dismissed from that job as well for stalking two women at work.

What prompts someone to stalk need not be as traumatic as a lost love or job. A retired couple reported being stalked by a business acquaintance after a minor disagreement. And a woman in her 70's was stalked by a woman of similar age for reasons she could never discern.

Men are stalked as well, and indeed are more often victims of violence by their stalkers, Dr. Hall said. One young man, she said, sought a restraining order to end the unrelenting pursuit by his former girlfriend. The judge, who told the man he should be "flattered by all the attention," nevertheless issued mutual restraining orders, which proved useless to the man. He was killed by the woman several weeks later.

Dr. Hall said that typically, when a man sought police protection from a woman who was stalking him, the authorities did not take him seriously. In her study of 16 men who were stalking victims, 56 percent were stalked by women; 44 percent were stalked by other men. She also said that when a woman stalks after the break-up of a relationship with a man, she will often go after the man's new girlfriend, "probably because women scare more easily than men do."

"The Psychology of Stalking," includes articles by 23 experts summarizing what they have learned about this noxious behavior, its underlying psychopathology and motives and the often devastating effects it has on its victims.

About one fact all the researchers agree. "There is no single profile of a stalker," said Dr. Kienlen, a contributor to the book. "Stalkers exhibit a broad range of behaviors, motivations and psychological traits."

Some stalkers have psychiatric illnesses, ranging from depression and schizophrenia to erotomania—a delusional belief that the person is loved by another—and most appear to have a personality disorder like extreme narcissism or dependency or an inability to sustain close relationships.

"Stalkers tend to have both—a mental illness and a personality disorder," Dr. Meloy, a psychiatrist affiliated with the University of California at San Diego, said in an interview. "And those who stalk strangers are more likely to be psychotic than those who stalk prior sexual intimates. The latter are more likely to be drug or alcohol abusers with a dependency personality disorder."

Dr. Kienlen conducted the first preliminary study of the backgrounds and psychological profiles of stalkers. More than half of the 24 male stalkers she interviewed had evidence of what psychologists call an attachment disorder stemming from the childhood loss or absence of a caring and consistent parent or guardian, usually in the first six years of life.

Although the theory of attachment disorder has its critics, Dr. Kienlen and other experts in stalking believe it may be a "predisposing factor" for stalking behavior by making it difficult for the person to establish and maintain healthy relationships. "Their parents may have divorced and the custodial parent had little contact with the child," she said. "The parents may have had a drug or alcohol problem; the child may have been physically, sexually or emotionally abused or even totally abandoned."

Dr. Kienlen said she had encountered three kinds of attachment disorders among stalkers. The "preoccupied" stalker has a poor self-image but a positive view of others and constantly seeks their approval and validation in order to feel good about himself. When rejected by others, the person stalks to restore his sense of self.

The "fearful" stalker has a poor self-image as well but also sees others as unreliable and unsupportive.

The stalker tends to get caught in a vicious cycle of wanting someone to boost his own self-image, then rejecting the person for not being trustworthy, which prompts the person to stalk because he again needs someone to boost his sagging ego.

The "dismissing" stalker thinks of other people as jerks and usually remains distant from them to maintain an inflated self-image. The stalker with dismissing attachment disorder who does form attachments becomes angry when a breakup occurs and may stalk out of revenge, to retaliate for being mistreated.

Most of the stalkers Dr. Kienlen interviewed also had extreme personality disturbances. The most frequent one encountered in stalkers was narcissistic personality disorder, which Dr. Kienlen said gave stalkers an inflated sense of self-worth and an intense need for other people to compliment and idolize them.

Other personality disorders experts frequently encounter in stalkers are extreme dependency, constantly needing the support, attention and approval of other people, and borderline personality disorder, having unstable moods and an exaggerated reaction to rejection and abandonment. Only about 10 percent of stalkers have an antisocial personality disorder, with an above-it-all detachment from other people that is most often encountered in criminals.

In 80 percent of the men Dr. Kienlen interviewed, there was also a precipitating factor, such as a recent loss that seriously upset them and seemed to have brought on their stalking behavior. The losses ranged from the break-up of an intimate relationship, a lost job and death of a parent to learning that they themselves had a serious illness.

"My theory is that in these vulnerable individuals, the losses damaged their sense of self-worth," Dr. Kienlen said. "To alleviate their grief or feelings of emptiness, they compensated by focusing on stalking. Sometimes the stalker blames the victim for the loss and stalks out of anger."

Battered Women Face Pit Bulls and Cobras

By JANE E. BRODY

THE cobra is a real snake in the grass, quiet and focused before striking its victim with little or no warning. The pit bull's fury smolders and builds, and once its teeth are sunk into its victim it won't let go. Men who batter women are either like cobras or pit bulls, say two professors of psychology at the University of Washington who have spent a decade studying violent marriages,

Tenacious stalkers and snakes in the grass.

and the distinction can make a difference in the severity of the harm they inflict, the ability of women to escape a relationship and the risks the women face if they do leave.

"Pit bulls are great guys, until they get into an intimate relationship," said Dr. Neil Jacobson who, with his colleague, Dr. John Gottman, elaborate on their study findings in a provocative new book, "When Men Batter Women (Simon and Schuster, $25). "O.J. Simpson is a classic pit bull. Pit bulls confine their monstrous behavior to the women they love, acting out of emotional dependence and a fear of abandonment. Pit bulls are the stalkers, the jealous husbands and boyfriends who are charming to everyone except their wives and girlfriends."

Mr. Simpson was acquitted in 1995 of charges that he murdered his former wife, Nicole Brown Simpson, and one of her friends, Ronald L. Goldman, but was found to be responsible for the deaths in a subsequent civil trial.

Pit bulls, the psychologists say, monitor the woman's every move. They tend to see betrayal at every turn and it infuriates them. And when their anger explodes into violence, they seem to lose control.

Cobras, on the other hand, are often sociopaths. They are cold and calculating con artists relatively free of the trappings of emotional dependence but with a high incidence of antisocial and criminal traits and sadistic behavior, the researchers found. Cobras' violence grows out of a pathological need to have their way, to be the boss and make sure that everyone, especially their wives and girlfriends, knows it and acts accordingly.

When they think their authority has been challenged, cobras strike swiftly and ferociously, the study revealed. Although they do not lose control like the pit bulls, they are more violent toward their wives, often threatening them with a knife or gun. They are also likely to be aggressive toward everyone in their lives, including strangers and even pets, as well as friends, relatives and co-workers. Cobras are the ones who kill the cat as a warning to wives that if they fail to toe the mark, this could happen to them.

In their study of 201 couples, including 63 couples where the wives were repeatedly beaten and emotionally abused, the Seattle-based psychologists discovered an extraordinary physiological difference between the two types of batterers.

Profiles of Abuse

After a decade of research, two psychology professors have found that abusive men tend to fall into one of two categories: "cobras" and "pit bulls," each with distinct characteristics.

PIT BULLS

■ Confine violent behavior to people they love.

■ Jealous and fear abandonment; try to deprive partners of independence.

■ Prone to rage, stalking and even public attacks.

■ Become physiologically aroused in an argument.

■ Some potential for rehabilitation.

■ Less likely to have criminal record; more likely to have abusive fathers.

Sources: Dr. Neil Jacobson and Dr. John Gottman

COBRAS

- Likely to be aggressive toward everyone, including pets.

- Not emotionally dependent, but insist that partners cater to every desire.

- More likely to use or threaten with knives or guns.

- Calm down internally as they become aggressive.

- Difficult to treat with therapy.

- More likely to have criminal records and abuse drugs and/or alcohol.

They hooked up the couples to polygraphs that recorded characteristics like heart rate, blood pressure and skin resistance while the couples argued nonviolently in a laboratory setting about volatile issues in their marriages. The researchers noted that, as expected, the batterers they call pit bulls became physiologically aroused as their anger intensified, but, surprisingly, those labeled cobras calmed down internally as they became increasingly aggressive.

When the police are called in response to violence inflicted by a cobra, they are likely to find a highly agitated woman and a calm, controlled man who blames the incident on his wife, which sometimes results in the arrest of the wrong person, the researchers said.

Prof. Amy Holtzworth-Munroe, a psychologist at Indiana University in Bloomington, said that understanding the types of batterers and how they got that way should help in the development of more effective treatment programs, as well as efforts to prevent domestic violence.

"Right now, we take a one-size-fits-all approach to treatment," Dr. Holtzworth-Munroe said. "If we in-crease our understanding of subtypes, we could match treatment protocols to them."

The psychologists were prompted to explore this societal scourge in detail by compelling statistics and myths about domestic violence, and frustration with the general failure of therapy and the law to deal effectively with batterers. They point to estimates that two million to four million wives are severely assaulted each year by their husbands, and half of all murdered women are the victims of their husbands, ex-husbands, boyfriends or ex-boyfriends. The comparable statistic for murdered men is only 6 percent.

Yet, in only one of six battering episodes are the police called and in only 6 percent of severely violent episodes does the batterer end up in the criminal justice system.

For example, Dr. Jacobson said, when O. J. Simpson was arrested in 1989 and pleaded no contest to spousal abuse, "he was given a slap in the wrist." "If the laws were different and enforced differently, battered women would be much safer," he said. "If wife-beating was an automatic felony and the perpetrators had a mandatory jail sentence, women would have a chance to experience life without an abusive husband and an opportunity to formulate a safety plan to escape from the relationship."

Instead, Dr. Jacobson said, "batterers are often referred to treatment programs that don't work, and judges and therapists alike are conned by these men, especially by the cobras," who have little trouble convincing everyone, including their wives, that it is safe for them to return home.

Dr. Daniel Saunders at the University of Michigan School of Social Work said: "Treatment evaluation studies are still in their infancy. We're still trying to find out what works and in what types of men." The evidence thus far indicates that a combination of arrest, prosecution, fines and counseling works better than any one approach alone, he said.

In the Seattle study, the actions and responses among violent couples were compared with those of three other groups: equally unhappy but nonviolent couples, couples who exhibited some aggressive behavior but not enough to be classified as violent and happily married couples.

Participants were recruited through advertisements and were simply told the study would examine conflicts in marriage. When they joined the study, the couples completed extensive interviews and participated in laboratory-staged arguments that were videotaped and analyzed by independent ob-

Exposing some myths of domestic violence.

servers who did not know how each couple was classified. A similar analysis was repeated two years later.

"There is occasional low-level violence in many marriages, with pushing or hitting with a pillow now and then out of frustration," Dr. Jacobson said. "This kind of behavior is found among about half of those who seek couples therapy, but it almost never develops into a battering relationship." Battering, the researchers insist, is not just a matter of physical aggression. Rather, Dr. Jacobson said, "it is aggression with the intent to control, subjugate or intimidate another human being, and in marriage it is almost always the man who fits this definition."

Once physical violence succeeds in intimidating the woman, it may even taper off, only to be replaced by a never-ending barrage of emotional abuse that is sufficient to remind the woman that the threat of physical violence is always present.

The two hallmarks of battering are fear and injury, Dr. Jacobson said. "Even though in 50 percent of the violent couples the wives were also violent, the men never showed fear in their voices or faces but the women virtually always were terrified and they get much more seriously injured," he noted.

Unlike the attacks by men, the violence of women is nearly always in response to battering by the man and is more self-defense than aggression, the researchers maintain. Yet, the men classified as pit bulls often profess that "they're the ones who are the victims in a violent relationship," Dr. Jacobson said. "O. J. Simpson said he felt like a battered husband. Cobras, on the other hand, know they are perpetrators and don't care."

While pit bulls may be easier to leave than cobras, in the long run they can be more dangerous. They are the ones who kill battered women on the courthouse steps when the women seek protection orders or divorces.

While the psychologists found that battered women are less likely to leave cobras, those who do escape face a shorter danger period because cobras generally stop trying to pursue them and go on to new conquests.

The histories of cobras and pit bulls also tend to differ. Cobras often had violent, traumatic childhoods, criminal records and a personal history of alcohol and drug abuse. Pit bulls, on the other hand, are less likely to have a history of delinquency or criminal behavior, but they are more likely than cobras to have had fathers who battered their mothers.

Drs. Jacobson and Gottman said their research shatters many prevailing myths about domestic violence. Contrary to the claims of batterers, their wives rarely do or say anything that would provoke a vicious attack in another kind of marriage. The same words and actions in a nonviolent marriage might trigger a disagreement or argument, but not a fist in the eye. Likewise, the psychologists state emphatically, there is nothing a woman can do or say to stave off or abort a battering episode. In many cases among their study subjects, when the woman tried to end an attack by leaving, the husband pursued her and intensified the beating.

Judging from the couples studied, the researchers concluded that battering almost never stops on its own. Although the frequency of physical attacks may diminish with time, in only one case did they stop altogether. Furthermore, even when physical attacks abated, emotional abuse continued and served to keep the wives intimidated and afraid. In fact, Dr. Jacobson said, emotional abuse can be even more damaging than physical abuse because the man is "always in her face, demeaning, degrading, humiliating, harassing and robbing her of her identity."

But in another myth-shattering discovery, the researchers found that a large number—38 percent—of women managed to escape from their abusive relationships within the two-year follow-up period. None, however, were the wives of cobras, who were terrified of their husbands' propensity to use lethal weapons. But at a subsequent contact five years after they entered the study, 25 percent of the cobra wives had also left their husbands. All told, 65 percent of the wives of violent men had left them at that point.

The researchers said those who left demonstrated extraordinary courage and resourcefulness, because it is upon leaving that the women face the greatest likelihood of being killed. But, as one woman who left said, "Death would be preferable to continue in this living hell."

Child Victims: In Search of Opportunities for Breaking the Cycle of Violence

Presentation by
Cathy Spatz Widom, Ph.D.
University of New York at Albany

April 8, 1997
Washington, D.C.

We have all read newspaper reports about the deaths of young children due to child abuse or neglect: Lisa Steinberg, Jessica Cortez, Emily Hernandez, Joey Wallace, Nadine Lockwood, and most recently, Elisa Izquierdo. But what happens to the children who survive? The babies abandoned on streets or in hospitals, children left unattended for days without food in filthy roach-infested apartments, or children brutally abused. These children may not be well known. Indeed in New York City, no one in the city's child welfare administration or the school system noticed the disappearance of 8-year-old Justina Morales for 15 months, although she was known to child welfare officials. As we now know, Justina Morales was murdered in December 1995 and her body disposed of in a trash can.[1]

The names of these children appear in distressing newspaper stories like the case of 16-year-old David Newbury and Mark Rea in Milwaukee, who sexually assaulted and clubbed to death a classmate. David's court record revealed a childhood history of beatings, cruel words, and indifference. Before being sentenced to life in prison, David told a probation officer, "I lived like I was treated."[2]

Today, I have three goals: to briefly describe how childhood victimization and violent criminal behavior are related, to illustrate promising strategies and opportunities to intervene, and to suggest some important principles to guide interventions prior to formulating or proposing new policy. This talk is an attempt to bridge the world of research with that of policy. You should know that I do not pretend to be exhaustive here in describing programs, but rather to illustrate with a few examples.

Over 10 years ago, as Jeremy Travis mentioned, with initial funding from the National Institute of Justice (NIJ), I began research to address the relationship between early childhood abuse and neglect and later delinquent and violent criminal behavior. This is a study of 1,575 children from a metropolitan area in

From *National Institute of Justice Reports*, November 1997, pp. 75-98. Reprinted by permission of the U.S. Department of Justice, Office of Justice Programs.

the Midwest who were followed for a 25-year period after the abuse or neglect incident. These were substantiated cases of physical and sexual abuse and neglect, which occurred early in the lives of these children (before age 12).[3] Using official criminal records of arrests, we found that childhood victimization increases the likelihood of delinquency, adult criminality, and violent criminal behavior. At the same time, however, we found that the relationship is not inevitable, suggesting an opportunity for long-range violence prevention through appropriate intervention.

I want to call your attention briefly to five major points.[4]

First, the risk of arrest: Childhood victimization clearly increases a person's risk of arrest. To place this in perspective, the odds are almost two times higher that an abused or neglected child will be arrested as a juvenile for a violent crime than a control group child.

Our research was conducted in a metropolitan county area in the Midwest, using court cases from the years 1967 to 1971. But others have found similar results. In New York, for example, as part of the Rochester Youth Development study, Thornberry and his colleagues collected information on child abuse and neglect for the children who were part of their study.[5] They also found that child maltreatment was a significant risk factor for delinquency. Similarly, another evaluation by Matt Zingraff and his colleagues, using maltreated children and two nonmaltreated comparison samples from another geographic area of the country, Mecklenburg County, North Carolina, found that maltreated children had higher rates of delinquency as well.[6] Thus, in three quite different prospective studies from different parts of the country using cases from different time periods, childhood abuse and neglect have been found to increase a person's risk of delinquency.

Second, we have also learned that abused and neglected children are arrested at an earlier age, have more arrests, and are more likely to be repeat violent offenders.[7] Abused and neglected children are involved in criminal behavior almost a year earlier than the control group children. This is important because we know that age of onset is often negatively correlated with the severity of the disorder.[8]

Third, there is a cycle of violence. And violence does beget violence. That is, being physically abused as a child leads to an increased risk of an arrest for violence. However, our findings indicate that being neglected as a child also increases the risk of arrest for violence. I'll come back to this.

Fourth, there are differential patterns for population subgroups. Childhood victimization seems to have pervasive consequences for criminal behavior and violence in some respects, that is, it affects females as well as males—and as you know, females are at low risk for being arrested, particularly for being arrested for a violent crime. On the other hand, there seems to be a differential impact of childhood victimization on the criminal consequences for African-American children as compared with white children.[9] This we do not yet understand.

Fifth and finally, other findings suggest that childhood victimization also has the potential to affect other domains of functioning. We've conducted in-person followup interviews with a subset of the original sample (work supported by the National Institute of Justice, the National Institute on Alcohol Abuse and Alcoholism (NIAAA), the National Institute of Mental Health (NIMH), and now the National Institute of Drug Abuse (NIDA)).[10] We have found that abused and neglected children are also likely to manifest cognitive and intellectual deficiencies;[11] mental health consequences including antisocial personality disorder,[12] posttraumatic stress disorder,[13] and higher rates of suicide attempts;[14] alcohol abuse for women;[15] unemployment; and lower rates of marital stability.[16] These outcomes reported so far most likely represent only the tip of the iceberg of areas potentially affected in a negative way by childhood victimization.

Enough of the bad news. The good news is that there is an emerging "science of prevention"[17] and that there are some programs that have been shown to be effective.

For the most part, our current system of interventions is highly reactive in nature, geared toward treatment, rather than proactive with preventive efforts aimed at reduced vulnerability and risk. In the case of child victims, the justice system gets the failures of other systems. By the time these children are treated or seen, it is often after referral by court personnel, when they are typically manifesting a long history of antisocial behavior.

However, at numerous points in a child's life and environment there are opportunities to intervene. This is particularly true for abused and neglected children and especially those who come to the attention of public officials.[18] I have selected a typical case to illustrate such opportunities for intervention.

This is the case of a male child who was brought to the attention of the courts through a neglect petition when he was 6 years old. His mother was unemployed and his father's whereabouts was unknown at the time. He had eight siblings, born during an 8-year time period. He was the fifth child. For some time before the neglect petition, he had been cared for by his maternal grandfather. By the time of his petition, he had been abandoned for some years. At the age of 7, he was made a ward of the county. During this time, his mother showed only sporadic interest in him, and indeed, many of the other children in the family were cared for by other people scattered throughout the city. Eventually, some of the other siblings were adopted. At age 9, he was picked up by the police for running away on two separate occasions. He was held overnight, and the incident was recorded. Then, he was sent to a foster home. During this time, his mother would take him away from the foster home, take him out of school, and return him to the foster mother with only the clothes on his back. At that time, the public school system referred him to the Children's Bureau because of the constant disruption of his school attendance due to his mother's moving from place to place. At age 12 and again at age 13 he was picked up and charged with being ungovernable. The first time, he was sent to a group home for a short stay. The second time, he was placed on probation. By age 20 he was well on his way to becoming a repeat violent offender. By age 32 he had 13 separate arrests for violence, and by all accounts he might be considered a dysfunctional young adult. By that time he had spent several years in correctional facilities.

What promising strategies or programs might have made a difference in his life? Before his birth, home visitors might have worked with his mother to improve her parenting skills through public health and family support system services. Home visitation is one type of program that involves several models. Some rely on public health nurses who establish contact with mothers during their pregnancy and provide frequent visits after birth, whereas others rely on paraprofessionals who meet with the mother after discharge from the hospital. One reason for using home visitation is to reach families who might not otherwise have access to services, such as rural families living in isolated areas, urban poor isolated families, or families who might be unwilling to travel to service providers, such as abusive or neglectful families.

Another advantage of the home visitation program is that, after having developed a relationship with the parent, home visitors can provide services and models for effective parenting. One program, developed by David Olds and his colleagues,[19] uses prenatal and infancy home visitation by nurses to prevent a wide range of health and development problems, including prevention of child abuse. The program was based on the premise that nurse home visitors were in an optimal position to identify and help change factors in the family environment that interfere with maternal health habits, infant caregiving, and parental personal accomplishment in the areas of work, education, and family planning. This intervention was assessed through a randomized trial with 400 first-time high-risk mothers. Compared with families without these services, home-visited clients had fewer low-birth-weight babies, fewer reported cases of child abuse and neglect, higher rates of child immunizations, and more age-appropriate child development.

Now our young man also might have been enrolled in a program for preschoolers at risk for impairment of intellectual functioning and eventual school failure, such as the Perry preschool project.[20] In this project, low-income, black, 3- and 4-year-olds were randomly assigned to preschool and control conditions. Children in the experimental group attended high-quality, cognitively oriented early childhood education for 1 to 2 academic years. Teachers made weekly home visits, and monthly parent meetings were held. Longitudinal followup data to age 19 indicate that the Perry preschool children showed lower rates of placement in special education classes, lower grade retention, better performance on standardized measures of achievement, better high school graduation rates, and lower rates of welfare assistance than the children with no preschool. Further followup at approximately age 27 showed that the preschool program had dramatically reduced the rate of arrests and chronic offending.[21]

Another opportunity that we missed for our young man was when the public school system, recognizing this child's inschool problems, complained about the disruptive influence of the child's mother. Truancy has been increasingly recognized as a major problem in our country. A number of communities have begun to design truancy-reduction programs that often involve schools, law enforcement, families, businesses, judicial and social service agencies, and community and youth service organizations. Such programs involve intensive monitoring, counseling, and other family-strengthening services that are offered to truants and their families. And in these cases, there is at least preliminary evidence to suggest that these programs may be effective.[22]

Although too late for our young man, a series of community-based interventions with children and adolescents, aimed at violence prevention, was initiated in 1992 at various sites across the country.[23] Now, these programs are not designed to intervene with abused and neglected children, yet we hope that the information obtained from the evaluations of these promising interventions will be helpful.

But for all of these promising strategies (and others not mentioned), we will need to use caution in moving from small pilot tests such as these to large-scale prevention trials. It is very tempting to generalize from programs that have shown promising results. However, it is very important to resist the temptation since there may be features of experimental projects that are difficult or even impossible to reproduce in a large-scale social program.

What have we learned from these promising strategies or interventions to help guide the development of further programs to break the cycle of violence? I'd like to mention six principles very briefly:

1. The earlier the intervention, the better. Interventions need to be instituted early—before the behaviors have stabilized and become less amenable to change.[24]

Early childhood is a period during which the central nervous system is changing rapidly and profoundly and the attitudes and habits of children are formed.[25] Without interventions, deficits or dysfunctional behaviors at one age lay the groundwork for subsequent dysfunctional behaviors.[26] For example, severe malnutrition in infancy or brain damage from physical abuse may lead to impaired cognitive and intellectual functioning, which in turn affects IQ and obviously affects school performance, which in turn affects that child's ability to function adequately as an adolescent and young adult. Services should begin early, preferably during the prenatal period or shortly after birth, and should extend through the early years of a child's life. Early interventions should focus on eliminating factors that decrease a child's capacity for normal cognitive and neurological maturation. Aiming early intervention efforts at childhood victims has the potential to influence their behavior before their first offense.

This is not to say that all children victims should automatically become suspects. But given the increased risks associated with early childhood victimization, police, teachers, and health workers need to recognize the signs of abuse and neglect and take action to intervene early. Later intervention should not be ignored, but later interventions are more labor intensive and more difficult since they must deal simultaneously with the existence of problem behaviors and the prevention of further additional problem behaviors. If earlier identification of abuse and neglect leads to positive interventions, then this should reduce the risk of future violent behavior.

2. Don't neglect neglected children. Increased attention needs to be paid to neglected children. Although neglect cases have not received as much attention as cases of physical or sexual abuse, some researchers have suggested that children who experience neglect may be as vulnerable to long-term problems and to dysfunctional behavior as are victims of physical or sexual abuse.[27] Our research demonstrated a clear link between neglect and later violent criminal behavior. These findings are of particular concern since the incidence of neglect is more than twice that of physical abuse, and neglect cases represent the majority of the cases taxing the child protection system. In contrast to the episodic and explosive nature of physical abuse, neglect is a chronic condition which, in some ways, may be more amenable to intervention strategies.

Few justice programs address the needs of neglected children. The disproportionate number of these cases has at least two consequences for public officials: First, they will be called upon to deal with more cases of abuse and neglect, and second, since childhood victimization in the form of neglect is linked to later criminal behavior, a larger share of tomorrow's offenders will be today's victims of neglect.

3. One size does not fit all. It is also important to recognize that one size does not fit all, for families or children. What works for one child in one context may not work for a different child in the same setting, the same child in another setting, or the same child in another period in his or her development. Characteristics of the child will influence the extent to which interventions may be effective. For example, temperament exacerbates in some cases or minimizes in other cases a child's level of risk to develop problem behavior.[28] We have found that there is a small group of children, less than 7 percent, within the larger group of abused and neglected children in our sample who have indications of severe behavior problems at an early age.[29] These children with behavior problems made more placement moves than children without such indication. And these children with behavior problems are seven times more likely to be arrested as a juvenile and four times more likely to be arrested for a violent crime than children without those indications. Now, whether frequent moves reflect an early predisposition of the child to antisocial behavior or whether they reflect a response to it, children with numerous placements are in need of special services and are not well served by routine responses. Rather than waiting until after multiple placement failures, better identification of these children prior to placement would permit assignment to specialized treatment programs based on an assessment of the child's needs, which includes taking into consideration the child's developmental status at the time.

To be effective, interventions need also to recognize that children do not develop in a vacuum but, rather, in a social context. Characteristics of parents or caretakers and of the neighborhood and the community in which the child lives also exert potent influences on the child's development. While the first important influence on the child is the family, children and families are interacting members of a larger social system including schools and communities. There is growing evidence that the long-term impact of childhood trauma, whether it is direct victimization as in child abuse and neglect or witnessing violence in one's family or community, may depend on characteristics or practices of the family or the community in which the child lives.[30] This takes me to the next point.

4. Surveillance is a double-edged sword. One advantage of home visitation programs is that they can provide a watchful eye in the home. Unusual bruises, signs of spousal abuse, or indications of drug abuse can be noted by an individual with a trained eye. Similarly, an advantage of better training for police officers and school teachers to identify child abuse and neglect is the potential for the provision of services to these children and their families. On the other hand, surveillance is a double-edged sword associated with potentially serious negative consequences, particularly when some segments of the population are at risk for different levels of surveillance. Families who, because of certain demographic characteristics such as poverty, unemployment, or single parenthood, have frequent contact with public service agencies are more often exposed to closer scrutiny. Special care needs to be taken, then, in responding to and handling cases of childhood victims to prevent damage from the destructive edge of the double-edged sword. Our differential findings regarding the long-term criminal consequences of abuse and neglect by ethnicity cannot be ignored. If there are differences in the community's or system's response to abused and neglected children as a function of differences in ethnic or racial backgrounds, then it is important to identify these differences, particularly if they relate to subsequent levels of violence in these children. At a minimum, intervention agents need to be sensitive to the possibilities of differential treatment on the basis of race or ethnic background and take steps to avoid such practices.

5. Interventions are not one-time efforts. Many intervention efforts involve a single dose of relatively short duration. However, we have learned that programs such as home visitation, the Perry preschool, and Head Start cannot be viewed as a "single shot in the arm" or a one-time inoculation procedure. Rather, interventions may require periodic "booster shots" and perhaps more long-term followup. The original Elmira study, continued through the child's second birthday, was associated with definite benefits.[31, 32] However, the effects disappeared when the children were reevaluated at 25 and 50 months of age.[33] Perhaps we need to view early childhood intervention programs in the same way that we view other services to children, such as fluoride treatment. They may need to be continued with varying intensities at various points in childhood and adolescence.

6. Resources should be accessible. It is not enough just to increase resources, because accessibility is as important as the resources themselves. Concrete barriers—such as transportation, language problems, and fragmented services—may prevent children at risk or their families from taking advantage of existing resources. But barriers can be psychological as well. According to one researcher,[34] schools that provide free meals for low-income children have found that these children will not eat the meals if other children or teachers know they are free. Max Frankel,[35] in a column entitled, "Less Medicare, More Magic," argued to preserve the universality of social security to avoid the stigmatization of the elderly poor. Likewise, the potential for stigma associated with early child and parent intervention programs would be minimized by universal coverage. Abusive and neglectful families

may be more likely to accept parenting and child intervention programs that are offered to all in the community rather than targeted ones that might embarrass or stigmatize. This may be particularly important for intrusive interventions in family life, such as home visitation programs. Programs offered to all children and all families would also avoid implications of discrimination as well. Service providers could determine the intensity of services required depending on the particular needs of the child, the particular family, and the resources of the community.

So, what do I conclude? Comprehensive parent and early childhood intervention programs are clearly the option of choice. Estimates of the cost of home visiting for 1 year are between $1,500 to $3,500 per family. Consider that the total number of newborns born in Washington, D.C., in 1992 was 10,960.[36] If early parent and child intervention services were provided to all mothers of newborns in the District, the total cost per year would be roughly $38.3 million, using the higher cost estimate. Assuming that such a program were to begin in 1998 and continue for 5 years, at the end of that time we would expect that the entering kindergarten class in the District in the fall of 2003 would show dramatically improved health and academic preparedness. Even though $38.3 million per year sounds like a lot for a social experiment, such a program would probably pay for itself. At least in the original Elmira project, the cost of this early prevention project for high-risk families was equivalent to government savings associated with lower utilization of Aid to Families with Dependent Children, food stamps, Medicaid, child protection services, as well as tax revenues due to maternal employment.[37] Furthermore, these cost savings do not take into account the costs associated with services for older children and adolescents involving special education, foster care, court expenses, and juvenile detention and incarceration.[38] John Leventhal,[39] a pediatrician at Yale, has suggested that home visiting for high-risk newborns and their families might be covered by medical insurance or managed care plans similar to the cost of medical care. He cites one report that estimated the total costs for each form of transplant—kidney, bone marrow, or liver—in the United States to be about $1 billion per year.[40] Home visiting, which clearly has the same potential to be life-saving for some children and to improve markedly the development of many others, is relatively inexpensive per family compared with transplantion. Leventhal suggests that in the course of a child's lifetime, a successful preventive service should be viewed as a modest investment to ensure that the child's first few years of life are spent in a safe and nurturing environment.[41]

Universal parent and child intervention programs beginning during pregnancy are clearly preferable. However, if policymakers are not persuaded by the substantial benefits likely to come from the kinds of intervention efforts suggested here, then the criminal justice literature indicates that interventions targeted at abused and neglected children at a minimum are critical since these children clearly are at high risk for hurting themselves and hurting others.

Problems with attempts to predict future delinquency or adult offending often complicate proposals for early intervention. The situation for victims of child abuse and neglect is different. Abuse and neglect cases are those in which a decision to intervene has already been made and where public officials are already involved. Nonetheless, one important unresolved issue for me is whether targeted intervention strategies can be developed that protect the privacy of the children and their families and guard against the potentially negative outcomes associated with increased surveillance.

I have two simple take-home messages. First, there are promising programs that we should evaluate and build upon. Second, children are able to change given the chance and a little help. Not all abused and neglected children grow up to become violent offenders. And while we do not yet fully understand the factors that make the difference in their lives, we need to intervene early—and the earlier, the better. This is consistent with other social goals: reducing crime, increasing educational achievement, and preventive health care. The cycle of violence hypothesis proposes that yesterday's and today's childhood victims will become tomorrow's offenders and perpetrators of violence. Rather than focusing on responses to child abuse or neglect in court proceedings that "treat" offenders, prevention efforts should target childhood victims to reduce their risk of becoming offenders in the future.

Question-and-Answer Session

Duane Ragan, Office for Victims of Crime, U.S. Department of Justice, Washington, D.C.: Did you include any of the children who had been in Head Start?

C.S.W.: I did not include Head Start evaluations in this talk, but certainly some of the children not in the Perry preschool program would have been in Head Start. I know there is controversy about the long-term effects of Head Start, but in some of the work that I've seen, the effects have been quite powerful. I didn't include them here because I simply didn't have the most up-to-date followups. Also, I really wanted to tie in the connection to the criminal justice community, the issue of reduced arrests and chronic offending.

Christopher Stone, Vera Institute of Justice, New York, New York: Do you know if there are any child welfare agencies in the country that have held themselves or are held accountable/responsible for the future development of the kids who are currently their wards?

C.S.W.: Remember, I'm a researcher; I don't work in child welfare. There are child welfare people here. Certainly, Nicholas Scoppetta in New York City now is trying to take a position, saying that "I'm going to be held accountable for this." I suspect that there are people who are doing that. Whether they are taking as public a stance as Scoppetta, I don't know. He is certainly getting heat.

Nicholas Scoppetta, Administration for Children's Services, New York, New York: The question was directed more toward holding us accountable for the future consequences of abuse and neglect. What I've been talking about is holding the system accountable for delivering what we are supposed to be doing, not simply the nobility of our intentions.

C.S.W.: Well, you see, I think that, if you don't have the kinds of slippages that you are having in the agency, if you are able to accomplish what you would like to do and do it early enough in the process when you have these definite cases of child abuse and neglect, you will see a reduction of problems in the future. So, if you will be held accountable for dealing properly and responsibly with those kids, then I think the rest will fall into place.

Edward Cotton, Illinois Department of Children and Family Services, Springfield, Illinois: I wondered whether, in the early intervention programs, particularly some of the models that are used nationally, you looked at strategies to use with dropouts. Since these programs are voluntary, the ones we looked at had extremely high dropout rates—whether at-risk families were identified in the hospital and said "no" or said "yes" and were never available after that. I guess I want to put things in perspective. These programs are voluntary, the dropout rate seems to be very high, and I wondered if you could discuss any strategies to address that. Because it doesn't matter if a program is great if people are not going to come to it or if they drop out of it.

C.S.W.: That's a good question. One of the things that I cut out of my presentation (but is in the paper) is a talk about some of these barriers. A woman named Karol Kumpfer[42] has done some work on parent-training programs that I think is creative. One thing that she has been able to do is to get very high parental attendance rates at her program meetings. One way she has done that is by really paying attention to some of the nitty-gritty issues like transportation, daycare, and all these other things that will actually enable parents to attend. That doesn't get at your issue, which is parents who simply don't want to or are not themselves "together" enough. I think (this is the caution that you heard here in this talk) we need to solve—we need to do some preliminary work to figure out what is the best way to get parents to enroll, to commit to being in these programs, and then to be kept involved in these programs. Because, clearly, if only a very small fraction of the families who are offered these services are taking the services, most likely those avoiding them are going to be the families who are most in need of the services (the most dysfunctional). Before we plunge into major programming—I guess I shouldn't have said 1998, then, for the newborns in the District—I think we need some preliminary work to deal with these very practical issues. But I don't know, other than Kumpfer's work, whether there is other literature that talks about that.

Donald Murray, National Association of Counties, Washington, D.C.: Dr. Widom, I was very interested in your highlighting the problems of accessibility to services. In so many of our communities we see a lot of fragmentation where the community doesn't have a strategy. In terms of holding the community accountable, making sure all the players are at the table, we're excited by what Governor Hunt in North Carolina is doing. I'm sure you've heard about it. At the county level, half the counties in the State (shooting for the whole State) have set up boards just to focus on children 0-to-3 years of age. He has put in a little less than $100 million, but so far the results have been spectacular.

C.S.W.: I certainly hope that someone is evaluating from when the program began to 5 years from now, so we can learn what were the good things that were done—what were the things that made a difference— so we can then take them to another community.

Donald Murray, National Association of Counties, Washington, D.C.: The central thing is getting the community to come up with a collaborative strategy based on the thinking of all segments of the community. That's usually not done. It's just a very simple idea.

David Lloyd, Family Advocacy Program, U.S. Department of Defense, Arlington, Virginia: I'm afraid that you picked a poor example: A child that's the fifth of eight children with umpteen different fathers already is in a family that is probably not going to be one that participates in any type of voluntary intervention program. It kind of reminds me of Richard Gelles's call for removing those children from their families permanently, thinking about terminating parental rights early, and moving them into adoption

(with the caveat of ensuring that they receive the treatment services to deal with what has already happened to them). Too many of those children do not receive this either in foster families or in adopted families.

But my larger concern has to do with the conflict that we have in child welfare philosophy. The good news, I guess, is that child abuse and neglect is a low base-rate phenomenon. Even if we double or triple the estimates of how frequently it occurs, it is still a relatively (thank goodness) infrequent phenomenon. Combined with that, we have kind of unitary terms to describe very discrete things happening. Neglect is not a unitary phenomenon. There are children neglected for their medical needs, which tend to be rather one-time-only issues. There are children whose educational needs have been neglected, and it is difficult to differentiate these children from truants when they hit a certain age level. Then there is neglect that is clearly poverty related; this probably should not be considered parental neglect but rather economic neglect or American society neglect. Then there is parental disinterest, which is, I think, the hardest one to deal with. It is the lack of attachment. Because we treat all forms of neglect the same, we don't really understand the phenomenon very well. Perhaps we would do better to really study the neglect cases, to really learn from those parents in the same way that we have interviews with serial killers, to try to learn what motivates them and to devise better strategies.

The evaluation of Hawaii Healthy Start over a longer time and some other early intervention programs leads me to a great deal of concern about whether we will get the payoff for the amount of money that it takes to do this with the hard-to-reach families, where the propensity for later delinquency and criminal behavior is the highest. I'm not at all convinced that having paraprofessionals work in a home where there are eight children of umpteen different fathers is really going to pay off when we have a low base-rate phenomenon—whether we are going to see that much change. There are a whole lot of other benefits from early intervention in addition to reduction of abuse and neglect and dealing with the consequences of abuse and neglect. But I think until we get our minds wrapped around what it is we are really trying to do in child welfare philosophy, we are going to continue to have a lot of problems in terms of preventing further delinquency and adult criminal behavior.

C.S.W.: Well, let me respond to that. First of all, although many of my cases do have multiple fathers for the children in the family, that wasn't one of the characteristics of the family that I described here. There were eight children; you're probably right—they probably could have been sired by different people. This case illustrates why I am arguing that it is not enough just to focus on the child. Successful interventions do not simply focus on a child. If one reads this literature, if one thinks about child development, it becomes apparent that the child is very much affected by the complicated dysfunctions of these parents as well as the communities. I think that it is a very important point. Also, we know a lot more about neglect than we did many years ago. There are many forms of neglect that the child welfare/child protection system does talk about. In my own work, however, I'm talking about a simple kind of neglect—it's a very powerful one, though. I'm talking about early neglect. We have eliminated the educational neglect that comes at a later point in time, especially if that's the only evidence of neglect. But these are cases of life-threatening failure to provide services to children: severe lack of food, clothing, shelter, and medical attention. I'm not talking about psychological maltreatment. My cases are from almost 30 years ago, now.

I think what is important is to recognize the effects of deprivation of these fundamental needs in early childhood. There was a psychologist by the name of Abraham Maslow who talked about a hierarchy of needs. At the very bottom of that hierarchy is the need for security, sustenance, the basic things in life. If we don't have that, if a child doesn't have food, clothing, shelter, or medical attention, how can that child go to school and be a well-functioning child? How can such children pay attention or keep their heads up in school?

We don't know enough about the linkages and effects because the field of child maltreatment, in terms of research, is relatively new and vastly underfunded. But I think that in the case of my research, which connects neglect of this sort with violent criminal behavior at a later point, we can't dismiss the connection.

Marc Mauer, The Sentencing Project, Washington, D.C.: Could you elaborate on what you spoke about as the potential negative consequences of increased surveillance? Wouldn't people make the argument that if more problems are found, the response should be more services? What is the problem with doing that?

C.S.W.: This is something that troubles me a lot. Although I really want to argue that we need to intervene in the lives of abused and neglected children, what stops me from endorsing that 100 percent (I don't know if you picked that up in my talk) is that we have these very troubling race-specific findings. Specifically, we find that for the African-American children in our sample (compared with the (control) African-American children—those are kids who grew up in the same neighborhoods, the only difference (at least on paper) is that one group was abused and one group doesn't have an official record of abuse), we find that the effects of childhood victimization are re-

ally enormous, very powerful, and much larger than the effects for white children in our sample who were similarly abused and neglected. We have been trying to find an explanation for this seeming difference in what should be a general phenomenon. It even seems to affect males *and* females. So why should it affect one group?

One of the things that we think about is relevant to something Janet Reno talks about—seeing a 3-year-old child or a 6-year-old child on the street at the wrong point in time. The community needs to respond to that child—take him or her home or whatever needs to be done. That is clearly a child in the wrong place. One hypothesis is that if we have a neglected child, it means that somebody's not paying attention to that child. That child may be out on the streets at the wrong time. If one has a child that is out on the streets, that child has more opportunities to get into trouble and to be picked up by the cops. And if that child happens to be an African-American, once that child gets connected to the juvenile justice system, it is very difficult to get out of the system. The child's attitudes may change, the child may develop hostilities, all kinds of things. So we are concerned that somehow, by following these children and their families, we may not be responding to them and giving them services in the same way.

That's why I say if we can find a way to target these children with full appreciation of the delicate balance between making things better or worse for them, then targeting would be the most effective. But I think we need to do a lot more creative work to figure out how to do that.

Marsha Renwanz, Office of Juvenile Justice and Delinquency Prevention, U.S. Department of Justice, Washington, D.C.: I've heard you speak several times and am always struck by the importance of your findings about neglect for the reasons that you mentioned, number of cases, etc. Given that we're now embarking on this nationwide experiment with welfare reform in the different States, do you have plans to look at several States in terms of risks of early neglect—catastrophic neglect for infants and toddlers—that you have identified? Will those risks be assessed by you or other researchers?

C.S.W.: There is a project that some people are working on in the District of Columbia to develop a proposal to provide services for abused and neglected children. The notion is that there will be an evaluation component to it, and I've been asked to help them with the evaluation component. I am way behind on all the other things that I was supposed to be doing when I was preparing this talk, so I'm trying to figure out how I can be involved. This is the only program that I know of, and that is in the infancy stage. But I am sure that there are lots of people in this room who know of programs in their communities. The real question is whether, as I said to the gentleman from North Carolina, there is a serious evaluation that is planned. And I'm even happy to say, "Let's have 2 years of this program without an evaluation"; get your program going. Maybe just collect some base-rate information. But let us evaluate these programs. Let us not simply run programs without learning something from them in a systematic way.

Rosemary Chalk, Board on Children, Youth, and Families, National Research Council, Washington, D.C.: I want to pursue the whole issue of targeted versus universal interventions. David Lloyd earlier expressed his skepticism about the home visitation approach, based on the results of the Hawaii effort. I think it's very important to distinguish the home visitation model used in Hawaii from that used in the Olds study. There are different types of skills involved, differences in terms of the timing of the intervention. Using the Olds model the intervention seems to have the greatest impact on adolescent first-time mothers, and the impact may have been moderated by their ability to delay a second pregnancy. So we may not be talking about eight children in the household, maybe now about four. We know that neglect occurs in families that have very high numbers of children—that's often a family characteristic. The whole issue of spacing pregnancies becomes a key outcome measure in looking at the effects of some of the home visitation interventions.

I haven't heard you say anything about neighborhoods. It may be that one strategy to use in trying to balance this question of targeting families versus universal interventions is to look at the kinds of neighborhoods in which cases of abuse and neglect tend to concentrate and see whether we can think of some selection criteria. If we have a neighborhood context, we might want to target the intervention on any first-time mothers in that neighborhood, regardless of their family situation or individual characteristics. We could use geographic criteria and look at the role of unrelated adults within that neighborhood as support systems and as support resources who may be helpful in maintaining the quality, timing, and dosage of the intervention that would be offered through some type of organizational approach in its initial stages.

C.S.W.: I'm glad you brought up the issue. I appreciate the point about the Hawaii program. One of the programs that I didn't mention follows a model that uses paraprofessionals versus the public health nurse model—they are very different. You can imagine different costs associated with them. One thing I think we need to do is to examine the extent to which these two models may have different effectiveness. If one

were to engage in a larger scale intervention, I would like to see both models tried and pitted against one another.

I did mention neighborhoods though, and I think that neighborhoods and communities are terribly important. There is a difficulty in targeting neighborhoods. I thought about saying, "Let's take six cities: D.C., Detroit, Gary, etc.," cities with big crime problems. The difficulty is that, if we target by neighborhood, we are essentially picking African-American and minority communities. I have a real problem with the issue of stigmatization.

James Comer, for example, in his work and programs on schools, specifically chose to do his work in the school system. He worked with the entire school system, so there would not be these issues of unwillingness to accept the resources that might be offered. I think taking a geographic area that does have a high crime problem (like D.C.), taking these kids and starting with the pregnant mother, one is going to get those very high-risk families. As long as we keep track, do a needs assessment at the beginning of such an experiment, and then follow through, we would be able to determine whether it is only the most high-risk mothers and families that are benefiting.

But in the United States 50 or 75 years ago, there were public health nurses going into communities and doing exactly what David Olds' program is doing now, especially in rural or isolated areas. So it is not drawing from the British or drawing from the French, it is going back to a historical time in the United States.

Rebecca Burkhalter, Burkhalter Associates, Inc., Washington, D.C.: My question relates to the fact that many of these children we are talking about as preschoolers or infants are going to be in the hands of daycare workers more than anyone else. I was involved in that for many years. One thing that disturbed me, and I am wondering if it has changed, was the absence of required skills and training in daycare workers. We really said, "Well, if she is a nice person. . . ." It didn't matter if she was qualified in early childhood development. If these people are going to be dealing with high-risk infants, they need to know something about children. Are we going to require more? And are we, as a Nation, going to feel that they are regular teachers and not just daycare workers and babysitters?

C.S.W.: I have no particular expertise to answer the question you're asking me. I would rather turn it back on the audience.

Shay Bilchik, Office of Juvenile Justice and Delinquency Prevention, U.S. Department of Justice, Washington, D.C.: To build upon a couple of points that were made about the Hawaii Healthy Start model versus home visitation through nurses (and targeting), right now we are in the middle of a project with David Olds in which we are replicating some of his work in six different communities, using that model in a targeted way through the Weed and Seed Office (partnering with Health and Human Services, the Weed and Seed Office, and the Office of Juvenile Justice and Delinquency Prevention). We are finding 100 first-time mothers in those communities to show how we could interrupt that pathway with delayed subsequent births and less welfare dependency. I know that David Olds is about to come out with a 15-year update on his original study that hopefully will show even more promising results.

C.S.W.: I'm very excited about that. I can't wait to see the results. But one thing that I think we have to remember, getting back to Rosemary's comment and others', is that anything that we can do to help the development of these children from a very early point is going to have positive benefits. So if we can have fewer low-birth-weight babies for these high-risk mothers, if we can have better health care—all of these things that one would think we would be able to do routinely—in turn are going to lead to healthier children, children who can perform better academically, and that is such a critical life point for these children. It is a time when they become so susceptible to delinquent peer groups and all the other bad things. Once they are in that risk category, it is simply a playing-out of problem behaviors.

Shay Bilchik, Office of Juvenile Justice and Delinquency Prevention, U.S. Department of Justice, Washington, D.C.: Cathy, the most promising part of your talk and of the work in this area is that it highlights the gap that exists between the ideal that you're talking about and what we are presently providing to these families. For policymakers it is critical to know that the gap is significant and that there needs to be a substantial investment just to get us to ground zero in doing this kind of work.

Notes

1. Cooper, M., "Girl's Slaying Spurs Inquiry on City Lapses," *The New York Times*, February 16, 1997, B1.
2. Terry, D., "When the Family Heirloom Is Homicide," *The New York Times*, December 12, 1994, B7.
3. Details of the design and description of the subjects are available in Widom, C.S., "Child Abuse, Neglect, and Adult Behavior: Design and Findings on Criminality, Violence and Child Abuse," *American Journal of Orthopsychiatry* 59 (1989):355–367.
4. For further information about these findings, see Widom, C.S., "The Cycle of Violence: Revisited Six Years Later," *Archives of Pediatrics and Adolescent Medicine* 150 (1996):390–395.
5. Smith, C., and T.P. Thornberry, "The Relationship between Child Maltreatment and Adolescent Involvement in Delinquency," *Criminology* 33 (1995):451–481.
6. Zingraff, M.T., J. Leiter, K.A. Myers, and M.C. Johnsen, "Child Maltreatment and Youthful Problem Behavior," *Criminology* 31 (1993):173–202.
7. Of the offenders in this study, abused and neglected children committed more offenses than controls (the average number of arrests was 6.9 versus 4.7, respectively). Abused and neglected children were also more likely to be recidivists (having more than two arrests) than nonabused and nonneglected individuals (17 percent versus 13 percent, respectively), chronic offenders with 5 or more arrests (20 percent versus 12 percent, respectively), and repeat violent offenders (9 percent versus 6 percent, respectively).
8. Loeber, R., and M. Stouthamer-Loeber, "Family Factors as Correlates and Predictors of Juvenile Conduct Problems and Delinquency," in *Crime and Justice: An Annual Review of Research*, ed. Michael Tonry and Norval Morris, Chicago: University of Chicago Press, 1987:29–149.
9. Maxfield, M.G. and C.S. Widom, "The Cycle of Violence: Revisited Six Years Later," *Archives of Pediatrics and Adolescent Medicine* 150 (1996):390–395.
10. This research was supported in part by grants from the National Institute of Justice (86–IJ–CX–0033, 89–IJ–CX–0007, and 93–IJ–CX–0031), the National Institute of Mental Health (MH49467), the National Institute of Alcohol Abuse and Alcoholism (AA09238), and the National Institute of Drug Abuse (DA10060). Points of view are those of the author and do not necessarily represent the position of the U.S. Department of Justice or the U.S. Department of Health and Human Services.
11. Perez, C.M., and C.S. Widom, "Childhood Victimization and Long-term Intellectual and Academic Outcomes," *Child Abuse and Neglect* 18 (1994):617–674.
12. Luntz, B., and C.S. Widom, "Antisocial Personality Disorder in Abused and Neglected Children Grown Up, *American Journal of Psychiatry* 151 (1994):670–674.
13. Widom C.S., "Exposure to Traumatic Events and Posttraumatic Stress Disorder in Abused and Neglected Children Followed-up, 1997," unpublished report.
14. Widom, C.S., "Childhood Victimization: Early Adversity and Subsequent Psychopathology," in *Adversity, Stress, and Psychopathology*, ed. B. Dohrenwend, New York: Oxford University Press, in press.
15. Widom, C.S., T. Ireland, and P.J. Glynn, "Alcohol Abuse in Abused and Neglected Children Followed-up: Are They at Increased Risk?" *Journal of Studies on Alcohol* 56 (1995):207–217.
16. Widom, "Childhood Victimization: Early Adversity and Subsequent Psychopathology."
17. Coie, J., N.F. Watt, S.G. West, J.D. Hawkins, J.R. Asarnow, H.J. Markman, S.L. Ramey, M.B. Shure, and B. Long, "The Science of Prevention: A Conceptual Framework and Some Directions for a National Research Program," *American Psychologist* 48 (1993):1013–1022.
18. One report by Meddin and Hansen found that the majority of abuse cases that were substantiated received no services at all (Meddin, B., and I. Hansen, "The Services Provided during a Child Abuse and/or Neglect Case Investigation and the Barriers That Exist to Service Provision," *Child Abuse and Neglect* 9 (1985):175–182).
19. Olds, D., C. Henderson, R. Tatelbaum, and R. Chamberlin, "Improving the Delivery of Prenatal Care and Outcomes of Pregnancy: A Randomized Trial of Nurse Home Visitation," *Pediatrics* 77 (1986):16–28.
20. Berrueta-Clement, J.R.B., L.J. Schweinhart, W.S. Barnett, A.S. Epstein, and D.P. Weikart, *Changed Lives: The Effects of the Perry Pre-School Program on Youths Through Age 19*, Ypsilanti, MI: High Scope Press, 1984, Monograph No. 8.
21. Schweinhart, L.J., H.B. Barnes, and D.P. Weikart, *Significant Benefits: The High Scope Perry Preschool Study through Age 27*, Ypsilanti, MI: High Scope Press, 1993.
22. Garry, E.M., *Truancy: First Step to a Lifetime of Problems*, Juvenile Justice Bulletin, Washington, D.C.: U.S. Department of Justice, Office of Juvenile Justice and Delinquency Prevention, October 1996, NCJ 161958.
23. Powell, K.E., and D.F. Hawkins, "Youth Violence Prevention: Descriptions and Baseline Data from 13 Evaluation Projects," *American Journal of Preventive Medicine*, Supplement to Vol. 12, No. 5 (September/October 1996).

24. Coie et al., "The Science of Prevention: A Conceptual Framework and Some Directions for a National Research Program," 1013–1022.

25. Carlson, M., F. Earls, and R.D. Todd, "The Importance of Regressive Changes in the Development of the Nervous System: Towards a Neurobiological Theory of Child Development," *Psychiatric Development* 6 (1988):1–22.

26. Widom, C.S. "Understanding the Consequences of Childhood Victimization," in *The Treatment of Child Abuse*, ed. R.M. Reese, Baltimore: Johns Hopkins University Press, in press.

27. Burgess, R.L., and R.D. Conger, "Family Interaction in Abusive, Neglectful, and Normal Families," *Child Development* 49 (1978):1163–1173.

28. Widom, "Understanding the Consequences of Childhood Victimization."

29. These behavior problems were noted in the juvenile probation department records or in the original case material and indicated that the child had engaged in chronic fighting, fire setting, destructiveness, or defiance of authority; had severe temper tantrums, uncontrolled anger, and sadistic tendencies (as in aggressiveness toward weaker children); or was extremely difficult to control.

30. Terr, L.A., "Chowchilla Revisited: The Effects of Psychiatric Trauma Four Years after a School-bus Kidnapping," *American Journal of Psychiatry* 140 (1983):1543–1550.

31. Olds, D., C. Henderson, and H. Kitzman, "Does Parental and Infancy Nurse Home Visitation Have Enduring Effects on Qualities of Parental Caregiving and Child Health at 25–50 Months of Life?" *Pediatrics* 93 (1994):89–98.

32. Olds, Henderson, Tatelbaum, and Chamberlin, "Improving the Delivery of Prenatal Care and Outcomes of Pregnancy: A Randomized Trial of Nurse Home Visitation," 16–28.

33. Olds, Henderson, and Kitzman, "Does Prenatal and Infancy Nurse Home Visitation Have Enduring Effects on Qualities of Parental Caregiving and Child Health at 25–50 Months of Life?" 89–98.

34. Masten, A., "Resilience in Individual Development: Successful Adaptation Despite Risk and Adversity," in *Educational Resilience in Inner-city America: Challenges and Prospects*, ed. M.C. Wang and E.W. Gordon, Hillsdale, NJ: Laurence Erlbaun Associates, Inc., 1994:3–25.

35. Frankel, M. "Less Medicare, More Magic," *The New York Times*, March 9, 1997, sec. 6, p. 30.

36. United States Bureau of the Census, *Statistical Abstract of the United States, 1995*, Washington, D.C.: U.S. Department of Commerce, Economics and Statistic Administration, Bureau of the Census, 1995.

37. The home visitation program in Elmira, New York, was analyzed and the net cost was determined: $3,173 for 2 years of intervention (including personnel salaries and benefits, travel expenses, supplies, staff training, and a modest overhead charge). By the time the children were age 4, low-income families who had received a nurse home visitor during pregnancy and through the second year of the child's life cost the government $3,313 less than comparison group children. Government savings were estimated as the difference in utilization of AFDC, food stamps, Medicaid, and child protection services minus tax revenues due to maternal employment (Olds, D., C. Henderson, C. Phelps, H. Kitzman, and C. Hanks, "Effect of Prenatal and Infancy Home Visitation on Government Spending," *Medical Care* 31 (1993):155–174).

38. Annual operating expenses per inmate in jails in 1993 were approximately $15,000 (Perkins, C.A., J.J. Stephan, and A.J.Beck, *Jails and Jail Inmates 1993–1994: Census of Jails and Survey of Jails*, Bulletin, Washington, D.C.: U.S. Department of Justice, Bureau of Justice Statistics, April 1995, NCJ 151651) and for State and Federal inmates they were approximately $18,000, based on average costs per day (Camp, C.G., and N.G. Camp, *The Correctional Yearbook*, South Salem, NY: Criminal Justice Institute, Inc. 1996).

39. Leventhal, J.M. "Twenty Years Later: We Do Know How to Prevent Child Abuse and Neglect," *Child Abuse and Neglect* 20 (1996):647–653.

40. Anders, G. "On Sale Now at Your HMO: Organ Transplants," *The Wall Street Journal*, January 17, 1995, B1 and B5.

41. Leventhal, "Twenty Years Later: We Do Know How to Prevent Child Abuse and Neglect," 651.

42. Kumpfer, K., V. Molgaard, and R. Spoth, "The Strengthening Families Program for the Prevention of Delinquency and Drug Use," in *Preventing Childhood Disorders, Substance Abuse and Delinquency*, ed. R. DeV. Peters and R.J. McMahon, Thousand Oaks, CA: Sage Publications, 1996.

Unit Selections

11. **Disrespect as Catalyst for Brutality,** Deborah Sontag and Dan Barry
12. **Advocacy and Law Enforcement: Partners against Domestic Violence,** Marie P. Defina and Leonard Wetherbee
13. **Incorporating Diversity: Police Response to Multicultural Changes in Their Communities,** Brad R. Bennett
14. **Afterburn: The Victimization of Police Families,** Andrew H. Ryan
15. **Marketing Community Policing: What Can We Expect?** Michael E. Clark
16. **A LEN Interview with Police Chief Randall Aragon of Whiteville, N.C.,** Peter C. Dodenhoff

Key Points to Consider

❖ Is there "community policing" in your community? If not, why not? If so, is it working?

❖ Should the police be involved in community problems not directly concerned with crime? Explain your response.

❖ What are the pros and cons of outside review of the police?

❖ What strategies can be implemented to deal with stress suffered by police officers and their families?

 **Links**   **www.dushkin.com/online/**

14. **ACLU Criminal Justice Home Page**
    http://aclu.org/issues/criminal/hmcj.html
15. **FBI Violent Criminal Apprehension Program**
    http://www.fbi.gov/vicap/vicap.htm
16. **Introduction to American Justice**
    http://www.uaa.alaska.edu/just/just110/home.html
17. **Law Enforcement Guide to the World Wide Web**
    http://leolinks.com
18. **National Institute of Justice**
    http://www.ojp.usdoj.gov/nij/lawedocs.htm

These sites are annotated on pages 4 and 5.

Police officers are the guardians of our freedoms under the Constitution and the law, and as such they have an awesome task. They are asked to prevent crime, protect citizens, arrest wrongdoers, preserve the peace, aid the sick, control juveniles, control traffic, and provide emergency services on a moment's notice. They are also asked to be ready to lay down their lives, if necessary.

In recent years the job of the police officer has become even more complex and dangerous, illegal drug use and trafficking is at epidemic levels, racial tensions are explosive, and violent crime continues to increase at alarming rates.

The role of the police in America is a difficult one, and as the police deal with a growing, diverse population, their job becomes more difficult. The need for a more professional, well-trained police officer is obvious.

The lead article in the unit, "Disrespect as Catalyst for Brutality" maintains that many New York City police officers see disrespect as a threat not just to their performance but sometimes to their lives.

"Advocacy and Law Enforcement: Partners against Domestic Violence" identifies a model for combatting family violence that combines the expertise of the police and civilian counselors. Brad Bennett, in his essay, "Incorporating Diversity: Police Response to Multicultural Changes in Their Communities," reports on a study done in California that shows how four police agencies responded to demographic changes in their communities. "Afterburn: The Victimization of Police Families," by Andrew Ryan, tells how "doing the police job" can have long-lasting effects on both officers and their families. What is community policing? "Marketing Community Policing: What Can We Expect?" asserts that much of the public, the media, and even the police remain unclear about what it is and what to expect of it. The unit closes with "A LEN Interview with Police Chief Randall Aragon of Whiteville, N.C." Chief Aragon, a strong proponent of Total Quality Management (TQM), maintains that it takes time to implement community-oriented policing effectively.

Disrespect as Catalyst for Brutality

**By DEBORAH SONTAG
and DAN BARRY**

After dropping her young daughter with a baby sitter, Taquana Harris rushed to her hostess job at the fashionable Bowery Bar one night last February, her leopard-print evening gown sweeping elegantly through the dark, icy streets of the East Village. Then a strange woman crudely grabbed her by the arm and demanded to know what she had done with the drugs.

Within seconds, Ms. Harris recalled, she found herself pinned to the steel grating of a bodega by two plainclothes officers engaged in a neighborhood drug sweep. Frustrated by the officers' refusal to hear her explanation for being on that particular block, Ms. Harris made a tactical mistake: she wisecracked. "Oh, I get it," she said. "You're trying to reach a quota."

One officer responded with pepper spray, blasting her in the face. Distraught and weeping, Ms. Harris was taken in handcuffs to the Ninth Precinct station house, where she

was charged with disorderly conduct and resisting arrest. Later that night, months before the charges were dropped and the city paid $50,000 to settle her claim of civil rights violations, one of the arresting officers left her with some parting words: "You don't talk to police officers the way you did."

The officer's comment, in an otherwise mundane case, drives to the heart of what links Ms. Harris's unsettling encounter to the worst cases of police brutality. However they end, be it with a strip search or a face slammed into the pavement, most misconduct cases begin with what the officers perceive as a challenge to their authority.

Such challenges lie at the root of so many civil rights lawsuits, and of so many academic studies of police behavior, that they are recognized as a phenomenon unto themselves. They provide the catalytic moment when, with the hint of power shifting from an officer to a citizen, rou-

tine encounters can escalate into explosive incidents. One officer may feel challenged by taunts, another by the simple question, "What did I do?"

These challenges continually test the relationship between civilians and the police, who are given guns, nightsticks and wide latitude to keep order. In New York City, that tenuous contract is tested even further by the often brash assertiveness of the city's residents. More so than elsewhere, experts say, the New York police are called on to show unnatural restraint in their dealings with the public.

The New York Police Academy tailors standard police training to instruct new officers on how to absorb verbal aggressiveness like a sponge, or, in the martial arts language they use, to "bend like the reed in the wind."

Once planted on the real streets of New York, however, the reeds are not so supple. Many officers see disrespect as a threat, not just to their job performance, but sometimes to their lives. For them, choosing to dominate testy citizens without overasserting themselves is not only an art but an attitude. Some situations, they believe, require forcefulness, and there is a fine line between appropriate and inappropriate force.

Officer Michael F. Wilson, a 13-year veteran of the force who teaches sociology at the Police Academy, said many officers struggle to rise above their visceral reactions to disrespect.

"Initially, when someone gives you major grief, you're stunned," he said. "It's like the first time you got punched as a kid. You're shocked, and your body wants to react. In the best of cases, though, there is this little person inside your head saying, 'It's not worth it. I put my hands on this person, I lose.'"

Spokesmen for the police argue that the thousands of police misconduct claims a year in New York City should be put in statistical context. Every year, the department makes 330,000 arrests and issues 1.5 million summonses for moving violations, and the great majority of those encounters are handled properly.

But critics say the recurrence of garden-variety misconduct cases like that of Ms. Harris's reflects the failure of the Police Department to alter something deeply embedded in the police culture: an us-versus-them mentality that makes many officers distrustful of those they encounter on the street. And they point out that, as the police aggressively enforce Mayor Rudolph W. Giuliani's "quality of life" strategy, the number of misconduct and excessive force claims has increased significantly, from 3,956 in 1993 to 5,596 last year.

An examination of dozens of police misconduct cases suggests that a variety of challenges to police authority—asking for a badge number, videotaping officers, leading them on a chase—can provoke an incident. Some officers feel irritated when someone files a complaint against them, others when a by-

stander intervenes in their handling of an encounter.

The officers' responses also vary, from the proper, nonconfrontational handling of a matter to a vindictive arrest, from a thwock with a flashlight to a debilitating beating.

One young man, Douglas Snyder, a New York University student, was kicked in the face until he lost consciousness after videotaping a police confrontation with squatters; the camera was smashed and urinated on. Another, Edward Dominguez, a high school student in the Bronx, was a passenger in a speeding car; an officer kicked him so hard in the groin that he lost a testicle.

When Authority Is Challenged, New York Police May Lash Out

In such encounters, the person usually ends up charged with one or more of what civil rights lawyers refer to as the triumvirate of charges: resisting arrest, disorderly conduct and the obstruction of governmental administration. Those charges are almost invariably dropped, but not before punishment has been delivered in the form of a humiliating strip search or a night spent in a holding pen.

In addition to traumatizing some law-abiding citizens, experts say,

these cases cost the city millions of dollars in lawsuits and immeasurable capital in public trust.

"I used to be the kind of person, when I see an officer, I smile," said Nancy Tong, a documentary filmmaker who was taken into custody for speaking disrespectfully to an officer. "I'm not that kind of person anymore."

New York's most notorious recent cases of police brutality stem from what the officers saw as challenges to their authority.

Prosecutors say that an officer's mistaken belief that Abner Louima was behaving aggressively toward him prompted the beating he gave the Haitian immigrant inside a Brooklyn station house. Francis X. Livoti, the officer dismissed this year for using a choke hold that led to the death of a Bronx man named Anthony Baez, explained that he moved to arrest Mr. Baez and his brother because, he said, they refused to stop playing football when ordered, "daring" him to "take some kind of action."

"Like Livoti, many officers experience rampant disrespect and view it as undermining their authority," said Stuart London, a lawyer who won Mr. Livoti an acquittal on murder charges and represents many officers accused of misconduct.

"Every day," Mr. London said, "throughout the city, you have officers who are routinely turning the other cheek. But sometimes they feel they have to take a stand in order to patrol effectively, and then something minor can really escalate."

Ill-Chosen Words

A Traffic Encounter Escalates in Chinatown

It was a hot August night three years ago when Ms. Tong, the filmmaker, was caught in bumper-to-bumper traffic on the narrow streets of Chinatown, and, she said in an interview, climbed from her car to peer at what lay ahead.

From behind her, a voice barked, "Get back in that car!"

Ms. Tong, 43, an immigrant from Hong Kong, shot back: "What's the big deal? It's a free country." When she turned around, she drew in her breath. She had unwittingly talked back to a police officer.

She ducked back into her car and when traffic began to move, the officer ordered her to pull over and demanded her license, which she had left at home. She asked what she had done. The officer got angry, she said, and told her driving was a privilege, not a right. He then told her the computer showed her license was suspended, which it was not, as he later admitted. Ordering her out of the car, he handcuffed her and took her into custody.

At the Sixth Precinct station house, she was strip-searched in a bathroom by a rubber-gloved matron, who took away her belt and keys. She was locked in a holding cell until the early hours of the next morning, then released with two tickets: one for driving without a license, the other for "failure to comply with an order." Both were later dismissed, and Ms. Tong sued the city.

"Unfortunately for them, I know a little bit about my rights," she said. "This is not China." She won a $35,000 settlement in 1996.

Ms. Tong's case typifies a pattern in which the blunt and often abrasive language of New York City aggravates an encounter with the police. Police experts say that the city's officers and residents expect one another to withstand a little verbal abuse. But some police officers perceive sarcasm and insult as direct challenges to their authority and, experts say, overreact.

"New Yorkers have big mouths," said Paul Chevigny, a law professor at New York University and an expert on police culture. "More of them are on the liberal side, and are more critical of authority, than in other places."

"In a way, I find New Yorkers charmingly naïve. They imagine they live in a city where they can challenge authority and not get hurt. They're wrong, and that's too bad."

Officer Wilson, the Police Academy instructor, said he urges young officers not to take things personally.

"I tell them people are not mouthing off at you, Mike Wilson, but at the uniform, the authority," he said.

Video Challenge

To Record
May Be to Provoke

A challenge to police authority does not have to be verbal. In several cases examined, people had their tape recorders or video cameras damaged or their tapes taken, suggesting that to record some officers at work is to provoke them.

During the city's celebration of the Fourth of July in 1995, some squatters reclaimed an East Village tenement from which they had been forcibly removed by the police several weeks earlier, then trumpeted their small victory by hurling bricks and firecrackers at the police. The department responded by sending hundreds of officers to the building, including dozens in riot gear.

Across the street, several college students had gathered on a rooftop to admire the fireworks over the East River, but turned to watching the struggle below. At one point, some police officers clambered up to the roof to question them, court records show, but left after being satisfied that the students were not involved in the fracas.

But Douglas Snyder, a New York University photography student, later said that he began to videotape the confrontation after seeing officers strike pedestrians with nightsticks and shields, just as the lights of a police helicopter above washed over him.

Minutes later, Mr. Snyder testified during a deposition this year, several police officers in riot gear stormed the roof with guns drawn. The officers screamed for everyone to "get down," several witnesses testified, then began kicking the students. Two officers ran over to Mr. Snyder and smashed his recorder, he said. Then one kicked him in the face until he lost consciousness.

Megan Doyle, Mr. Snyder's girlfriend at the time, began to scream. She later testified that officers threw her to the ground and put a gun to her head, calling her "slut" and "whore." Then she, Mr. Snyder and several other students were handcuffed, arrested and held for several hours on charges of disorderly conduct.

The morning after the encounter, Mr. Snyder found his smashed camera on the roof. The tape was missing.

The charges were dropped several weeks later, and a few months ago the city paid $50,000 to Ms. Doyle and $42,500 to Mr. Snyder to settle their lawsuits.

Question Authority?

Power to Arrest
Can Be Abused

Dr. James O'Keefe, the director of training at the Police Academy, says the academy works to instill in officers a wary respect for the public, and to convey the lesson that emotion should never overtake reason.

For decades, the academy operated like a boot camp, in which verbal abuse was thought to prepare recruits for the streets. But officials came to suspect that the approach also taught officers to treat citizens in a similarly harsh manner.

After a phase using transactional analysis, an approach based on a form of popular psychotherapy, the academy now uses the martial arts paradigm to convey the importance of bending like a reed. In classes and role-playing situations, officers are taught that verbal attacks don't threaten them, and that their role in a confrontation is to end it, not win it.

But those officers who respond inappropriately to challenges have more at their disposal than flashlights and batons to exact punishment. Officer Wilson spells out to recruits why they always have the upper hand. "At the end of the day," he tells them, "you have the power of arrest."

In most police misconduct cases, civil rights lawyers said, that power seems to be abused. In such cases, officers often level charges to punish someone who has shown them disrespect, or to cover up their mishandling of an encounter, the lawyers said.

In Los Angeles, Merrick Bobb, a special counsel to the city, tracks the use of such charges as resisting arrest or disorderly conduct, noting when they are leveled and dropped, as one way to identify problem officers.

"You find clearly that often those contempt-of-cop arrests are filed by the police officer as a way to cover a use of force that may be questionable," Mr. Bobb said. "You also find that these charges get dropped because they are not valid."

New York City does no such tracking, although the police misconduct files suggest a similar pattern.

The case of Sahar Sarid is one example. Manhattan prosecutors recently declined to prosecute Mr. Sarid, 22, for resisting arrest after an encounter with the police that landed him in a hospital emergency room earlier this year. His mistake, he said, was responding to a request for his license and registration with a question, "Why?"

A month after emigrating from Israel, Mr. Sarid became confused by Manhattan traffic patterns and unknowingly drove the wrong way down East 62d Street before being stopped by the police on York Avenue. When he questioned the order to produce his license, an officer

punched him in the arm, he said. He was directed to pull over in a bus stop, he said, only to get a ticket later for illegally parking there.

Mr. Sarid then climbed out of his car, he said, and refused to get back in, telling the officers he feared getting struck again. That, he said, pushed the officers to kick his legs out from under him, beat him with their fists, handcuff him and twist his fingers. "Go back to the Middle East," he said he was told.

On the way to the station house, the arresting officer warned Mr. Sarid not to bleed all over his cruiser, and then punched him again, he said. Terrified, he began to hyperventilate, and was taken to New York Hospital instead. Hospital records show that he was treated for a bloody nose and abrasions on the cheek and forehead.

Mr. Sarid sought the assistance of Dov Hikind, a Brooklyn Assemblyman who helped him find a lawyer. A strong supporter of the police, Mr. Hikind scoffed at the idea that Mr. Sarid had done anything wrong. "This is one of the most abusive cases I've ever seen," he said. "If this guy resisted arrest, why did they drop the charges?"

Hell on Wheels

Bronx Car Chase Ends In Injury and Arrest

Among the most provocative ways to challenge police authority, as Rodney G. King learned, is to engage officers in a car chase. As Jerome H. Skolnick and James J. Fyfe noted in "Above the Law" (The Free Press, 1993), their study of police conduct, "Fleeing motorists become prime candidates for painful lessons at the end of police nightsticks."

Edward Dominguez, 17, and his brother-in-law, Vicente Fernandez, then 20, did not consider themselves to be fleeing motorists on a spring

night in 1993, just speeding drivers traveling a deserted highway at 70 miles an hour. Mr. Fernandez, a Dominican immigrant who works in his father's supermarket, had just picked up Mr. Dominguez, an American-born Dominican, from his job at one of his father's Mexican restaurants in the Bronx.

The men remember making a U-turn on Gun Hill Road, but said they were unaware at the time that a police cruiser began following them after the illegal maneuver. During testimony in a Police Department trial, however, the officers said they were forced to chase the young men at high speed on the Bronx River Parkway until Mr. Fernandez's car broke down.

With guns drawn, two officers pulled the two young men from the car, threw them on the ground and handcuffed them, both sides said. Mr. Fernandez was struck twice in the head with a police revolver, which left him with a bump on his forehead and a cut on the back of his head, according to hospital records.

With both men face down on the ground, Officer Francisco Rodriguez repeatedly asked where they had stolen the car, ignoring Mr. Fernandez's claim that it was his mother's. When Mr. Dominguez asked what they had done wrong, he said, the officer told him to shut up and spread his legs.

Then, Mr. Dominguez said, the officer kicked him hard in the groin, causing excruciating pain. One testicle swelled so much that weeks later it had to be removed.

At the police station house, a nauseated Mr. Dominguez told Sgt. Henry Pelayo that he was in pain from an officer's abuse. The sergeant, Mr. Dominguez said, told him no one had harmed him. When the young man insisted, according to prosecutors, the sergeant placed his hand on his gun and said: "No, you fell! Nobody hit you. You fell."

About 3 A.M., the young men were released to Mr. Dominguez's father, who drove them to the hospital. Mr. Dominguez's sister called the Civilian Complaint Review Board and filed a complaint. By dawn, the incident was under investigation, and the young men were interviewed by the police as they sat in wheelchairs in the emergency room.

A year and a half later, during the officers' departmental trial, Rae Downes Koshetz, the Deputy Commissioner in Charge of Trials, found the young men's complaints about their injuries at the hands of the officers to be "plausible, promptly made, unexplained by the respondents, and corroborated by independent medical evidence."

She found Officer Rodriguez guilty of physical abuse and of calling Mr. Fernandez a "Dominican faggot." Referring to the "gratuitous nature of the misconduct and the serious injury inflicted on Dominguez," she recommended that he lose 30 days' pay and be placed on probation for a year.

She found Sergeant Pelayo guilty of bullying and threatening the men, of "misconduct per se" and of condoning the misconduct committed at the scene. She recommended suspension without pay for 20 days, which Commissioner William J. Bratton upgraded to a 30-day suspension.

Both men were subsequently indicted by the Bronx District Attorney's office, and a trial date will be set in two weeks. They remain on the force. Officer Rodriguez's lawyer would not comment; Sergeant Pelayo's lawyer said his client was innocent.

Mr. Dominguez, meanwhile, dropped out of high school in his senior year, had a psychological breakdown and, at 21, is supported by his father. He was briefly married, but the marriage ended because he was unable to father a child due to his injury, he said.

He was born and raised in New York, but is considering moving to the Dominican Republic for a fresh start.

Advocacy and Law Enforcement
Partners Against Domestic Violence
By MARIE P. DEFINA and LEONARD WETHERBEE

Photo © Don Ennis

Domestic disturbances generate some of the most frustrating calls for police officers. Such calls often are repetitious as officers respond to the same homes over and over, take up valuable time that could be spent on other investigative matters, and frequently produce no legal action against offenders.

In the late 1980s, increased public awareness that violence in the home is a criminal matter, not a private one, fueled changes in Massachusetts state law.[1] Under the revised law, officers no longer are restricted to mediating a volatile situation or merely walking the perpetrator around to cool off. Now, officers may arrest a battering spouse on probable cause. With the burden of pressing charges lifted from the victim, who is often reluctant to proceed against an abusive mate, the number of arrests for domestic violence has increased statewide.[2] Other legislative mandates have enhanced law enforcement's efforts to thwart domestic violence. These include:

- Changes in firearms regulations, which allow for "immediate suspension and surrender (when the order is served) of [the offender's] license to carry firearms and/or [firearms identification] cards as well as any firearms, rifles, shotguns, machine guns, and ammunition . . . if the plaintiff can demonstrate a substantial likelihood of immediate danger of abuse"[3]
- Bail reform allowing pretrial release of domestic violence offenders to be based on hearings about the defendant's alleged dangerousness[4]
- Special training of officers assigned to domestic violence cases in every police department in the state[5]

Nevertheless, 5 years after the state legislature enacted these changes, police officers still met victim resistance to arresting their abusive partners. And, even though the number of arrests for domestic violence increased, the number of repeat offenses did not decrease as hoped.

While the revised state laws dramatically increased the tools available to police, law enforcement officials in the cities of Concord and Newton, Massachusetts, felt that something else needed to be done. Officers still left the scene of domestic disturbances frustrated that they could not do more, wondering how to convince a victim to leave.

In the upper middle-class communities of Newton and Concord,

From *FBI Law Enforcement Bulletin*, October 1997, pp. 22-26. Reprinted by permission of the U.S. Department of Justice, Federal Bureau of Investigation.

police encountered additional obstacles unique to their wealthy suburbs. They found some victims of domestic violence reluctant to call the police because they wanted to preserve appearances (not wanting a patrol car in the driveway); others did not seek help because they doubted that action would be taken against abusers who were influential in the community. The willingness of victims to call police proved contingent on several factors, including whether:

- The incident would be reported in the local newspaper
- Family pressure against disclosure was brought to bear on the victim
- The victim had peer support
- The victim was willing or able to sustain the possible emotional and financial loss associated with disclosure
- The victim perceived negative impact on the perpetrator's job or community standing.

Further, police in Concord and Newton were surprised to find that many well-educated citizens did not believe domestic violence posed a serious problem in their communities. Despite the relative affluence of the citizens in the community, there were fewer resources for battered individuals in suburbia than in the inner city, and individuals at risk seemed reluctant to seek out the available resources for fear of being traced by the abuser.

When victims did choose to contact such crisis intervention services as shelters, counselors, and legal aid, these agencies could be reached only during business hours. This often meant a time lag of as much as 72 hours existed between the violent act and the delivery of ancillary services to the victim.

Due to the complex psychological dynamics underlying domestic abuse, the emotional and economic loss associated with family violence,[6] and the potential lethality of future violence, these communities needed a multilevel response *delivered within a*

critical window of time. Because the responding officer's role ends with arrest and containment of the abuser, police in these two communities looked for help outside their departments to strengthen and improve the total response to the domestic violence call.

THE PARTNERSHIP APPROACH

The chief of the Concord Police Department (CPD) approached the problem with the community policing philosophy in mind, seeking to be part of the problem-solving process by developing a partnership with residents. The CPD began to collaborate with the Domestic Violence Training and Resource Institute (DVTRI), a local, all-volunteer, nonprofit, grassroots organization that deals specifically with crisis intervention for domestic abuse victims. The neighboring Newton Police Department (NPD) also joined the partnership. Both police departments appointed lieutenants to serve as domestic violence coordinators to oversee the implementation process and act as liaisons with the civilian organization.

Working Together

Whenever people from different disciplines join forces to address an issue, problems can arise from the clash between their divergent mindsets and approaches. The initial task of the partnership between the police and the civilian advocacy group was to identify such problem areas and propose solutions.

Historically, civilian advocacy groups and law enforcement officers have tended to mistrust one another. Most law enforcement personnel have not been trained in the psychological theories of domestic abuse. Likewise, civilians usually do not understand the policies and procedures of basic law enforcement.

In seeking models for interdisciplinary cooperation, neither the domestic violence coordinators nor the DVTRI could find suitable examples. Training curricula and related materials generally were limited to one discipline and did not integrate perspectives from other areas. In addition, like many smaller police departments, the CPD and NPD do not have civilian volunteer programs operating within the station on a 24-hour basis, so concerns arose over security, domain, and space availability.

Ms. Defina founded the Domestic Violence Training and Resource Institute, in Concord, Massachusetts, and now serves as its executive director.

Chief Wetherbee commands the Concord, Massachusetts, Police Department.

To overcome these difficulties, the partners sought to build trust among participating groups by forging a style of communication and a method of working together. First, they pioneered a model for policies and procedures, working out the details of the interaction between the

> **The partnership has enhanced the services available and increased their accessibility to victims in these suburban communities.**

police departments and the civilian group. Then, to bridge the gap between the advocacy group and the law enforcement personnel, they devised training curricula that cross traditional role lines. Next, the Concord Police Department provided secure space within the police station accessible to DVTRI peer advocates around the clock. Finally, the partnership established criteria to measure the success of the program in reaching its projected goals.

TRAINING

To take advantage of the expertise and insight of both the civilian domestic violence counselors and the police personnel involved, the partnership established two training programs. One program concentrated on educating police officers about domestic violence, and the other trained civilian volunteers as peer advocates.

For Police Officers

The director of the Domestic Violence Training and Resource Institute devised a 16-hour curriculum for all sworn police personnel in Concord and Newton. The classwork not only addressed the legislative changes regarding spousal abuse but also delved into the underlying issues of domestic violence.

Through role-playing exercises, officers experienced the victim's dilemma by assuming the identity of a battered spouse. These exercises proved highly effective in raising police sensitivity to victims and in curbing the impulse to ask judgmental and blaming questions, such as "Why do you stay with him?" Instead, officers learned how to identify and deal effectively with batterers' controlling and manipulative behaviors.

The training also helped police officers overcome the frustration they typically felt at the scene of a domestic disturbance when they were unable to resolve the crisis. Leaving an abusive partner is a process, not an event. Law enforcement officers, by orientation, respond to crisis events with the expectation of an immediate resolution, but that is an inappropriate expectation for the unique nature of this crime. Officers learned that an interdisciplinary team approach is logical and necessary to address the complex and multiple needs that must be met during a domestic violence crisis and before a victim can safely leave a relationship. This insight provided the extra dimension that police in Concord and Newton had been seeking in their response to domestic violence calls.

For Civilian Volunteers

The DVTRI then recruited and trained a cadre of civilian volunteers for the Certified Peer Advocate Program (CPAP). After extensive character and psychological screening, volunteers attended a rigorous program consisting of 55 hours of classroom instruction, followed by 187 practicum hours. Upon successful completion of the program, volunteers become certified by the DVTRI to work with police and other service providers for victims of domestic violence.

The primary goal of the CPAP is to provide around-the-clock crisis intervention services, victim rights information, and extensive safety planning for domestic violence victims. Safety planning involves reviewing predictable behaviors or actions that occur between the abuser and the victim. The advocate then helps develop a plan of action the victim can take that would lend to her safety. For example, safety plans might include devising an escape route, designating a person to call in the event of an emergency, or locating a safe place to hide keys, money, and important documents. In addition, the CPAP provides ongoing follow-up services for victims; furnishes referrals for legal aid, shelters, and counseling; sends advocates to court with victims of battering; and runs support group services and life skills workshops.

The DVTRI also offers a safe space network for those in need of immediate, short-term shelter. This network of homes scattered throughout several communities provides domestic violence victims a safe place to stay for several days until other accommodations become available. Also, victims in transit who need a place to stay on their way to another destination can use the safe space Network.

ASSISTING VICTIMS

The partnership between the police and the DVTRI provides services to domestic violence victims in three basic ways. First, when a domestic disturbance call comes into the police department, officers respond to the location and secure the site. Responding officers tell the victim about the available advocacy services. If the victim chooses to obtain the services of a civilian volunteer, the police notify the DVTRI.

Second, victims sometimes do not want to involve the police at their homes. In these instances, the victims can call or visit the police station to request an advocate, or they can contact the DVTRI directly.

Finally, local hospital emergency rooms and other service providers within the communities, including the local clergy, may refer victims to the DVTRI. They may do so with or without the intercession of the police department.

PUBLICITY

Crisis intervention services can be useful only if the intended recipients know about them, and several avenues provided publicity for the Certified Peer Advocate Program early on. Through direct contact with domestic violence victims, word spread. The local media picked up the story and reported on the police-civilian advocate partnership.

The participating agencies also developed a pamphlet describing available services and how to obtain them. Many local clergy members who participated in the peer advocate training agreed to keep materials about CPAP in their offices to use when counseling victims. In addition, the Concord Police Department posted the information on its Internet home page.[7]

CONCLUSION

From a law enforcement perspective, the partnership among the Concord and Newton Police Departments and the DVTRI proved to be a logical and necessary choice. Now, the police can offer victims a range of services—from resource information to emotional support to safety planning—without any critical lapse of time. The partnership has enhanced the services available and increased their accessibility to victims in these suburban communities. It also has helped to educate citizens about the nature and prevalence of domestic violence, a crime that occurs even in their seemingly serene backyards.

The success of this partnership has born statistical fruit already. From April 1994, when the program began, through October 1995, the number of repeat assaults in Concord has dropped 80 percent.[8] While the number of repeat assaults fell, the prosecution rate climbed due to greater willingness of victims, now backed by advocate support, to testify against abusers and to follow through on obtaining restraining orders. In the first 9 months of the partnership, 57 individuals requested the services of a peer advocate. By the end of 1995, more than 350 adults and 450 children had been served by the Certified Peer Advocate Program.

Combining police and civilian resources in this way can generate significant long-term changes in social attitude and behavior. With a unified voice, the police and peer advocates speak the powerful message that domestic violence will not be tolerated.

Endnotes

1. MGL 209A.
2. Susan Schechter and Lisa Klee Mihaly, "Ending Violence Against Women and Children in Massachusetts Families: Critical Steps for the Next Five Years," Massachusetts Coalition of Battered Women Service Groups, November 1992, 1.
3. MGL 209A, Sections 3B, 129B, and 131 CH 140.
4. MGL c. 276, s. 58A; See also Samuel E. Zoll, Chief Justice, District Court, Commonwealth of Massachusetts, "New Law Regarding Bail and Dangerousness," Trial Court of the Commonwealth, District Court Department, August 1994.
5. Scott Harshbarger, Attorney General, Commonwealth of Massachusetts, "Domestic Violence: Strategies for Prevention and Enforcement," Paper presented at Attorney General's Conference, Northeastern University, Burlington, MA, October 21, 1994.
6. Susan F. Turner and Constance Hoenk Shapiro, "Battered Women: Mourning the Death of a Relationship," The National Association of Social Workers, Inc., 1986.
7. The Concord, MA, home page address is http://www.concordma.com.
8. Domestic Violence Training and Resource Institute, Annual Report for 1995, Concord, MA.

Incorporating Diversity
Police Response to Multicultural Changes in Their Communities

BRAD R. BENNETT, D.P.A.

A great demographic change is taking place in the United States, making the population much more multicultural and diverse than it used to be. As with other kinds of social changes, law enforcement agencies must adapt to the population shifts in their communities.

This article discusses the findings of a study undertaken to determine how law enforcement agencies in four California cities responded to demographic changes that took place in their communities between 1980 and 1994. The departments in San Jose, Long Beach, Stockton, and Garden Grove[1] now police cities where African Americans, Asians, and Hispanics represent almost 50 percent of the population, an average of a 17-percent increase in the ethnic population since 1980. The departments have employed a number of strategies to best serve their changing communities.

REPRESENTATION AND INCORPORATION

All four police departments have made concerted efforts to incorporate into their organizations the varied and diverse members of their communities. Through recruiting and hiring strategies, citizen participation, training programs both for employees and community members, community outreach initiatives, and community policing, each department has embraced its diverse community groups.

Recruiting and Hiring

San Jose developed a philosophy that recognized and espouses the value of a diversified work force. This philosophy provided the fundamental ingredient that fostered the attitude necessary to lay the foundation for a successful recruiting and hiring strategy. Many of San Jose's recruiting efforts involve officers as culturally diverse as the applicants they seek. The recruiters seek out potential applicants by attending events, such as festivals and job fairs, frequented by people from a variety of ethnic backgrounds, by advertising in bilingual publications, and by offering incentives to applicants who speak more than one language.

In addition to these fairly traditional approaches, San Jose also developed some unique ways to recruit and promote ethnically diverse employees. The department's program rewards officers with up to 40 hours of paid leave if the individuals they recruit become police officers. The department also helps all officer candidates to overcome obstacles, cultural or otherwise, in preparing for the department's written tests. Mentors from ethnically diverse police officers associations within the department help newly hired officers acclimate to the department.

San Jose's efforts to incorporate representatives of diverse groups do not stop at the entry level. The department continually monitors the composition of special units, such as the detective, gang, training, and personnel units, to ensure that they represent the department and the community. Officers can serve in special units for only 3 years so that all members of the department have an opportunity to do so.

The department also incorporates diversity into its promotional procedures. Recruiting efforts and community relations are enhanced when community members from diverse backgrounds see people similar to themselves in a variety of positions and ranks throughout the department.

Similar to San Jose, the Long Beach, Garden Grove, and Stockton Police Departments have taken steps to recruit and hire personnel who reflect the cultural composition of their communities. Special emphasis has been placed on recruiting Asian applicants because of the large increase in Asian populations in these communities over the past decade.

All three departments hired individuals specifically to work with the Asian community and to attract more Asian applicants. Community leaders in Long Beach also help by training people within their cultural groups so they can qualify as potential candidates for positions within the police department and in city government in general. In addition, Long Beach established an Asian Affairs Advisory Committee, while Garden Grove works with the City Cultural Cohesiveness Committee to improve its recruiting efforts.

Citizen Participation

All four departments have undertaken successful efforts that bring di-

From *FBI Law Enforcement Bulletin,* December 1995, pp. 1-6. Reprinted by permission of the U.S. Department of Justice, Federal Bureau of Investigation.

verse individuals into their organizations at different levels. These include civilian community service officer, reserve officer, police cadet, Law Enforcement Explorer, and Police Athletic League programs. Such initiatives provide excellent opportunities for police departments to familiarize citizens with agency operations.

These police departments also use a variety of methods for determining the concerns of community members. Forming advisory groups representative of the entire community has proven to be one effective way to establish collaborative relationships with diverse groups. Advisory groups give residents a voice and help them ensure that the department understands their unique needs and serves them in a professional manner. Such groups also prompt police agencies to be more open and responsive to the community.

In addition to forming advisory boards, departments developed neighborhood groups and solicited information through focus groups and citizen surveys. As many agencies move toward a more service-oriented, community-involved approach to policing, it will become increasingly important for the police to try to represent the wide variety of community groups in the ranks of employees and to incorporate the voices of the full range of citizens.

TRAINING

All four police departments conduct training programs to teach employees about the many cultures within their communities. The length of the programs varies tremendously, from a few-hour presentation to a week-long course.

In the two larger departments, San Jose and Long Beach, the programs are components of advanced officer training and are offered only to sworn personnel. The two smaller agencies, Stockton and Garden Grove, provide training to all employees. Most of the programs call on community members to facilitate the training, and the departments have developed rather uncommon approaches to their cultural diversity training.

In San Jose, the police chief sought input from members of the advisory broad to design the cultural diversity training program for the department. Based on their suggestions, the training starts with a segment on change. It ad-

dresses a wide range of concerns relevant to individual and organizational change, including understanding the process of change and overcoming resistance. The initial instruction and the discussions that arose from it helped to eliminate many of the barriers that often occur when dealing with new issues, ideas, and approaches.

The Long Beach Police Department collaborated with the National Conference of Christians and Jews to develop its 40-hour cultural awareness training course for all department employees. In addition to general topics related to cultural diversity, the program addresses some nontraditional subjects of interest, such as Anglo cultures, the police culture, the homeless, and various religions.

> " ... to be responsive to all citizens, police departments must find out what their communities need."

Long Beach also emphasizes cultural diversity awareness in its basic recruit training academy. Recruits received 8 hours of classroom instruction devoted to diversity awareness, and then they spent 16 training hours with citizens from the various ethnic groups within the city. Recruits and citizens thus have an opportunity to interact in a nonconfrontational, positive way.

In addition to cultural awareness training, all four departments encourage or provide training in the various languages spoken within their communities. Bilingual or multilingual officers can be very helpful to their departments and their communities. Unfortunately, as communities become more and more diverse, the number of languages spoken increases as well, and it becomes difficult for agencies to cope. Still, by encouraging all officers to learn other languages, departments can facilitate communication with the full spectrum of community members.

COMMUNITY OUTREACH

To respond to the needs of their diverse communities, the police agencies in the study tried a variety of approaches, including police substations, citizen police academies, and youth programs. Many of these initiatives did not target ethnic neighborhoods in particular; instead, they impacted the police department's responsiveness to all community members.

Police Substations

The San Jose and Garden Grove departments have placed substations in areas where very distinct populations live. Police employees, representatives from other government agencies, and citizen volunteers who speak the residents' languages staff the substations.

Staff members work closely with merchants, apartment complex owners, and residents to ensure police responsiveness to the needs of each community. Especially in large cities, substations provide citizens the opportunity to access needed government services. They also enable government employees to establish personal relationships with community members.

Citizen Police Academies

A number of police departments across the United States have adopted citizen police academies. Through these academies, police agencies seek to educate community members about the roles and responsibilities of police officers and to familiarize the public with the departments and how they work within the community.

San Jose and Garden Grove both have citizen police academies. San Jose includes a wide variety of community members in its classes. Garden Grove requires members of its community policing advisory board to attend the academy to acquaint them with the functions, policies, and operations of the police department.

As noted, to be responsive to all citizens, police departments must find out what their communities need. Similarly, departments also should educate their communities about the functions of the police department, as well as any changes that occur within the department. An open exchange of information between each community and its police department promotes understanding and greater cooperation.

Youth Programs

All four departments have developed youth-centered programs to enhance their relationships with young people in their communities. These programs generally focus on at-risk youth, who often come from culturally diverse backgrounds.

Initiatives include assigning beat officers to schools, conducting educational programs, and sponsoring Police Athletic Leagues. Officers teach Drug and Alcohol Resistance Education (D.A.R.E.), participate in after-school activities, and become involved in the schools as role models, mentors, and counselors.

Involving diverse youth in Law Enforcement Explorer and police cadet programs also has proven advantageous. Youngsters learn self-discipline and often develop improved self-esteem. For students interested in law enforcement careers, these programs expose them to the department and provide them opportunities to learn about policing.

Through these programs, the departments have focused on getting the police and young people together in positive circumstances. Relationships between police and children have improved tremendously in the schools where officers have been assigned. Young people and officers get involved with each other in positive settings that benefit both groups. Positive contacts made through these programs often translate into improved relationships between officers and the children's families as they interact outside the school environment.

COMMUNITY POLICING

Many members of the law enforcement profession believe that community policing provides the best method for being responsive to and involved in the community. As an organizational philosophy, it promotes a set of values and corresponding procedures that form the basis for police-community interaction to solve problems. Community policing reverses the notion that the police have sole responsibility for maintaining public order, recognizing instead that the community at large is responsible for the conditions that generate crime.

Empowering the community to solve its own problems is the key to making community policing work. This means that the police and members of the community—neighbors, families, individuals, schools, organizations, churches, and businesses—must accept the challenge to assume joint responsibility for the community's safety and well-being.

The four departments studied, similar to many police agencies across the country, have taken steps to implement community policing. Many of the initiatives already described are components of those efforts. Most of the agency personnel interviewed for this study believe that this approach offers the best opportunity for responding effectively to changing and diverse communities. Only by listening to and working with community members can the police determine what needs to be done and how best to do it.

Officers in San Jose, Stockton, and Garden Grove were reassigned from normal patrol duties to specific neighborhoods. These officers formed partnerships with community groups to identify and solve neighborhood problems. The police arranged their priorities based on the problems identified by residents. Some of the strategies employed by these departments for solving community problems included community surveys, meetings, education, and involvement; neighborhood cleanups; citizen patrols; school and youth programs; government and social service involvement; and community empowerment initiatives.

> ## "A common theme became apparent during the study of these four California police departments: Leadership makes a difference."

The San Jose, Stockton, Long Beach, and Garden Grove departments are all moving toward implementing community policing departmentwide. These departments believe that to be successful they must involve all stakeholders in tailoring their philosophies and processes

to meet the specific needs of their communities. Department employees, as well as community members, must participate in the development of community policing as a law enforcement approach in order for it to be effective. Such participation raises two important sets of expectations—those between individual employees and the police organization and those between the community members and the organization. Police leaders must work to balance these expectations in order to move effectively toward community policing.

To begin this process, the agencies formed internal committees composed of a cross-section of department members to determine the particular approach most suitable for each department. After establishing a general internal philosophy and approach, representatives from the agencies then met with community members to design specific strategies for the various communities within their cities.

Everyone involved in implementing community policing should recognize that it is not a fixed or standardized program. It is not a structured model of policing that can be replicated and transferred from agency to agency with ease. Rather, departments must adopt philosophies and approaches that meet the unique needs of their communities. Only in this way will community policing provide the promised benefits for police departments who want to serve their diverse communities effectively.

LEADERSHIP

A common theme became apparent during the study of these four California police departments: Leadership makes a difference. New leaders in each organization led all four departments in making significant strides toward enhanced responsiveness to their communities. Interviews with department members revealed that what distinguished the new leaders from their predecessors was the ability to translate intentions into realities. Because they could deal effectively with their constituencies both inside and outside the organization, these leaders could turn their visions for their departments into action and reality.[2]

The current leaders reorganized the influence of relationships among the agency, the individual employees, and

Increased Population Diversity

During the 1980s, 6 million people legally immigrated to the United States. In the previous two decades combined, only 7.4 million immigrants legally entered the country. Census information shows that between 1980 and 1990 the country's population of Asians doubled, from 1.5 percent to 3 percent of the U.S. population. The Hispanic population grew by half, from 6.4 percent to 9 percent of the population by 1990. Despite the rapid growth among immigrant groups, African Americans continue to be the largest minority group in the United States, representing 12.1 percent of the population in 1990.

The diversity of the United States is expected to expand even more. Projections by the U.S. Census Bureau suggest that Asians will continue to be the fastest-growing race in America,

reaching 11 percent of the population by the year 2050. Hispanics are expected to eclipse African Americans as the largest minority group by the year 2010 and to increase to 21 percent of the population by 2050. By that year, the number of African Americans probably will rise to 16 percent of the total population, while the number of whites will fall from 75 percent to 53 percent of the population. By 2050, the U.S. population will be divided almost evenly between minorities and non-Hispanic whites.[4]

Source: Chris Swingle, "U.S. Minorities Expected to Grow by 2050," *Democrat and Chronicle*, Rochester, New York, December 1992, 1.

---

the community members on organizational responsiveness. The leaders first addressed internal issues, because it is important to attend to employees' needs before addressing the needs of the community. Next, they developed strategies for dealing with police-community relationships.

These strategies reflect both a concern for community problems and a social responsibility that goes beyond law enforcement. They include service dimensions that recognize that crime prevention is a community matter and suggest that the police broaden their approach beyond merely responding to crime. The approaches adopted by the leaders of all four agencies recognize that the police must become more problem-oriented; they must scrutinize problems, obtain as much information as

possible from everyone involved or affected, and only then develop solutions.[3]

CONCLUSION

All four agencies set the goal of being responsive to their changing communities. As shown by the various strategies and programs employed by each agency, there are many ways to achieve that goal. Developing positive relationships with young people from diverse backgrounds, actively seeking input on departmental operations from the full spectrum of community members, conducting imaginative police training in the areas of cultural sensitivity and improved communication, and adopting the community policing phi-

losophy moved these agencies toward their goals.

There is no guarantee that every effort to improve police service to a changing and diverse society will be successful. Yet, these four agencies show that imaginative and resourceful moves toward responding to changes in their communities can be made.

The United States historically has been noted for incorporating people from all over the world into a common society. Once again, the country is being called upon to open its arms to people from many backgrounds, and police departments must do their part. By embracing all segments of their communities, agencies can tap into the vast resources of their many members. By drawing on those strengths, the police and the public can work together to make communities safer for everyone.

Ethnic Changes in Total Population

	1980 Ethnic Population	1990 Ethnic Population	Increase
San Jose	36%	50.4%	14.4%
Long Beach	33%	50.5%	17.5%
Stockton	43%	56.0%	13.0%
Garden Grove	22%	45.3%	23.3%

Endnotes

1. The 1990 census showed the population of these cities as: San Jose, 782,248; Long Beach, 429,423; Stockton, 226,255; and Garden Grove, 149,700.
2. Warren Bennis, "The Artform of Leadership," in *Public Administration in Action*, ed. Robert B. Denhardt and Barry Hammond (Pacific Grove, CA: Brooks/Cole Publishing, 1992), 311–315.
3. Roy Roberg and Jack Kuykendall, *Police Organization and Management, Behavior, Theory, and Processes* (Pacific Grove, CA: Brooks/Cole Publishing, 1990), 48–52.

AFTERBURN:

the victimization of police families

By Andrew H. Ryan, Ph.D., Chief Psychologist, South Carolina Criminal Justice Academy, Office of Human Services & Assessment, Columbia, South Carolina

We know you are a different breed—not only in our minds but in your own. We know you are exposed to the things of which nightmares are made, and that you have become the primary victim of violent crime. We know that your family is victimized by these events, as well. The research tells us that you have chosen one of the five most stressful professions, and that many of you do not survive the career for many reasons previously considered unrelated to the events of your job. Too often, the services that could make a difference are either unavailable or unapproachable, as the nature of the profession tends to dissuade its members from seeking help. It is your story that this article addresses, with a focus on how we can better serve and protect our most valued commodity—the police family.

The story began when a police officer responded to a call where a woman had threatened homicide and suicide. She had just learned that her child was terminally ill, and did not want the child to suffer.

It was a typical South Carolina day in the midst of mosquito season. She chose as her setting for this crisis the woods near her parents' home, where she grew up. Having exhausted all her coping skills, she saw no other way to ease the pain.

When the officer arrived, she turned her gun on him, initiating an eight-hour standoff. Additional officers called to the scene took armed defensive positions, while the first officer negotiated for the lives of the woman and her child. Able to provide a solution where there were no solutions earlier, he saved her life, the child's life and, possibly, his own and those of his fellow officers—all without a shot being fired.

I would like to report that the story had a happy ending, but the reality is that it was not the end, but the beginning . . . the beginning of an "Afterburn."

Whom Can You Talk To?

When he went home that night and tried to relate the story to his wife, she did not want to listen; she said she could not bear to relive the story she had already seen on TV. As her husband recounted the details of the woman's plight, she became overwhelmed and ran into the bathroom, locking the door and running water to drown out his words. The officer's overwhelming need to talk led to a breakdown in the open communications of the family.

In no other profession can you save a life in the line of duty, exchange high fives with your peers, receive media recognition as a hero and then, almost within hours, have the aftermath of the event leave emotional scars on you and your family. The total effects on your family and friends are immeasurable.[1]

The "AFTERBURN" training program for law enforcement, recently presented as a national teleconference, stresses a multidisciplinary approach to addressing the needs of police officers and their families following the officer's involvement in or exposure to violent crime.[2] If we are to provide meaningful assistance, we will need the combined resources of mental health professionals, the clergy and law enforcement, as well as the attention of our politicians, to prioritize and coordinate the services.

The fields of victimization and psychotraumatology have dramatically expanded in the past 20 years. Initially, the focus was on the individual who suffered direct or threatened physical, emotional or psychological harm as a result of a serious or violent crime. Today, although these victims are still the primary focus, the secondary victims of crime are recognized as being in need of similar services.

Traditionally, violence involved physical force with the intent to harm another, and the plight of the victim was understood in terms of physical violation. However, injury to victims of violence involves not only physical violation, but psychological violation as well. The aftermath of violence for victims must be understood by considering threats not only to their bodily integrity but also to their psychological integrity. Victims may be forced to cope with the possible loss of physical functioning, financial stability and even the possible breakdown of the cognitive structures that are instrumental in providing psychological stability.[3]

One way to begin to understand the reactions—and thus the needs—of primary and secondary victims is to recognize that anxiety and fear are the predominant emotional responses of victims of violence. Coping with violent victimization involves coming to grips with the ensuing cognitive disorganization precipitated by the experience. For victims of violence, intense anxiety—with all its emotional, physiological and behavioral manifestations—reflects a disruption in their worldview and beliefs about society. The key to their recovery process is in the re-establishment of an integrated worldview. A police officer's exposure to violent crime may have an even more powerful effect on the police family, as family members are more likely to personalize the event and identify with the officer as the victim.

The Heavy Badge

Although the average police badge weighs only 2 ounces overall, with larger models running to perhaps 4 ounces, Dr. Gary Aumiller notes that when that badge is pinned on, it carries a weight unknown to most law enforcement officers. The true weight of the badge is not found in the gym or measured on a scale, and cannot be overcome by muscle. This weight requires a strength and conditioning for which few officers are trained.

The heaviness of the badge makes law enforcement officers different from other professionals; it is pinned not just on a chest, but on a life style. These life style difficulties can act to victimize not only officers, but their families as well. Over the course of the last 15 years, police psychologists have identified 10 areas that make the badge heavy and the police family different:

1. Law enforcement officers are seen as authority figures.

2. The wearing of a badge, uniform and gun makes a law enforcement officer separate from society.

3. Law enforcement officers work in a quasi-military, structured institution.

4. Shiftwork is not normal.

5. Law enforcement work encourages camaraderie, which can be a double-edged sword.

6. Officers have a different kind of stress in their jobs, described by some police psychologists as "burst stress."

7. Law enforcement officers have a job that requires extreme restraint under highly emotional circumstances.

8. The law enforcement officer works in a fact-based world, with everything compared to written law.

9. The "at-work" world of the officer is very negative.

10. The children of law enforcement officers may have a more difficult adjustment to adulthood.[4]

Being a law enforcement officer is more than what is taught at the academy or on the job. The work has many effects that need to be overcome so as not to affect the officer's personal life and victimize his family.

What About the Kids?

As Ellen Kirschman has written, "If families are at-risk for 'catching' trauma, children are the most vulnerable family members because they are still learning how to manage their emotions. Children and adolescents, however mature they appear, usually don't possess the social or psychological sophistication to understand what has happened to them or to their families when traumatic stress occurs."[5] The family is a child's "safe harbor," and it is within the family environment that children learn to deal with stressful events. We must provide these children with a sense of normalcy, understand their emotions and why they are reacting the way they do, not hide the truth from them and, most of all, know when to get them professional help.

The Family

Exposure to violent crime, others' pain and suffering, and man's inhumanity to man all potentially impose a heavy toll on the police officer as a primary victim and family members as secondary victims. The impact of violent crime can be severe; a significant number of officers involved in a critical incident will show transitory post-traumatic stress symptoms. Significantly, secondary victims also feel the emotional pain and, without assistance, will become emotionally depleted over time.

The consequences of this victimization do not manifest themselves solely on the job, but throughout the officer's life. He may also be asked to return to the job of helping before he has healed himself. Depression, anxiety and anger—all of which are normal symptoms among victims of crime—can alter one's approach to life. Unfortunately, the police officer is not afforded the luxury of suffering through the

pain; he must endure and go back to serving other victims. So, too, the police family must go on as if nothing has changed.

In reality, of course, much has changed. The family dynamics have been altered and may never be the same. What, then, is the percentage of family members with the same symptoms?

The importance of assessing and treating the spouses/mates of trauma survivors has been successfully argued by many researchers.[6] Additionally, the author has found no significant differences in levels of depression, post-traumatic stress disorder (PTSD), communication, attitudes toward police issues and stress symptoms between police officers and their wives.[7]

The same argument has also been extended to the entire family of the officer. For example, Brende and Goldsmith discuss the "ripple effect" of traumatic events, in which the officer's entire family is affected by the traumatic event.[8] Such "post-traumatic family victimization cycles" require proper intervention, and include therapy considerations such as identifying intra-family alienation, defining a healing community, resolving shame and secrets, and breaking the repetition cycle.

These findings lend some support to the argument that officers' families may be secondary victims of trauma and should no longer be ignored by police psychologists and support personnel.

Couples and families are being recognized more and more as desired units of treatment and support following a traumatic event. Therefore, it is imperative that all service providers—especially police psychologists—look beyond the immediate officer-victim's needs to recognize the needs of his spouse/mate and children. It is important to note that treatment of these couples and families may require special interventions that go beyond traditional couples or family therapy to focus more on multidisciplinary psychoeducational and self-help principles.

Brooks discusses several "pitfalls" of past family therapy with Vietnam veterans, which may provide some insight into treating officer families.[9] Specifically, family therapy for Vietnam veterans has often consisted of a linear view that focuses on "what the family can do to help"—implying that the veteran's military experience is the cause of the family disruption. Similarly, guidelines for "communicating with the veteran" are often presented to the family. Brooks asserts that this linear view is also evidenced in "spouse/mate support models" for PTSD intervention, which clearly locate causality for problems with the veteran and his Vietnam experience. Similarly, communication problems are considered to lie with the veteran; when responsibility is partly on the spouse/mate, it is only in the sense that she is not responding to the veteran's deviant behaviors. In summary, this view has been one of "veteran as problem/family as victim."

Service providers and police psychologists working with law enforcement families need to heed this warning. Moreover, many law enforcement intervention programs take this same linear view with the police officer and his family. Immersion into a culture where one is surrounded by other officers, coupled with an expectation that he should be able to suppress his feelings and distance himself emotionally, may lead the officer to resist involvement in family therapy. Police psychologists must not only recognize the need for couples and family therapy following a trauma, but also consider the unique contextual variables associated with the police culture and the effect this may have on treatment.

A final consideration in the service to police families comes from an area familiar to many of us in law enforcement—the need for peer teams. The officer's extended family—the other officers within the agency—are a valuable commodity in that the police have been taking care of themselves for years. This tradition should not be discouraged. Rather, it should be used to expand the network of support and referral services. Together, teams work to prevent the negative impact of acute stress, as well as accelerate the recovery process in a person or group that has experienced a critical incident.

In light of the known effects of PTSD on family members, Critical Incident Stress Management (CISM) focuses on a broader systemic approach to mitigating potential harm. The value of CISM is being realized by increasing numbers of police departments across the nation. In order to facilitate this support for family members, additional specialists—including

chaplains, family counselors and school psychologists—may serve in a supporting role to the team supervisor when expertise with children/families is necessary. CISM in a family context would help avoid some of the pitfalls of the traditional linear model just discussed and would certainly go a long way toward the development of a multi-disciplinary/multiprocess model for the inoculation against, and early intervention in, PTSD.

For these reasons, it is important that we be open to getting help at the earliest signs of difficulty in the officer's work, social or home life. AFTERBURN and programs like it establish a protocol for early intervention and pre-event education, and encourage the development of departmental policies and training guidelines for use by all victim service providers. The time for a more diversified multidisciplinary approach is here. We must begin now to prepare our police families for what is to come.

The Future

Society has succeeded in promoting the myth of superhuman cops who are invincible in every way. Unfortunately, this myth serves only to expose the officer and his family to more stress, thereby setting him up for failure.

The reality of "doing the job" can have debilitating, long-lasting effects on the officer and the same consequences for his family.

Family members, significant others and co-workers are all burned by their vicarious exposure to crime and their direct exposure to the officer. The total impact of crime on law enforcement families is just beginning to be understood. The ripple does not stop with the officer. It spreads to the family, the agency and, eventually, the community.

Programs such as AFTERBURN are attempts to bring deserving recognition to *all* victims of crime today. We have ignored the police family far too long. Moreover, we have failed to realize the valuable resource we have in the police family.

Recognition of the afterburn is not the final solution, of course; it is only

the beginning. Careers, families and communities—not to mention countless dollars—can be saved when we begin using the resources already available. Early intervention and crisis-response programs can mitigate and sometimes prevent the unnecessary loss of our most valuable resource in law enforcement.

1. This story was recently related by Sherie Carny, director of Victim Services, South Carolina Attorney General's Office.
2. "Afterburn: The Victimization of Police Families," a national teleconference, was funded by a grant from the State Victim Assistance Program and produced by the South Carolina Department of Public Safety, Criminal Justice Academy Division, with the SC Educational Television Network. It aired on May 21, 1997, and is available by contacting the author at 803–896–7727.
3. G.S. Everly and J.M. Lating, *Psychotraumatology: Key Papers and Core Concepts In Post-Traumatic Stress* (New York, NY: Plenum Press, 1995).
4. G.S. Aumiller and D.A. Goldfarb, *The Heavy Badge,* unpublished manuscript, 1997.
5. E. Kirschman, *I Love a Cop—What Police Families Need to Know* (New York, NY: Guilford Publications, Inc., 1997).
6. N.K. Bohl and R.M. Solomon, "Impact of a Husband's Critical Incident on the Family," paper presented at the FBI "Law Enforcement Family: Issues and Answers" Conference, Quantic, VA, July 1993; E.M. Carroll, D.W. Foy, B.J. Cannon and G. Zwier, "Assessment Issues Involving the Families of Trauma Victims," *Journal of Traumatic Stress*, 1991, 4: 25–40; K. Coughlan and C. Parkin, "Women Partners of Vietnam Vets," *Journal of Psychosocial Nursing*, 1987, 25: 25–27; L.J. Maloney, "Post-Traumatic Stresses on Women Partners of Vietnam Veterans," *Smith College Studies in Social Work*, 1988, 58: 122–143.
7. A.H. Ryan, Jr., "Post-Traumatic Stress Disorder and Related Symptomology in Traumatized Police Officers and Their Spouses/Mates," presented at the FBI "Law Enforcement Family: Issues and Answers" Conference, Quantico, VA, 1994.
8. J.O. Brende and R. Goldsmith, "Post-Traumatic Stress Disorder in Families," *Journal of Contemporary Psychotherapy*, 1991, 21: 115–124.
9. G.R. Brooks, "Therapy Pitfalls with Vietnam Veteran Families: Linearity, Contextual Naivete and Gender Role Blindness," *Journal of Family Psychology*, 1991, 4: 446–461.

Community Policing Partnerships

Marketing Community Policing: What Can We Expect?

NEW YORK, N.Y.

Over the past decade or so, it has become increasingly clear that police and communities can and will work together to reduce crime and improve neighborhood safety.

From New York to San Diego, community policing strategies have gone a long way toward this goal, with hundreds of police departments having formally adopted the philosophy.

The country's embrace of community policing, however, seems to have left considerable confusion in its wake. While practitioners and policymakers debate and refine the philosophy, and the strategies underlying it, much of the public, media and even police remain unclear about what it is and what to expect of it.

What is community policing?

Practitioners generally refer to community policing's four key elements as: 1) increased police presence—especially visible presence—at the neighborhood level; 2) increased problem solving—actually solving crimes and reducing chronic crime conditions rather than primarily focusing on making arrests; 3) increased partnership between police and communities, especially those directly affected by serious crime conditions; and 4) emphasizing crime prevention rather than only addressing crimes after they occur.

Why the confusion?

While most of these concepts are well-understood by community policing proponents, many police officers and citizens still lack a practical understanding of what to expect from their departments under this model of policing.

Much of the confusion stems from the lack of a consistent and well-thought-out marketing approach. In an age of information overload and bombardment by multiple media, there has been little effort to nationally publicize the particulars of com-

munity policing and what specifically to expect from it. As a result, the public—as well as many political leaders and police officials—has tried to simplify community policing's message to "Officer-Friendly" type programs, more and better equipment, and/or a return to cops walking beats.

If community policing is not reducible to any one of these elements, then what are realistic expectations of this new, smarter law enforcement strategy? The question is best answered from the perspectives of its two principal markets: the community and police.

What can citizens expect of community policing?

Because of its promise to actually solve crimes and improve police-community working relations, community policing's success can be measured in the following ways:

- actual reductions in crime levels, especially in chronic crime conditions that

communities have identified as disruptive, such as open drug traffic, illicit gun traffic, visible prostitution, graffiti and double-parking, and minor quality-of-life offenses such as public drunkenness, drug use, vagrancy, loitering and menacing behavior;

- an increase in targeted, strategic partnerships between police and community groups to reduce drug use and traffic, and illicit gun traffic and ownership. Improved community-police relations are reasonable expectations of success, but meet-and-greet church breakfasts, and traditional public relations activities are secondary to working together to actually prevent and reduce crimes that disturb community life; and

- increased street police presence in targeted areas. While this is a reasonable expectation of such practical partnerships, it is unlikely to be equally possible across an entire jurisdiction.

What can police expect of the community?

Photo courtesy of the Maryland State Police Department.

From *Community Policing Exchange,* May/June 1998, p. 5. © 1998 by the Community Policing Exchange. Reprinted by permission.

Far less attention has been devoted to what the police should be able to expect from their new community partners. For community policing to work, citizens must also contribute to the partnership, producing outcomes such as the following:

- **Organized action.** Organized communities are more capable of effectively and efficiently bringing their own resources to bear on crime conditions than are disorganized ones. Block, neighborhood or civic associations that involve residents in a regular, democratic and participatory way can agree on priority problems and how to best tackle and correct them. Well-organized citizen action converts random individual acts into planned, organized anti-crime and crime prevention efforts.
- **Increased competence** in dealing with crime and law enforcement. Well-organized community residents learn the basics of tackling crime problems safely, effectively and in collaboration with law enforcement. They learn how to report crimes confidentially and without unnecessary risks; work with local police and prosecutors; sustain action and accountability over time, hopefully increasing the number of involved residents; and use a community's unique resources to prevent and reduce crime. Reasonable expectations of competent communities include trained civilian patrols; well-planned mobilizations and rallies against crime hot spots; regular, accurate and useful information-sharing with police and prosecutors; use of civil and other actions to deny criminals access to or use of targeted spaces; lobbying and advocacy for law enforcement; regular court monitoring to assure proper prosecution and correction; and increased citizen involvement in prevention activities to reduce illegal behavior.

Marketing Strategies

These practical expectations of community policing must be widely understood, communicated, discussed and agreed on to become long-lasting. To accomplish these goals, community policing advocates, policymakers and practitioners should embrace the methods of modern marketing technology. Such strategies include the following:

- **Market research.** The modern marketing tools of survey research, focus groups, polling and the like are all tools that should be used more widely if community policing's message is to become a reality. Questions to ask include the following: What do cops and communities want? What do they consider valuable? How are they willing to work together? How do they measure success?
- **Education and communication.** Posters, mass media advertising, cultivation, educational materials and training are all tools that could be used far more effectively to help focus public attention on the new roles expected of police and community residents. Exploring what we expect the police to do differently and what we expect community residents to do differently should remain the key focus.
- **Consensus and accountability for results.** Many communities—especially urban neighborhoods hard-hit by wide-spread drug-traffic, violence and related crime—have already voted with their feet on what they consider to be top crime priorities and effective community policing. But in a democratic society, long-range, lasting change toward the community policing model assumes much broader discussion, understanding and support. It also assumes regular accountability on the part of practitioners, law enforcement and citizens for agreed-on results. Communities should regularly monitor and assess the performance of police services using "report cards" based on such realistic measures of success as those outlined above.

Community policing, to date, has been characterized by intensive but relatively closed discussions among those of us who believe in it or attempt to practice it. To achieve lasting change, we must turn now to the far more difficult task of involving the entire citizenry in defining, measuring and carrying it out. *By Michael E. Clark*

The Citizens Committee for New York City has been involved in community policing since 1984. For more information, contact Michael E. Clark, President, Citizens Committee for New York City, 305 Seventh Ave., New York, NY 1001. Phone: (212) 989-0909. Fax: (212) 989-0983.

Law Enforcement News interview
by Peter C. Dodenhoff

Chief Randall Aragon of the Whiteville, N.C., Police Department is a fascinating amalgam of seeming contradictions. All of his 23 years in law enforcement have been served in the South, yet he was born and raised in the tough East New York section of Brooklyn, N.Y. He got his initial law enforcement training during a hitch in the military police, but has a decided penchant for the strategies and jargon of the business world, and prefers to think of himself as a "CEO" and his town's residents as "customers." He is a past age-group winner of the state's "Toughest Cop Alive" competition, yet carries himself with an unassuming sensitivity that befits a man whose agency is a two-time winner of the Governor's Award for Excellence in Community-Oriented Policing.

Aragon is a leading apostle of problem-oriented community policing, and the success that he and his staff have achieved in Whiteville has become the envy of countless other agencies. All of his officers are officially known, in both title and job description, as Community Policing Officers, and must complete training and a formal exam to earn that status. Even Whiteville's sergeants are called Community Policing Sergeants.

The 52-year-old Chief was brought in to head a department suffering the ravages of low morale, nagging crime problems and shaky citizen confidence. He had already overhauled one police force and was being asked to live up to a reputation for success that preceded him to Whiteville.

In any department, Aragon believes the transformation process begins with a firm foundation—the proven business practice known as Total Quality Management. Aragon and the Whiteville P.D. spent more than a year building the foundation, based on the TQM principles of participative management, continuous process improvement and the use of teams—teams to design the transition to community policing, to set goals and objectives, even to design evaluation standards that would work in a community-policing context. It all comes down to what Aragon concedes is a written off "Dilbert" word: empowerment, giving every member of the organization a clear sense that they have a hand and a stake in how things get done.

The process is not without its risks. Aragon warned Whiteville's mayor that crime rates might go up at first, but explained that it would be due to the citizens' restored faith in reporting crimes to the police. There were also no guarantees that every member of the organization would buy into the new philosophy, but careful selection, focused training and a measured approach to change helped with believers. Policing is a risk-taking venture, he says, and chiefs who are unwilling to take risks should not assume the mantle of leadership in the first place. If he had it to do over again, Aragon says he would do things the same way, mistakes and all. Mistakes are a learning tool, he points out, and helped him develop his 20 "success insurance strategies" for community policing.

Aragon harbors no doubts that his approach to instilling a community-oriented footing can work in any agency (with allowances for tailoring to fit local needs). That belief is currently being put to the test in a rather unusual way. Earlier this year, Aragon was appointed as Whiteville's Public Safety Director, a post that puts him in overall command of both the police and fire departments. It should surprise no one to learn that he has already begun working on a TQM approach aimed at giving Whiteville its very own community-oriented Fire Department. Just give him time.

A *LEN* interview with

Police Chief Randall Aragon of Whiteville, N.C.

"We keep hearing leaders say they've been doing community policing for years when really, you know, they've been riding around waving and walking up to people and saying hello. That's not community policing; that's public relations."

LAW ENFORCEMENT NEWS: Whiteville's community-oriented policing effort took roughly two years from concept to award-winning implementation. Should one be surprised that it took that long, or that it happened as quickly as it did?

ARAGON: It's hard to place a definite time frame on how long it should take to finalize your community-policing effort. One thing any leader needs to

keep in mind as one of the "success insurance strategies" is to take things slow. In essence, you have to draw your resources into accepting or adopting community-oriented policing. It's not an easy effort; in fact, it's a very risky effort. My theme is getting the foundation laid, and getting it solid and committed and firm, and only after that pulling your staff into adopting community-oriented policing. I hear war stories from a lot of leaders about how they thrust their

"Making small mistakes—of course, not the disastrous ones—will actually cement the agency and bring you together as more of a team, as long as you realize where you faltered."

people into it, that it's an overnight evolution. Everyone's so surprised that it's sometimes a big-risk venture. So my theme is, take your time, no matter how long it takes; get your foundation right first.

LEN: Is community-oriented policing still evolving in Whiteville even as we speak?

ARAGON: No, we're right now at a citywide, department-wide approach. Every zone in our city is now involved in community-oriented policing somehow. Every patrol or uniformed officer is practicing community-oriented policing to the nth degree, really. We're kind of refining along the way. We started officially in 1994, and for maybe a year and a half I was developing a positive organizational culture. That is what I recommend. I preach that when I teach, and when we go and mentor other cities that have come in and visited us: Get the foundation right. A lot of leaders are very out of touch with what this means. You've got to get your folks to willingly achieve organizational objectives. Leadership involves influencing people to achieve organizational objectives. What I recommend is the TQM approach, Total Quality Management. I really am an ardent believer in TQM. We use that to get everybody to understand what commitment is, and how important it is to buy into a concept and work in teams. A lot of readers read all these glowing reviews about community policing, and they really don't know how to get it started. We spent a good year-and-a-half getting the foundation right, and then after that we started slowly talking about community-oriented policing and what it really is, and that became a learning process. Only after that, about a year later, did we start using it and bringing it into the department.

LEN: For those readers who are unfamiliar with the nuts and bolts of TQM, could you explain how it served as a key ingredient in the success of community policing?

ARAGON: The traditional leader comes from a do-it-or-else kind of situation—I'm the boss and this is what we expect. The TQM concept focuses really on three things: the use of participative management; continuous process improvement and the use of teams. Jablonsky, one of the gurus of TQM, states something like it's a cooperative form of doing business that re-

lies on the talents and capabilities of both management and labor in continuously improving productivity and quality through the use of teams. If you can pick through that, you'll see these three elements, participative management, continuous process improvement and the use of teams. And I wanted our people to fully understand what empowerment is. You've heard that; it's the Dilbert word, empowerment, and it's written off. But empowerment is a force that energizes. It's the power to fully take a personal interest and responsibility in achieving the goals of the organization because they know they have a hand in how things get done. It's that simple. And how do you achieve that? Well, we got that through adopting these TQM principles. To this day it's part of our training. We don't send anybody to a three-week course; we just can't afford that. However, our orientation training includes that; in fact, we even have the principles of it on our rookie exam. With our department, you receive about six weeks of training with a field training officer after you graduate from the police academy. That six weeks includes learning about TQM and what it means, and then it's on our written rookie exam.

Customer orientation

LEN: That would certainly seem to set rookies on the right course coming out of the academy. It puts a service-orientation right there on the table.

ARAGON: Yes, and we have evolved to the point that we have brought citizens to a higher level; they're called customers in Whiteville. You know, a lot of cities from around the state come in and visit us to learn what we're doing, and they say, "Hey, there's some kind of revolution going on down there, and it's a good revolution." And when they leave, they adopt this customer term. We want our citizens to believe that they are truly believed by us to be our customers. We want them to think—this is what we preach—that we don't hold a monopoly on law enforcement services. When we project that, which we're doing, our customers feel so elated, you know, they just brag: "They call us customers, just like the local electric company."

"If you're going to be a leader, there's risk; it comes with it. You take the risk and use proper judgment. If you don't want to take a risk, I don't think you need to be a leader."

LEN: Does it surprise you at all that Whiteville and its Police Department have become a magnet for other localities that want to figure out how to replicate your success?

ARAGON: It did in the beginning. You know, we thought we were just doing the right thing, and it was something that we needed to do. We accepted it as being the way you do business. But then, after I published a few articles, we started getting calls from all over the United States. People wanted me to send them checklists, and they started coming down to our state to visit. Our guys couldn't wait to be part of this orientation. We know we've got a lot of strategies that are just working superbly. We're not giving away secrets, really. We're trying to enhance everybody's quality of life throughout the United States.

LEN: It seems that the implementation went through with minimal resistance. Was it the groundwork that was laid, or perhaps were the men and women of the Whiteville P.D. just hungry for meaningful change?

ARAGON: They were hungry for change, but not everybody. There were just a select few that had heard about community policing, so I drew upon those informal leaders to bring them into the fold. One of the success strategies is development of a transition team, a cross-section of the whole agency to actually bring us where we wanted to go and come up with the vision, rather than make it a chief's thing. So many leaders really start out on the wrong foot by making it the chief's thing. We wanted it to be a staff concept. So again, jumping back to the TQM principles of teamwork, we developed a transition team with a team leader. I was on the team as a facilitator, but they developed the direction we should go in. So here's the entire department looking at a team of their own people. We had civilians on it, we had ranking people, non-ranking people. It was just a cross-section. They were plotting the course—and don't forget, they were getting the TQM training also. The ideas were self-generated, and then the empowerment kicked in, so it wasn't just the chief's thing or a top echelon thing.

It works everywhere

LEN: Is this something that worked in large part because the Whiteville, P.D. is the size that it is, or would this kind of an evolutionary, participatory process work in a larger organization?

ARAGON: It will work everywhere, and we've proven that. High Point's top leaders came down to us and then we did a follow-up visit to them, and we explained exactly what we're doing here. It's kind of like one-size-fits-all when it comes down to the concept. The procedures might have to be tailored a little bit, but the concept is basically the same of having a trained team that knows what empowerment is, knows the principles of TQM and so forth, and then putting them on a course. Of course, High Point's strategies are going to be different, but they have a transition team going, and they're doing the same thing. A lot of agencies don't do that. They start out with a general order that says "We're going to do community policing." To me, policing is a risk anyway. Don't front-load it.

LEN: You routinely refer to police chiefs as CEOs. That's business jargon. Is it a tell-tale sign of where you're coming from in terms of running a department?

ARAGON: Precisely. I feel like it's a business venture. A police chief is a businessman; his profits are the positive satisfactions received by the customer. So I try, using the TQM principle, to condition myself and my staff to give it a business aura. I know we've got to be regimented, but I try to lose that air as much as possible and approach it as a businessman. When people ask, "You're what?" I say, "I'm the CEO," and it makes me proud to know that I am.

LEN: You were hired in Whiteville specifically to implement a community-policing philosophy. Whose idea was it to shift the department to this footing: the officers, the community, local political leaders, or some combination of all of these?

ARAGON: All of the above. There was a lot of discontent a few years ago, and very bad morale. A bunch of lawsuits had developed and the Chief had resigned. In fact, one editorial indicated the department was a shambles. It needed to go in a different direction, and more than anything, the department unquestionably needed a renewal of its self-esteem from the bottom up. The city manager I worked for had heard about community policing, and he thought that would be the cure for it, and he knew that I had some experience in it.

LEN: I was about to ask if the fact that you were hired specifically to implement community policing in Whiteville suggested that you had already done it successfully in another agency. . . .

ARAGON: I had taught it in college, and I had implemented it in another agency, Selma, N.D., prior to coming to Whiteville. Of course at that point it was just getting started; it was becoming a very important evolution in the United States. You kept hearing about agencies that were doing it, but not to the magnitude that we've implemented it in Whiteville. But I had the experience and a little bit of know-how.

Mistakes & all

LEN: You've been quoted as saying that if you had it to do all over again, you'd do it the same way. Mistakes and all? Isn't that a rather bold assessment on your part?

ARAGON: By making some of the mistakes that we did, it made us better. I remember being asked that in past interviews by psychiatrists: "If you had to do it all over again, would you do anything different?" And I said the same thing: No, I wouldn't. And he'd say that sounds kind of ridiculous. Well, let me tell you this. I'm a product of my mistakes, and I wouldn't appreciate where I'm at if I didn't make those mistakes.

The mistakes we made along the way are why I developed the 20 success insurance strategies, to help people to try and not lose productivity, and not have that down time if they can help it. We've had some

setbacks, nothing disastrous, but some where we wasted a month or two, and we maybe could have been there quicker. Making small mistakes—of course, not the disastrous ones—will actually cement the agency and bring you together as more of a team, as long as you realize where you faltered. So that's why I'm saying, yes, I would do the Whiteville model again, even with the small setbacks we've had, because it's made us a stronger unit.

LEN: The demographics of Whiteville are interesting, to put it mildly. It's a relatively small city of about 6,000, with a fairly standard racial and ethnic makeup. But as a county seat and a local commercial hub, that population probably doubles or triples during the course of a business day, which changes the whole picture a little. In keeping with that, what aspects of community policing in Whiteville are a textbook approach, and what aspects would you describe as a custom fit or unique to your city?

ARAGON: That's a good question. We're not a huge city, but during the day, we have 15,000, 20,000 or 25,000 people come to the city to go to work, eat and shop, and that's where you've got to tailor your approach according to your demographics. We might only have 6,000, 6,500 living here, but during the daytime, it's a booming metropolis, because if you're going to buy anything in the county, you're probably going to come to the city of Whiteville. We have some of the sections of the city where we have 30 to 60 thousand cars passing in one 24-hour period. So, of course, we have our crashes—about 800 a year. We have the larcenies, we have the damage to property, all those things of a city maybe four or five times larger, and it happens with people who don't live here. So we had to tailor our needs and our efforts because of that. Now you might have some city that is the county seat and it's just like a Mayberry situation where nothing ever really happens. That CEO is going to have to tailor his community policing effort and maybe do something less aggressive in the crime control strategy part of it because of the way it is. But we had a unique situation

> "Our community-policing officers had nothing but glowing reviews about what they did; and how uplifting it is to them when they go home at night knowing that they've worked a little area that they are fully in control of and are held accountable for. We want everybody to realize that they've contributed, and it wasn't just lip service."

here and what we did worked for us. It's all part of tailoring your effort and how you adapt it.

Target-specific beginnings

LEN: Of the 6,500 or so people who make up Whiteville's full-time population, many of them live in Federally subsidized, low-income housing, a potentially significant factor in terms of how that segment of the population may wish to be policed. . . .

ARAGON: Our community policing efforts initially became target-specific in the at-risk areas of the city, the public housing areas. I believe you'll find that most cities end up starting it in those areas, and then expanding it to a citywide approach. We started in the at-risk areas where the low income, the high crime and the high fear of crime area were—and that's posed an unfortunate dilemma. What we now find is that we could not withdraw our resources from those areas; our communities wouldn't tolerate that. It's worked in those areas on the east side and west side of our city, where we do have Federally subsidized areas. They're light-years different from what they used to be due to our efforts. That's a success story that anybody who begins it and adopts the right strategy will see. But I want to bring to the forefront that any city, any CEO who adopts a target-specific approach that is working in one specific area with community policing and doesn't expand it citywide is really doing all of their customers a disservice. A lot of CEO's don't realize that it needs to be citywide and department-wide eventually. You just can't have some officers doing community policing and some not. That's where you start your inner turmoil.

A risk-taking venture

LEN: So as the philosophy is being implemented, it should be made clear to all employees that community policing will become everyone's way of doing business at some point?

ARAGON: Yes. It's not just a temporary measure that's going to fade away. It's going to end up that everybody wearing a uniform is going to be understanding what the philosophy is and what the strategies are to achieve that end. You have a lot of conflict, but to me, policing is a risk-taking adventure anyway, both internally and externally. You do have backlash. And that's one of the biggest things that can spell disaster, the backlash that comes internally and externally. It's one thing we're experts on.

LEN: Some people, some CEOs, to use your term, are experts on taking risks while others are experts on avoiding risk. . . .

ARAGON: I know, and I've learned after my many years of leadership how to balance that. If you're going to be a leader, there's risk; it comes with it. You take the risk and use proper judgment. And if you don't want to take a risk, I don't think you need to be a leader; you need to be a follower and settle for that.

LEN: Were there any ways in which the demographics of Whiteville made implementation of community policing a challenge?

Aragon: "I constantly reinvent myself."

ARAGON: We had to tailor it quite a bit. You know, I mentioned earlier about "one size fits all." What I meant by that was that you have to build the positive organizational culture, you've got to use some kind of total quality management technique. You can't use "one size fits all" as far as developing your community-policing effort. We have some areas in the city that are literally crime-free, and we had to balance the fact that some areas, even though they're not crime-ridden or at risk, we had to give them some attention because that would create a backlash on us. We knew we had traffic problems, we knew we had a lot of larcenies—we have malls. Most of the larcenies we have are shoplifting and gas drive-offs, and it's hard to prevent that. That's something the business needs to take some proactive steps on. So what we zoomed in on was doing something in the schools, doing something in the neighborhoods themselves, getting out there and making sure that every single customer knew we were moving in to help them in a partnership to solve their community problems jointly. That was our biggest thrust, getting out into the communities. When I and some of my staff go out and do our lectures and talks, we keep hearing CEOs say that they've been doing community policing for years. We laugh; it's kind of like an insult. Those leaders say they've been doing it for years when really, you know, they've been riding around waving and walking up to people and saying hello. That's not community policing; that's public relations. And that's another side that bothers me.

Everyone's interests at heart

LEN: Obviously the 15,000 or so extra people [who] come to Whiteville in the course of a day have to be considered part of your service population somehow, because even though they're not residents or local tax-payers, they nonetheless do consume services. The community is spoken for in terms of neighborhood watch groups and community councils and so forth, but who looks out for the interests of the transient or commuter population in Whiteville when it comes to crafting community policing?

ARAGON: Well, another technique we use is called our leadership council. The leadership council is part of our "big six," and once again that's a principle of community policing, the big six, which involves the business community, elected officials, the media, officers, our customers and other officials. We meet quarterly. Again, I'm the facilitator on that, and my staff will be there, along with all these other folks I mentioned. This is when we have the big forum to determine if we are meeting the needs of not only our people who physically reside here, but also the needs of the customers who come in and want to patronize and purchase and go to school, etc. So you're right. You can lose sight of the fact that those people are also part of what makes the city so valuable quality-of-life-wise. It's the ones who just spend a few minutes in town. But we've been successful even there; the feedback we're getting from this is superb.

LEN: Even if a city's residents overwhelmingly said they were satisfied with their police service, it wouldn't be quite the same if that were offset by 10,000 commuters saying that the city and its police force stink. . . .

ARAGON: Yes, but we don't have that. I'll be out doing talks and I'll hear somebody from another town say, you know, "We're all so proud that y'all are doing this, and we wish our city would do this." And then I think, well, I've talked to their city, and the city doesn't want to take that step. You kind of wonder why they don't. I've heard all kinds of different stories: that they're not big enough, or "Well, I've been doing that for years." Yeah, you've been doing that for years; you've been shaking hands, doing the grin-and-wave routine. That's not community policing, and their customers become kind of like stepchildren because they're not giving them the full service that they can.

LEN: Often, too, it seems, when people say, "Well, we've been doing that," in the next breath they'll say, "But it doesn't work," as if to draw a sweeping con-

clusion based on shaking a few hands and checking in on merchants from time to time.

ARAGON: That's just it, and you know they're not going to change. They're not getting the full worth of their police force because they think they're doing something that's been around for 20 years.

Undefeated champs

LEN: The news item that first brought you to our attention was your winning a second consecutive Governor's Award for Excellence in Community Policing—the first two years that the award has been offered, in fact. At some point are you folks going to retire as undefeated champions and give someone else a chance to win?

ARAGON: Well, the second year, when the assessment team left, they didn't give us the positive air that the first one did. So the talk of this department was, well, we didn't get a good feeling from the assessment team, and besides, they've got to give it to somebody else; they don't want us to monopolize it, you know. So I just convinced myself that somebody else would get it. Then, boom! We ended up getting it. And, as I found that out later, we totally maxed all the points. This did not come by accident. We worked hard for it, but we know we're doing the right thing. That's what makes us feel good. It wasn't just a bunch of eyewash. They interviewed people at random—our community-policing officers, as we call them—and every CPO interviewed had nothing but glowing reviews about what they did, and how uplifting it is to them when they go home at night knowing that they've worked a little area that they are fully in control of and are held accountable for. That's the nature of the game. When you go home, we want everybody to realize that they've contributed, and it wasn't just lip service.

The bottom line

LEN: To continue in the business metaphor you favor, there should be a bottom line here, with customer satisfaction being just one part of it. At the same time, an impact on crime rates would seem to be a must. What have your community policing efforts achieved in practical, bottom-line terms—crime rates, fear of crime and quality-of-life considerations?

ARAGON: Community policing is meant to do several things: to prevent and control crime, to restore and maintain order and to reduce the citizens' fear of crime. That's what we're after; that's the bottom line of everything in law enforcement. What you will see when you adopt a community policing effort, and this is a teachable fact, is that reported crime will go up the first three to five years in your jurisdiction. That's a definite, and a total paradox. I had to brief my mayor and my manager before we even began. I said, "Look, let me just lay this out. If crime goes up for the next few years, don't think we're losing." And they were just shaking their heads. Our mayor's a super man; he's been there 16 terms, and he says, "What are you talking about?" I had to explain that people are going to report things once they realize how competent we are in our services. They're going to report things they never reported in their life. In 1996, crime increased 6 percent over the prior year. And last year, crime went up 5 percent. So we have had somewhat of an increase. But let me tell you something. The fear of crime has plummeted. That is what we're really after. Sure, I want crime to go down; we do want that. But the key is, although crime is going up somewhat, the fear of crime is going down.

LEN: Is that something you've measured, or is it more of a gut feeling on your part?

ARAGON: It's been gut feeling, but we recently had a high-powered survey of the community done, and in essence it stated that the Whiteville Police Department are heroes. There's just a whole positive feeling toward the officers' work, toward the theme of community policing and everything it stands for: preventing and controlling crime, restoring and maintaining order and reducing citizens' fear of crime. They like what we're doing, and they wouldn't want us to change what we're doing. In fact, the statistician doing the survey was astounded. He'd never done one that received so many positive reviews.

We're also going up for national accreditation this November for the first time; that's something we've been working for 3½ years. As part of that, we did an employee survey, and we're exceeding our greatest expectations as far as positive reviews even from our employees. So we're not only making our customers happy; the employees are happy, too. Sometimes just the opposite happens. You'll be satisfying your customers and you'll have all this internal backlash. Or you've got your employees feeling good, and the customers can't stand to walk out to the police department and to make contact with them. We're doing it on both fronts, so if that's a measure of success, we've got it.

LEN: What about the third factor you cited, the quality-of-life considerations? How are things playing out in that regard?

ARAGON: If we didn't have that I'd be very disappointed. The customers themselves have indicated that they feel the quality of life has been enhanced, that their neighborhoods are in better shape than they've ever been, and that they feel more esteem and more commitment to their own neighborhoods. That was due to community-policing efforts.

A smooth fit

LEN: Many observers have taken issue with the idea of implementing community-oriented policing in the context of a traditional rank and organizational structure. How did that work out with the Whiteville P.D.? Where did you have to make changes? Where did it fit smoothly?

ARAGON: We didn't change our organizational structure in terms of the hierarchy. Sergeants remained sergeants and lieutenants remained lieutenants. The thing that we did at the bottom end was with the officers, as I mentioned earlier. You need to go in and look at your job descriptions. Officers are traditionally called officers, and they have certain duties. They will be able to effect an arrest, chase the bad guy, and all the things that go along with catching crooks. What we had to add in there was the fact that they had to communicate, develop community watches, do introductory visits, do all these things that are involved in community policing. So the only significant thing we did in the job structure is that the bottom-line officer, who was just called a policeman or a patrolman, is now called a community policing officer. The sergeants are the same way; they're called community policing sergeants. We're very liberal when it comes to uniforms—that's another TQM thing. In North Carolina, we usually have very mild winters. Some days you could wear pullover knit shirts with a collar. It's part of the uniform, a black golf shirt with a nice embroidered badge. But where it used to read "Patrolman," it now reads "Community Policing Officer." The thing is, if you're going to expect community policing to work out, let's call them that.

That's been the biggest structural change; I haven't changed the organization beyond that. And in most police organizations, I believe, community policing would fall right into place in the paramilitary setup. It's just a matter of making sure people have the right job description.

LEN: Several years ago, the Governor of North Carolina came out and said he was putting a high priority on the development and implementation of community policing in the state. Apart from the fact that this seems a rather bold and uncommon pronouncement for a governor, has this commitment translated into resources for local governments?

ARAGON: Most definitely. The Governor has firmly stated that he will support it as a priority, and it's held up. We have received a lot of grant money from the state Department of Crime Control and Public Safety, which is where the Federal funds go, to be meted out as needed. So he's been true. Gov. Jim Hunt has walked his talk, as has his staff, and he's made it very clear that if you wish to pursue this, he's going to support it and get you the resources you need.

LEN: The Governor is limited to two successive terms. Do you get any sense that the emphasis on community policing would outlast his tenure?

ARAGON: I think it's going to continue. He's not given up the reins on community-oriented policing by any means. Of course, his term is going to be over in a year or so, but if the new governor, whoever that's going to be, has been keeping his eyes and ears open, he's going to have to be very supportive of this movement because it's just getting better and better. You know and I know that this cornucopia of funding for community policing is going to close some day, and you're going to have to start footing your own bill. The seed money, as we call it, is going to end sooner or later. That's a big question facing a lot of city councils and budgetary operators: When it stops, what are we going to do with all these people we have on grants?

LEN: A lot of departments are already facing the music. . . .

ARAGON: I've seen good friends of mine, other CEOs, that had 10, 11, 12 officers, and they're going to be stripped because their government can't afford the cost. And that's a shame because it's from tiny acorns that mighty oaks grow.

> When we hire officers, we hire them based on whether they can solve problems. We ask them that. It used to be: "Can you shoot?" "Can you communicate?" Now it's also, "Can you solve problems?"

Opportunity knocks

LEN: Is it, perhaps, a case of being "confronted with insurmountable opportunities," where, if the departments had done their homework and successfully implemented community policing when they had the Federally funded officers on hand, it would now offer a chance to see if the baby could walk on its own after the officers leave?

ARAGON: It goes back to what I mentioned earlier. If you started with this approach five or six years ago, and you had done as some CEOs have done, with a little target-specific section working community policing, maybe two, three or four officers—many big agencies devote a section of the department to it while everybody else is doing the traditional policing, going call to call 24-by-7. They're not developing their preventive tools and they're not solving problems; they're just fighting fires. That's going to hit some day and the loan is going to come due because they have not spread this philosophy department-wide. They started it as a small team and they're still doing it. And the thing is, what are you going to have? You're going to have that little section of the community that's had attention from the community-policing officers, while the rest of the city is still doing traditional policing, going from call to call to call. And when the grants stop, what do they have? They've still got problems. If they were to evolve totally, with the whole city using the effort, they probably won't mind if they lose a couple of officers. They wouldn't have that problem. But they haven't been proactive, if you see what I'm saying.

LEN: In other words, some chiefs and departments have been wasting a lot of time during three years of grant funding by not pushing the envelope of community policing. . . .

ARAGON: If you got your seed money and two or three officers, and no one else is doing community policing, what do they have when it's over? They've got community policing in only one section of the city. You're really just displacing the criminals. One of the principles I preach is that a lot of times you're just displacing the crooks, and they just go into another sector of the community. Really, the bottom line is that if you got the seed money, develop your effort to be city-wide. This way, down the road, whether you keep your staff the same or do away with it by attrition, you've got the entire city thinking, sleeping, working toward problem-solving.

LEN: And thereby give the department a far better chance of maintaining course and speed in terms of serving its customers, even after the grant money runs out?

ARAGON: Yes, and that's the point. That's why we are totally community policing. Every officer that works at the Police Department has his own neighborhood. And we're holding them to solving problems and preventing crime and reducing crime. In fact, they are rated as to how they perform. Just to give you one example, we have officers who shine their shoes, they look sharp, they keep their hair cut, their cars clean. But come evaluation time, they don't receive good evaluations because holistically, they've done the traditional policing effort; they haven't actually solved community problems in their area. The area hasn't received the attention. They haven't made the introductory visits they're supposed to do, which means getting out of the car, introducing themselves to their customers, developing a community watch with an adequate number of people, etc. They're catching the bad guys, which is required, but the whole picture has not been attended to.

Measuring up

LEN: Normally, one would think that developing the kind of evaluation measure you're describing would be at best problematic, maybe even next to impossible, given that officers would say you can't measure these things. But might it be possible that, given the teamwork approaches and participatory nature of management that TQM has built into your organization, that the evaluation methodologies were more or less agreed to by all parties concerned?

ARAGON: Exactly. In our TQM approach, we make sure up front that there's agreed-upon objectives and goals. We look at them during the year, and at the end of the year we actually pull that out. Then the officers are evaluated based on the agreed-upon goal and objectives, which are the typical community-policing objectives: visitations, developing community watches, preventing crime, customer satisfaction. We look at that and we grade them. Essentially, we were counting beans, like, did you arrest your bad guys? That's important, of course. Crooks still go to jail in community policing; we don't make any bones about that. Now, though, they go to jail even better. Now the customers tell us who's doing what—unlike before, when we had to practically pull teeth, begging them to help. They're coming to us because they're confident in what we're doing.

LEN: And, of course, officers are all taught these principles in their rookie training or their field training, so there should really be no surprises. When it comes time for evaluation, everybody knows what the criteria for success or failure will be.

ARAGON: Exactly. Even when we hire officers, we hire them based on whether they can solve problems; that's one of the key issues. We ask that. It used to be: "Can you shoot?" "Can you communicate?" Now it's also, "Can you solve problems?" And you'll have the types who say, "What?" That's the one you don't hire. And when you do hire them and they fall into accepting this, and you see that they can do it, first you've got to train them right. In our basic training after they finish at the police academy, we have a minimal FTO training course, which is six weeks of riding with another FTO. Part of that is community-policing training, which we tailor for us, and they are actually tested on their knowledge of community policing. They have to ride a bike. They have to go on visitations with a veteran officer. And when they pass two tests—the traditional test for officers, what we call the rookie exam, and the community-policing test—they get a little green tag to put on their epaulet, which signifies that they've received the community-policing training and passed it. So there's actually an empowerment thing; they receive an award for learning a new concept.

Now we've got to go into their job and set goals and objectives for the year, and then, as you mentioned, we see if they actually achieve these goals and objectives. Many times officers are just looked at in terms of how many arrests have you made. Have you shined your shoes? Have you washed your car? Do you write a good police report? That's important, but how about whether you have solved problems in your community? Have you actually brought your community together to be a partnership? Have you got them working as a team? That's also what we're after. Some officers that we've rated got less than the maximum score because, again, they may have shined their shoes, washed their cars and written their reports right, but they haven't gotten out and done the COP tasks. If you're not going to have that follow-up, then don't even start the program, because you're just wasting your time and their time. And one other thing I wanted to bring out is that you've got to have enough time to do community policing. If your agency is going on calls 24-7, and there's nothing but that, you [had] better talk to your policy-makers and your legislative advisers, because you can't develop community policing. You've got to have someone commit the time. And that's one thing a lot of CEOs don't even understand. You've got to have uncommitted time because you actually have to get out and go and visit your customers and develop meetings and so on. I would say the greater percentage of U.S. departments have uncommitted time; they just need to use it.

Required reading

LEN: Your insights into community policing are an outgrowth, no doubt, of being a well-read police executive. Could you identify a handful of books that you feel are essential reading for any CEO looking to emulate your community-policing success?

ARAGON: Off the top of my head, there are three books. No. 1 is a very good book that I'm now reading for the third time because I missed some things: "The Five Pillars of TQM: How to Make Total Quality Management Work for You," by Bill Creech. I'm an ardent believer in his principles, and it's one of the best books on TQM. In fact, he's probably going to owe me some royalties. Second would be "Community Policing: How to Get Started," by Robert Trojanowicz and Bonnie Bucqueroux. I teach from that. There are many other good books, but this is the essence. And last would be "The Seven Habits of Highly Effective People," by Stephen R. Covey." I'm currently back in school trying to become a "Seven Habits" instructor.

Creech's book on TQM and Steve Covey's "Seven Habits" will get you into developing that positive organizational culture, and then Trojanowicz's will ease you into community policing. Taken together they form a kind of CEO's survival kit on community policing. I've read many others, but those are the giants. I'm a life-long learner, and I constantly reinvent myself. I just thirst for knowledge, and I never know all the answers. When I do, I'm going to hang it up.

Gimme some skin: Sensor patch may help spot parolees' drug use

Philadelphia will be the test site for the latest technological advance to make sure parolees are drug-free—a black patch the size of a wristwatch that is designed to detect indications of drug use and relay this information along with person's whereabouts to authorities.

The patch, which is attached to the wrist or ankle, determines drug-use status, whether the patch is in contact with skin and skin temperature—measures to ensure that the device is being worn. Its surface is coated with an antibody that interacts with cocaine and other drugs. If drug metabolites are present in a person's sweat, colored particles are released from the patch and detected by a built-in sensor.

The sensor relays information to a transmitter that is similar to a pager and worn on the subject's belt. A signal is sent via wireless e-mail to alert authorities of drug use, even if officials are several states away, identifying who the user is and where he is located within a radius of 150 feet.

Authorities say the device, which can be adapted to detect other drugs such as heroin and amphetamines, will help probation and parole officers keep tabs on their charges, which is now done mostly through urinalysis drug screening.

"It could open up a new and possibly foolproof method of monitoring substance abuse," said Saralynn Borrowman, program manager for investigative sciences at the National Institute of Justice.

The patch could also make the task of monitoring ex-offenders' drug use easier, cheaper and faster, they add,

and thus more effective. "People have found that the closer you make the consequences and the behavior, the more likely it is to influence behavior," said Jerome Jaffe, former head of the Federal Center for Substance Abuse Treatment who is now a professor of psychiatry at the University of Maryland.

The sweat patch offers "real-time" data about drug use, said David A. Kidwell, who heads research at the Naval Research Academy in Washington. Other drug screening methods, such as those that utilize urine and hair samples, are "always after the fact" and sometimes "beatable," he told The Philadelphia Inquirer.

In the pilot program, the patch will be used to detect alcohol use as part of a test to iron out kinks in the technology. Kidwell said that no decision has been made on how many subjects might take part in the pilot. But he said laboratory tests conducted so far show that "what we have works."

The patch, which has been in development for nearly three years, may not be available for widespread use for another two years, Kidwell said. Still unknown is whether the patch will be comfortable to the wearer, whether it can be somehow disabled or fooled and what kind of maintenance they might require, he added.

Kidwell, who plans to conduct the pilot test in collaboration with the Institute for Addictive Disorders at Allegheny University of the Health Sciences, also has proposed another pilot project in New Orleans in conjunction with the district attorney's office there.

Unit 4

Unit Selections

17. **Adversarial Justice,** Franklin Strier
18. **How to Improve the Jury System,** Thomas F. Hogan, Gregory E. Mize, and Kathleen Clark
19. **Jury Nullification: A Perversion of Justice?** Andrew D. Leipold
20. **Confronting the Breakdown of Law and Order,** Bruce Wiseman
21. **A Little Learning,** James Q. Wilson

Key Points to Consider

❖ Is the American jury system in trouble? Defend your answer.

❖ Explain your understanding of "adversarial justice."

❖ In your view, is "jury nullification" ever justified? Why or why not?

 **Links**   **www.dushkin.com/online/**

19. **Center for Rational Correctional Policy**
    http://pierce.simplenet.com
20. **Justice Information Center**
    http://www.ncjrs.org
21. **National Center for Policy Analysis**
    http://www.public-policy.org/~ncpa/pd/law/index3.html
22. **U.S. Department of Justice**
    http://www.usdoj.gov

These sites are annotated on pages 4 and 5.

The courts are an equal partner in the American justice system. Just as the police have the responsibility of guarding our liberties by enforcing the law, the courts play an important role in defending these liberties by applying the law. The courts are where civilized "wars" are fought, individual rights are protected, and disputes are peacefully settled.

The articles in this unit discuss several issues concerning the judicial process. Ours is an adversary system of justice, and the protagonists, the state, and the defendant are usually represented by counsel.

The lead article, "Adversarial Justice," asserts that the reliance we place on our adversarial trial court system to deliver just decisions is a misguided leap of faith. Author Franklin Strier maintains that the

exclusive responsibility for presenting evidence is assigned to attorneys, whose goal is victory, not enlightenment. Noting deficiencies in the jury trial, the authors of "How to Improve the Jury System" recommend allowing jurors to take notes and to submit written questions for witnesses. Focusing again on the jury, what is "jury nullification"? Andrew Leipold discusses the nullification decision, which occurs when jurors in a criminal case acquit the defendant, despite their belief that he or she was guilty of the crime charged.

The very idea of justice is perverted by psychiatry in the courtroom, according to "Confronting the Breakdown of Law and Order." The unit closes with Professor James Q. Wilson's "A Little Learning," which focuses on expert witnesses in court.

Judicial System

ADVERSARIAL JUSTICE

Franklin Strier

Franklin Strier is professor of law at California State University, Dominquez Hills, California, and editor of the Journal of Business and Management. *His newest book is* Reconstructing Justice: An Agenda for Trial Reform *(Greenwood, 1994).*

We take it as axiomatic that our trial courts dispense justice. The very legitimacy of the courts depends on that expectation. Yet the reliance we place in our adversarial trial court system to deliver just decisions is a misguided leap of faith. This is neither a radical nor novel perspective. Consider, for example, this observation by the eminent jurist Karl Llewellyn:

> The adversary trail seems from outside like back-handedness or trickery which approaches a travesty on justice; a dragging, awkward, unreliable machinery at best; at worst, one which is manipulated. In consequence . . . there is not one sole excrescence of trial machinery that will find one sole jot of support from any person in the court except the lawyer.[1]

Several inherent flaws of the adversary trial system support Llewellyn's assessment, but none more forcefully than the system's weakness in exposing the truth. In a trial, justice without truth is serendipitous. Benjamin Disraeli said, "Justice is truth in action." The U.S. Supreme Court has concurred, frequently stating that the central purpose of the trial is the determination of truth. As the O.J. Simpson trial careens fitfully but inexorably to its uncertain denouement, what and how much truth will it reveal? How good is it, or any American trial, at finding the truth? The sobering reality is that our trials, especially jury trials, are decidedly fickle vehicles to the truth. Justice is the casualty.

Paradoxes and false presumptions suffuse the theories and concepts undergirding our trial system. One such presumption is sometimes referred to as the *fight theory*, which holds that truth is best revealed in the courtroom through the clash of opposing views, rather than through investigation by the judge or other neutral third parties. Adversary theory presumes that the personal motivation of attorneys will generate the most assiduous search for favorable evidence. Essentially, this is the legal version of the "invisible hand" theory: Each party pursuing his or her own self-interest will adduce the most favorable evidence and generate the best arguments, yielding the fairest possible trial and a just result. By the same token, statements of the opposition will be vigorously monitored. Because the parties (rather than the judge) control the proceedings, rigorous cross-examination of adverse testimony is assumed.

The problem with the fight theory is that it is neither logically supportable nor empirically verifiable. Federal judge Jerome Frank, former chairman of the SEC and an oft-quoted critic of the adversary system, challenged the fight theory. His premise was simple: "The partisanship of the opposing lawyers blocks the uncovering of vital evidence or leads to a presentation of vital testimony in a way that distorts it."[2] He concluded: "To treat a lawsuit as, above all, a fight, surely cannot be the best way to discover facts. Improvement in fact-finding will necessitate some considerable diminution of the martial spirit in litigation."[3]

Other critics disparage the fight theory. Judge Marvin Frankel, a leader in the movement to give truth a greater value in trials, was shocked by the wanton leap of logic necessary to subscribe to the fight theory. After noting that other truth seekers do not use adversary means, he observed:

> We . . . would fear for our lives if physicians, disagreeing about the cause of our chest pains, sought to resolve the issue by our forms of interrogation, badgering, and other forensics. But for the defendant whose life is at stake—and for the public concerned the defendant is a homicidal menace—this is thought to be the perfect form of inquiry. We live, at any rate, as if we believe this.[4]

Commenting on the implausibility of the truth-from-fight assump-

---

1. Karl Llewellyn, *Jurisprudence: Realism of Theory and Practice* (Chicago: University of Chicago Press, 1962), 446–47.

2. Jerome Frank, *Courts On Trial* (Princeton, N. J.: Princeton University Press, 1949), 81.
3. Frank, *Courts,* 102.
4. Frank, *Courts,* 102.

tion, Thurman Arnold wrote in *The Symbols of Government:*

> Bitter partisanship in opposite directions is supposed to bring out the truth. Of course no rational human being would apply such a theory to his own affairs.... Mutual exaggeration of opposing claims violate(s) the whole theory of rational, scientific investigation. Yet in spite of this most obvious fact, the ordinary teacher of law will insist (1) that combat makes for clarity, (2) that heated arguments bring out the truth, and (3) that anyone who doesn't believe this is a loose thinker.[5]

Our use of the fight theory results in a paradox: Trial procedure assigns exclusive responsibility for presenting the evidence to those with no legal or professional obligation to seek the truth—the attorneys. Their goal is victory, not enlightenment. Studies show that attorneys often spend more time trying to hide or distort facts than revealing them. In every trial, at least one attorney usually tries to suppress or cloud unfavorable evidence.

A tenet of the adversary system is that each side's attorney will fight as hard as he can. Thus the attorney's duty of "zealous advocacy" is prescribed in the various professional codes that purport to delineate ethical conduct for attorneys. But this makes adversarial excess endemic to the system. And although we expect attorneys to adhere to the rules of evidence and confine their strategies to the ethical boundaries of the rules, they often bend the rules and stretch the strategies.

PRETRIAL ABUSE

Attorney abuses begin before the trial, during the discovery process. Under discovery, a litigant may request of the opposing party any relevant information (not protected by privilege) which that party has or to which that party has access. One objective was to do away with the element of unfair surprise in a trial. Initially, discovery was hailed as a boon to truth seeking, fairness, and the expedited disposition of cases. No longer. Discovery abuses now constitute the single greatest source of dispute, delay, cost, and trickery in the adversary system. Excessive discovery tactics either bully the opposition into submission or limit and distort the flow of information. Either result defeats the principal purposes for which discovery was designed.

Attorneys often use written interrogatories as tactical weapons by smothering a relatively impecunious adversary with extensive discovery demands and resultant costs. A survey of Chicago litigators found widespread use of another discovery tool, the deposition (direct questioning of a party or witness), as an aggressive weapon. The idea, said one respondent, is to "see if you can get them mad," to put them "through the wringer, through the mud," so that "they are frightened to be a witness and ... are a much worse witness."[6] Responding attorneys employ an equally mischievous array of tactics. These include creating false, diversionary leads; providing the bare minimum of information; and making the acquisition of that information as difficult and expensive as possible.

In criminal cases, the prosecution always has the constitutional duty to disclose exonerating evidence. But many states now make pretrial discovery a "two-way street," requiring that the defense grant similar discovery rights to the prosecution. California is one of the recent states to mandate reciprocal discovery. The intentional breach of this duty by the defense in the Simpson case may bear heavily on the outcome. During his opening statement, defense attorney Johnnie Cochran flagrantly broke the discovery law by referring to intended witnesses and their prospective testimonies without first disclosing their identities and/or statements to the prosecution for discovery. These witnesses, Cochran said, would offer testimony exculpating Simpson or casting great doubt upon the prosecution's evidence. Cochran further suggested that the prosecution had hidden this evidence.

The prosecution expostulated convulsively. The government was unaware of some of the new witnesses. How could it hide that of which it was unaware? The other new witnesses were known miscreants or felons and thus were completely unreliable.

When the prosecution asked for sanctions against the defense, Judge Lance Ito found himself in an extremely delicate situation. Some sanctions were clearly in order, yet they could not be so severe as to produce bias against the defendant

---

Trial procedure assigns exclusive responsibility for presenting the evidence to those with no legal or professional obligation to seek the truth—the attorneys. Their goal is victory, not enlightenment.

---

5. Thurman Arnold, *The Symbols Of Government* (New York: Harcourt, Brace & Co., 1962), 183–85.

6. Wayne Brazil, "Civil Discovery: Lawyers' Views on Its Effectiveness, Its Principal Problems and Abuses," *American Bar Foundation Research Journal* 787 (1980).

and create grounds for appellate reversal. After all, it was the defense attorney, not the defendant, who was the misfeasor in this procedural breach. The judge mulled it over for a day, then imposed two sanctions: First, he granted the prosecution ten minutes of "reopening" statements—in essence, a rebuttal; second, he admonished the jury to disregard the defense counsel's opening statements as they pertained to six of the potential witnesses.

Significantly, the judge did not mention what the testimony of these potential witnesses was to be. Thus, the jury does not know what weight to attach to the admonition. The warning will, therefore, have little corrective impact on the effect of the defense's opening statements (save suggesting to the jury that the defense counsel is somewhat untrustworthy). The ultimate effect of this gambit by the defense may never be known, but it is likely to be an affordable "cost of doing business."

Discovery abuse epitomizes the adversary system. Indeed, some attorneys argue that adversarial professionalism *commands* the use of such devices whenever they offer significant advantages. Whatever the validity of this contention, the intense competitive pressures of the adversary system make resort to obstructionist discovery devices a constant temptation and a common occurrence.

Pretrial adversarial excesses continue during voir dire (jury selection), a fertile area for trial attorneys to ply their trade. Attorneys may dismiss prospective jurors by challenges. Those whose responses to the voir dire questions indicate probable bias are challenged for *cause.* Attorneys may perceive that other prospective jurors would not view their client's case favorably but are not sufficiently biased to challenge for cause. Such individuals can be removed by *peremptory* challenges. Unlike challenges for cause, peremptory challenges require no stated reason by the requesting attorney; however, they are limited in

> *Discovery abuse epitomizes the adversary system. Indeed, some attorneys argue that adversarial professionalism* commands *the use of such devices whenever they offer significant advantages.*

number—a common number is six for each side. But in cases of serious crimes, the number may be twelve or more. (There were twenty in the Simpson case.) Because of their limited availability, a premium is put on the attorney's skill in using peremptory challenges.

Statute and case law require the panel from which the jury is selected to be drawn from a representative cross section of the community in which the case is filed. To this end, courts use voter registration lists as the primary source for jury panels. Theoretically, the varying views within the community, if represented on the jury, make for vigorous and salutary debate. The hope is that conflicting prejudices will cancel each other out.

By strategic use of peremptory challenges, an attorney tries to assemble a jury receptive to his case. As candid practitioners readily admit, lawyers conduct voir dire not to get unbiased jurors but to get jurors favorably biased. Attorneys also seek competitive advantage by attempting to influence prospective jurors while interviewing them. Their tactics are designed to *create* bias in prospective jurors—via indoctrination, education, and socialization—rather than merely detect it.

Trial advocacy tracts (some even appearing in law school textbooks) are replete with advice on achieving an illegitimate goal: gaining adversarial advantage during voir dire. Several studies support the conclusion that the vast majority of the attorney's efforts during voir dire are indeed undertaken for gaining adversarial advantage rather than screening for bias. For example, one

survey found that over 80 percent of attorneys' time during voir dire was used to indoctrinate prospective jurors. These findings were confirmed by an extensive survey of Los Angeles jurors (hereafter "the Los Angeles survey") that I conducted in 1987–88. (With over 3,800 jurors responding, it was the largest of its kind.)[7] More than one-third of the jurors agreed that "one or both attorneys were trying to persuade me in addition to probing for bias." This suggests that numerous attorneys are using voir dire for inappropriate didactic purposes.

TRUTH CORRUPTION

Once trial begins, tricks by attorneys can escalate—thanks in large part to the bench's historically lax enforcement of professional conduct rules. When infractions occur, they are routinely winked at by judges and bar association ethics committees. As a result, trial lawyers ostensibly enjoy a unique privilege in plying their trade: They are largely unanswerable to society for behavior that would be morally questionable elsewhere. This led the venerable jurist Felix Cohen to lament: "How the edifice of justice can be supported by the efforts of liars at the bar and ex-liars on the bench is one of the paradoxes of legal logic which the man on the street has never solved."

---

7. Franklin Strier, "Through the Jurors' Eyes," *ABA Journal,* October 1988, 78–81.

Space does not permit even a modest catalog of truth-corrupting tactics, but mention of a few common artifices will suffice:

Coaching witnesses. A standard practice is for attorneys to interview their witnesses in preparation for testimony. The practice is known by a variety of sobriquets—"rehearsing," "horse shedding," "prepping," and "sandpapering"—but the most common term is "coaching." The dangers of coaching are substantial: An attorney who knows the testimony of all friendly witnesses can orchestrate a common story that can avoid contradictions. In the course of coaching their witnesses, attorneys suggest "better" answers that, if not clearly contravening the witness' intended answer, subtly but effectively shade, dissemble, or distort the truth. The Simpson prosecutors continued to accuse the defense counsel of coaching those defense witnesses whose changed stories benefited the defendant.

Attorney statements. Judges frequently tell jurors that attorney statements are not evidence. That is not enough. Jurors should also be informed that *attorneys are not under oath and do not have to believe their own statements.* Few jurors appreciate this. That is why attorneys are so effective when they (permissibly) impeach the credibility of witnesses they know to be telling the truth.

Similarly effective is the presumptuous question, one of the more insidious tools in the cross-examining attorney's arsenal. The presumptuous question implies a serious charge against the witness for which the attorney has little or no proof. An example: "Isn't it true that you have accused men of rape before?" Such innuendos are particularly effective against expert witnesses. A recent study found that by merely posing these questions, an attorney could severely diminish an expert's credibility, *even when the witness denied the allegation and his attorney's objection to the charge was*

sustained. This clearly indicates that the presumptuous cross-examination question is a dirty trick that can sway jurors' evaluations of a witness' credibility.

Explanations for the effectiveness of this tactic vary. Communications research suggests people believe that when a speaker offers a premise, he has an evidentiary basis for it. With their pristine mind-sets, jurors assume that the derogatory premise of an attorney's question is supported by information. Another explanation lies in the possible confusion of jurors as to the sources of their infor-

---

The longer the trial, the less likely jurors will be able to distinguish information suggested by an attorney's presumptuous question from that imparted by the witness' answer.

---

mation. The longer the trial, the less likely jurors will be able to distinguish information suggested by an attorney's presumptuous question from that imparted by the witness' answer.

Witness abuse. Cross-examining attorneys often regard witnesses as if they were open garbage cans and treat them accordingly. Early in the Simpson trial, for example, the defense resorted to hardball tactics against witnesses. Recall the derisive browbeating of police detectives by defense counsel. And when Simpson's friend, Ron Shipp, testified that O.J. had disclosed his dream of killing Nicole, the defense counsel on cross-examination accused Shipp of being an alcoholic, a deadbeat, an ingrate, and a perfidious grasper who knowingly betrayed his friend to advance his own aspirations as an actor.

Emotional appeals. In the Los Angeles survey, two-fifths of the ju-

rors felt "one or both attorneys were trying harder to distort or selectively hide facts rather than seeking to reveal the truth so the jury could make an informed judgment." Jurors rank ordered the tactics used to accomplish this obfuscation. "Appeals to the emotions of the jurors" and "repeated interruptions and disruptive tactics" came in first and second, respectively.

An emotional appeal to the jury, of course, is the time-honored ploy of the trial attorney with a weak case. How it will "play with the jury" becomes the overarching con-

sideration in presenting evidence. Surely one of the most emotional moments in the Simpson trial appears to have been skillfully choreographed by the prosecution to have maximum impact on the jury. Assistant District Attorney Christopher Darden questioned Denise Brown, the sister of Nicole Brown Simpson, on the first Friday afternoon of the trial. After recounting O.J.'s past physical abuses of Nicole, Denise dissolved in tears. Darden then immediately asked for and received a recess, knowing that the jurors would carry that last compelling tableau with them over the entire weekend.

Adversarial trials conduce such drama because they are staged like theatrical performances. The show is the action taking place in the arena, bounded on the jury's right by the witness stand and judge's bench, and on the left by the attorneys' tables. Indisputably, the attorneys are the performers. Only they are allowed to walk freely in the arena, to and from the witness stand, the bench, and the jury box. They gesture, flail, and point. But mostly they talk: They bluster, blather, harangue, sermonize, and beguile. They laugh, cry, and bristle; they make the jurors laugh, cry, and bristle. Bar associations unabashedly offer "courtroom acting" classes to attorneys that satisfy continuing-education requirements. It is the greatest show in town because it involves real people with real problems and high stakes: prison or freedom; child custody or childlessness; recompense for serious bodily injury or destitution and welfare. Should matters of such consequence be resolved by a process that elevates showmanship over dispassionate and rational inquiry?

Dumb shows. The "repeated interruptions and disruptive tactics" referred to in the Los Angeles survey can come in many forms. Sometimes referred to as "dumb shows," this category consists of indecorous behavior intended to distract or mislead the jury, such as dropping books or making bogus objections. The legendary Clarence Darrow used a novel subterfuge. Before trial, he would insert a nearly invisible wire in his cigar. When his opponent began interrogating a witness, Darrow would smoke the cigar. Eventually, all eyes would follow the cigar ash, which, magically, never dropped.

Changing the story. In the unique, "fact-finding" inquiry that is the trial, attorneys selectively present evidence only to the extent that it furthers their version of the facts. The objective is to craft a credible story for the jury. In developing its story, the Simpson prosecution team chose an interesting strategy. Knowing it had to tarnish an American icon, the prosecution eschewed the conventional wisdom of beginning its case with evidence of the murder in favor of presenting evidence of antecedent wife beating.

Sometimes the attorneys' stories change as the trial progresses. An

---

Adversarial trials are staged like theatrical performances.

Arizona trial judge offers his impression of how this happens:

> The sporting lawyer's concern is whether the story is convincing, whether it adequately meets the opposing story, not whether it is true or false. Thus it is not at all unusual to hear a courtroom story unfold like a novel, changing as the trial proceeds. Sometimes the story becomes clearer, sometimes fuzzier, sometimes contradicted as it is orchestrated by the lawyer-maestros. As one side crafts a story, the other side expresses outrage at the opponent's fiction and responds by fictionalizing its own story. The story is not as dismaying as the attorney's acquiescence in it. In this sort of liar's paradise, truth ceases to be a Heidegerian revelation; instead, trial evidence becomes a progressive sedimentation, with new layers of lies overlaying the original ones.[8]

The defense's story certainly changed in the Simpson trial. Defense counsel Robert Shapiro initially said O.J. was asleep at the alleged time of the murder. Later, defense counsel Johnnie Cochran claimed O.J. was swinging golf clubs in his yard at that time. We can only speculate as to why the story changed. We know the change occurred after the judge ruled that O.J.'s exercise videotape—recorded shortly before the murders—could be shown to the jury. This evidence would obviously refute the claim that O.J. was so racked with arthritis at the time as to be incapable of a double murder with a knife. Once the arthritis claim was dropped, there was no disadvantage in maintaining O.J. was swinging golf clubs at the time of the murder. Further, it helped explain why O.J. was outside his house when he called his girlfriend on his cellular phone.

Partisan expertise. Will technological advances improve trial truth seeking? Even with the advent of more accurate fact-finding techniques such as DNA testing, the adversarial process will continue to subvert the truth by subordinating it to competing values. Peter Sperlich, who writes on the use of scientific evidence, says: "The adversary system maximizes the opportunities to obscure the facts, coopt the experts, and propagandize the judge. . . . The greatest single obstacle to complete and accurate scientific information . . . is the adversary system."[9]

When expert witnesses are pushed into advocacy roles, attorneys and the system corrupt the value of the witness' expertise. Attention is too often focused on the personal characteristics of expert witnesses instead of the quality of their evidence. In a 1987 book compiling papers and comments on social research and the courts, the authors reached consensus on these points: (1) scientists serving as expert witnesses must expect to be used (and misused) for partisan purposes; and (2) the adversary system is not a reliable means of bringing all the relevant scientific data to the adjudicator's attention or of separating valid research from unwarranted conclusions.

With judges being generally passive, the scope of zealous advocacy

---

8. R. J. Gerber, "Victory vs. Truth: The Adversary System and Its Ethics," 19(3) *Arizona State Law Journal* 3, 19 (1987).

9. Peter Sperlich, "Scientific Evidence in the Courts: The Disutility of Adversary Proceedings," *Judicature*, 66(10) (May 1983), 472, 474, 475.

trial tactics is limited only by the often-fertile imaginations of the litigation attorneys. Censuring individual practitioners or even the entire litigation bar for this state of affairs misses the source of the problem. After all, trial lawyers merely play their assigned roles within the adversary system. We should not condemn the attorney for engaging in morally questionable but nevertheless permissible trial tactics. Rather, we should decry the system that sanctions such tactics.

PROBLEMS WITH THE JURY SYSTEM

Any discussion of the adversary system is incomplete without considering the impact of the jury. Juries became enshrined in the Constitution because they were our bulwark during colonial times against the arbitrary and unjust decisions of the local judges appointed by the English Crown. Now we have representative democracy and many other constitutional protections against government encroachment. (Instructively, the courts of most other democracies do not use juries as we know them; none, including England, use them as extensively.) So the primary purpose of the jury is no longer protection against the government. Rather, it is a vehicle to attainment of an ideal: integration of community values, via the perspectives of common citizens, into the administration of justice. To this end, the law seeks juries composed of a representative cross section of the community where the trial is held.

Whether the jury system achieves or even approximates this ideal is highly debatable. Exemptions from service routinely afforded professionals and other potentially competent jurors both dilute the quality of juries and remove the very individuals particularly able to inject the community values that the law seeks. Most important, juries are usually selected partly or fully by the attorneys. It would betray great naïveté to contend that, in any given trial, the trial attorney's allegiance to the ideal of a representative, impartial jury is more than coincidental.

The main focus, however, should not be the jurors themselves. We should instead vet the jury system. Specifically, does current jury procedure facilitate or inhibit the realization of the ideal? And does this procedure make sense within the context of an adversarial trial?

The jury is called the trial's "fact finder." But unlike fact-finding in any other inquiry, the jury does not find, or investigate, any facts. Instead, it is the passive recipient of information, called evidence, introduced by the partisan attorneys. Although no appellate court has ruled that questions from jurors are forbidden, the vast majority of courts do not allow them or do not inform jurors of the right to ask questions. Incredibly, juries enter deliberations without the opportunity to fill in missing information or clarify uncertainties.

The restriction on questions is only the overture to a litany of ill-founded constraints imposed on jurors. No matter how lengthy or complex the evidence, most courts do not allow jurors to take notes or do not advise them of the right if it is permitted. Nor do they permit jurors to see a transcript of the testimony or a notebook of exhibits. Trials operate under the myth of perfect juror recall—yet another blatantly erroneous presumption.

There's more: Our trials litigate everything at once. All evidence on all possible issues is heard in one continuous trial. Evidence on any issue can be introduced at any time between opening and closing statements. No juror-friendly, logical order to the presentation of witnesses or evidence is required. As a consequence of this implausible scheme of "fact-finding," jurors tend to forget evidence or apply it to the wrong issue. Historian Carl Becker's commentary on the jury system resonates with truth: "Trial by jury, as a method of determining facts, is antiquated and inherently absurd—so much so that no lawyer, judge, scholar, prescription-clerk, cook, or mechanic in a garage would ever think for a moment of employing that method for determining the facts in any situation that concerned him."[10]

Being laypersons rather than experts, jurors are frequently overwhelmed by technical or complex evidence. This would include the DNA evidence that expert witnesses hired by the opposing sides "explained" in the Simpson jury. Unfortunately, these experts often compound instead of ease the jury's task: How is a juror to know if the most persuasive expert is the most authoritative? Also troubling is the potential degree to which the experts' hefty fees may flavor their testimonies.

Equally confounding the jury's search for truth is all the relevant evidence that they *cannot* hear. Because nontruth values such as individual dignity and privacy coexist with truth in the philosophical underpinning of our trial system, large gobs of highly probative evidence can be withheld from the fact finder. As illustration, the sanctity of the family dictates that spouses need not reveal spousal communications. The judge also has great discretion to exclude relevant evidence if he believes its probative value is outweighed by the danger of unfairly prejudicing, confusing, or misleading the jury.

But substantially more evidence is kept inadmissible by exclusionary rules based on erroneous presumptions. These exclusions both compromise the search for truth and profoundly beggar the justice of the final decision. For instance, a procedural rule intentionally blindfolds jurors as to whether civil-case defendants carry insurance. (It is presumed that such information would

---

10. Quoted in Frank, *Courts*, 124.

In this sort of liar's paradise, truth ceases to be a Heidegerian revelation; instead, trial evidence becomes a progressive sedimentation, with new layers of lies overlaying the original ones.

unduly influence the jury's award.) The problem is that juries go ahead and make their own assumptions anyway, thereby unwittingly corrupting the decision-making process even more.

Simpson case watchers will note the magnitude of relevant evidence that may be excluded by the granddaddy of all exclusions, the hearsay rule. A historical distrust of jurors' ability to properly discount hearsay forms the basis of the exclusion. Yet no empirical consensus supports this contention. That is why legal scholars since Jeremy Bentham have advocated that hearsay be excluded only when more direct proof is available.

Jury problems in divining the facts pale in comparison with understanding the judge's instruction on the law to be applied. *Most judicial instructions are worthless.* Rather than explain or clarify the law, the judge's instructions usually confuse the jurors with jargon-laden, incomprehensible language. That is because they are worded to avoid appellate reversal, not to educate the jurors. Consequently, jurors commonly deliberate and vote in ignorance of the law, referring instead to their personal values and biases or succumbing to the emotions evoked by the pandering of the attorneys.

Let us pause to reassess the two preeminent features of the adversarial trial. First, we have the partisan opposing attorneys. With the qualified exception of prosecutors, they have no obligation to the truth but do have an overriding professional and financial incentive to do all they can to win within the decidedly loose bounds of zealous advocacy.

Second, we have the lay jury. It cannot independently investigate but must rely exclusively on the staged, colored, and filtered versions of the facts presented by the attorneys.

This relationship profoundly affects trial outcomes. *The adversary and jury systems combine to deliver a witch's brew of trial justice.* Crafty attorneys have long prevailed in contravention of the merits of the cases they tried before juries by employing superior forensic skills or tricks or pandering to the basest of the jurors' emotions. Not only does the legal profession condone these tactics, it instructs in their use through law school courses and practitioner seminars. Over one-third of the Los Angeles survey jurors believed that the outcome of the case they sat on was dictated by a disparity in skills between the opposing attorneys. Two-fifths said the skills disparity was partly or completely responsible for a "wrong" decision with respect to the verdict or size of an award. These findings are unsurprising in light of adversary system theory, which holds that the optimal benefits of the system are realizable only in the presence of a supposition of epic proportions: Opposing litigants will be represented by competent attorneys of roughly equal skills. No more reason exists to believe this myth than to believe that opposing litigants will have roughly equal resources.

The mismatched attorney phenomenon is not entirely random. The wealthier the litigant, the better the available legal representation. I refer not only to better attorneys, but also to more persuasive expert witnesses and to other litigation

support services that help "scientifically" select the most favorably disposed jurors. These factors have certainly benefited wealthy litigants, such as William Kennedy Smith. It is no small curiosity that our legal system espouses equality of treatment (equal justice); yet our trial mechanism, more than any other, skews trial outcomes in favor of the side with the better attorney and more money.

REFORMS

Though failing, the trial system is not irreparable. I list below a few reform proposals.[11] The aim of all of them is to distribute some of the powers now wielded exclusively by attorneys to the judge and jury. As the impartial players in the trial, they are best suited to seek justice; the attorneys are not. Writes University of Chicago law professor Albert Alschuler:

> Although the adversary system may need a watchman, the task need not be assigned to the watched. Lawyers are simply not the appropriate figures to correct the defects of our adversary system. Their hearts will never be in it, and more importantly, it is unfair to both their clients and themselves to require them to serve two masters.[12]

Action from judges is the key to reform. Few people realize how extensive the judge's inherent authority is. All that is required for its exercise is the courage to impose rationality on the system.

If we are going to continue assigning weighty responsibilities to juries for little pay and much disrup-

11. For a full discussion of proposed reforms, see Franklin Strier, *Reconstructing Justice: An Agenda for Trial Reform* (Westport, Conn.: Quorum Books, 1994), chapter 7.
12. Albert Alschuler, "The Preservation of Clients' Confidences: One Value among Many or a Categorical Imperative?" 52 *University of Colorado Law Review* 349, 354 (1981).

tion of their lives, let's at least facilitate their task. All exclusionary evidence rules should be reevaluated to test whether their underlying presumptions correspond with reality. If we truly value the jury system, we should dare to embrace the revolutionary notion that jurors can actually be trusted with hearsay and other evidence commonly excluded, if the judge provides appropriate cautionary instructions. On balance, is justice really served by completely barring potentially decisive evidence because some jurors may ignore these instructions? Jurors should also be allowed to ask questions. When attorney incompetence leaves critical questions unasked, thereby threatening a possible miscarriage of justice, the judge should ask the questions.

The judge can order that all evidence on the same issue be presented at the same time by both sides. Imagine how much more lucid and judicable a trial would be with the following procedures. Witnesses with opposing testimony—including expert witnesses—would testify consecutively. Jurors would have a qualified opportunity to ask them questions. If helpful, the judge could call *neutral* expert witnesses to testify. At the end of each day and during deliberations, jurors could retrieve any or all of the testimony plus pictures of the exhibits from computers in the jury room. In order to provide a framework for processing the evidence, written copies of the judge's instructions would be simplified and given to the jurors *before* as well as after hearing the evidence.

Two important reforms should be made in jury selection. First, trial venues should no longer be changed because of pretrial publicity. In the age of mass media and instant communications, everyone hears about a high-profile case immediately.

> *Action from judges is the key to reform. Few people realize how extensive the judge's inherent authority is. All that is required for its exercise is the courage to impose rationality on the system.*

Deadly riots followed the first Rodney King trial because it had been moved from a minority community to a predominantly white one; the resulting jury had no African Americans. Now it has been bruited about that Los Angeles District Attorney Gil Garcetti moved the Simpson trial from the west side of Los Angeles (predominantly white) to the more mixed downtown area because he felt a conviction by a predominantly white jury would lack credibility. This may be a valid political judgment, but it has little to do with the law. It certainly contravenes the ideal of a jury representing a cross section of the community where the crime occurred.

Many experts believe most trials are won during jury selection. This militates in favor of the second jury selection reform—eliminating peremptory challenges. (Peremptories remove prospective jurors for reasons other than overt bias.) Inevitable disparities in the jury selection skills of attorneys probably skew the final jury more in a particular direction than the full panel from which it has been drawn. Now, the advent of expensive jury consultants gives an unfair advantage to wealthy clientele both in jury selection and in strategy suggestions during trial.

* * *

These and other reforms will be vigorously opposed. Who gains the most by preservation of the status quo? Not the judges. A recent extensive survey I conducted of the California judiciary confirms the earlier findings of a nationwide Harris survey that judges favor many trial reform proposals. Narrowing further the search for the antireform interests, contemplate who is most adversely affected by an obviously projury reform—videotaped testimony. Prerecorded testimony (i.e., before jury selection) would have the following benefits for juries and the quality of trial justice:

• Jurors would not be inconvenienced by interruptions for sidebar conferences, attorney objections, witness delays, and so forth.

• The resulting compression of evidence presentation time would give the jurors a more comprehensive view of the entire case.

• The court no longer need resort to the absurd fiction that jurors can actually follow the judge's instructions to disregard what they have already heard ("unringing the bell").

• All improper attorney questions and bogus objections intended solely for effect could be eliminated from the jury's purview.

Note that by virtue of the last benefit, any inappropriate nonverbal behavior (gestures, facial expressions) by attorneys or their clients could also be eliminated. Is there any remaining doubt as to who wants to keep trial procedure as is?

COMMENTARY

How to Improve the Jury System

by Thomas F. Hogan, Gregory E. Mize, and Kathleen Clark

The subject of the American jury system raises conflicting cultural sentiments. While the jury trial is revered as the most democratic institution in our society, a summons for jury service is dreaded as an unwelcome intrusion into our lives. Jury verdicts, respected because they are reached by a group of peers, are also ridiculed in recent high-profile trials.

Amid this cultural cognitive disconnect, however, there is no major movement to abolish the right to a trial by jury. Rather, across the country, communities and their courts are joining forces to fix the system. Recent efforts in Washington, D.C., Arizona, California, Colorado, New York, and other states have all focused on modernizing the jury system by making it more convenient, democratic, and educational for the jurors.

The ongoing jury reform experience in Washington, D.C., provides a look at jury service through the eyes of the juror and reveals that community-wide collaboration may be the most effective way to reconnect our actions and our values about the duty to serve.

In late 1996, the Council for Court Excellence assembled a committee and charged it with recommending improvements to the jury systems in Washington, D.C. Then, in February 1998, after a full year of study, the D.C. Jury Project published its comprehensive research report, which includes 32 specific recommendations to the bench and bar on how to modernize jury trials in the local and federal courts.

In the District of Columbia, where well-intentioned committees addressing worthy problems are hardly uncommon, nothing unusual has happened. Or has it? This report, entitled *Juries for the Year 2000 and Beyond,* may not become another denizen of the library shelf after all.

What makes the D.C. Jury Project's recommendations worthy of thoughtful consideration by the local and national legal communities? First and foremost, the quality of analysis regarding an impressive number of important issues in *Juries for the Year 2000 and Beyond* renders it both readable and well worth reading.

The revered constitutional institution of the jury trial, under recent media attack, deserves a renewed opportunity to thrive. Modernization efforts such as this could be a good opportunity. Besides offering rather mundane and unexceptionable recommendations, such as improving the quality and scope of the juror source list and providing comfortable facilities for jurors, the report probes deep into the history of the jury selection process and takes a stand on the complex issue of peremptory challenges.

Second, the courts and the bar should consider the message in this report because of who the authors are. The 36 diverse members of the D.C. Jury Project, collaborating in a way not previously experienced by these authors, were able to avoid the typical chasm that exists between the legal and civic communities. When jurors, lawyers, and judges take the time to actually listen to one another, then their conclusions deserve special attention.

Substantive recommendations aside for a moment, one of the most gratifying and productive aspects of the D.C. Jury Project was the makeup of the committee. Instead of assembling a generic group composed entirely of like-

Improving the Jury System

There is a national movement to modernize the jury system and reconnect our actions and our values about the duty to serve.

Recommendations include improving the quality and scope of the juror source list and providing comfortable facilities for jurors.

Jurors need practical training and easier access to information about the particulars of the cases before them.

minded lawyers and judges, the Council for Court Excellence actively recruited citizens with jury service experience as well as academicians with an interest in the field. Additionally, attorneys and businesspeople from a variety of backgrounds and viewpoints were called upon. Federal and local trial judges were included. Court administrators and jury officers rounded out the group.

The diversity of professional experience and personal background among Jury Project members was not an effort to have token representatives on the committee. Rather, the wide range of viewpoints enhanced the effectiveness of the collaborative effort. Each member was respected for his own perspective, but everyone understood that the purpose was to reach common/higher ground for the good of the overall system.

Not unlike a jury deliberation, we went about our work methodically, setting aside, when our convictions allowed, personal interests or biases that would impede true progress. It was clear at the outset that the citizen-juror members of the group were the real experts among us.

Also like deliberating jurors, committee members accepted the challenge with honesty and integrity. They struggled at times with controversial issues and differences of opinion yet continued to search for the right answers—overcoming the destructive chasm that so often divides the civic and the legal communities. Because this uncommon level of commitment and vision came from such a diverse committee and because former jurors contributed so significantly to the conclusions, the bench and bar need to listen to their consumers by giving

careful consideration to all of the recommendations in *Jurors for the Year 2000 and Beyond.*

PEREMPTORY CHALLENGES

One lesson learned from this collaborative effort involves group dynamics. Since the committee comprised people who often sit opposite one other in the courtroom, perspectives and theories were bound to collide. Over time, though, committee members developed a sense of trust and respect for one another. Improper gamesmanship, cynicism, and distrust were replaced by year's end with a refreshing dose of candor and a willingness to listen. At no point in the process was this lesson in group dynamics more evident than in our discussion of jury selection and peremptory challenges.

Many members of the D.C. Jury Project believe that peremptory challenges should be abolished, and an overwhelming majority believe that if not eliminated, they should be drastically reduced.

Several two- or three-hour meetings were devoted to this topic, and the discussions were both enlightened and forthright. After much study, soul-searching, and listening to our juror colleagues, a majority of the Jury Project reached the conclusion that the peremptory challenge is inconsistent with the fundamental precepts of an impartial jury.

In *Batson v. Kentucky* (1986) and subsequent decisions over the past decade, the Supreme Court has affirmed the constitutional principle that peremptory strikes of jurors may not be exercised in our nation's trial

courts to discriminate against jurors based on their race or gender, and that parties are not constitutionally entitled to peremptory strikes. Justice Thurgood Marshall, concurring in the *Batson* decision, forcefully advocated ridding trials of peremptory strikes. "The decision today will not end the racial discrimination that peremptories inject into the jury-selection process," he wrote. "That goal can be accomplished only by eliminating peremptory challenges entirely.... Misuse of the peremptory challenge to exclude black jurors has become both common and flagrant."

Indeed, in the experience of most trial judges on the Jury Project, attorneys in both civil and criminal cases continue to exercise peremptory strikes in a manner that, at a minimum, suggests the appearance that prospective jurors are being peremptorily stricken on the grounds of race, gender, or both. The District of Columbia Court of Appeals, as well as numerous state and federal appellate courts throughout the nation, repeatedly have found that such discrimination routinely occurs.

It is important to note that the use and abuse of peremptory challenges leaves prospective jurors and the public in general with the perception that people are being arbitrarily and discriminatorily denied the opportunity for jury service. Such a perception inevitably undermines confidence in our courts and the administration of justice.

In *The Future of Peremptory Challenges,* the Court Manager 16 (1997), G. Thomas Munsterman, director of the Center for Jury Studies of the National Center for State Courts, writes:

> The peremptory challenge is a curious feature of our jury system. Starting with randomly selected names from broadbased lists, we work hard to assemble a demographically representative panel from which to select a jury. We defend every step of the process used to arrive at that point. Then comes the swift sword of the peremptory challenge, cutting jurors from the panel with nary an explanation.

No one has recently written more thoroughly or compellingly of the need to eliminate peremptory challenges than Judge Morris Hoffman, a state trial judge in Denver, Colorado.

In *Peremptory Challenges Should Be Abolished: A Trial Judge's Perspective,* 64 U. Chi. L. Rev. 809 (1997), Hoffman carefully traces the history of the peremptory challenge and demon-

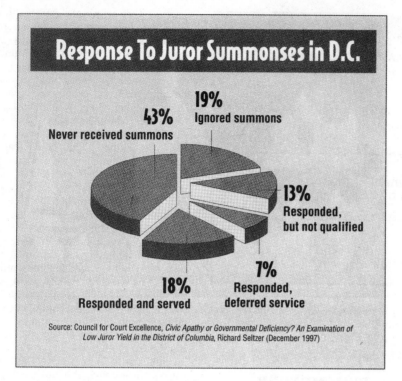

Response To Juror Summonses in D.C.

43%
Never received summons

19%
Ignored summons

13%
Responded,
but not qualified

18%
Responded and served

7%
Responded,
deferred service

Source: Council for Court Excellence, *Civic Apathy or Governmental Deficiency? An Examination of
Low Juror Yield in the District of Columbia*, Richard Seltzer (December 1997)

strates that it is not rooted in principles of fairness, impartiality, or protection of the rights of the accused; rather, it stems from "the now meaningless and quite undemocratic concept of royal infallibility," having been "invented two hundred years before the notion of jury impartiality" was conceived.

He also observes that "the Supreme Court has consistently and unflinchingly held that the peremptory challenge is neither a constitutionally necessary component of a defendant's right to an impartial jury, nor even so fundamental as to be part of federal common law."

Indeed, there was no discussion whatsoever of peremptory challenges in the *Federalist* papers or during the Constitutional Convention, and the Constitution is "utterly silent" on the matter. As Hoffman forcefully demonstrates, efforts to subvert constitutional rights, *not* to defend them, have invigorated and sustained the practice of peremptory challenges as the "last best tool of Jim Crow" in American trials. Such challenges provide "an incredibly efficient final racial filter" to keep African Americans off juries in the South and throughout the United States.

Against this background, Hoffman shows that peremptory challenges have never had a legitimate purpose and have none today. Their genesis in England was to serve as a basis to excuse jurors for *cause*. Peremptory challenges are "decidedly undemocratic,"

are "susceptible to significant abuse by authorities," and are "inherently irrational." There is evidence that, notwithstanding the *Batson* decision and its progeny, they are used "in the same old way" they always have been used, "save for some nominal and meaningless extra hoops now required by *Batson*."

Judge Hoffman concludes, as do many members of the D.C. Jury Project, that the peremptory challenge is inconsistent with fundamental precepts of an impartial jury because (1) it reflects an inappropriate distrust of jurors, causing "perfectly acceptable, perfectly fair and perfectly impartial prospective jurors to be excluded in droves" and to become frustrated and cynical about the justice system; (2) it improperly shifts the focus on jury selection from the individual to the group; and (3) it injects an inappropriate level of adversariness into the jury selection process, tending to result in the selection not of impartial jurors but of jurors who are biased for one side or the other.

The foregoing considerations have persuaded a substantial majority of the D.C. Jury Project that peremptory strikes should be eliminated or drastically reduced in the District of Columbia. The project is also persuaded, however, that if peremptory strikes are eliminated, it is vital to improve the ability to ascertain grounds for strikes of jurors for cause. Relevant information about jurors should be obtained by (1) using a written questionnaire

completed by all jurors and given to the court and parties upon the jury panel's arrival in the courtroom and (2) requiring that each juror be examined at least once during the voir dire process and attorneys be given a meaningful opportunity to ask follow-up questions of all jurors.

The process should be conducted so that no jurors will be called to the bench more than once. Moreover, to assure to the extent possible that prospective jurors who may be biased or partial are in fact stricken for cause, an expanded legal standard governing for-cause strikes should be established. It should mandate that when a prospective juror's demeanor or substantive response to a question during voir dire presents *any* reasonable doubt as to whether the juror can be fair and impartial, the trial judge shall strike the juror for cause at the request of any party, or on the court's own motion.

Throughout the report, the primary theme is that jurors need more institutionalized respect. When jurors arrive in a courtroom, we thank them for coming and remind them of their importance in the trial process. They are, we say with sincerity, the "other judges." Then, in more than a handful of instances, jurors and their needs are promptly forgotten. Our other actions—from the jury selection process throughout deliberations—send quite a different message about how important jurors really are.

No longer treated like judges, jurors are expected to endure a jury selection process that insults their intelligence and infects the entire judicial process with the stench of unfairness. They will likely spend countless hours waiting in the lounge or the jury room, often with no word of when they will be needed. During trial, we ask them to absorb complex and contradictory information, many times without the appropriate tools they need to fully understand and retain such information.

As Stephen Adler wrote in *The Jury*, "To build a better jury system, we need to grant jurors the perquisites of power: reasonable creature comforts, practical training in the nature of their endeavor, and easier access to information about the particulars of the cases before them." Fortunately, many judges in the District of Columbia and around the country have found ways to do this. In searching for ways to enhance the jury service experience and improve the quality of justice, the Jury Project learned from these judges.

For years, jurors have been viewed as passive recipients of often complex information. Recently, however, increasing numbers of judges and attorneys across the nation have recognized the juror education that takes place during trial.

Jurors, like students, need appropriate tools to make informed and rational decisions. We wouldn't send our children to school without pencils and paper. Why should jurors not have basic tools to do their important job? The Jury Project recommends that jurors be allowed to take notes and submit written questions for witnesses, that judges minimize sidebar conferences while the jury is in the room, that the court provide exhibit notebooks and interim summations in extended trials, and that judges offer to assist a jury that reports itself at an impasse.

How to efficiently incorporate these procedures into trials can be a part of every judge's training. What jurors want and need to do their job effectively is for such practices to be uniform throughout the court system. A citizen should have the same treatment no matter whose courtroom he reports to for jury service.

We recognize that receptivity to these recommendations will vary among those who read and ponder their contents. A recommendation may strike one person as unremarkable and a long-accepted custom, while another recommendation may appear radical or unreachable. The prime audience for one recommendation may be a juror administrator or data system designer. In other instances, a recommendation will be most relevant to a newer member of the bench or to a continuing legal education coordinator.

In any event, whether you are a jurist, policymaker, barrister, or citizen, we hope that you will engage yourself in this continuing project. In so doing, we believe, you will experience what we have: an opportunity to revisit important first principles of our jury system, join hands with a broad and talented spectrum of Washingtonians, and seek to make a genuine difference in the administration of justice in our courts. Welcome aboard.

Judge Thomas F. Hogan, of the U.S. District Court for the District of Columbia, and Judge Gregory E. Mize, of the D.C. Superior Court, are cochairs of the D.C. Jury Project. Kathleen Clark is a senior analyst for the D.C. Jury Project and is on the Council for Court Excellence.

JURY NULLIFICATION:
A Perversion of Justice?

Trial reforms may have to be enacted to reverse the trend of defendants being set free despite convincing evidence of guilt.

by Andrew D. Leipold

CONSIDER the following two cases. In the first, a man helps his terminally ill wife commit suicide. The prosecutor brings criminal charges against him, and the case looks strong. The defendant freely admits he prepared the toxic mix of drugs for his wife, knowing it would kill her. He argues, however, that he acted out of mercy, because his wife was suffering from a ter-

Dr. Leipold is associate professor of law, University of Illinois at Urbana-Champaign.

minal illness and no longer wanted to live in pain. The defendant takes the stand in his own defense at trial and, during his testimony, breaks into tears, saying he loved his wife, but saw no way to help her except by hastening her death. The jurors believe the defendant is sincere and, although they agree that he has violated the criminal law, return a verdict of not guilty.

Case two: A group of men are charged with vandalizing a grocery store. It was owned by immigrants, and there is strong

suspicion that the crime was motivated by the ethnic unrest that has been infecting the community. Although there is compelling evidence linking the defendants to the vandalism, they have the good fortune of being tried by a jury that shares their dislike of immigrants. Jury deliberations are brief, and the defendants walk away free.

These two cases are examples of jury nullification, which occurs when the jurors in a criminal case acquit the defendant, despite their belief that he or she was guilty

DEFENDANTS　DEFENDANTS　DEFENDANTS　DEFENDANTS

NOT GUILTY　NOT GUILTY　NOT GUILTY　NOT GUILTY

of the crime charged. In every state and Federal court, a jury has the power to decide that, no matter what the law provides and no matter what the evidence proves, a defendant should not be convicted. As the above examples show, sometimes the nullification decision is based on mercy for the defendant, sometimes on dislike for the victim. Juries also have been known to nullify when the defendant engaged in civil disobedience and the jurors agreed with the actions (an environmentalist interfering with logging efforts, for instance) or wanted to send a wake-up call to the police or prosecutor who used questionable methods to gather evidence.

There has been a lot of discussion about jury nullification lately. When juries acquitted O.J. Simpson (in his criminal trial) and the Los Angeles police officers who beat Rodney King, there were loud and sharp claims in newspapers and coffee shops that these verdicts were based on racial prejudice, class bias, an irrational desire to punish the police, or naivete about police practices, not on the evidence presented. A *Yale Law Journal* article, "Racially Based Jury Nullification: Black Power in the Criminal Justice System," by Paul Butler of George Washington University Law School, has helped fuel the debate. He not only recognizes that juries sometimes *do* make decisions that are not based on the evidence, but argues that African-American juries at times *should* use the nullification power when a black defendant is accused of a non-violent crime. These events and discussions have led some people to brink of

despair about juries: "It seems like guilt or innocence doesn't matter anymore," they think. "Today, trials are about politics and about power; the only thing that matters is who is on the jury."

It would be easy to draw this conclusion from watching the nightly news—easy, but wrong. The truth is that juries rarely acquit against the evidence, at least in serious cases. Most jurors are quite sensible and recognize that, if they acquit a factually guilty defendant, they may be turning a dangerous person loose, perhaps into their own neighborhoods. Juries may be merciful, but they are not stupid. More to the point, most garden-variety street crimes don't raise any issues that might lead a jury to nullify. Most crime is intra-racial, so any ethnic kinship a jury might feel for the defendant is blunted by the greater sympathy for the victim. Most crimes also have no political overtones or present obvious examples of police misconduct or prosecutorial overreaching. Perhaps most importantly, the majority of criminal cases never go before a jury. Most criminal charges end in a guilty plea prior to trial, often as a result of an agreement between the prosecutor and defendant. While it is true that prosecutors sometimes offer an attractive plea bargain because they are worried about what a jury will do (what lawyers euphemistically refer to as the "risks of litigation"), instances of nullification are rare enough that most plea agreements probably don't change much.

While the *instances* of jury nullification are small, the problems created by the *existence* of the nullification doctrine are

very large. In an effort to protect the jury's right to acquit for any reason it wants, courts have created an elaborate series of rules that prevent the public from looking behind a verdict to the jury's reasoning. These rules create far more problems for the administration of the criminal law than jury nullification does, yet get relatively little attention.

Let's go back to the second case mentioned above and assume that the jurors considering the vandalism case really want to convict the thugs who committed the crime. What stands in their way now are not any feelings of mercy or spite, but the trial judge. In any trial, a judge is asked to rule on a series of questions about what evidence should be admitted, questions the lawyers can ask, and legal instructions the jury should get at the end of the case. Assume in the vandalism case the judge gives the jury the wrong instruction, misinterpreting the vandalism statute and telling the jury they must make certain findings the law doesn't really require them to make. The jurors go back to deliberate and, duti-

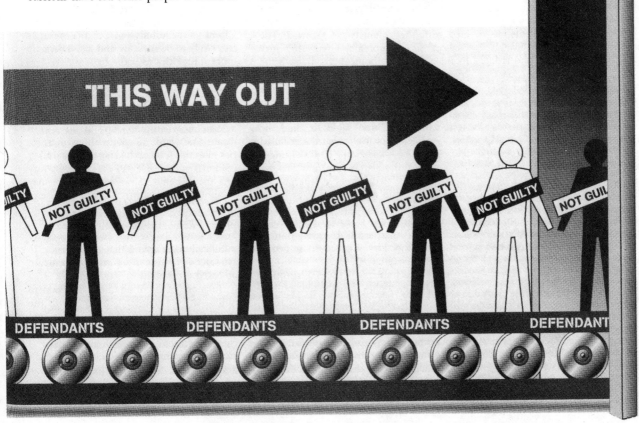

fully following their (faulty) instructions, return a verdict of not guilty.

Most would agree that this was a "bad" verdict—if the jury were given the proper instructions, they probably would have convicted, but because of the error, they let otherwise guilty people go free. This sounds like a perfect case for an appeal, except for one thing: the prosecutor absolutely is barred from asking a higher court to review the jury instructions. Because of the double jeopardy clause of the Constitution ("nor shall any person be subject for the same offense to be twice put in jeopardy of life or limb"), once a jury has returned a verdict of not guilty, the prosecutor is prohibited from bringing the defendant to trial a second time or even asking the court of appeals to consider the errors that were made at trial.

What does this have to do with jury nullification? Simple: I think that the main reason we bar prosecutors from making an appeal from an acquittal is to protect the jury's power to nullify. We are so anxious to preserve the jury's discretion to nullify in the occasional case that we put up with other, probably more numerous, acquittals that are the product of bad legal rulings at trial. *This,* I would argue, is the real cost of jury nullification—not the convictions that are lost when the jury deliberately acquits against the evidence, but those lost when the jury wants to convict, but erroneously is prevented by the trial court from doing so.

This conclusion—that the ban on government appeals is attributable to our desire to protect the nullification power—seems surprising (and a bit suspicious), because we normally think of the double jeopardy clause as a protection for defendants, to prevent them from being dragged through a trial twice, with all the expense and risk associated with it. While this might make sense as a plain reading of the double jeopardy clause, the Supreme Court never has taken the provision quite that literally. In fact, we allow a prosecutor to put a defendant through more than one trial in all kinds of cases: when the defendant successfully has appealed from a conviction, the government usually can bring him or her to trial a second time; when the first trial results in a hung jury, the prosecution usually can try a defendant again; and when the trial judge declares a mistrial at the defendant's request, he or she usually can be tried a second time (unless the government was trying to provoke a mistrial). Even when the defendant is acquitted by a jury in state court, there is no double jeopardy bar to a second trial in Federal court under the "dual sovereignty doctrine." (Recall that the officers in the Rodney King case were acquitted first in state court, then later convicted on Federal charges.)

Despite these exceptions to the double jeopardy clause, the Supreme Court has re-

mained steadfast in its view that a jury acquittal prevents the government from appealing, even to correct pure legal errors like bad jury instructions. When all the explanations for the rule are picked apart and held up to the light, the best explanation is this: We don't allow the government to appeal from an acquittal, no matter how serious the legal errors made at trial, because *maybe,* just maybe, the jurors decided to exercise their power of nullification. If the jury nullified, it would make no sense to allow a government appeal, because the evidence and the legal instructions were irrelevant; the jury decided to acquit for reasons unrelated to the cold legal requirements of guilt. Since juries never explain their verdicts in the courtroom (they just announce "guilty" or "not guilty"), we never really can be sure when one is based on mercy rather than bad legal rulings.

All of this would make great sense if the Constitution gave juries the right to nullify or even if the nullification power were an idea so good that we were willing to put up with the type of "bad" acquittal described above. I believe nullification fails on both fronts: the power is not protected by the Constitution nor does it bring enough social benefits to make the current protected status worth the costs.

The right that isn't

The notion that juries can acquit a defendant for any reason at all is older than our nation. By the late 17th century, English judges had decided that jurors must be left to their own devices and consciences when rendering verdicts, and the idea traveled with the colonists to America. The concept of a supremely powerful jury found a welcome home here. It gave the colonists the power to convict those who misbehaved, while still nullifying the charges against those who broke what many colonists felt were oppressive laws. At the time, the jury's right to "find the law"—to decide for itself what the criminal law should be—was quite logical. Judges often were untrained in the law, making them no better than jurors at interpreting and applying the often-complex common law. As a result, there was a great deal of writing in the decades around the Revolutionary War that seemed to support a "right" of the jury to acquit someone against the evidence.

Yet, if the framers of the Constitution and the Bill of Rights thought that nullification was an important part of the right to trial by jury, they were awfully quiet about it. There is very little in the debates surrounding the drafting or ratification to suggest that they even thought about the issue, much less intended to incorporate it in the Constitution. While the Supreme Court, in construing the constitutional

right to a jury, has been curiously closed-mouthed about the topic, the one time the Court spoke clearly, it decisively stated that a jury's *power* to nullify does not mean that a defendant has the *right* to be tried before a jury with that power. In the 1895 decision of *Sparf and Hansen v. United States,* the Court laid the groundwork for the rule that still prevails in most of the country—judges are not required to tell juries that they have the power to acquit against the evidence nor are they required to let lawyers argue to the jury in favor of nullification. The message is clear—even if courts can't stop juries from nullifying, they are under no legal obligation to help juries exercise the power.

Just because something is not protected constitutionally does not make it a bad idea. In many cases, I think that jury nullification is an excellent concept. If I were on the jury of the man accused of helping his wife commit suicide and I believed he did it out of love for the victim, I would vote to acquit in a heartbeat. Prosecutors are not infallible. At times, they make bad judgments; occasionally, they are mean-spirited; and sometimes, they get so used to the unending stream of bad people and violent acts they miss the human and moral dimension of actions that normally are crimes. So, even if I had the power to prevent all juries from acquitting against the evidence, I probably would not use it.

Nevertheless, jury nullification is a dangerous power, and when any power is left in the hands of an unaccountable group, there is cause for worry. The biggest concern, mentioned above, is that procedural rules now in place—like prohibiting the appeal of acquittals—make jury verdicts less likely to be accurate and fair. There are other difficulties as well:

First, we don't know how the power is used. Because juries almost never explain their verdicts, it is impossible to say how often nullification occurs. Our inability to determine when and why it does also means that we do not know how often juries use this power for good ends rather than evil ones. For every case where a jury acts morally and shows mercy, there may be another where a jury acquits because of hatred toward the victim or favoritism to the defendant. It takes strong faith in human nature to support a doctrine like jury nullification, knowing that the decision to set someone free can be made on a whim or based on prejudice.

In most cases, of course, a decision to nullify will be neither good nor evil; the morality and wisdom of the decision will depend on our individual views. Some will cheer when an abortion clinic protester is acquitted against the evidence, others will despair; some will think justice is done when a man who assaulted a homosexual couple is convicted only of the lowest possible charge (another form of nullification), others will see it as a hateful sign of the times; and many will be shocked when an accused rapist or wife beater is set free because the jury believed that the victim was asking for it. What we think doesn't matter, though. If we want juries with the unreviewable power to acquit when the charges are unfair, we must accept juries that have the power to make decisions others find distasteful and stupid.

Second, juries often don't have enough evidence to make a reasoned nullification decision. Even if we take a kinder view toward juries, there still are reasons to be troubled by the breadth of their discretion. If a jury is to make a reasoned nullification decision, there is certain information it needs to have. Let's say a jury has before it a simple drug possession case by a college-bound high school senior. The evidence looks strong, but the thought of ruining a promising future troubles the jurors. The young man had only a small amount of drugs, looks remorseful, and has a supportive family with him in court. Rather than send another teenager to jail, the jury decides to nullify.

If the jury's perception were accurate, perhaps it made the right call. The problem is what a jury sees might not be the full story. The jurors might not learn that the defendant has had scrapes with the law before, that he is a troublemaker at home and at school, and that, in fact, the police found a load of drugs in the car, which were not introduced at trial because the car was searched illegally. If the jury had known these things, its feelings of mercy quickly might have evaporated. However, there usually will be no evidence introduced of these other facts because they are irrelevant to the technical question of guilt or innocence. Stated differently, because the jury has no right to nullify, evidence that might inform the exercise of that power usually is not admitted at trial, nor are defense lawyers usually permitted to make overt appeals to the nullification power. Juries therefore make the nullification decision in the dark, letting some go free who are not worthy of mercy and convicting some who might be more deserving of it.

Third, encouraging nullification encourages lawlessness. The urge to nullify may tug at our hearts because it is so easy to imagine cases where we would do so ourselves if we were jurors. Consider a woman who is walking alone when she is surrounded by a gang of thugs. The terrified woman brandishes a gun and the gangsters flee, but as they do, she shoots one, causing great bodily harm. In many states, the woman could be prosecuted for assault with a deadly weapon because once the thugs turned and ran, she no longer had the right to use deadly force in self-defense. Yet, many of us would not be troubled with

such legal niceties and would cheerfully acquit if given the chance.

In more reflective moments, though, we should wonder why we let a jury make this decision. We have an elected legislature to pass laws and elected or appointed judges to interpret them. The wisdom of the people's representatives has been that when a person no longer is in danger, he or she may not use force in self-defense. That decision may be right or wrong, but it was arrived at through a legitimate, representative process. Why, then, should the jury be able to ignore that mandate because they sympathize with the woman and detest thugs? The jury is unelected, unaccountable, and has no obligation to think through the effect an acquittal will have on others. Perhaps it will be that thugs will accost fewer women; perhaps the effect will be to blur the line further between legitimate self-defense and vigilantism.

Reasonable people can disagree on the proper reach of the criminal laws. Nevertheless, the place for them to disagree is in public, where the reasons for expansions and contractions of the laws can be scrutinized and debated by those who will be affected by the verdicts juries reach. It is enough that we ask juries to decide whether the defendant before them is guilty of the crime charged. To expect them to make a reasoned decision on the wisdom of the law itself, with virtually none of the information that normally would be required in making such a decision, calls for more wisdom from most juries than fairly can be expected.

A possible solution

There is a way to retain the best features of jury nullification while avoiding some of the problems. If we really want to allow juries to acquit someone against the evidence, we should pass a law making nullification an affirmative defense, much like we do for self-defense, duress, and necessity. (The nullification probably would be classified as an "excuse" rather than a "justification," but in either case, it would serve as a defense to the crime charged.) The statute could be drafted in any way that we wished. It could be a defense, for example, if the defendant reasonably believed that his or her actions were for the benefit of the victim (the mercy killing case), if the harm caused by the defendant's actions were so slight as not to justify punishment (a case of simple marijuana possession for the college-bound high school student), or if the jury believed the defendant already has suffered enough and further punishment would be excessive (a father prosecuted for manslaughter because he failed to strap his child in a car safety seat). A jury would not be required to accept the defense in any of these cases, but, by allowing a defendant to raise an affirmative defense, the

statute would permit the attorneys to submit evidence on the question and the jury to make a more informed decision.

Making nullification an affirmative defense would have two other benefits. First, it would allow judges to make more explicit to the jury that, when the evidence points to guilt, they have the *duty* to convict unless there is a defense. This might help avoid some of the abuses of nullification like that described in case number two above. Second, the focus on nullification might allow some clever lawyer to argue to the Supreme Court that government appeals of acquittals should not be barred by the double jeopardy clause. If I am right that the ban on appeals is explained best by the desire to protect the nullification power and if the power to nullify is not protected by the Constitution—there is little in the historical record to support it—then the government should be able to argue to a court of appeals that the acquittal was based on bad evidence rulings, bad jury instructions, improper defense tactics, or any other legal ground.

I suspect that neither of these things will happen. The rule against appealing from an acquittal is ingrained deeply in constitutional law, and no argument by an academic is likely to change that. Nor do I think there is any danger that states will rush to pass nullification statutes. Broadening the rights of a criminal defendant is not exactly in vogue among politicians, and creating any additional defenses, especially one as open-ended as a nullification defense, would be wildly unpopular with the law- and-order crowd. On the other hand, there are groups, like the Fully Informed Jury Association, that for the last several years have been promoting aggressively the idea of nullification in the legislatures, at shopping malls, and in front of courthouses where potential jurors walk. They argue, at times quite persuasively, that dispersing the criminal justice power into the hands of juries is one way to keep government in check and to ensure that, if bad laws or bad prosecution decisions are made, there will be a backstop that will prevent unjust convictions. As long as we have even modest amounts of mistrust about governments, such efforts will strike a responsive cord.

Whether anything changes or not, jury nullification remains a fascinating and important topic because juries are one of the few institutions that make critically important decisions, yet are almost entirely unaccountable. Understanding how and when they decide to free a person who they believe committed a crime tells us something about how we feel about our laws, prosecutors, police, and the entire justice system. Punishing the guilty and protecting the innocent are among the highest duties of government. Deciding who is to be punished—and who should not—is at the core of those duties. Anything that helps accomplish that task better is worthy of consideration.

Confronting the BREAKDOWN OF LAW AND ORDER

The courts and psychiatry have bent over backwards in their interpretations of sanity and responsibility, thus perverting the idea of justice.

by Bruce Wiseman

DURING THE 1995 New Mexico legislative session, State Sen. Duncan Scott proposed an amendment to a bill stating: "When a psychologist or psychiatrist testifies during a defendant's competency hearing, the psychologist or psychiatrist shall wear a cone-shaped hat that is not less than 2 feet tall. The surface of the hat shall be imprinted with stars and lightning bolts. . . ."

While the New Mexico State Senate was voting in favor of the "Wizard's hat" amendment, a Florida columnist proposed another solution. He recommended that the confusion created by psychiatric "experts" be reduced by placing a red light and a digital display above the witness stand indicating the price paid for the testimony.

The New Mexico bill was not signed into law, and digital displays and red lights have not been installed. Both solutions might have reminded judges and juries of the actual value of "expert" psychiatric and psychological testimony.

Justice is based on the concept that each man is responsible for what he does and accountable for his actions. However, psychiatry has pushed society to a state of chaos wherein no one is responsible for anything. A wife can mutilate her husband; children can kill their parents; and a man can shoot the President—yet, psychiatrists claim the perpetrators are themselves the victims, and therefore not guilty. Psychiatric testimony often serves to occlude the fact that a crime has been committed, prolong litigation, and drive the cost of justice even higher.

Psychiatrists' inability to assess and predict human behavior is a well-documented fact. In one typical study, two "skilled psychiatrists" each chose six of 20 patients as being depressed—but they were not the *same* six.

Psychiatric testimony is valueless in adjudicating criminal intent. In 1988, psychologist Jay Ziskin indicated: "Studies show that professional clinicians do not in fact make more accurate clinical judgments than lay persons." Defense attorneys are aware of this and have been known to "shop around" for a psychiatric report that will serve their purposes. Hence, the red light to expose the nature of the witness and the digital display to advise the jury at what price the criminal's "illness" was manufactured.

"What amazes me is that, in any trial I've ever heard of, the defense psychiatrist always says the accused is insane, and the prosecuting psychiatrist always says he's sane," Jeffery Harris, executive director of the Attorney General's Task Force on Violent Crime, points out. "This happened invariably, in 100% of the cases, thus far exceeding the laws of chance. You have to ask yourself, 'What is going on here?' "

Even when courts do not accept the psychobabble, its introduction into the legal process has come close to destroying Americans' faith in justice. Examples include the "Twinkie" defense, blaming the sugar in the snack cake for driving the accused to crime, and the murder trial in which a psychiatrist testified that a man murdered his wife because of the movie (which made its debut one month after the crime), "Crocodile Dundee."

Psychiatrists even have given Americans another reason to stay indoors during the winter's cold. According to psychiatrist Marc Sageman, murders committed during cold weather are not a crime. In 1995, he testified that Joseph Harris killed his ex-supervisor, her boyfriend, and two former coworkers because he "hated the onset of winter."

The justice system has been subverted so thoroughly that gross injustices such as in the New York trial of April Dell'Olio are common. Dell'Olio was acquitted of murder by reason of insanity and, because two psychiatrists testified she did not pose a danger to society, was released with no incarceration whatsoever. Presiding Judge Kevin Dowd said the insanity defense laws forced him to treat the killing "with the psychiatric equivalent that April had a 'bad hair day' on Oct. 20, 1992."

These two psychiatrists provided "expert" testimony on a matter they knew themselves unqualified to adjudicate. In 1979, an American Psychiatric Association

Mr. Wiseman, national president, Citizens Commission on Human Rights, Los Angeles, Calif., is the author of Psychiatry—The Ultimate Betrayal.

task force admitted to the U.S. Supreme Court that "psychiatric expertise in the prediction of 'dangerousness' is not established and clinicians should avoid 'conclusionary judgments in this regard.' "

The Supreme Court concurred, stating that "professional literature uniformly established that such predictions are fundamentally of very low reliability, and that psychiatric testimony and expertise are irrelevant to such predictions. In view of these findings, psychiatric testimony on the issue of future criminal behavior only distorts the fact finding process."

It was not always this way. Once, there was no set definition of insanity, and the courts had difficulty in determining who was or was not conscious of what they were doing.

That changed in 1843, when Daniel M'-Naughten shot the British Prime Minister's secretary and was acquitted on the grounds of insanity. Fearing the ruling would establish a precedent making it easier to excuse criminal behavior, the English Parliament passed a measure known as the "right-wrong" test. As this legislation contained the words "at the time of committing the act," it opened the door to the "temporary insanity" plea.

This concept reached the U.S. in 1859. Congressman Daniel Sickles shot and killed Phillip Barton Key, the U.S. Attorney for the District of Columbia, over an affair he had been having with Sickles' wife. Sickles was acquitted, becoming the first American beneficiary of the temporary insanity plea.

In 1929, the Court of Appeals for the District of Columbia adopted the "irresistible impulse" rule. Such an impulse could "override the reason and judgment and obliterate the sense of right and wrong." The British Royal Commission on Capital Punishment expanded this defense in 1953 to excuse a criminal who systematically planned out a crime, stating that "The criminal act may be the reverse of impulsive. It may be coolly and carefully prepared; yet it is still the act of a madman." The insanity, it said, lay in "psychosis due to disease of the brain."

Almost half a century and billions of research dollars later, psychiatry still hopes to prove one day that this "disease" has a biological or organic cause. Even if its comparison to a medical illness were supported by scientific research, the theory remains flawed. While cancer and other medical conditions may cause tremendous pain and mental anguish, they are not used as a justification for murder.

Despite the faulty logic, the U.S. Court of Appeals in Washington, D.C., adopted this standard in 1954. Judge David Bazelon ruled that an accused is blameless if the crime was "the product of a mental disease or mental defect." This became known as the "Durham Rule."

Abe Fortas, the court-appointed defense attorney in *Durham v. United States,* assessed the impact of the decision: "What then is the basic significance of the Durham case? It is, I suggest, that the law has recognized modern psychiatry. . . . Its importance is that it is a charter, a bill of rights, for psychiatry and an offer of limited partnership between criminal law and psychiatry." Psychiatry had arrived.

The two key parties to the Durham Rule had direct tie-ins with psychiatry. Bazelon was undergoing psychiatric treatment. Fortas, who later became an associate justice on the Supreme Court, served on the Board of Trustees at the William Alanson White Psychiatric Foundation.

With psychiatric testimony such an obvious impediment to the legal process, one may ask how it insinuated itself into the courts. Human nature plays a role. Who among us has not committed an act of which we are not proud—and who among us has not wished the blame lay elsewhere?

Through manipulation of this human trait, psychiatrists were able to foster agreement with their explanations for criminal behavior and forward their goal of psychiatric imperialism. This goal was expressed by court psychiatrist Erwin Stransky in a 1918 issue of *The General Magazine for Psychiatry:*

"Therefore the forensic activity of the psychiatrist can become a good part of applied psychiatry . . . by helping diplomatically to restrain and to dominate the human mind in the sense of race hygiene and protection of the society. . . .

"[The psychiatrist] will continuously educate judges, plaintiffs and defenders to such a degree, that actually he becomes gently and slowly, the leading element of the trial; then he will fill charges, defense and verdict, with his ideas, having the outstanding high goal in mind, to direct all and everything into the port of the higher manbreeding where the medico is the safest pilot. In this way the psychiatrist in the courtroom can fulfill a great deal of his mission as educator of man, if he only wants to, 'wants' in the sense of medical imperialism which is the imperialism of culture. . . ."

Stransky's views on medical imperialism and racial hygiene are of the same doctrine the Nazis used to justify the Holocaust. Under it, the Jewish people were guilty of the "crime" of birth.

Stransky's goals were reinforced and expanded in an address by psychiatrist J.R. Rees to the annual meeting of the National Council for Mental Hygiene on June 18, 1940. Rees, who later became co-founder of the World Federation of Mental Health (WFMH), stated that psychiatry had made "a useful attack on a number of professions. The two easiest of them naturally are the teaching profession and the

Church; the two most difficult are law and medicine.

"If we are to infiltrate the professional and social activities of other people, I think we must imitate the Totalitarians and organize some kind of fifth column activity!" This required a "long-term plan of propaganda" in which psychiatrists had "better be secretive."

When G. Brock Chisholm—Rees' partner in founding the WFMH—delivered a 1946 speech at the William Alanson White Psychiatric Foundation, he revealed that the destruction of morality was no accident. "The reinterpretation and eventually eradication of the concept of right and wrong," Chisholm said, are the key objectives "of practically all effective psychotherapy."

Insight also was provided as to why psychiatrists are willing to prostitute themselves in court and why a judge undergoing psychiatric treatment would rule that criminals should be excused of their crimes. Psychiatrists and psychologists, Chisholm stated, "have escaped these moral chains" and "patients they have treated successfully have done the same."

The appeal of "insanity" and "diminished capacity" defenses once was limited by the fact that, while the criminal could escape prison, he risked indefinite incarceration in a state mental hospital. This changed when psychiatric lobbyists pressed Congress to pass the Community Mental Health Centers Act in 1963.

Following passage, it became the practice to send patients home with their "medications," and the insanity defense became very attractive indeed. One study of 55 murderers found not guilty by reason of insanity and placed in mental institutions between 1965 and 1976 revealed that the average time served in the hospital was 500 days.

As for the killers psychiatry sees fit to unleash upon society, many go on and kill again. Edward Kemper was discharged from a California state hospital five years after murdering his grandparents. He then killed and decapitated two women and a 15-year-old girl. Shortly afterward, two court psychiatrists testified that there was no "reason to consider him to be of any danger to himself or any other member of society." In the following two months, Kemper brutally murdered five more women.

Psychiatry's contribution to the breakdown of law and order is not limited to the courts. It is the driving force behind the destruction of personal responsibility in all sectors of society. As such, it is eroding the very fabric of civilization.

When psychiatry invaded American schools in the early 1960s, academics took a back seat to psychiatric goals. Scholastic Achievement Test scores plummeted, and high schools now graduate students who can not read. As Chisholm projected, children are taught that right and wrong are "value judgments" secondary to what makes them feel good. School officials, who once disciplined children for running in the halls, hired uniformed police and installed metal detectors.

The drug culture's role in crime is well-known; less so is the role psychiatry played in its creation. Psychologists and psychiatrists spoke of the "great importance" of mescaline and peyote. LSD later was developed for psychiatric use, and the late Harvard psychologist, Timothy Leary, is known best for persuading the nation's young to "turn on, tune in, and drop out" on LSD.

Major tranquilizers such as Thorazine began to appear in the 1950s and were heralded by psychiatrists as "miracle drugs." In the 1960s, minor tranquilizers such as Valium and Librium were promoted as psychiatry's "solution" for stress. Anti-depressants were touted as the cure for the blues, and medicine chests swelled.

In essence, psychiatry made it acceptable to escape one's problems with a drug. By the time these substances reached the public along with marijuana, cocaine, and the other "street" drugs, the stage had been set. Why should children say no to drugs? After all, their parents took them. The only difference was the pusher.

The names of the drugs have changed, but psychiatry's role as the pusher has not. News of some new psychiatric "miracle drug" or a new use for an old one is a media favorite. School children are forced to take psychiatric drugs for "illnesses" such as "Disorder of Written Expression," "Mathematics Disorder," and "Unspecified Learning Disorder." No longer is the message that mind-altering drugs are unacceptable—they are necessary.

"Psychiatrists will testify as long as attorneys will pay, and attorneys will pay as long as psychiatrists prostitute themselves."

These "learning disorders" are listed along with 371 additional reasons why the individual can not be responsible in the *American Psychiatric Association's Diagnostic and Statistical Manual for Mental Disorders* (DSM). According to psychiatrist Al Parides, the DSM is "a masterpiece of political maneuvering" that attempts to "medicalize many problems that don't have demonstrable, biological causes." Majority vote—not scientific proof—is the only requisite for inclusion.

Every human emotion and activity—criminal or not—is classified as a reason for psychiatric care. Criminal "disorders" include "Pyromania Disorder," "Kleptomania Disorder," and "Pedophilia Disorder." Life "disorders" include "Oppositional De-fiance Disorder," "Attention Deficit Hyperactivity Disorder," "Obsessive Compulsive Disorder," and "Unspecified Mental Disorder." There even are psychiatric labels for those who drink too much coffee, eat junk food, or are happy.

As these "disorders" are promoted, more and more Americans become convinced they are but "victims" of a "mental illness." They now have an alibi for any shortcomings in life, and it is difficult to bring them back into the fold of personal accountability.

It is as professor of psychiatry emeritus Thomas Szasz warned: "We have to restore the idea of responsibility, which is corrupted and confused by psychiatry, by the idea that something happened to you when you were a child and therefore you are not responsible 30 years later."

While psychiatry masquerades as a science, it is an ideology that does not have society's best interests at heart. Some legislation and court rulings have sought to limit the insanity defense, but these measures are not enough. Psychiatrists will testify as long as attorneys will pay, and attorneys will pay as long as psychiatrists prostitute themselves.

What is painfully clear is that psychiatry and its kindred "sciences" must be thrown out of every sector of the courts and society. Contrary to psychiatric ideology, man is not just another helpless creature, without will or conscience, to be manipulated according to someone else's design. Underneath whatever confusions he may have, he knows he has the courage to confront and solve his problems, as well as the ability to discern between what is right and what is wrong. Underneath it all, he knows that the ultimate betrayal is to try to persuade him otherwise.

MORAL JUDGMENT

A Little Learning

*When judges allow 'experts' to exhibit
their private theories in court,
justice is the victim.*

JAMES Q. WILSON

IN 1976 Beverly Ibn-Tamas shot and killed her husband, Yusef, in his medical office in Washington, D.C. She was convicted of second-degree murder and sentenced to spend one to five years in prison. Beverly testified that she had been subjected to repeated beatings and threats during her four-year marriage to Yusef. Other witnesses, including Yusef's first wife, also testified to his violent behavior. Events on the day of the shooting were disputed, but what is clear is that Beverly shot Yusef twice, once from close range. Obviously, however, the jury did not think the crime was premeditated (hence second rather than first degree), and the judge found her a sympathetic defendant (hence the short sentence). Beverly's lawyers appealed, however, claiming that the court had improperly excluded the testimony of Dr. Lenore Walker, a psychologist who described a condition called battered-woman syndrome, and who had frequently served as an expert witness.

A divided appeals court told the trial court to hold an evidentiary hearing on the issue of admitting Dr. Walker's testimony. It did and concluded that Dr. Walker had not established that her methodology was generally accepted by experts in the field. The conviction was upheld. Beverly served one year in prison.

When expert witnesses offer to testify, the judge must rule on the admissibility of their testimony. In doing so, he must answer, among others, these questions: Is the testimony based on facts that are "beyond the ken of the average layman"? Does the expert have sufficient skill and knowledge in this field to make the testimony valuable to the jury? Will the testimony unduly prejudice the jury? The appeals court said that Dr. Walker's testimony might have "enhanced Mrs. Ibn-Tamas's general credibility" and "supported her testimony" that her husband's behavior had led her to believe she was in imminent danger." The court compared Beverly to Patty Hearst, who had argued three years earlier in her trial for bank robbery that expert testimony would "explain the effects kid-napping, prolonged incarceration, and psychological and physical abuse may have had on the defendant's mental state at the time of the robbery."

Just what could expert testimony have said about this "mental state" that "the average layman" could otherwise not know? The appeals court did not really answer that question, and based on what one can learn from Beverly Ibn-Tamas's trial, the answer in her case seems to be—nothing at all.

A few years later, however, the New Jersey Supreme Court undertook to give an answer in reviewing the case of Gladys Kelly, who had been convicted of reckless manslaughter and sentenced to five years in prison for having stabbed her husband to death with a pair of scissors. Gladys claimed that during their seven-year marriage her husband, Ernest, had abused her. Though some of her claims were disputed, let us assume they were true. On the fatal day they had a fight on the street that began with an argument over money. Ernest pushed Gladys to the ground, but two bystanders separated them. Gladys went off to find her daughter and returned with a pair of scissors. At this point the facts are unclear. The defense claimed that Ernest rushed at Gladys with his hands raised and that she, fearing for her safety, stabbed him. The prosecution claimed that Gladys started the fight, chased Ernest after threatening to kill him, and then stabbed him. The state Supreme Court reversed the conviction because expert testimony by Dr. Lois Veronen about battered-woman syndrome had been excluded.

In reaching this decision, the court drew heavily on amicus briefs filed by the American Civil Liberties Union, the New Jersey Coalition for Battered Women, and the American Psy-

Mr. Wilson is James Collins Professor of Management and Public Policy at UCLA and the author of Moral Judgment, published by Basic Books, a division of HarperCollins Publishers, Inc.

From *National Review*, June 2, 1997, pp. 37-39. Adapted from *Moral Judgment* by James Q. Wilson. © 1997 by James Q. Wilson. Reprinted by permission of BasicBooks, a division of HarperCollins Publishers, Inc.

chological Association. It discussed the lamentable extent of wife abuse in the United States, complained of the bias against women in the law-enforcement agencies charged with investigating abuse cases, and reviewed the theory of battered-woman syndrome. As interesting as these observations were, they did not address the central issue: whether expert testimony would have aided the jury in reaching its verdict. Since the jury had refused to convict Gladys of murder (instead agreeing on a verdict of reckless manslaughter), it had already accepted a mitigation, no doubt one arising out of her history and circumstances. And since the judge had sentenced her to the minimum term, he also must have understood that there were mitigating factors. The expert testimony, then, had to be designed to aid the jury in deciding that this was justifiable homicide—a case of self-defense.

But what could Dr. Veronen have contributed to that issue? Not that Gladys's fear of being killed by Ernest was reasonable (traditionally a requirement in pleading self-defense); all the facts bearing on that—and they were disputed facts—were already available to the jury. The Supreme Court conceded that. The value it found in the proffered testimony was that it would help dispel two "myths": the first being the "popular misconception" that battered women are "masochistic and actually enjoy their beatings, that they purposely provoke their husbands into violent behavior"; the second, that "women who remain in battering relationships are free to leave their abusers at any time."

As evidence for the first of these myths, the court cited a book by Dr. Walker. But in fact there is no evidence in Dr. Walker's book that the public believes battered women are masochists who enjoy provoking their husbands. Subsequent research has failed to find such evidence.

The second so-called myth raises a serious question that is not easily answered. No doubt many people, hearing of the abuse a woman has endured, ask themselves why she doesn't simply leave. The explanation advanced by Dr. Walker and others is that battered women suffer from "learned helplessness." The phrase was coined by Professor Martin Seligman, a psychologist at the University of Pennsylvania, after studying the behavior of dogs who were confined in harnesses in such a way that they could not escape painful electrical shocks. They soon ceased to struggle, and when presented with a way out they chose not to take it. When the experiment was over, they had to be dragged from their cages. The dogs had lost their will to control their environment. Professor Seligman later described depression in humans as learned helplessness. Dr. Walker asserts that women who have experienced the battering cycle—an increase in marital tension, then a physical attack, followed by a period of loving contrition—become helpless in much the same way as do shocked dogs. They believe they can neither control their environment nor predict the effects of their own behavior. Poverty, concern for their children, and the indifference of police and social-welfare agencies may reinforce this sense of helplessness.

No doubt some battered women (and some women who have never been battered) display these symptoms. But the evidence supporting the view that most battered women feel helpless is sketchy. Mary Ann Dutton, a psychologist deeply sympathetic to the plight of battered women, has written that women exposed to violence and abuse "do not respond similarly" because there is no "singular 'battered-woman profile.' " Some feel psychologically trapped and try to stick it out, others solicit help from friends or call the police; still others resist and fight back. Some go to shelters, some do not. Many of these coping strategies turn out to be ineffective; but, by choosing them, abused women do reveal themselves not to be as passive as shocked dogs in a cage. Some evidence suggests that it is precisely the most severely abused women who are most likely to leave their husbands. We do not yet have good ways of predicting who will leave a relationship and who will remain helplessly trapped within it.

Moreover, killing one's abuser seems quite inconsistent with the theory of learned helplessness. Dr. Seligman's helpless dogs did not bite their abusers, but Dr. Walker's helpless women killed theirs. Dr. Walker's own evidence seems to contradict her conclusions. A helpless woman should feel that her life is governed by external forces rather than by her own choices, but the battered women Dr. Walker studied displayed an internal, not external, locus of control. People who believe that they, and not external forces, govern their lives cannot plausibly be called helpless, especially when in some cases—the women who kill their husbands—they act on that belief.

None of these issues have prevented appellate courts from accepting the view that there is a phenomenon called battered-woman syndrome about which expert testimony will have significant probative value.

THE position that so many judges and legislators have taken is scientifically suspect, philosophically debatable, and legally unnecessary. The science is suspect for a variety of reasons [see "Trial by Expert," *NR,* March 10]; indeed, the problems with bringing social science into the courtrooms are perfectly illustrated by battered-woman syndrome. We do not know what proportion of battered women develop a syndrome (and how many develop the syndrome without being battered), and the evidence for the existence of a syndrome was mostly elicited by interviewers who were predisposed to find it. The American Psychiatric Association has declined to include the syndrome in its *Diagnostic and Statistical Manual (DSM-IV)* despite intense lobbying by its supporters. Dr. Walker herself is an advocate, who displays a tendency to find a "syndrome" where the facts do not support it. When she discovered that many of her women did not display feelings of helplessness and did not have low self-esteem, she expressed surprise and went on to dispute or discount the women's own accounts. She explained that in "reality" these women have no control over their lives, whatever they might say to the contrary; in fact, their denial of helplessness reflects their desire to "gain approval" from Dr. Walker. By 1989, five years after she expressed her surprise at the poor fit between her hypothesis and the data, she had overcome whatever reservations the data had occasioned and now wrote confidently that the "typical battered woman has poor self-image and self-esteem."

Philosophically, it is hard to see why a jury should consider such a syndrome to be an excusing condition if some women (and for all we know, most women) who are battered and who kill their abusers do not suffer from the syndrome. Syndrome sufferers would have the benefit of expert witnesses testifying on their behalf, while equally abused but non-syndrome women would not. Describing a battered woman as some courts have done—as dependent, brainwashed, terror-stricken, or psychologically paralyzed—reproduces rather than eliminates the very stereotypes to which most of us object. Anne Coughlin states it well: the battered-woman claim, designed "ostensibly to refute a variety of misogynist stereotypes," requires accused women "to embrace precisely those insulting stereotypes that the defense was supposed to explode, and it endorses the assumption that women are incapable of the rational self-governance exercised by men." The syndrome defense is, by definition, not available to a woman with a sturdily independent cast of mind and a record of making her own decisions and managing her own affairs. If she kills an abusive mate, she is on her own in claiming self-defense; it is only the passive weak-willed woman who can use the syndrome to bolster her self-defense claim.

A jury that is free to acquit a guilty but likable defendant is also free to convict an innocent but detestable one.

Legally, the syndrome may add something to the traditional claim of self-defense, but that something is ill-defined. It is a mistake to say that the old law of self-defense was inherently masculine. As Professor Susan Estrich has pointed out, the rules of self-defense "exist not so much to define manly behavior as to limit manly instincts—in order to preserve human life." It might be manly, she observes, to respond to an insult with deadly force, but it is illegal because the law requires that there be imminent danger of death or grave bodily injury.

It would be difficult to cite or imagine a criminal defense that was applicable solely to a female defendant. Ordinary fair play, to say nothing of the equal-protection clause of the Constitution, suggests that a defense available to one sex be available to both. In February 1989 Paul Kacsmar killed his brother, Francis. At his trial he claimed he acted in self-defense. Paul, a man in his forties, lived with his mother and brother in Pittsburgh. Paul was ill (he had suffered a stroke) and a somewhat wimpy fellow; Francis was a combat veteran who liked to practice judo. They did not get along. Francis thought of himself as the head of the house; Paul resented his claims. There were many arguments over the years and a few fights. Most of the fights involved pushing and shoving, but sometimes punches were thrown, usually by Francis. Paul denied ever being the aggressor and claimed that Francis sometimes threatened to "beat the hell out of him." On the night of the shooting,

Francis accused Paul of not doing his share of the housework. The argument escalated, and Francis hit Paul a few times with his fist. After Paul broke free, he ran to his room, picked up a gun, came back downstairs, and without warning shot the unarmed Francis five times.

Paul was convicted of voluntary manslaughter and sentenced to five to ten years in prison. On appeal, a Pennsylvania superior court reversed his conviction on the grounds that the trial judge had not admitted expert testimony that Paul suffered from "battered-person syndrome." The court reasoned that if a woman could suffer from battered-woman syndrome, a man could suffer from battered-person syndrome. The Pennsylvania court repeated the erroneous cliché that expert testimony on such syndromes can dispel the "myths" that abused people are "masochists who are responsible for the abuse." It did not explain who held such a myth or why anyone would suppose that Kacsmar's jury had entertained it.

When such cases as Gladys Kelly's or Paul Kacsmar's came to the attention of appellate judges cognizant of the problem of abuse, they had two choices: they could reassert the traditional law of self-defense and remind lawyers and trial judges that there were ample ways for getting such a defense to the jurors and clarifying for them the distinctions between justification, excuse, and mitigation; or they could help invent a new standard of personal accountability based on poor social-science research and dubious theorizing and commend it to trial judges and jurors without clarifying its relationship to the law of self-defense or foreseeing its capacity for protean transformation and growth.

THEY chose the latter course. By itself this change might have had little effect, but it was compounded by the willingness of many jurors to judge the motives as well as the actions of defendants. Jurors will judge the moral worthiness of victims despite the fact that the law rests on the proposition that, except for certain conditions (for example, the victim was trying to kill his killer), all lives are of equal moral worth. They will often weigh the motives and character of both victim and defendant and adjust their verdicts accordingly; in extreme cases they will engage in what legal scholars call jury nullification by acquitting a defendant despite overwhelming evidence of guilt. Our sympathy for some defendants may lead us to feel that the jury's refusal to convict despite conclusive evidence is a sign of its humanity. But a jury that is free to acquit a guilty but likable defendant is also free to convict an innocent but detestable one.

Justice is a difficult ideal, vulnerable to attack by benevolence on one side and vengeance on the other. To the extent that the criminal courts allow victims to be put on trial, they foster this siege and allow an affluent defendant to introduce expert witnesses and other evidence that engages the sympathies of jurors while debasing standards of conduct. The law is, or ought to be, a tough master that, by holding us all to a high standard of personal accountability, produces the behavior we wish to see and reduces the opportunity for privilege to corrupt the system.

Unit Selections

22. **Restoring the Balance: Juvenile and Community Justice,** Gordon Bazemore and Susan E. Day
23. **Juvenile Offenders: Should They Be Tried in Adult Courts?** Michael P. Brown
24. **A Decline in Crime?** Timothy W. Maier and Michael Rust
25. **Kids and Guns: From Playgrounds to Battlegrounds,** Stuart Greenbaum
26. **With Juvenile Courts in Chaos, Critics Propose Their Demise,** Fox Butterfield
27. **Now, Justice Is Served by Youths, for Youths,** Regina Marcazzo
28. **Preventing Crime, Saving Children: Sticking to the Basics,** John J. Dilulio Jr.
29. **Pairing Juvenile Offenders with Volunteer Advocates,** Kim G. Frentz

Key Points to Consider

❖ What reform efforts are currently under way in the juvenile justice system?

❖ What are some recent trends in juvenile delinquency? In what ways will the juvenile justice system be affected by these trends?

❖ Is the departure of the juvenile justice system from its original purpose warranted? Why or why not?

❖ What do you think of the "Youth Court" concept? Be specific.

 **Links** | **www.dushkin.com/online/**

23. **Crime Connections on the Web!**
    http://www.appstate.edu/~robinsnmb/crime.htm
24. **Gang Land: The Jerry Capeci Page**
    http://www.ganglandnews.com
25. **Institute for Intergovernmental Research**
    http://www.iir.com
26. **National Network for Family Resiliency**
    http://www.nnfr.org
27. **Partnership against Violence Network**
    http://www.pavnet.org

These sites are annotated on pages 4 and 5.

Although there were variations within specific offense categories, the overall arrest rate for juvenile violent crime remained relatively constant for several decades. Then, in the late 1980s, something changed, bringing more and more juveniles charged with a violent offense into the justice system. The juvenile justice system is a twentieth-century response to the problems of dealing with children in trouble with the law or children who need society's protection.

Juvenile court procedure differs from the procedure in adult courts because juvenile courts are based on the philosophy that their function is to treat and to help, not to punish and to abandon,

offenders? The next essay "Juvenile offenders: Should They Be Tried in Adult Courts?" deals with this question. It appears that a "get tough" approach to deal with young law violators seen throughout the criminal justice system is society's reaction to violent, uncaring youths. Timothy Maier and Michael Rust in "A Decline in Crime?" assert that recent killings by children horrified Americans and have spurred lawmakers to push what some call "feel-good" legislation to curb criminal violence. "Kids and Guns: From Playgrounds to Battlegrounds" identifies that guns are now the weapon of choice for youth. This lethal mix of kids and guns has reached a crisis in the United States, according to the author.

the offender. Recently, operations of the juvenile court have received criticism, and a number of significant Supreme Court decisions have changed the way that the courts must approach the rights of children.

Despite these changes, however, the major thrust of the juvenile justice system remains one of diversion and treatment rather than adjudication and incarceration, although there is a trend toward dealing more punitively with serious juvenile offenders. This unit's opening essay, "Restoring the Balance: Juvenile and Community Justice," proposes an alternative approach to addressing juvenile crime that focuses on the interests of multiple justice clients. This restorative sanctioning model could provide a clear alternative to punishment-centered sanctioning approaches now dominant in juvenile justice and could ultimately redefine the sanctioning function.

Is throwing teens into adult courts—and adult prisons—the best way to deal with juvenile

Judges and politicians are debating a solution to violent teenage crime that was once unthinkable: abolishing the system and trying most minors as adults. "With Juvenile Courts in Chaos, Critics Propose Their Demise" sheds light on this debate. Regina Marcazzo, in "Now, Justice Is Served by Youths, for Youths" describes the Youth Court. This is a judicial innovation in which minors who choose to plead guilty to misdemeanors are given the option of being sentenced by their peers.

The key to preventing youth crime and substance abuse among young people is discussed in John J. Dilulio Jr.'s "Preventing Crime, Saving Children: Sticking to the Basics." He maintains that improving the day-to-day link between responsible adults and young people is essential. The unit closes with Kim Frentz describing an effective one-to-one mentoring program in "Pairing Juvenile Offenders with Volunteer Advocates." Thanks to this effort, she reports, kids are improving in school, enhancing their coping skills, and staying out of trouble.

Restoring the Balance: Juvenile and Community Justice

by Gordon Bazemore and Susan E. Day

The problem of crime can no longer be simplified to the problem of the criminal.

Leslie Wilkins

Offender-based control strategies are incomplete, since they take a 'closed system' view of correctional interventions: change the offender and not the community.

James Byrne

In a democratic society, citizens' expectations of government agencies are critically important. Unfortunately, within our juvenile justice system, community needs have been lost in the decade-long debate over the future of the juvenile court and the relative efficacy of punishment versus treatment. A number of politicians and policymakers argue for criminalizing our juvenile justice system through "get tough," adult sentences for juvenile offenders. Some even advocate abolishing the juvenile justice system and its foundation, the independent juvenile court.

On the other hand, many proponents of the juvenile court call for reaffirming the traditional treatment mission. Increasingly, the public and even many juvenile justice professionals perceive that treatment and punishment options are, as one judge aptly put it, "bad choices between sending kids to jail or sending them to the beach."

It is doubtful that either traditional treatment or criminalized retributive models can restore public confidence in the juvenile justice system. Only through extensive, meaningful citizen participation will public expectations and community needs be met. For most juvenile justice systems, achieving this level of involvement will require substantial restructuring.

This article describes an alternative approach to addressing juvenile crime that focuses on the interests of multiple justice clients. Alternatively

Gordon Bazemore is associate professor in the School of Public Administration at Florida Atlantic University. He is currently editing a book on international juvenile justice reform. Dr. Bazemore is principal investigator of a national action research project funded by OJJDP to pilot systemic reform based on restorative justice principles. He has directed several evaluations of juvenile justice, policing, and minority overrepresentation programs.

Susan E. Day is director of the Florida Youth Restoration Project, a community service program for delinquent youth in Palm Beach County, Florida. She serves as program manager for the Balanced and Restorative Justice Project.

From *Juvenile Justice*, December 1996, pp. 3-14. Reprinted by permission of the U.S. Department of Justice, Office of Juvenile Justice and Delinquency Prevention.

referred to as restorative justice, the balanced approach, and balanced and restorative justice (BRJ), this model is viewed by a growing number of juvenile justice professionals as a way to reengage the community in the juvenile justice process.

The Limits of Current Paradigms

Crime should never be the sole or even primary business of the State if real differences are sought in the well-being of individuals, families, and communities. The structure, procedures, and evidentiary rules of the formal criminal justice process coupled with most justice officials' lack of knowledge and connection to (the parties) affected by crime preclude the State from acting alone to achieve transformative changes.

Judge Barry Stuart

Worse still, we fear that even when something does work, it is seen to do so only in the eyes of certain professionals, while 'outside' the system, ordinary citizens are left without a role or voice in the criminal justice process.

John Braithewaite and Stephen Mugford

If juvenile justice is underfunded, it is also underconceptualized.

Advocates of reaffirming treatment argue that the system is failing because it lacks adequate resources. Critics and defenders of juvenile justice, however, argue that juvenile justice systems have failed to articulate a vision of success. If juvenile justice is underfunded, it is also underconceptualized. As closed-system paradigms, the treatment and retributive models are insular and one-dimensional. They are insular because they are offender-focused and one-dimensional because they fail to address the community's diverse interests.

Although the punitive approach may appease public demand for retri-

bution, it does little to rehabilitate or reintegrate juvenile offenders. Punishment is often used inappropriately, resulting in amply documented negative effects. Ironically, retributive punishment may encourage offenders to focus on themselves rather than on their victims. Even increasing its severity may have little impact if we have miscalculated the extent to which sanctions such as incarceration are experienced as punishment.[1]

In the public mind, punishment is at least somewhat related to offense. In contrast, treatment appears to address only the needs of the offender. Treatment programs often ask little of the offender beyond participating in counseling, remedial services, or recreational programs. Even when such programs "work," they make little difference in the lives of victims of juvenile crime, citizens concerned with the safety of their neighborhoods, or individuals who want young offenders held accountable for their actions.[2]

In fact, both punitive and treatment models focus little attention on the needs of victims and victimized communities. Neither model engages them as clients or as coparticipants in the justice process. Whether treatment or punishment is emphasized, the offender is the passive and solitary recipient of intervention and service. Increasingly reliant on facilities, treatment programs, and professional experts, juvenile justice systems exclude victims and other community members from what could be meaningful roles in sanctioning, rehabilitation, and public safety.

Fortunately, treatment and retributive models are not the only options for juvenile justice. The alternative, a community-oriented system, would involve citizens in setting clear limits on antisocial behavior and determining consequences for offenders. Victims' needs for reparation, validation, and healing would be at the core of a

community justice system, which would work toward building crime-resistant communities whose residents feel safe. It would emphasize the need for building relationships and involving youth in work, service, and other roles that facilitate bonding with law-abiding adults. Finally, a community justice system would articulate more meaningful roles in rehabilitating offenders and improving community safety for employers, civic groups, religious communities, families, and other citizens.

Toward Community Juvenile Justice: A Balanced and Restorative Approach

Government is responsible for preserving *order* but the community is responsible for establishing *peace*.

Daniel Van Ness

• In inner-city Pittsburgh, young offenders in an intensive day treatment program solicit input from community organizations about service projects they would like to see completed in the neighborhood. They work with community residents on projects that include home repair and gardening for the elderly, voter registration drives, painting homes and public buildings, and planting and cultivating community gardens.

• In Florida, young offenders sponsored by the Florida Department of Juvenile Justice and supervised by The 100 Black Men of Palm Beach County, Inc., plan and execute projects that serve as shelters for abused, abandoned, and HIV-positive and AIDS-infected infants and children. In Palm Beach County, victim advocates train juvenile justice staff on sensitivity in their interaction with victims and help prepare victim awareness curriculums for youth in residential programs.

• In cities and towns in Pennsylvania, Montana, Minnesota, Australia, and New Zealand, family members and other citizens acquainted with a juvenile offender or victim of a juvenile crime gather to determine the best response to the offense. Held in schools, churches, or other community facilities, these family group conferences are facilitated by a community justice coordinator or police officer and ensure that offenders hear community disapproval of their behavior. Participants develop an

new partnership between youth and victim advocates, concerned citizens, and community groups.

The balanced and restorative justice model is centered around community-oriented responses to crime.[3] Jurisdictions implementing it represent a diverse range of urban, suburban, and rural communities. These communities share a common commit-

ers them to do so. As Judge Barry Stuart notes:

> When members fail to assume responsibility for decisions affecting the community, community life will be characterized by the absence of a collective sense of caring, a lack of respect for diverse values, and ultimately a lack of any sense of belonging. . . . Conflict, if resolved through a process that constructively engages the parties involved, can be a fundamental building ingredient of any relationship. As members increase their ability to resolve disputes creatively, the ability of the community to effectively sanction crime, rehabilitate offenders, and promote public safety increases.[5]

Punitive and treatment models focus little attention on the needs of victims.

agreement for repairing the damage to victim and community and a plan for reintegrating the offender.

• In Minnesota, Department of Corrections staff collaborate with local police and citizen groups to establish family group conferencing programs and inform the community about offender monitoring and victim support. In Dakota County, a suburb of Minneapolis, retailers and senior citizens whose businesses and homes have been damaged by burglary or vandalism call a crime repair hotline to request a work crew of probationers to repair the damage.

• In Deschutes County, Oregon, offender work crews cut and deliver firewood to senior citizens and worked with a local contractor to build a homeless shelter.

• In more than 150 cities and towns throughout North America, victims and offenders meet with volunteer mediators to develop an agreement for restitution. At these meetings, victims express their feelings about the crime and gain information about the offense.

• In several cities in Montana, college students and other young adults in the Montana Conservation Corps supervise juvenile offenders working on environmental restoration, trail building, and other community service projects. They also serve as mentors.

While many professionals have become demoralized as juvenile justice systems are threatened with extinction, others are seeking to create a

ment to restructuring juvenile justice on the basis of a new mission (balanced approach) and a new value framework (restorative justice).

Restorative and Community Justice

From the perspective of restorative justice, the most significant aspect of crime is that it victimizes citizens and communities. The justice system should focus on repairing this harm by ensuring that offenders are held accountable for making amends for the damage and suffering they have caused. The most important issue in a restorative response to crime is not deciding whether to punish or treat offenders. Rather, as Howard Zehr suggests, the three primary questions to be answered are "What is the harm?" "What needs to be done to make it right?" and "Who is responsible?"[4]

A restorative system would help to ensure that offenders make amends to their victims. Juvenile justice cannot do this alone, however. Restorative justice requires that not only government but victims, offenders, and communities be actively involved in the justice process. In fact, some have argued that the health of a community is determined by the extent to which citizens participate in community decisions. An effective justice system strengthens the capacity of communities to respond to crime and empow-

The most unique feature of restorative justice is its elevation of the role of victims in the justice system. Victim rights has become a popular slogan, but victim needs are addressed by the system only after the needs of judges, prosecutors, probation officers, treatment providers, and even offenders are considered. Restorative justice does not define victim rights as the absence of offender rights; it focuses on the needs of victim, community, and offender. To bring balance to the present offender-driven system, however, it is necessary to give priority to victims' needs for physical, material, and emotional healing.

The Balanced Approach Mission

The balanced approach is a back-to-basics mission for juvenile justice that supports a community's need to sanction crime, rehabilitate offenders, and ensure public safety. Toward these ends, it articulates three goals for juvenile justice: accountability, public safety, and competency development (see figure 1).[6] Balance is attainable when administrators ensure that equitable resources are allocated to each goal.

• **Accountability.** Crime is sanctioned most effectively when offenders take responsibility for their crimes and the harm caused to victims, when offenders make amends by restoring losses, and when communities and victims take active roles in the sanctioning process. Because the offender's obligation is defined primarily as an obligation to his victims rather than to the State, accountability cannot be equated with responsiveness to juvenile justice professionals by obeying a curfew, complying with drug screening, or writing an essay. Nor can it be equated with punish-

the mere absence of bad behavior. It should increase the capacity of adults and communities to involve young people in work, service, dispute resolution, community problem solving, and cognitive skills building.

• **Public safety.** Assuring public safety requires more than mere incapacitation. Communities cannot be kept safe simply by locking up offend-

groups to enhance the role of juvenile justice professionals as resources in prevention and positive youth development.

The principle behind BRJ is that justice is best served when victims, offenders, and communities receive equitable attention in the justice process. The needs of one client cannot be met unless the needs of other clients are addressed. Crime severs bonds between victims, offenders, and families. Although offenders must take full responsibility for their acts, the responsibility for restoring mutual respect, understanding, and support among those involved must be shared by the community.

The health of a community is determined by the extent to which citizens participate in community decisions.

ment. It is easier to make offenders take their punishment than it is to get them to take responsibility for their actions.

• **Competency.** The most successful rehabilitation ensures that young offenders make measurable gains in educational, vocational, social, civic, and other competencies that enhance their capacity to function as productive adults. When competency is defined as the capacity to do something well that others value, the standard for achieving success is measured in the community. Competency is not

ers. Locked facilities must be part of any public safety strategy, but they are the least cost-effective component. A balanced strategy invests heavily in strengthening a community's capacity to prevent and control crime. A problem-oriented focus ensures that the time of offenders under supervision in the community is structured around such activities as work, education, and service. Adults, including parents, are assigned clear roles in monitoring offenders. A balanced strategy cultivates new relationships with schools, employers, and other community

Small Changes Yield Large Results

The change at the heart of BRJ is embodied in the community-building interventions described above. BRJ collaborators, including juvenile justice and other service professionals, have discovered that even small changes in how they conduct business can have immediate and lasting effects on the dynamics of community relationships.

Communities in the United States and across the globe are making dramatic policy changes on the basis of restorative priorities. In 1989, New Zealand began requiring that all juvenile offenders over age 14 (except in the most serious cases) be referred to a family group conference in which restorative goals are addressed in meetings that include victims, offenders, support groups, families, policymakers, social workers, and others. The New Zealand law appears to have drastically reduced court workloads and the use of incarceration.[7]

Fourteen States have enacted legislation adopting the balanced approach as the mission of their juvenile justice systems. A number of States have administrative rules or statewide policies that require case managers and other decisionmakers to consider the goals of the balanced approach in dispositional recommendations. In Pennsylvania and Montana, decisionmakers are

Figure 1

Restorative Justice

Competency

Public Safety

Accountability

Table 1
The Participants in a Balanced and Restorative Juvenile Justice System

Crime Victims	Offenders	Citizens, Families, and Community Groups
◆ Receive support, assistance, compensation, information, and services. ◆ Receive restitution or other reparation from the offender. ◆ Are involved and are encouraged to give input at all points in the system as to how the offender will repair the harm done. ◆ Have the opportunity to face the offenders and tell their story. ◆ Feel satisfied with the justice process. ◆ Provide guidance and consultation to juvenile justice professionals on planning and advisory groups.	◆ Complete restitution to their victims. ◆ Provide meaningful service to repay the debt to their communities. ◆ Face the personal harm caused by their crimes by participating in victim offender mediation or other victim awareness programs. ◆ Complete work experience and active and productive tasks that increase skills and improve the community. ◆ Are monitored by community adults as well as juvenile justice providers and supervised to the greatest extent possible in the community. ◆ Improve decisionmaking skills and have opportunities to help others.	◆ Are involved to the greatest extent possible in rehabilitation, community safety initiatives, and holding offenders accountable. ◆ Work with offenders on local community service projects. ◆ Provide support to victims. ◆ Provide support to offenders as mentors, employers, and advocates. ◆ Provide work for offenders to pay restitution to victims and service opportunities that allow offenders to make meaningful contributions to the quality of community life. ◆ Assist families to support the offender in obligation to repair the harm and increase competencies. ◆ Advise courts and corrections and play an active role in disposition.

---

using balanced approach criteria as funding guidelines and have formed statewide groups to oversee the development of restorative justice efforts.

Balanced and restorative justice cannot be achieved by mandates or legislation alone. As the three jurisdictions that constitute the OJJDP-funded demonstration effort are learning, the new model cannot be implemented overnight. Working with different juvenile justice systems in diverse communities, administrators in Palm Beach County, Florida, Dakota County, Minnesota, and Allegheny County, Pennsylvania, are pursuing varied approaches to systemic change to build a restorative model from the ground up. These administrators have made significant progress but acknowledge that the kind of change envisioned by BRJ is quite different from past practices. This change is especially striking in the model's focus on citizen involvement, including restructuring juvenile justice agencies to more effectively engage the community.

Balanced and Restorative Justice: New Roles for Citizens and Professionals

I'm glad to see somebody is finally trying to instill some responsibility

in these kids. I'm happy to help when it's obvious that we're trying to make taxpayers out of these kids, rather than tax liabilities.

Community Member

In the mediation session I learned that the offender was just a little kid and not the threat I thought he was. I also learned he had some needs that weren't being met. . . . For the first time (I've been a victim before), it seemed like someone was responding to my needs and listening to me.

Youth Crime Victim

When I first walked into the conferencing meeting and saw the victim and her friends and then saw my grandfather there I wished I could have gone to jail instead. But once everybody had talked about the crime I began to realize that Mrs. B was really hurt and scared by what I had done. I had to work hard to earn the money to pay her back and to do the community service hours (but the work on the crew was pretty fun) and I thought it was fair after all.

Juvenile Offender

Now I know what my job is really about! As a manager, I have a better sense of how to allocate, or reallocate, our resources. And my staff are getting a better sense of what their role is and how this fits with

my vision of what the community's role should be. We know we're really 'out of balance,' but for the first time we have a plan to move forward without chasing every fad and new program that comes along. We can also talk to the community about what we're doing in a way that they understand and want to help.

Manager of a Local Juvenile Justice System

As a community justice model, balanced and restorative justice offers a new vision of how victims, offenders, and others can be involved in the juvenile justice process. As table 1 illustrates, this vision is best understood by examining how the model is viewed by its participants.

Balanced and restorative justice is a work in progress. No juvenile justice system is completely balanced or fully restorative. But if juvenile justice systems, including those most committed to the model, fail to meet the standards they have set for community and client involvement, it is not because the model is utopian. It is because administrators are constrained by management protocols designed to deliver services based on the treatment and retributive paradigms.

Figure 2
What's New About the Balanced Approach?

Current System	Balanced and Restorative Justice
	New Values
Resource Allocation and Staffing Patterns	*New* Clients
	New Performance Outcomes
Programs and Practices	*New* Decisionmaking
	New Resource Allocation and Staffing Patterns
Performance Outcomes?	

The innovation of balanced and restorative justice lies in its agenda for restructuring the juvenile justice system to make it community-focused rather than bureaucracy-driven. This agenda demands new values, clients, performance objectives, decisionmaking processes, program priorities, staff roles, and patterns of resource allocation. As figure 2 suggests, while most juvenile justice agencies determine intervention priorities on the basis of current staff roles and resource allocations, juvenile justice managers who adopt the balanced approach mission are committed to making their agencies and systems value- and client-driven and outcome-oriented. Decisions are based on the premise that programs are means to accomplish restorative outcomes that address community needs (see table 2).

From a community justice perspective, the value of a program and the quality of its implementation is gauged in large measure by the extent to which it involves community members at all levels of implementation.

Citizen Involvement and Client Focus

In the total quality management (TQM) movement,[8] the concept of a client involves three components: a recipient of service, a target of intervention and change, and a coparticipant who must have input into the process and be involved to the greatest extent possible in decisionmaking.

The input of each client group is needed to stimulate and maintain community involvement. Currently few citizens are involved at significant levels in juvenile justice because they are seldom asked. Although many professionals would welcome community involvement and may work hard at collaboration and service brokerage, such efforts often fail to include employers, clergy, civic leaders, and neighborhood residents. Too often, juvenile justice agencies are unable to find appropriate roles for community members who are not social service professionals or time to support their efforts. Short-term involvement is often uninteresting because it is not linked to interventions that achieve significant outcomes for offenders or victims. When citizens are asked to participate, it is often on the basis of civic duty rather than personal commitment. As Braithwaite and Mugford observe, citizens are more willing to become involved if they have a personal interest in the offender, victim, or the family.[9]

Crimes typically evoke a community of concern for the victim, the offender, families and friends, and interested citizens and community groups. As the New Zealand experiment with family group conferencing illustrates, these personal communities can be a primary resource in resolving youth crimes. It is around such microcommunities that citizen participation in justice decisionmaking is being built.[10]

BRJ practices and programs invite a high level of citizen participation. Community involvement is never easy, but it is satisfying for citizens to help young offenders make restitution to their victims.

The more active roles for offenders, victims, and community in the juvenile justice process, noted in table 1, have implications for the roles of juvenile justice professionals. The most important and difficult challenge in moving toward balanced and restorative justice will be to alter the job descriptions and professional orientations of juvenile justice staff. For those accustomed to working with offenders individually or in programs and facilities, the role change implied by the need to engage victims and communities may be dramatic. Essentially, this change may be best understood as moving from direct service provider or service broker to community justice facilitator.[11]

As table 3 suggests, the new roles involve juvenile justice professionals in activities with each of the three justice clients. These activities include a variety of efforts to enhance preventive capacity and to help adults provide offenders with opportunities for competency development.

Getting There

> Some may say this [movement toward restorative justice] is Utopian. While this may be true, in a climate of failure and irrational extremism in the response to juvenile crime, there may be *nothing so practical as a good Utopia*.
> Lode Walgrave

Robert Fulcrum tells the story of a reporter visiting the cathedral in Chartres, France, during the cathedral's construction. Hoping to get a sense of how those working on this magnificent structure understood and experienced their contribution to its completion, the reporter began asking several workmen about their jobs. The first, a stonecutter, said that his job was simply to cut the stone into square blocks for someone else to use in the foundation; the job was monotonous, and he had been doing the same thing day in and day out. Next, the reporter asked a workman who was painting stone blocks on the front of the building about his job. "I just paint these blocks and nothing more," he said. "There is not much to it."

Frustrated that these workmen had little to say about the significance of working on this historical effort, the reporter moved to another part of the building and approached a man carefully cutting stained glass windows. Surely, this man felt that his work was the artistic opportunity of a lifetime. Once again the reporter was disappointed; the man said that he was very tired and somewhat bored with his task. Finally, as he walked out of the cathedral in despair, the reporter passed an elderly woman stooped and working rapidly to clean up the debris left from the stone and glass cutters, painters, and other artisans. He asked what it was that she was doing. Her answer was that she was building the most magnificent cathedral in the history of the world to the glory of God.

As this story illustrates, the key to progress toward restorative justice is viewing small steps as the building blocks of a more effective juvenile justice system.

Will balanced and restorative justice work? BRJ is not a treatment program but a model for system reform. It cannot be assessed by using traditional program evaluation technologies. The success of a restorative justice system should be measured not only by recidivism but also by victim satisfaction, offender accountability, competency development, and public safety.[12] The success of BRJ will depend on the consistency and integrity of implementation, how well its core philosophy is understood,

Table 2
Outcome Measures and Priorities for Practice in the Balanced Approach

Competency Development

Intermediate Outcome

Measures	Priorities for Practice
♦ Proportion of youth on supervision completing successful work experience or employment (quality of experience?). ♦ Proportion of youth on supervision completing meaningful work/service project. ♦ Extent of bonding between youth under supervision and community adults. ♦ Increase in empathy and improvement in skills. ♦ Demonstrated improvement in conflict resolution and anger management. ♦ Measured increase in educational, interpersonal, citizenship, and other competencies.	♦ Structured work experience and employment programs. ♦ Service/active learning. ♦ Cognitive and decisionmaking programs. ♦ Dispute resolution training. ♦ Intergenerational projects. ♦ Cross-age tutoring. ♦ Conservation and environmental awareness.

Accountability

Intermediate Outcome

Measures	Priorities for Practice
♦ Proportion of offenders completing fair and appropriate restitution orders or agreements. ♦ Proportion of victims given input into the process. ♦ Proportion of victims satisfied with the process. ♦ Proportion of offenders showing measured increase in victim awareness and empathy. ♦ Proportion of offenders and victims completing mediation or other resolution and community service. ♦ Proportion of offenders completing meaningful community service projects (number of such projects completed).	♦ Restitution to victims. ♦ Restorative community service. ♦ Victim offender mediation. ♦ Direct service to victims or surrogate victims. ♦ Victim awareness panels or victim offender groups in treatment programs.

Public Safety

Intermediate Outcome

Measures	Priorities for Practice
♦ Proportion of offenders reoffending while under juvenile justice supervision. ♦ Number of citizens involved in preventive and monitoring activities. ♦ Decrease in community fear and increase in understanding of juvenile justice. ♦ Decrease in school violence and increase in school and community-based conflict resolution. ♦ Increase in competency, empathy, and internal controls for offenders under supervision.	♦ Structuring time of offenders being supervised in the community: work experience, community service, and alternative education. ♦ Effective use of natural surveillance and community guardians such as employers, relatives, churches, and mentors. ♦ Continuum of graduated community-based sanctions and surveillance. ♦ Prevention and capacity building in schools and other community groups.

<table>
<tr><td colspan="2">

Table 3
New Roles in the Balanced and Restorative Justice Model

The Coparticipants

</td></tr>
<tr><td>Victim</td><td>Active participant in defining the harm of the crime and shaping the obligations placed on the offender.</td></tr>
<tr><td>Community</td><td>Responsible for supporting and assisting victims, holding offenders accountable, and ensuring opportunities for offenders to make amends.</td></tr>
<tr><td>Offender</td><td>Active participant in reparation and competency development.</td></tr>
</table>

Juvenile Justice Professional

Sanctioning	Facilitate mediation, ensure restoration, develop creative or restorative community service options, engage community members, and educate the community on its role.
Rehabilitation	Develop new roles for young offenders that allow them to practice and demonstrate competency, assess and build on youth and community strengths, and develop community partnerships.
Public Safety	Develop incentives and consequences to ensure offender compliance with supervision objectives, help school and family control and maintain offenders in the community, and develop prevention capacity of local organizations.

how effectively it is adapted to local conditions, and whether restorative justice is given a chance. Although restorative justice may not lead to immediate reductions in recidivism, the standard of comparison should be the current system. As a First Nations Community Justice Coordinator in Yukon, Canada, reminds us:

So we make mistakes. Can you— the current system—say you don't make mistakes? . . . If you don't think you do, walk through our community. Every family will have something to teach you. . . . By getting involved, by all of us taking responsibility, it is not that we won't make mistakes, we would be doing it together, as a *community* instead of having it done to us. . . . We need to make *real differences* in the way people act and the way we treat others. . . . Only if we empower them and support them can they break out of this trap.[13]

It is the failure of the current paradigms that has moved some policy-makers toward radical measures to abolish the juvenile justice system. Those who wish to preserve it see balanced and restorative justice as a means to do so by crafting a new system in which juvenile justice reflects community justice.

Notes

1. For commentary on closed-system approaches to community corrections, see J. Byrne, "Reintegrating the Concept of Community in Community Corrections," *Crime and Delinquency* 35 (1989): 471–499; see also A.J. Reiss and M. Tonry, "Why Are Communities Important in Understanding Crime?" *Communities and Crime* (Chicago: University of Chicago Press, 1986). Like treatment, punishment will remain an essential component of any juvenile justice system. However, punitive measures focused primarily on incarceration represent only one limited approach to meeting community needs to sanction crime. For commentary on more educative and expressive approaches to setting tolerance limits for crime, see J. Braithewaite, *Crime, Shame and Reintegration* (Cambridge, England: Cambridge University Press, 1989); L. Wilkins, *Punishment, Crime and Market Forces* (Brookfield, VT: Dartmouth Publish-

ing Company, 1991); G. Bazemore and M. Umbreit, "Rethinking the Sanctioning Function in Juvenile Court: Retributive or Restorative Responses to Youth Crime," *Crime and Delinquency* 41 (1995): 296–316. The counterdeterrent effects of retributive punishment, including stigmatization, weakening bonds, and conventional peer and adult relations, are also well documented. Finally, empirical evidence that criminal justice decisionmakers typically overestimate the perceived punitive effects of incarceration is provided in M. Crouch, "Is Incarceration Really Worse? Analysis of Offenders' Preferences for Prison Over Probation," *Justice Quarterly* 10 (1993): 67–88.

2. The critique of the individual treatment model presented here is not premised on the largely discredited "nothing works" perspective, nor do we question the need for an effective rehabilitative model for juvenile justice. Rather, our criticisms of traditional counseling-based treatment are based primarily upon the very limited context of intervention in most treatment programs and on the deficit assumptions about offenders on which most of these programs are based. A more comprehensive agenda for rehabilitation and reintegration would focus more on relationship building and the development of roles for delinquent youth that allow them to demonstrate competency while forming bonds with conventional peers and adults. A competency development component of such a reintegrative and restorative agenda is outlined in G. Bazemore and P. Cruise, "Reinventing Rehabilitation: Exploring a Competency Development Model for Juvenile Justice Intervention," *Perspectives* 19 (1995): 4; and G. Bazemore and C. Terry, "Developing Delinquent Youth: A Reintegrative Model for Rehabilitation and a New Role for the Juvenile Justice System," *Child Welfare* (forthcoming).

3. Balanced and Restorative Justice (BRJ) is also the title of a national action research project funded through the Technical Assistance and Training Prevention division of the Office of Juvenile Justice and Delinquency Prevention. This project provides national training and information dissemination as well as support and assistance to demonstration projects currently implementing BRJ.

4. H. Zehr, *Changing Lenses: A New Focus for Crime and Justice* (Scottsdale, PA: Herald Press, 1990).

5. Judge B. Stuart, notes from presentation at the annual conference of the Society for Professionals in Dispute Resolution (Toronto, Canada, 1993): 7.

6. In a balanced system, programs and practices aimed at repairing harm to victims should, as Troy Armstrong has phrased it, "resonate with" practices aimed at rehabilitative and public safety objectives. Specifically, holding offenders accountable is a first step in the rehabilitative process. Developing capacities for competent behavior in offenders increases community safety by increasing connectedness and concern for others as well as life skills. Enhanced community safety is often necessary to carry out meaningful community sanction-

ing, offender reintegration, and victim support and restoration. For a detailed discussion of the balanced approach mission, see D. Maloney and G. Bazemore, "Rehabilitating Community Service: Toward Restorative Service in a Balanced Justice System," *Federal Probation* (1994); G. Bazemore, "On Mission Statements and Reform in Juvenile Justice: The Case of the Balanced Approach," *Federal Probation* (1992); G. Bazemore and C. Washington, "Charting the Future of the Juvenile Justice System: Reinventing Mission and Management," *Spectrum: The Journal of State Government* (1995). Table 2 of this paper provides a general summary of how performance objectives on each goal can be measured.

7. F.W.M. McElrae, "Restorative Justice—The New Zealand Youth Court: A Model for Development in Other Courts?" *Journal of Judicial Administration* 4 (1994), Australian Institute of Judicial Administration, Melbourne, Australia.

8. W.E. Deming, *Out of Crisis* (Cambridge, MA: MIT Center for Advanced Engineering, 1986); L. Martin, *Total Quality Management in Organizations* (Newbury Park, CA: Sage, 1993).

9. J. Braithewaite and S. Mugford, "Conditions of Successful Reintegration Ceremonies: Dealing with Juvenile Offenders," *British Journal of Criminology* (1995): 34. The authors give examples of how relatives, friends, and acquaintances of young offenders, victims, and their families become vital resources in restoring and meeting the needs of crime victims while also helping offenders when asked to participate in family group conferences.

10. For a more detailed description of the New Zealand and Australian models of family group conferencing, including research findings and critical concerns about implementation, see G. Maxwell and A. Morris, *Family, Victims, and Culture: Youth Justice in New Zealand* (Wellington, New Zealand: Social Policy Agency and Victoria University, Institute of Criminology, 1993); C. Alder and J. Wundersitz, *Family Group Conferencing: The Way Forward or Misplaced Optimism?* (Canberra, Australia: Australian Institute of Criminology, 1994); M. Umbreit and S. Stacy, "Family Group Conferencing Comes to the U.S.: A Comparison With Victim Offender Mediation," *Juvenile and Family Court Journal* (forthcoming).

11. The transformation from service provider to the facilitator role is used to describe changes in probation services in the Vermont Department of Corrections' restructuring of the State's probation system through Community Reparative Boards.

12. Answering the question "Does it work?" in a restorative community justice framework must give consideration to improvements in the capacity of community groups and citizens to prevent, sanction, and control crime. For example, the development of community support groups of nonprofessional citizens is generally not viewed as a success outcome, but such measures may be a more critical gauge of long-term community safety than reductions in recidivism of offenders in treatment programs.

13. Rose Couch, Community Justice Coordinator, Quanlin Dun First Nations, Yukon, Canada. As quoted in B. Stuart, "Sentencing Circles: Making 'Real Differences'," monograph, Territorial Court of Yukon, Whitehorse, Yukon, Canada.

Supplemental Reading

Bazemore, G., and M.S. Umbreit. (1995). "Rethinking the Sanctioning Function in Juvenile Court: Retributive or Restorative Responses to Youth Crime." *Crime and Delinquency* 41(3): 296–316. This article proposes restorative justice as an alternative model for the juvenile courts to address limitations of sanctioning choices inherent in individual treatment and retributive justice paradigms. NCJ 156328

Bazemore, G., and M.S. Umbreit. (1994). *Balanced and Restorative Justice*. Washington, DC: U.S. Department of Justice, Office of Juvenile Justice and Delinquency Prevention. Community supervision of juvenile offenders based on the balanced and restorative justice approach is discussed in this examination of the Balanced and Restorative Justice Project being developed as an outgrowth of the Office of Juvenile Justice and Delinquency Prevention's juvenile restitution training and technical assistance program. NCJ 149727

Cragg. W. (1992). *Practice of Punishment: Towards a Theory of Restorative Justice*. New York: Routledge. This book develops a theory of punishment in which the central function of law is to reduce the need to use force in the resolution of disputes. The author examines traditional approaches to punishment to determine why they have failed to provide a coherent and humane approach to sentencing and corrections. NCJ 143921

Umbreit, M.S. (1995). "Holding Juvenile Offenders Accountable: A Restorative Justice Perspective." *Juvenile and Family Court Journal* 46(2): 31–42. This article defines accountability for juvenile offenders as an intervention strategy within the context of the restorative justice paradigm, in which the meaning of accountability shifts from incurring a debt to society to incurring a responsibility for making amends to the victimized person. NCJ 156121

Umbreit, M.S., R.B. Coates, and B. Kalanj. (1994). *Victim Meets Offender: The Impact of Restorative Justice and Mediation*. Monsey, NY: Willow Tree Press. This book reports findings from a study of victim-offender reconciliation and mediation programs for juvenile offenders in California, Minnesota, New Mexico, and Texas. NCJ 147713

LAW & JUSTICE

JUVENILE OFFENDERS:

Should They Be Tried in Adult Courts?

The "get tough" approach to dealing with young law violators seen throughout the criminal justice system is society's reaction to violent, uncaring youths.

by Michael P. Brown

CHILDREN have been described as our future, our greatest resource, and our hope for a better tomorrow. For many Americans, though, children invoke fear. They represent violence, a segment of society lacking in self-control and devoid of ethics and morals, and the failure of the family to instill traditional values—chief among them being the value of human life and respect for others.

Fear of crime, especially random violence perpetrated by young Americans, is among the nation's greatest concerns. It has served as the motivation for countless numbers of people to change their lifestyles, take self-defense classes, install home security systems, and carry handguns for protection. Moreover, fear of crime has influenced politicians and laypersons to adopt the position that a conservative jus-

Dr. Brown is professor of criminal justice, Ball State University, Muncie, Ind.

tice system, which seeks to punish and deter, holds the most promise in curtailing juvenile crime. Waiving juveniles to criminal (*i.e.,* adult) court and imposing criminal penalties, according to the conservative position, are effective ways for society to express outrage for the transgressions of "out-of-control" youth and to placate its desire for retribution. Others, however, contend that treating juveniles as adults is going too far. Although many of these juveniles are incarcerated for their crimes, which the law allows, they often are the easy victims of homosexual rape and other forms of violence at the hands of hardened adult criminals.

The criminal sanctioning of juvenile offenders is not a contemporary phenomenon. Juveniles have been punished as adults for centuries. Prior to the 17th century, for instance, children were seen as being different from adults only in their size. Hence, they were held essentially to the

same behavioral standards as adults. Youngsters were perceived of as being miniature adults and, therefore, subject to the same punishments as offenders who were decades their senior. Childhood was considered to end at about age five.

It was not until the 17th century that European church and community leaders successfully advanced the notion that children were weak and innocent and in need of the guidance, protection, and socialization of adults. Consequently, childhood was prolonged, education became a priority, and societal norms emerged specifying age-appropriate behavior. Youngsters no longer were viewed as miniature adults. For the first time in recorded history, they were a separate and distinct group.

By the 18th century, English common law characterized those under the age of seven as being incapable of forming criminal intent. For an act to be considered criminal, there must be *actus reus* (the criminal act itself), *mens rea* (the intent to commit the criminal act), and *corpus delecti* (the interaction between the act and the intent to commit it). Therefore, since youths were considered to be incapable of forming *mens rea,* they were legally unable to commit a crime or to be criminally sanctioned. Between the ages of seven and 14, children were presumed to be without criminal intent unless it could be proven that they knew the difference between right and wrong. At age 14, they legally were considered adults, capable of forming criminal intent and therefore justly sentenced to serve time in jail and prison alongside other adults.

By the early 1800s, there was the belief that juvenile and adult offenders should be incarcerated separately. At that time, special correctional institutions for youthful offenders were established in the U.S. It was not until 1899, though, that the first juvenile court was established. This uniquely American institution was based on the premise that youthful offenders should be treated differently than their adult counterparts. Instead of deciding guilt or innocence, the court would ascertain whether youths were in need of treatment. Under the driving philosophy of the new court, *parens patriae,* it would serve as the benevolent parent—all-knowing and all-loving, wanting only that which is in the best interest of children. Consequently, instead of harsh, punitive sanctions that sought to deter, the court would seek long-term behavioral change by providing the guidance youths so woefully lacked from their natural parents. Sentences were to be customized to meet the needs of each juvenile so as to optimize the rehabilitative effects of court intervention.

For most juveniles, the *parens patriae* doctrine still serves as the foundation upon which their sentences are based. Such an orientation is not deemed appropriate, however, for those juveniles waived to criminal court. Provisions that allow juveniles to be waived are, on the one hand, in contrast with the original intent and purpose of the juvenile justice system. On the other, they are consistent with the manner in which youthful offenders were sanctioned in the past.

The present-day controversy surrounding waivers appears to be a consequence of at least two factors converging. First, the definitions of childhood and age-appropriate behavior are in a state of flux. Young people are said to be more predisposed toward violence today than they were in the past. National crime data sources seem to support this notion. Violent juvenile crime has increased by nearly 70% since 1986. Moreover, the violence perpetrated by juveniles is portrayed by the mass media as being more heinous than at any other time in history. People are fearful of falling victim to a generation that seemingly holds beliefs and values that diverge drastically from those of normative society.

Second, the "get tough" approach to dealing with law violators—as seen throughout the criminal justice system—increasingly is being applied to juvenile offenders as well. Although a conservative approach to juvenile crime is not new, it is in sharp contrast to the predominant way in which the juvenile justice system has responded to youthful offenders in the U.S. for nearly 100 years. While it is true that waivers have been in existence for more than 70 years, they are used more today than in the past. This has drawn attention to how society's response to juvenile offenders is changing from primarily being oriented toward rehabilitation to increasingly becoming prone to subjecting juveniles to conservative criminal court practices.

"Legal adults"

Every state and the District of Columbia have at least one provision (some states have as many as three) to waive certain juveniles to criminal court. Juveniles may become "legal adults" through judicial waiver, prosecutorial discretion, or statutory exclusion. A judicial waiver involves the juvenile court waiving jurisdiction over a case and sending it to criminal court for

prosecution. In all but three states, juvenile court judges have been entrusted with the power to waive juveniles to criminal court. Prosecutorial discretion (also known as concurrent jurisdiction) refers to the prosecutor deciding in which court—juvenile or criminal—charges will be filed. Ten states and the District of Columbia give prosecutors this authority. Statutory exclusion involves state legislatures designating certain offenses for which criminal prosecution is required. Thirty-six states and the District of Columbia have enacted legislation that excludes certain offenses from juvenile court jurisdiction.

> ## "... The majority of those juveniles waived to criminal court will re-enter society stigmatized by their criminal label...."

Age and offense seriousness traditionally have been the criteria by which juveniles are waived to criminal court. Twenty-one states and the District of Columbia have no minimum age requirements for transferring juveniles to criminal court. Among the remaining 29 states, minimum age requirements range from seven to 16. The largest proportion of cases waived to criminal court are serious crimes such as murder; offenses involving serious personal injury (such as aggravated assault); property crimes; public order offenses (such as disorderly conduct, obstruction of justice, and weapons offenses); and drug offenses. Additionally, some minor offenses (such as fish and game violations), which do not fall within the jurisdiction of the juvenile court, are tried in criminal court. Moreover, some states permit juveniles to be waived if their current charge is a felony and there is evidence of prior felony convictions. Furthermore, most states have a provision that allows juveniles to be waived to criminal court if there is reason to believe that offenders are not amenable to treatment.

Using the most recent available data, the Office of Juvenile Justice and Delinquency Prevention (JJDP) reports that, from 1985 to 1994, the number of delinquency cases waived to criminal court rose from 7,200 to 12,300, a 71% increase. Despite this growth, the percentage of cases waived to criminal court during this 10-year period remained relatively constant, ranging from a low of 1.2% to a high of 1.5% of all formally handled delinquency cases.

Over this span, the types of offenses waived to criminal court have changed considerably. While 54% of the cases waived in 1985 were for property crimes, the percentage dropped to 37% by 1994. Cases involving murder and personal injury rose from 33 to 44%. The percentage of drug offenses more than doubled, from five to 11%. Public order offenses remained relatively constant—nine percent in 1985 and eight percent in 1994.

The percentage of cases involving youthful offenders under the age of 16 increased from six to 12%. Males consistently have comprised the majority of cases waived to criminal court—95% in 1985 and 96% in 1994. Of the juveniles waived to criminal court in 1985, 57% were white, 42% black, and two percent of other racial and ethnic groups. By 1994, the percentage of white and black juvenile offenders became more similar (49 and 48%, respectively), and youths from other racial and ethnic groups increased to four percent. (Figures have been rounded off to nearest full percentage point.)

Waiving juveniles to criminal court often is justified on the grounds that they are deserving of more punitive criminal court sanctions and that the "get tough" approach to fighting crime will serve to deter future criminal conduct. Decades of research has yielded mixed findings regarding whether juveniles are sentenced more harshly by criminal courts and are less likely to recidivate. Most studies indicate that juveniles waived to criminal court do not receive substantially more punitive sanctions. In fact, many studies have reported that juveniles are more likely to receive probation instead of incarceration. Of those incarcerated, most receive terms of confinement comparable to those imposed in juvenile court. Moreover, research has revealed that juveniles waived to criminal court are no less likely to recidivate than those sanctioned in juvenile court.

The methods by which the justice system responds to unlawful conduct are not determined in a vacuum. They are a reflection of societal attitudes. In the past, waiving juveniles to criminal court was considered an option after all other avenues of treatment in the juvenile court had been explored. Today, the situation is drastically different. The conservative environment that currently exists not only makes it more acceptable, it is an expectation that judges and prosecutors will act decisively by waiving certain juveniles to criminal court. Hence, waivers no longer are viewed as a last resort. In fact, the use of waivers has been expanded to include first-time juvenile offenders. The establishment of exclusionary statutes, requiring certain juveniles to be waived automatically, eliminates the possibility of the exercise of discretion by those who know youngsters best—juvenile court judges and prosecutors. It is estimated that exclusionary statutes have resulted in more juveniles waived to criminal court than judicial waivers and prosecutorial discretion combined.

Waiving juveniles to criminal court is not the answer to the crime situation. At best, waivers are a short-term solution to a complex social condition that will not be simplified by transferring juveniles to the jurisdiction of the criminal court. At best, they merely serve to mollify the public's desire for retribution. After all, the majority of those juveniles waived to criminal court will re-enter society stigmatized by their criminal label and, in all likelihood, more dangerous than they were before being sanctioned as adults. This is especially true of youths who have served time in prison alongside adults.

Nevertheless, it is unlikely that waivers will be repealed. Therefore, it is incumbent upon decision-makers to make an informed, socially responsible use of waivers. In so doing, they would be restricted to those who pose the greatest risk to the safety and security of society—violent youth such as murderers, rapists, and robbers who show no apparent promise for reformation.

As for the others, juvenile court intervention holds the most promise for transforming troubled youths into productive, law-abiding adults. The OJJDP, based upon the results of numerous studies, has proposed a multifaced strategy for dealing with youthful offenders:

Strengthen the family unit. Parents are primarily responsible for instilling in their children socially redeeming morals and values. Parenting classes may be necessary when mothers and/or fathers lack the skills, abilities, and maturity to socialize their offspring properly. When a functional family is nonexistent, a surrogate one should be established to fill that void in a child's upbringing.

Support core social institutions. Capable, productive, and responsible youths are influenced positively by schools, religious institutions, and community-based organizations. Social institutions impart law-abiding beliefs and values and offer youths legitimate opportunities for economic gain.

Promote delinquency prevention. Communities must be proactive by responding to children who are at risk of committing delinquent acts. Although youths have a responsibility to live within the boundaries of the law, social institutions have a similar responsibility to engage youngsters in activities that encourage productive, law-abiding behavior.

Encourage an effective and immediate justice system response to delinquency. When delinquency occurs, the justice system must respond immediately to prevent future such actions and suppress escalation in their seriousness. The justice system should act in concert with conventional social institutions to enlist the influences that the family and religious organizations, for instance, have on the lives of youths.

Identify and control those youths who already are serious offenders. Youths who have not responded to traditional juvenile court intervention efforts or have demonstrated an unwillingness to abide by the rules of nonsecure community-based treatment efforts should be isolated in secure juvenile facilities for the protection of society. Deviating somewhat from the OJJDP's proposal, this intervention effort would be restricted to nonviolent offenders.

The alternative to waiving juveniles to criminal court is a comprehensive community response to juvenile unlawfulness that views juvenile and criminal justice as components of a larger whole—society. Moreover, it sees crime as a community problem with a community solution, instead of viewing it solely as a justice system problem with a justice system solution.

Many people will resist the notion of instituting alternatives to criminal court waivers. A community response to juvenile crime requires the commitment of the entire society. Therefore, it needs more effort than simply waiving juveniles to criminal court. Nevertheless, it holds the promise of returning children to their natural and rightful position as our future, our greatest resource, and our hope for a better tomorrow.

A Decline in Crime?

Killings by children have horrified Americans and spurred lawmakers to push what some call "feel-good" legislation aimed at curbing criminal violence.

By Timothy W. Maier and Michael Rust

The pain and horror of those few unbelievable minutes outside a Jonesboro, Ark., middle school, where a 13-year-old boy and his 11-year-old friend are alleged to have killed four schoolmates and a teacher, left Americans with the same anguished questions that have become all too familiar. What has happened to young people and why? The media-soaked society that flashes images of children killed by other children around the globe quickly supplied the usual roster of suspects. Too many guns? Too few stay-at-home parents? Too much Nintendo? Or just too much of an increasingly desensitized and coarsened modern world?

Through the shock, familiar remedies are paraded by the usual suspects. Pass more laws; restore the old morality. Liberals call as usual for more gun control; conservatives assure us that home-schooling is an answer. But a look at violence in America and how it affects young people shows complexity and supplies very few easy answers.

One startling fact to keep in mind is that violent crime is down for the sixth year in a row. What's more, juvenile homicides declined 31 percent from 1993 to 1996 and juvenile crime in general dropped 18 percent from 1994 to 1996.

Preliminary statistics for this year from the FBI *Uniform Crime Report* show another 5 percent dip in all violent crime during the first six months in 1997. Violent crime, which includes aggravated assault, rape and murder, is down 7 percent for 1996. But these figures are cold comfort to Americans confronted by seemingly meaningless and random acts of violence. "We are a violent culture," says Richard Maxwell Brown, a historian at the University of Oregon. But the irony is that horrific events like that at Jonesboro are not necessarily barometers of societal trends. "This Arkansas case is clearly a different thing," Carnegie-Mellon University criminologist Alfred Bloomstein tells **Insight**. "The trend in violent crime is downward. Individual events don't create the trend." While it's true, as Bloomstein points out, that millions of schoolchildren return safely from school every day, that is small comfort for parents who wait for them with increasing anxiety.

"I don't like to think our schools are unsafe. However, some schools are not as safe as they were 10 years ago," says Patrick Lacy, a Virginia school-board attorney. If events such

Youth violence arrests are down

130,000
120,000
110,000
100,000

125,085
119,678
104,137
106,190
102,231

'92   '93   '94   '95   '96

As is violent crime

5.0
4.5
4.0
3.5
3.0

Millions of murders, rapes, robberies and assaults

'90 '91 '92 '93 '94 '95 '96

SOURCES: Justice Policy Institute and Bureau of Justice Statistics

GRAPHIC BY CHARLES HAZARD

as Jonesboro inspire legislation, it isn't necessarily a bad thing, he says, citing the federal law requiring all school districts to mandate one-year expulsion of any child who carries a gun to school.

"I don't think we are going to see a wave of 11-year-old killers," adds criminologist Henry Brownstein of the University of Baltimore, author of *The Rise and Fall of Violence*, "Most 11-year-olds are not that dangerous. But violence is not new to these types of kids because they usually have experienced high levels of violence at home." Brownstein warns statistics also don't show youth violence undergoing the "technical change" from settling scores with a fistfight until now when "they whip out of their pocket a 9mm handgun."

Caution also is echoed by Alan McEvoy of Ohio's Wittenberg University, who says crime numbers show only "a modest decline." McEvoy, the author of several books on youth violence and past president of the Safe Schools Coalition, a national nonprofit organization devoted to reducing violence, says that "violent crime is still off the charts and is at an unacceptable high level."

But that perception, says Tom Riley, senior analyst of the Statistical Assessment Service in Washington, is related to media coverage. "The amount of crime seen on TV is the amount of crime people think is out there," he says, noting the media generally have been "slow to catch on when crime goes up," as in the late 1980s, and "slow to catch on when crime is going down," such as in 1993. For example, Riley says, in 1990 one in nine crime stories dealt with murder, but by 1995 about 27 percent of crime stories dealt with murder.

But the United States homicide rate of 9.3 percent in 1992 is far higher per 100,000 than those of European and Asian countries with reliable statistics. In 1992, for example, Japan had the lowest homicide rate in the industrialized world, at 0.6 per 100,000 followed by Great Britain at 0.7 per 100,000, Germany at one per 100,000 and France at 1.1 per

FBI statistics show that on average, before a perpetrator goes to prison he has committed about 15 offenses that went unpunished by the law.

100,000, according to the Population Reference Bureau in Washington.

The recent FBI statistics also were heavily influenced by what happened in New York, where Mayor Rudy Giuliani coasted to an easy re-election last year on the basis of his success in cutting crime. (Between 1992 and 1995, New York accounted for 22 percent of the national decline in violent crime.) Violent crime in the Big Apple dropped 16 percent last year, which featured prominently in the national downturn.

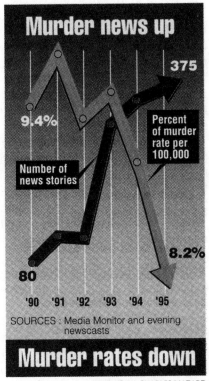

GRAPHIC BY CHARLES HAZARD

Giuliani and former New York City Police Commissioner William J. Bratton implemented aggressive community policing that is tough on juvenile crime and conducts "relentless pursuits" by treating minor crimes with the same intolerance as major felonies—an approach modeled after the broken-window theory that links crime with disorder. In fact, FBI statistics show that on average, before a perpetrator goes to prison he has committed about 15 offenses that went unpunished.

Gun-control advocates such as Sarah Brady were quick to point to the Brady Law, named for her husband, James, who was shot in the 1981 assassination attempt on President Reagan, as one reason behind the decline in crime. Last year the Supreme Court ruled that it is unconstitutional for the federal government to require states to conduct Brady Law background checks on gun purchasers, but most states say they will conduct the checks voluntarily.

As president of the Washington-based Handgun Control Inc., Brady credits the bill with preventing 250,000 convicted felons, people with histories of mental illness and juveniles from obtaining handguns, despite that the record shows there have been only seven prosecutions under the law, of which only three persons went to prison for illegally obtaining a handgun. "The important thing," Brady claims, "is we are headed in the right direction."

University of Chicago economist John Lott disputes the impact of gun legislation, claiming the decline of violent crime can be traced to going the other way by legalizing carrying of concealed weapons. His study shows that in states permitting citizens to carry a concealed handgun, murders declined by 8.5 percent, rapes by 5 percent and aggravated assaults by 7 percent. "I don't see any gain from having rules to prohibit the sale of guns," insists Lott. "We don't find any evidence that the Brady Law has any impact on violent crime. The Brady Law did not have any effect on murder or robbery." Brady critics also point to the fact that Washington, where the Brady attack occurred, has one of the strictest gun laws, yet the number of slayings increased from 361 in 1995 to 397 in 1996.

Bloomstein maintains that while universal gun control is not feasible, preventing "access to guns by kids is doable." The image of the youthful suspects in Jonesboro cradling weapons at very young ages provides a disquieting backdrop to these discussions. "Kids get them from somebody, and we can be quite severe on who sells guns to kids or makes them accessible," says Bloomstein. One proposal is to make guns, in effect, child-proof, by installing locks and magnetic rings which enable only the owner of the gun to fire the weapon.

Merely appearing to deal with crime is a political winner. Little wonder that legislators were quick to respond to the Arkansas tragedy. On March 31, Capitol Hill lawmakers called for a ban on the import and sale of high-capacity ammunition clips that fire more than 10 rounds, the type used in the Jonesboro shooting. "No weapon used has the killing power this weapon has," declared California Democratic Sen. Dianne Feinstein as she deftly loaded an AK-47 assault rifle with a 75-round drum—enough firepower to mow down most of the Senate in less than a minute.

While guns were being brandished in the Capitol, the nation's legislative bandwagon rolled. Congress is considering building more juvenile prisons, while Sen. Jeff Sessions, an Alabama Republican, wants juvenile offenders to be prosecuted as adults from age 14. Every state has this option on the books already except Hawaii and New Mexico, and 20 states have no age limits. States long ago joined the movement for a legislative fix, but it is continuing. A proposal in Mississippi calls for prosecutors to seek the death penalty in school killings. This was in reaction to the shooting deaths of

Public concern that crime is a problem trumps the statistics that say otherwise. This may be true because many citizens are fearful that violence will touch their lives.

two girls on Oct. 1 at a high school in Pearl, Miss.

But increased penalties and expanded police powers come at a price. Even New York's successful campaign against crime also generated a greater number of complaints of police misconduct. Polls indicate that most citizens believe it's a small price to pay, but "there is the danger of sacrificing civil liberties by caving in to harsher penalties for juvenile offenders, which I find extreme and awful," says McEvoy. The Jonesboro killings show "what we should do is try to find out how they got to this point in the first place. These Arkansas kids were isolated, and they gave off clues, and no one paid attention. I hate to see a policy formed based on a singular event. We have to look at what are the patterns here and what we can do intelligently to intervene without sacrificing our civil liberties."

A state judge also wonders if, like Megan's Law, the Arkansas case will be the poster child for more federal intervention. "It's all feel-good legislation," the judge tells Insight. "You got every law you need right now on the books. Now it's just feel-good time."

Perhaps there is something unique about the American interpretation of the right to use deadly force in self-defense. In his 1992 book, *No Duty to Retreat*, historian Raymond Maxwell Brown described how standing one's ground long ago became a principle of American law

as well as a characteristic of the national ethos. The struggle to settle and subdue a wilderness continent caused English common law to be adapted to American conditions. By 1921, the long history of "no duty to retreat" was recognized by the Supreme Court. It came in a case from Texas (of course) that involved a fatal stabbing, and Justice Oliver Wendell Holmes, discussing his majority opinion in a letter to British socialist Harold Laski, wrote that "it is well settled" in Texas that "a man is not born to run away."

The American expansion of the original English principle, Brown wrote, "helps explain why our country has been the most violent among its peer group of the industrialized urbanized democracies of the world." The no-duty-to-retreat assumption "has long since become second nature to most Americans," he wrote. "It is an expression of a characteristically American approach to life."

This isn't all bad; Brown went on to point out that social activists and reformers long have been united by a common temper bound to this spirit. But adolescents and prepubescents are not likely to appreciate a restoration of historical perspectives. He reminds Insight that, in the medieval and early modern periods, children who committed crimes were treated as adults starting from the age of 6 or 7. In Jonesboro, where an 11- and a 13-year-old apparently wielded weapons very effectively, "maybe we need to return to the older period in which children were treated like adults."

"With the kid killing, you wonder how much they understand the finality of death," says Joel Jacobsen, assistant attorney general of New Mexico. "They just don't have the experience to say that this really has consequences that go on for decades." And Jacobsen, the biographer of one of America's most famous young killers, Billy the Kid, speculates that just as with the famous Kid—who killed four to 10 people between the ages of 18 and 21—a youthful belief in one's own invincibility may have played a role.

The life story of the Kid, whose real name was William Bonney, strikes contemporary chords. Jacobsen's 1994 book, *Such Men as Billy the Kid*, describes how Bonney was like many of his peers in "wishing to do the right thing but capable of rationalizing almost anything." The product of a dysfunctional family—his mother died, and his stepfather was neglectful—Bonney at age 18 killed a saloon bully, his first homicide. A legendary shootist during the infamous Lincoln County War, the Kid later tried to go straight, but opportunistic politicians reneged on a bargain to exchange a pardon for information. The Kid resorted to crime until Sheriff Pat Garrett put a bullet in him on a dark night July 14, 1881.

Billy, like many of today's young guns, was "obviously someone who could kill without conscience, without feeling that he had done anything wrong," says Jacobsen, who observes the same phenomenon today. Killers often rationalize that the victim "deserves to die, so I'll take it upon myself to see that he gets what he deserves," he says. But this also is true of arguments for capital punishment, adds Jacobsen. This "is a very uncomfortable thought, but it's almost an expression of the same sort of cultural impulse that we have the right to decide."

And there is no denying that cold calculation plays a role in some youth violence. In New Mexico, there has been a "perverse incentive" in which gangs recruit children under age 13 as killers, knowing the youngsters will receive at most two years in a youth facility, says Jacobsen. Sarnoff Menick, a psychologist at the University of Southern California, conducted a study of criminal records of felons in Copenhagen and Philadelphia. He found that those who were not punished committed three times as many crimes as those who were consistently punished with either fines or jail time. However, the study noted that the severity of the punishment had little effect.

Bloomstein says the decline in crime has to do more with demographics and the stabilization of the crack wars than with any political initiative. The 1980s "Just Say No" campaign, which sent older dealers to prison, along with the introduction of cheap crack cocaine, destabilized the market and led to turf wars, he says. Criminologist James Fyfe of Temple University, a former New York City homicide detective, predicts it will be demographics that cause violent crime to increase within 15 years, as schools grow more overcrowded.

And, it always should be remembered, numbers never tell the full story. The horror of Jonesboro goes far beyond the number of victims or alleged perpetrators. Apart from how many youths are committing how many crimes, there's what Jacobsen calls "the total pointlessness" of much of it. "Not all antisocial behavior is criminal," he says. "There are a lot of things they can do to get their kicks at the expense of somebody else without breaking a law."

Meanwhile, public concern that crime is a bigger and bigger problem trumps the formal statistics that say otherwise. This may be true because so many ordinary citizens are fearful that widely publicized violence will touch their own lives. If the polls are correct, few miss the coarsening of the culture, the deterioration of civility and growing indifference to the ancient verities on which moral standards and laws once were based.

Kids and Guns: From Playgrounds to Battlegrounds

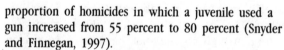

by Stuart Greenbaum

Late last year an 11-year-old boy was shot and killed. An 18-year-old allegedly killed the boy because he had shorted him on drug money (Thomas and Martin, 1996). The shooting should have rocked the Chicago neighborhood where it took place, except that this kind of thing happens all too often.

The lethal mix of children and guns has reached a crisis in the United States. Teenage boys are more likely to die of gunshot wounds than from all natural causes combined. The number of children dying from gunshot wounds and the number of children committing homicides continue to rise at alarming rates (McEnery, 1996).

Buying guns illegally is relatively easy for juveniles.

Guns are now the weapon of choice for youth. As can be seen in the figure in the following box, "Juvenile Gun Homicides", gun homicides by juveniles have tripled since 1983, while homicides involving other weapons have declined. From 1983 through 1995, the

Stuart Greenbaum is president of Greenbaum Public Relations, a Sacramento, California, firm that specializes in public interest concerns, including high-risk youth services. A 20-year veteran of public safety communication, Mr. Greenbaum is a cofounder and past communications director of the National School Safety Center at Pepperdine University.

proportion of homicides in which a juvenile used a gun increased from 55 percent to 80 percent (Snyder and Finnegan, 1997).

Disputes that would previously have ended in fist fights are now more likely to lead to shootings. A 1993 Louis Harris poll showed that 35 percent of children ages 6 to 12 fear their lives will be cut short by gun violence (Louis Harris and Associates, Inc., 1993). A 1990 Centers for Disease Control and Prevention study found that one in five 9th through 12th graders reported carrying a weapon in the past month; one in five of those carried a firearm (Centers for Disease Control and Prevention, 1991).

"No corner of America is safe from increasing levels of criminal violence, including violence committed by and against juveniles," Attorney General Janet Reno has observed. "Parents are afraid to let their children walk to school alone. Children hesitate to play in neighborhood playgrounds. The elderly lock themselves in their homes, and innocent Americans of all ages find their lives changed by the fear of crime" (Coordinating Council on Juvenile Justice and Delinquency Prevention, 1996).

The number of murdered juveniles increased 47 percent between 1980 and 1994, according to figures from *Juvenile Offenders and Victims: 1996 Update on Violence* (Snyder et al., 1996). The Summary, which cites data from the Federal Bureau of Investigation's Uniform Crime Reporting Program, notes that from 1980 through 1994 an estimated 326,170 persons were murdered in the United States. Of these, 9 percent (30,200) were youth under age 18. While there was a 1-percent increase from 1980 through 1994 in the total number of murders, the rate of juveniles murdered increased from five per day to seven per day. Fifty-three percent of the juveniles killed in 1994 were teenagers ages 15 to 17, while 30 percent were younger than age 6. In 1994, one in five murdered juveniles was killed by a juvenile offender.

Recently, however, there has been good news. Between 1994 and 1995, juvenile arrests for murder declined 14 percent, resulting in the number of juvenile murder arrests in 1995 being 9 percent below the 1991 figure. Overall arrests for violent juvenile crime decreased 3 percent between 1994 and 1995—the first decline in 9 years. These efforts must continue, however, as even these reduced rates are substantially higher than 1986 levels (Snyder, 1997).

Often, teenagers turn guns on themselves. In 1991, 1,889 teens ages 15 to 19 committed suicide—a rate of 11 per 100,000 (Allen-Hagen et al., 1994). Between 1980 and 1994, the suicide rate for 15- to 19-year-olds rose 29 percent, with an increase in firearms-related suicides accounting for 96 percent of the rise (Centers for Disease Control and Prevention, 1996). The risk of suicide is five times greater for individuals living in households with guns than for those in households without guns (Kellerman et al., 1992).

What is causing this epidemic of violence and how can it be stopped? The deterioration of the traditional family and the impact of drugs, gangs, poverty, and violence in the media are among the factors cited as contributing to the violent behavior of today's teens. Many of these children—victims and perpetrators—come from one- or no-parent families (McEnery, 1996).

Programs to get guns out of the hands of young people are being put into place.

Guns are readily available to juveniles. Although Federal law mandates that a person must be at least 18 years old to purchase a shotgun or rifle, and at least 21 years old to buy a handgun, law enforcement officials and youth themselves report that buying guns illegally is relatively easy for juveniles. Increasingly, juveniles believe they need guns for protection or carry them as status symbols. As more guns appear in the community, a local arms race ensues.

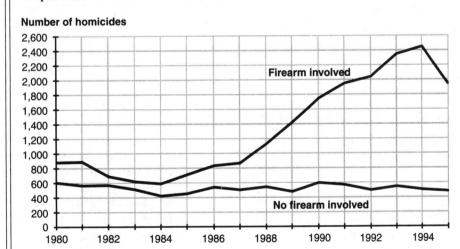

Juvenile Gun Homicides

Gun homicides by juveniles have tripled since 1983, while homicides involving other weapons have declined.

Number of homicides

Firearm involved

No firearm involved

◆ From 1983 through 1995, the proportion of homicides in which a juvenile used a gun increased from 55 to 80 percent.

Source: Snyder, H.N., and T.A. Finnegan. 1997. *Easy Access to the FBI's Supplementary Homicide Reports: 1980–1995* (data presentation and analysis package). Washington, DC: U.S. Department of Justice, Office of Justice Programs, Office of Juvenile Justice and Delinquency Prevention.

This article describes some promising steps that have been taken to curb the violence endangering our youth and our communities. It also provides information about a number of initiatives that have focused on gun violence in particular.

U.S. Attorneys Join the Fight

Local, State, and national programs to get guns out of the hands of young people are being put in place. In a report to the Attorney General and the President, U.S. Attorneys outlined the following ways in which they are supporting State and local programs:

◆ Disrupting the markets that provide guns to youth.

◆ Taking guns out of the hands of young people through coordination with State and local law enforcement officials.

◆ Working with State and local prosecutors to enhance enforcement of their laws.

◆ Encouraging and providing financial support for State and local efforts to trace the sources of guns taken from juveniles.

◆ Launching targeted enforcement efforts in places where young people should feel safe, such as their homes, schools, and recreation centers.

◆ Participating in prevention efforts directed at juveniles in our communities through mentoring, adopt-a-school (in which schools are "adopted" by civic groups or businesses), and Neighborhood Watch programs.

◆ Promoting increased personal responsibility and safety through public outreach and information on the consequences of juvenile handgun possession (Office of Juvenile Justice and Delinquency Prevention, 1996).

The experience of victimization by violence is far too common among children.

These approaches, also supported by other components of the U.S. Department of Justice (DOJ), are critical elements of a comprehensive youth gun violence reduction strategy.

To advance the U.S. Attorneys' violence prevention efforts and to help States and local jurisdictions respond to the problem of juvenile firearms violence, the Office of Juvenile Justice and Delinquency Prevention (OJJDP) published *Reducing Youth Gun Violence:*

An Overview of Programs and Initiatives (Office of Juvenile Justice and Delinquency Prevention, 1996). This report provides information on a wide array of strategies—from school-based prevention to gun market interception. In addition to program descriptions, the report includes a directory of youth gun violence prevention organizations and a bibliography of research, evaluation, and publications on youth and guns.

Promising Programs

Many State and local programs designed to take guns out of the hands of teenagers have proven successful. In the Kansas City (Missouri) Gun Experiment, the U.S. Attorney's Office and the Kansas City Police Department worked with local agencies to focus law enforcement efforts on high-crime neighborhoods. Under this initiative, developed with Weed and Seed funding from the Bureau of Justice Assistance, traffic law violators were routinely stopped, as were youth violating curfews and individuals involved in other infractions of the law. During these stops, police looked for violations that established legal authority to search a car or pedestrian for illegal guns. These special gun-interception teams were 10 times more cost-effective than regular police patrols.

The success of the Kansas City Gun Experiment is striking. An evaluation funded by the National Institute of Justice (NIJ) found that crime in the 80-block target neighborhood, which had a homicide rate 20 times the national average, was cut in half in 6 months. Significantly, the program did not merely displace crime to other locations. Gun crimes did not increase in any of the seven surrounding patrol beats. The active involvement of community and religious leaders in the development of the program resulted in broad support for the program in the community, which had objected to past police crackdowns on guns (Sherman et al., 1995).

In Boston, where juveniles in high-risk neighborhoods frequently carry guns, NIJ has launched a problem-solving project to devise, implement, and assess strategic interventions to disrupt illicit firearms markets and deter youth violence. Its initial focus was analyzing the supply and demand for guns. Strategic interventions by police, probation, and parole officers have presented gang members–prevalent among both victims and offenders–with a clear choice: Stop the flow of guns and stop the violence or face rapid, focused, and comprehensive law enforcement and corrections attention. Although it is too soon to evaluate the long-term effectiveness of this strategy, its immediate impact is encouraging; youth violence in Boston appears to have been substantially reduced (Kennedy, 1997).

NIJ's promising initiative in Boston was highlighted at OJJDP's August 1996 national satellite teleconference, Reducing Youth Gun Violence, which was viewed by more than 8,000 participants at 271 downlink sites. The teleconference, which is available on videotape from OJJDP's Juvenile Justice Clearinghouse, also featured the Detroit-based Handgun Intervention Program, carried out by volunteers in Michigan's 36th District Court, and the Shock Mentor Program, a collaborative effort among Prince George's County, Maryland, Public Schools, the Washington, D.C., chapter of Concerned Black Men, Inc., and Prince George's Hospital Center.

Partnerships To Reduce Juvenile Gun Violence

Based on a review of research and programs conducted by OJJDP and summarized in *Reducing Youth Gun Violence: An Overview of Programs and Initiatives,* OJJDP has started a new initiative, Partnerships To Reduce Juvenile Gun Violence. This effort is intended to increase the effectiveness of existing youth gun violence reduction strategies by enhancing and co-

ordinating prevention, intervention, and suppression strategies and by strengthening linkages among the community, law enforcement, and the juvenile justice system. Its comprehensive approach addresses three critical factors: juveniles' access to guns, the reasons young people carry guns, and the reasons they choose to use guns to resolve conflicts. Partnerships have been forged through recent OJJDP grants to the Center for Community Alternatives in Syracuse, New York; the City of East Baton Rouge, Louisiana; the Council on Alcoholism and Drug Abuse of Northwest Louisiana; and Youth ALIVE!, which services Oakland and Los Angeles, California.

Child abuse and neglect nearly doubled between 1986 and 1993.

OJJDP is funding an evaluation of Partnerships To Reduce Juvenile Gun Violence to document and analyze the process of community mobilization, planning, and collaboration needed to develop a comprehensive approach to combating youth gun violence.

The fundamental challenge in reducing juvenile firearm possession is to convince youth that they can survive in their neighborhoods without being armed. Community-based programs such as those listed above are working to dispel the perception by many juveniles that the authorities can neither protect them nor maintain order in their neighborhoods. A number of communities have implemented programs that address the risk of victimization, improve school safety, and foster a secure community environment.

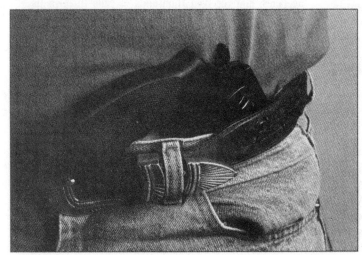

Victimization and the Cycle of Violence

The experience of victimization by violence is far too common among children in America. A survey of inner-city high school students revealed that 45 percent had been threatened with a gun or shot at, and one in three had been beaten up on their way to school (Sheley and Wright, 1993). According to a survey released by the U.S. Department of Health and Human Services, child abuse and neglect nearly doubled between 1986 and 1993 (Sedlak and Broadhurst, 1996). Investigations by child protective services agencies in 49 States determined that more than 1 million children were victims of substantiated or indicated child abuse and neglect in 1995 (National Center on Child Abuse and Neglect, 1997).

Public information campaigns can empower citizens to reach informed judgments.

OJJDP and NIJ have supported several studies focusing on this cycle of violence. The research indicates a relationship between experiences of childhood violence and subsequent delinquent behavior. OJJDP's Rochester (New York) Youth Development Study found that children who had been victims of violence were 24 percent more likely to report engaging in violent behavior as adolescents than those who had not been maltreated in childhood (Thornberry, 1994). An NIJ longitudinal study of childhood victimization found that child abuse increases the likelihood of future delinquency and adult criminality by nearly 40 percent (Widom, 1992).

With funding support from OJJDP, the New Haven (Connecticut) Department of Police Services and the Yale Child Study Center established the Child Development-Community Policing (CD-CP) program to address the adverse impact of continued exposure to violence on children and their families and to interrupt the cycle of violence affecting so many of our children. Reflecting New Haven's commendable commitment to community policing, the program brings law enforcement and mental health professionals together to help children who are victims, witnesses, and (in some instances) perpetrators of violent acts. The CD-CP program serves as a model for police-mental health partnerships across the Nation and is being replicated under the CD-CP grant in Buffalo, New York; Charlotte, North Carolina; Nashville, Tennessee; and Portland, Oregon (Marans and Berkman, 1997). In fiscal year 1997, OJJDP is enhancing the CD-CP program to provide training to school personnel, probation and parole officers, and prosecutors.

Public Information Campaigns

Researchers have found that long-term public education campaigns on violence prevention, family education, alcohol and drug prevention, and gun safety curriculums in schools are effective in helping to reduce delinquency (American Academy of Pediatrics, 1992; Centers for Disease Control and Prevention, 1991; Christoffel, 1991; DeJong, 1994). This may be especially true for education campaigns to prevent gun violence, because public awareness of positive activities can reduce fear, which is a powerful factor in juveniles choosing to carry guns. Involving teenagers in the development and operation of these programs is a critical ingredient to a program's success (Treanor and Bijlefeld, 1989). The public and private sectors, including the media, also can play significant roles in program design and implementation.

The goal of public information and education efforts should be threefold: to change public perceptions about youth violence and guns, to educate the community about the problem, and to convince youth and adults that their involvement is essential to the success of any program to curb possession and use of guns by youth. Public information campaigns can empower citizens to reach informed judgments about effective ways of preventing firearms violence by and against juveniles.

Public information campaigns to reduce gun violence should:

◆ Provide accurate information to key policymakers about the causes, nature, and extent of juvenile delinquency and victimization, particularly gun-related violence.

◆ Communicate that juvenile gun violence and victimization are preventable.

◆ Publicize strategies and results of successful programs and encourage their replication.

◆ Motivate individuals, government agencies, and community service organizations to work collaboratively to address the problem as a key to ensuring public safety.

A number of public information campaigns have been launched or are being developed. In California, the statewide Campaign To Prevent Handgun Violence Against Kids has produced 30-second television public service announcements (PSA's) in English and Spanish; communicated critical information on youth gun violence to elected officials, media leaders, and public agencies; and received thousands of calls through its hotline and information service (Office of Juvenile Justice and Delinquency Prevention, 1996).

To assist communities in their public education efforts, the Center to Prevent Handgun Violence collaborated with Disney Educational Productions (1994) to produce *Under the Gun: A Story About Violence Prevention.* The video, intended for educational and law enforcement agencies, refutes the notion that guns are glamorous and that carrying guns makes communities safer.

OJJDP and the Bureau of Justice Assistance are funding a public-private partnership to create and market PSA's with a three-part message designed to persuade young people to turn away from violence, educate parents and other community residents about solutions to youth violence, and show teens, parents, and youth-serving professionals how they can become part of the solution.

Conclusion

As disturbing as youth gun violence is, it need not be inevitable. It is preventable–as many programs throughout the United States are beginning to demonstrate. With the public alarmed about the problem, public servants and practitioners might bear in mind the Greek philosopher Solon's words, "There can be no justice until those of us who are unaffected by crime become as indignant as those who are."

References

Allen-Hagen, B., M. Sickmund, and H.N. Snyder. 1994 (November). *Juveniles and Violence: Juvenile Offending and Victimization.* Fact Sheet. Washington, DC: U.S. Department of Justice, Office of Justice Programs, Office of Juvenile Justice and Delinquency Prevention.

American Academy of Pediatrics, Committee on Adolescence. 1992. Firearms and adolescence. *Pediatrics* 89(4):784-787.

Centers for Disease Control and Prevention. 1996 (November). *National Summary of Injury Mortality Data, 1987–1994.* Atlanta, GA: Centers for Disease Control and Prevention, National Center for Injury Prevention and Control.

Centers for Disease Control and Prevention. 1991. Weapon carrying among high school students: United States, 1990. *Morbidity and Mortality Weekly Report* 40(40):681-684.

Christoffel, K.K. 1991. Toward reducing pediatric injuries from firearms: Charting a legislative and regulatory course. *Pediatrics* 88(2):294-305.

Coordinating Council on Juvenile Justice and Delinquency Prevention. 1996 (March). *Combating Violence and Delinquency: The National Juvenile Justice Action Plan.* Report. Washington, DC: U.S. Department of Justice, Office of Justice Programs, Office of Juvenile Justice and Delinquency Prevention.

DeJong, W. 1994 (November). *Preventing Interpersonal Violence Among Youth: An Introduction to School, Community and Mass Media Strategies.* NIJ Issues and Practices. Washington, DC: U.S. Department of Justice, Office of Justice Programs, National Institute of Justice.

Disney Educational Productions. 1994. *Under the Gun: A Story About Violence Prevention.* Burbank: The Walt Disney Company.

Kellermann, A.L., F.P. Rivara, G. Somes, D.T. Reay, J. Francisco, G. Banton, J. Prodzinski, C. Fligner, and B.B. Hackman. 1992. Suicide in the home in relation to gun ownership. *New England Journal of Medicine* 327:467-472.

Kennedy, D.M. 1997 (March). *Juvenile Gun Violence and Gun Markets in Boston.* Research Preview. Washington, DC: U.S. Department of Justice, Office of Justice Programs, National Institute of Justice.

Louis Harris and Associates, Inc. 1993. *A Survey of Experiences, Perceptions and Apprehensions About Guns Among Young People in America.* New York, NY: Louis Harris and Associates, Inc., and LH Research, Inc.

Marans, S., and M. Berkman. 1997 (March). *Child Development-Community Policing: Partnership in a Climate of Violence.* Bulletin. Washington, DC: U.S. Department of Justice, Office of Justice Programs, Office of Juvenile Justice and Delinquency Prevention.

McEnery, R. Today's schoolyard bully just might be armed. *Asbury Park Press.* Feb. 28, 1996.

National Center on Child Abuse and Neglect. 1997. *Child Maltreatment 1995: Reports from the States to the National Child Abuse and Neglect Data System.* Washington, DC: U.S. Department of Health and Human Services, National Center on Child Abuse and Neglect.

Office of Juvenile Justice and Delinquency Prevention. 1996 (May). *Reducing Youth Gun Violence: An Overview of Programs and Initiatives.* Program Report. Washington, DC: U.S. Department of Justice, Office of Justice Programs, Office of Juvenile Justice and Delinquency Prevention.

Sedlak, A.J., and D.D. Broadhurst. 1996 (September). *Third National Incidence Study of Child Abuse and Neglect.* Washington, DC: U.S. Department of Health and Human Services, National Center on Child Abuse and Neglect.

Sheley, J.F., and J.D. Wright. 1993 (December). *Gun Acquisition and Possession in Selected Juvenile Samples.* Research in Brief. Washington, DC: U.S. Department of Justice, Office of Justice Programs, National Institute of Justice and Office of Juvenile Justice and Delinquency Prevention.

Sherman, L.W., J.W. Shaw, and D.P. Rogan. 1995 (January). *The Kansas City Gun Experiment.* Research in Brief. Washington, DC: U.S. Department of Justice, Office of Justice Programs, National Institute of Justice.

Snyder, H.N. 1997 (February). *Juvenile Arrests 1995.* Bulletin. Washington, DC: U.S. Department of Justice, Office of Justice Programs, Office of Juvenile Justice and Delinquency Prevention.

Snyder, H.N., and M. Sickmund. 1995 (August). *Juvenile Offenders and Victims: A National Report.* Washington, DC: U.S. Department of Justice, Office of Justice Programs, Office of Juvenile Justice and Delinquency Prevention.

Snyder, H.N., M. Sickmund, and E. Poe-Yamagata. 1996 (February). *Juvenile Offenders and Victims: 1996 Update on Violence.* Statistics Summary. Washington, DC: U.S. Department of Justice, Office of Justice Programs, Office of Juvenile Justice and Delinquency Prevention.

Snyder, H.N., and T.A. Finnegan. 1997. *Easy Access to the FBI's Supplementary Homicide Reports: 1980-1995* (data presentation and analysis package). Washington, DC: U.S. Department of Justice, Office of Justice Programs, Office of Juvenile Justice and Delinquency Prevention.

Thomas, J., and A. Martin. Notorious block's deadly legacy, West Adams Street's world of fear, drugs, death. *Chicago Tribune.* Nov. 23, 1996.

Thornberry, T. 1994 (December). *Violent Families and Youth Violence.* Fact Sheet. Washington, DC: U.S. Department of Justice, Office of Justice Programs, Office of Juvenile Justice and Delinquency Prevention.

Treanor, W.W., and M. Bijlefeld. 1989. *Kids and Guns: A Child Safety Scandal.* Washington, DC: American Youth Work Center and Educational Fund to End Handgun Violence.

Widom, C.S. 1992 (October). *The Cycle of Violence.* Research in Brief. Washington, DC: U.S. Department of Justice, Office of Justice Programs, National Institute of Justice.

With Juvenile Courts in Chaos, Critics Propose Their Demise

JUSTICE BESIEGED

By FOX BUTTERFIELD

CHICAGO—The nation's juvenile courts, long a troubled backwater of the criminal justice system, have been so overwhelmed by the increase in violent teen-age crime and the breakdown of the family that judges and politicians are debating a solution that was once unthinkable: abolishing the system and trying most minors as adults.

The crisis began building a decade ago, when prosecutors responded to the growth in high-profile youth crime by pushing for the trials of greater numbers of children, dramatically raising caseloads.

But the courts have become so choked that by all accounts they are even less effective than before, with more juveniles prosecuted but fewer convicted and no evidence of a drop in rearrest rates for those who go to prison.

The resulting situation angers people across the political spectrum, from those who believe the juvenile court is too lenient, to those who feel it fails to prevent troubled children from becoming ensnared in a life of crime.

In interviews around the country, judges, probation officers, prosecutors and defense lawyers described a juvenile court system in perhaps the worst chaos of its history.

In Chicago, where the first juvenile court was created in 1899, judges today preside over assembly-line justice, hearing an average of 60 cases a day, about six minutes per case. In New Orleans, public defenders have to represent their poor clients with no office, no telephone, no court records and little chance to discuss the case before trial. In New York, where the recent case of Malcolm Shabazz—who admitted setting the fire that killed his grandmother, Malcolm X's widow—focused new attention on Family Court, some officials say it is time to junk the system.

Almost everywhere, with juvenile courts starved for money, record-keeping is so primitive that often the judge, the prosecutor and the defense attorney have different records on the same defendant, making an accurate assessment of the case impossible. And because the courts cannot afford their own warrant squads, young defendants sometimes fail to show up for trial or simply skip out of the courtroom with virtual impunity.

Despite calls for tougher justice, the overcrowding and lack of resources mean that only a small percentage of the young people who move through the juvenile justice system are imprisoned, although there are other forms of punishment, the most common of which is probation.

Of the 1,555,200 delinquency cases referred by the police to prosecutors nationwide in 1994, 855,200, or just over half, resulted in what in adult criminal courts would be called indictments, said Jeffrey Butts, at the National Center for Juvenile Justice. Of these, Mr. Butts said, 495,000 defendants were found guilty.

In turn, 141,300 of these cases resulted in a juvenile's being incarcerated. That is 9 percent of those originally sent to prosecutors by the police.

By contrast, in adult criminal court, which is explicitly intended to be punitive, 90 percent to 95 percent of defendants who have been indicted plead guilty in a plea bargain, often as a way to win a lighter punishment. The philosophy of juvenile court traditionally was to rehabilitate rather than punish young offenders, a premise that has come under attack in recent years.

Congress is poised to pass legislation, backed by President Clinton, that would provide Federal grants to states that sharply increase the number of young people they try in adult court. The legislation, already passed by the House and likely to be adopted soon by the Senate, would further undermine the authority of the juvenile court at a time when many specialists predict there will be a new wave of youth crime, as the number of teen-agers increases by 15 percent in the next decade.

"The Family Court is bankrupt," said Peter Reinharz, chief of New York City's juvenile prosecution unit. "It's time to sell everything off and start over."

Mr. Reinharz is a longtime critic of the juvenile court, but even its staunchest defenders are now troubled by what they see.

"It is no longer just the chronic problems that have long plagued the court, like overcrowding and making do with less," said Bart Lubow, a senior associate of the Annie E. Casey Foundation who has studied juvenile courts around the nation. "Now there's a crisis of confidence, since the very notion that has been its cornerstone, that children are different from adults and therefore need to be treated differently, is in question."

Among the issues swirling in the nation's 3,000 juvenile courts are the following:

• As pressure to get tough on young criminals has increased, the number of juveniles arrested who are prosecuted in court has climbed to 55 percent in 1994 from 45 percent in 1985.

But the percentage of young people convicted has not kept pace, rising to 33 percent in 1994 from 31 percent a decade earlier.

In Chicago, the figures show an even more dramatic effect of overloading the system. The Cook County State's Attorney has increased the number of juveniles he prosecutes to 85 percent of all those sent to him by the police, but about 70 percent of these cases are dismissed for lack of evidence or the failure of witnesses to appear, according to a new study by the Children and Family Justice Center of

the Northwestern University School of Law.

"This is the dirty little secret of Cook County," said David Reed, the lead author of the report. "You have lots more cases but almost the same number of judges and prosecutors, and they can only do so much work and prove a certain number guilty. So all these kids are brought in on criminal charges and then most are let go. It fosters cynicism about the court, makes the public and crime victims mad and teaches young people that justice is a joke."

• With an angry public demanding harsher punishments, it is becoming increasingly difficult for judges to differentiate between defendants who may have committed a youthful indiscretion and those who are on their way to a lifetime of crime. The distinction is critical. Almost 60 percent of those teenagers sent to juvenile court for the first time never return. But every time a young person is sent back to court, his likelihood of being arrested again increases until recidivism rates reach 75 percent by a fifth appearance, said Howard Snyder, of the National Center for Juvenile Justice.

• Despite a rush by legislators in all 50 states over the past decade to pass laws trying young people in adult court, there is no evidence that being convicted in adult court or sentenced to adult prison is more effective in reducing youth crime than the juvenile justice route. A new study of 5,476 juvenile criminals in Florida, which followed them from their arrest in 1987 through 1994, concluded that those tried as adults committed new crimes sooner after their release from prison, and perpetrated more serious and violent crimes, than those tried as juveniles.

Charles Frazier, a sociology professor at the University of Florida and a co-author of the report, said that keeping young people in the juvenile justice system works better because juvenile institutions provide more education and psychological treatment for inmates, helping offenders rehabilitate themselves. By

contrast, adult prisons now are more punitive and have largely abandoned trying to change criminals' behavior.

"Ultimately, you are going to release all these people back into the community, and the juvenile justice system does a better job of reclaiming them," Professor Frazier said.

19th-Century Origin
Firmly but Gently Disciplining Youths

The criticism of the juvenile court misses a fundamental point, some specialists believe. With the breakdown of the family, can any court system, juvenile or adult, do the job society once did: instill discipline and values in children, punish them if they are bad and then help redeem them?

"The juvenile court was set up 100 years ago, in a very different America, to help cure kids of immigrant families with manageable problems, like truancy, petty thefts and fighting," said Jeffrey Fagan, the director of the Center for Violence Research and Prevention at Columbia University.

As envisioned by the pioneering social worker, Jane Addams, the juvenile court was to be a surrogate parent and the judge a kindly doctor, seeking to understand the social conditions that had led the child astray, the way a doctor would study a disease. This paternalism was reflected in the informality of the courtroom, with the judge sitting at an ordinary table, not behind a bench, and wearing only street clothes, not a robe.

The court's guiding principle was to do what was "in the best interest of the child," not to protect the community or insure the child's constitutional rights. So punishments were kept light, since children were thought to still be in the process of forming their personalities, and thus more amenable to reform than adults. And all proceedings and records were kept confidential.

An antiseptic nomenclature was even invented to avoid stigmatizing children. A boy was "taken into custody," not arrested. He had a "petition of delinquency" drawn against him, rather than being charged. And there were no convictions, only "adjudications," and no sentences, only "placements."

But today, poverty, joblessness and violent teen-age crime seem far worse than they were in the 1890's, often making the court's customs appear a quaint anachronism.

Also, as a result, Professor Fagan said, "The juvenile court can no longer do what it was set up to do. It certainly can't do what the public expects it to do, control juvenile crime."

Statistics only hint at the magnitude of the troubles the court is asked to resolve.

Since 1960, the number of delinquency cases handled by juvenile courts nationwide has risen almost four times, to 1.55 million in 1994. During the same period, the number of cases involving abused or neglected children, which are also handled by juvenile courts, has increased five times faster than even the delinquency cases, said Mr. Butts of the National Center for Juvenile Justice. And these abused and neglected children are often the very ones who become delinquents.

Among delinquency cases, violent crimes are rising the fastest. From 1985 to 1994, juvenile crimes involving weapons soared 156 per-

cent, murders jumped 144 percent and aggravated assaults were up 134 percent. Property crimes were up 25 percent.

A Case in Point
In a Chicago Court, Beating the System

Perhaps the most revealing place to see the troubles is in Chicago, home to the nation's oldest and largest juvenile court. The Chicago court is not the best; that may be in Louisville, San Jose or Oakland, where the judges command wide respect. Nor is it the most beleaguered; that distinction may belong to Baltimore or New Orleans. Cook County is just a good example of what goes on in a high-volume juvenile court.

A tiny 13-year-old defendant, so short he could barely see Judge William Hibbler seated behind the bench, was on trial for murder.

The defendant—who will remain unidentified in accordance with the court's rules of confidentiality—was wearing an Atlanta Braves baseball jacket, and he looked more like a team mascot than a hardened criminal. But the teen-ager was charged with first-degree murder for shooting a man who was trying to buy crack cocaine.

At an even younger age, he was arrested for armed robbery and burglary, though without being sent to prison. This time, after his arrest for murder, he had been allowed to return home because the court had failed to give him a hearing within the 36-hour limit specified for juveniles.

While free awaiting trial for murder, he had stolen a car.

Neither his mother nor father was in court. His father had died of alcohol poisoning; his mother, a crack addict, was in a boot camp on a drug charge.

Judge Hibbler, the presiding judge of the delinquency division of the Cook County Juvenile Court, wore a black robe, a small sign of how the court has shifted from its original

The Juvenile Caseload: A Closer Look

THE DELINQUENCY CASELOAD HAS SURGED...
Estimated number of delinquency cases handled in juvenile courts around the country. A youth may be involved in more than one case.

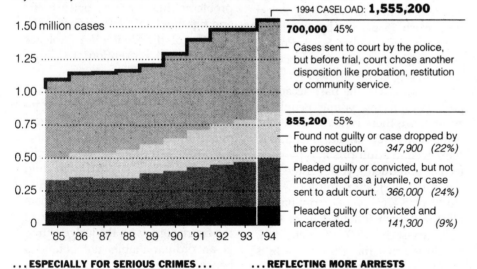

1994 CASELOAD: **1,555,200**

700,000 45%
Cases sent to court by the police, but before trial, court chose another disposition like probation, restitution or community service.

855,200 55%
Found not guilty or case dropped by the prosecution.   *347,900 (22%)*

Pleaded guilty or convicted, but not incarcerated as a juvenile, or case sent to adult court.   *366,000 (24%)*

Pleaded guilty or convicted and incarcerated.   *141,300 (9%)*

...ESPECIALLY FOR SERIOUS CRIMES...
Change in cases for selected crimes.

VIOLENT CRIME*	CASES IN 1994	CHANGE SINCE '85
Murder	3,000	+144%
Aggravated assault	85,300	134
Robbery	37,000	53
Forcible rape	5,400	25
OTHER SERIOUS CRIME		
Weapons offenses	48,800	+156%
Simple assault	177,700	91

*The four crimes in the F.B.I.'s violent crime index.

...REFLECTING MORE ARRESTS
Arrests per 100,000 for violent crimes.*

Ages 10 to 17

All ages

Sources: National Center for Juvenile Justice; Office of Juvenile Justice and Delinquency Prevention; F.B.I.

The New York Times

informality and evolved, in the judge's phrase, into more of a "mini criminal court."

The courtroom is inside the Cook County Juvenile Center, a modern structure a block long and eight stories high that from the outside looks more like an office building than a courthouse with a juvenile jail attached. The building was recently reconstructed as part of an effort to reverse the turmoil overtaking juvenile court.

Inside, however, the waiting rooms are still painted a dingy brown and are jammed with largely black and Hispanic families, many of them holding crying babies. In the men's rooms the toilets are broken and the metal mirrors are scrawled with graffiti.

These dilapidated conditions, said Mr. Lubow of the Casey Foundation, "basically say to the families and kids who come to juvenile court that we don't take them seriously, that we value them less as people."

Now, after talking with his lawyer, the youth begrudgingly confessed to murder as part of a plea bargain. Judge Hibbler then solemnly ordered that he "be committed to the Illinois Department of Corrections, Juvenile Division, till 21 years of age."

The boy smirked. He knew he had beaten the system again. He could be free in as little as five years. Without the plea bargain, he could have been transferred to adult court and faced a minimum sentence of 20 years.

It was the kind of case that infuriates conservatives and others, suggesting that juvenile court is little more than a revolving door.

But it was also the kind of case that makes children's rights advocates argue that juvenile court is failing to help young people from troubled families by intervening early enough to prevent them from becoming ensnared in a life of crime.

Even many judges themselves, who are often the only defenders of the juvenile court, concur that the court is foundering. But the judges

tend to blame the politicians who have passed laws to try more teenagers in adult courts.

"There is a crisis," Judge Hibbler acknowledged. But, he contended, "Children don't stop being children just because they commit a crime, and calling for an end of the juvenile court is the same as saying we should do away with grammar schools and junior high schools and just put everyone in college."

Clogging the Courts
Convictions Flat As Caseload Soars

In the traditional juvenile court, probation officers played a key role.

They presided at what is still widely called "intake," or arraignment in adult terms. After the police decided which juveniles to send to court—usually about half were dismissed with the equivalent of a parking ticket—the probation officers would screen out children whose crimes were petty or who had no record. Nationwide, they filtered out about half the cases referred by the police.

But in Chicago in the late 1980's, in response to the epidemic of crack cocaine and the rise of teen-age gun violence, Richard M. Daley, then the Cook County State's Attorney, wrestled this power away from the court probation department. To appear tough on crime, he began prosecuting 97 percent of the cases forwarded to him by the police, according to an analysis by The Chicago Sun-Times.

Mr. Daley is now mayor of Chicago, and that figure is down to 85 percent, the State's Attorney's office says.

But Bernardine Dohrn, the director of the Children and Family Justice Center at Northwestern University, said that prosecuting such a high proportion of cases has overwhelmed the court, resulting in about 70 percent of the cases filed by the State's Attorney being dropped before trial.

A new study by Ms. Dohrn's center has found that while the number of delinquency cases heard each month has more than tripled in the last decade, the number of convictions has remained almost flat.

"They are clogging the system," Ms. Dohrn said, "and when you do this wholesale, you drive kids into the system who don't belong there and you don't find the kids who aren't in school and are getting into serious trouble. They are able to pass through for a long time without being stopped. So it's a double whammy, and dangerous."

Probation officers are also supposed to enforce the most commonly used punishment in juvenile court, probation—a court order requiring a young person to go to school or find a job and obey a home curfew the rest of the day.

But no one likes probation: not judges, who want more innovative alternatives; not the offenders, who chafe at the loss of freedom, and not the police or prosecutors, who regard probation as a farce. Worst of all, probation further undercuts the credibility of the court.

For judges, probation is part of a terrible dilemma. "I really have only two major choices," said Glenda Hatchett, the presiding judge of the Fulton County Juvenile Court in Atlanta.

"I can place these kids in incarceration, where they will learn to become better criminals, or I can send them home on probation, back to where they got in trouble in the first place," Judge Hatchett said.

Because governments have always regarded the juvenile court as a "poor stepchild" of the criminal justice system, Judge Hatchett said, there isn't money for the kinds of programs she believes would help, by reaching at-risk children and their parents when the children are 4, 5 or 6 years old, before it is too late.

Shifting Roles

Probation Officers Become Enforcers

Laura Donnelly is a Chicago probation officer with a master's degree in social work.

That makes her part of a vanishing breed, because today more and more probation officers have degrees in criminal justice. The change reflects the transition of the juvenile court from its origins in social welfare, treating the best interests of the child, to a criminal justice agency.

Ms. Donnelly has a caseload of 45 youths whom she visits a few times a month at home, school or work to make sure they are where they are supposed to be. Three of her clients have disappeared completely. She is confident she could find them, if she had enough time, which she does not.

She could also get a court-ordered arrest warrant, but the juvenile court cannot afford its own warrant squad, and police officers she knows are reluctant to spend time looking for children on warrants, unless the person is arrested on a new charge.

"A lot of officers don't want to waste their time on kiddie court when the judge is going to release the kid anyway," she said.

Ms. Donnelly stopped by a house on Chicago's South Side where one of her clients lived with his grandmother and 13 cousins, since his mother was a crack addict who couldn't be found. A husky 16-year-old, the boy was on probation for selling crack and was confined to his home 24 hours a day unless accompanied by his grandmother.

A charge of auto theft had been dropped when he repeatedly failed to appear for trial and the witnesses in the case tired of going to court without any result. That is a common way for young defendants to win.

Ms. Donnelly reminded the boy that he had another court date in two days, relating to a charge of theft and battery incurred while he was supposed to have been confined to home. He had forgotten about the appearance.

It was another day's work for Ms. Donnelly. "These kids have had nothing but chaos in their lives," she said. "That's what we have to overcome, to give them as much structure and consistency as we can."

"But how," she asked, "do you replace the absence of the family?" Sometimes she thinks the only answer is to move in herself. But she knows that would not work either.

A Move for Change

Young Suspects In Adult Courts

All these troubles have sparked a growing movement to drastically restructure and perhaps abolish the juvenile court.

Leading the charge are conservative politicians who have passed laws in all 50 states allowing juveniles to be tried in adult court and sent to adult prison.

In Illinois a person under 17 may be tried in adult court for crimes including murder, carjacking and armed robbery as well as possession of drugs or weapons within 1,000 feet of a school or housing project, a provision that disproportionately affects minorities. Illinois also has a version for juveniles of the "three strikes and you're out" law.

Congress is poised to pass the most Draconian law yet, with provisions for $1.5 billion in Federal grants to states that try larger number[s] of young people in adult court and making 14-year-olds subject to trial in Federal court if they commit certain felonies.

"It's the end of the juvenile court," said Ira Schwartz, dean of the School of Social Work at the University of Pennsylvania. "All you would have left is a court for larceny." Such a truncated court would not be financially viable and would probably be scrapped, he suggested.

At the same time, some left-wing legal scholars have also called for abolishing the juvenile court, though for very different reasons. Barry Feld, a professor of law at the University of Minnesota, believes that young people often fail to get adequate legal representation in juvenile court and would fare better in adult court, where they would be more likely to be assigned decent lawyers.

Under his plan, as a further protective measure, juveniles in adult court would be given a "youth discount," or lighter sentences, depending on their age.

Some children's advocates who in the past championed the juvenile court have begun urging still another solution—that the court scale back its judicial role and transfer its functions to community groups or social service agencies that would provide better treatment for young people in trouble.

In the rush to try juveniles in adult courts, some critical questions go unasked. For example, are 13- and 14-year olds really competent to stand trial like adults?

Often such young defendants cannot tell a coherent story to help defend themselves, said Thomas Grisso, a psychiatry professor at the University of Massachusetts Medical Center. What then should the court do? Wait till they are more mature?

As a result of all this ferment, Mr. Schwartz said, "What we have right now in the juvenile court is chaos, with every state moving piecemeal on its own." A century after the creation of the juvenile court, he said, "Unless we take it more seriously, what we are headed for is its abolition by default."

Now, Justice Is Served By Youths, For Youths

By REGINA MARCAZZO

RIVERHEAD

THE nearly empty room at Riverhead Town Hall was silent as the officers of the court entered on a recent Wednesday to decide the fate of a 15-year-old boy charged with possession of marijuana.

Leading the procession was the judge, Sabina Sapienza, in her black robe. All of the other court officers wore blue golf shirts with gold letters and an emblem of the scales of justice.

The judge is 18 and a recent Shoreham-Wading River High School graduate. None of the others is old enough to take a legal drink.

But it was not a mock trial; this was real justice being dispensed. It was the third case ever tried by the new Riverhead Youth Court, a judicial innovation in which minors who choose to plead guilty to misdemeanors are given the option of being sentenced by their peers.

The defendant decided to go before the Youth Court when given the option upon his arrest by the Riverhead police. "I figured this was better than a real court," the defendant said while waiting outside the courtroom during deliberations by the jury, which on this night included three officers of the newly formed

Town of Brookhaven youth court, who had come to get a taste of participation in a real trial.

Three youth courts have been established on Long Island with funding through Federal grant money administered by the New York State Division of Criminal Justice Services.

Youth court defendants are juveniles who agree along with their parents to have their cases heard using the unconventional method. They must be first-time nonviolent offenders who plead guilty to nothing more than a misdemeanor. Cases can be referred through the probation department and other sources such as a local school district.

"The feedback that we've gotten on the youth courts has been overwhelmingly positive," said Scott Sandman, a spokesman for the State Division of Criminal Justice.

"It's a movement that's going around the country," said Vincent Iaria, the Suffolk County Director of Probation. "If you have peer involvement not only will people learn about the system and take it seriously, they'll also have to do meaningful punishment decided by their peers. It helps the delinquent to see it's a crime against the community. It's a crime against all of us, including their fellow peers."

Besides the defendant in the Riverhead marijuana case and his

mother, who sat next to him throughout the session, the case involved two prosecuting attorneys, two defense attorneys, the five jurors, a clerk and the judge. The only adults with any significant role in the proceedings were Dan Rodgers and John Shields, volunteer attorneys who coached the young prosecution and defense teams and answered questions asked by the jurors during deliberations. The two adults have the right to intervene in case of some miscarriage of justice.

"The toughest critics on kids are the kids," said Mr. Rodgers, a criminal attorney in Riverhead who volunteered to be a mentor to Youth Court members and said he found the process rewarding and worthwhile. "The message gets across loud and clear."

"I think it's fantastic," said Mr. Shields, another volunteer mentor and also a Southampton Town deputy town attorney. "I've seen some performances here that are equal if not better than law competitions I've seen."

The defendant's two young attorneys argued for leniency after presenting three witnesses, including the defendant, to testify that the 15-year-old was cooperative, helpful at home, active in sports and not planning to break the law again.

"He has admitted that he made a stupid mistake," said Lauren Paladino, a recent Riverhead High School graduate, issuing her closing statement for the defense. "I'm sure most of you have been in the same spot."

From the stand, the defendant told the jury that his desire for a career in law enforcement was strengthened by the experience. "I want to stop kids from messing up like me," he said. When asked if he would be a repeat offender, he said: "I was arrested and handcuffed. That scared me a lot."

Officer Scott Wicklund of the Riverhead Town Police also took the witness stand to testify about the arrest and the defendant's cooperation. "I really firmly believe in this," Officer Wicklund said of the court, adding that he felt more nervous testifying in youth court than he did in the conventional court system.

During deliberations, where Mr. Rodgers and Judy Doll, who supervises the youth court program for Riverhead Town, dispensed advice and answers, the jury talked about how they wanted to be sure the defendant learned from the experience and did not get in trouble again. They did not buy the defense's requested sentence: 10 hours of community service working with the defendant's choice group, the elderly. Instead they went with the suggestion of the prosecuting attorney Ed Libassi, a recent Shoreham-Wad-

ing River High School graduate who will attend John Jay College in New York in September to pursue a police science degree. He recommended 25 hours of community service.

The defendant was given 10 hours of cleaning and washing Riverhead Town Police vehicles, 8 hours working inside the police department and 7 hours at the town's animal control center. The defendant was also ordered to take a tour of the local jail and serve as a juror on a later case.

Outside in the hallway throughout the trial was a woman whose daughter was serving as a juror as part of a shoplifting sentence handed down in an earlier youth court session. The daughter had also been sentenced to four hours of community service and was sent to a recovery program on shoplifting.

"I think it means more to them when they're told through their peers," the mother said.

The mother of a another youth court defendant whose case was being heard that night said she noticed a positive change in her son even before the trial.

"I think that he got a lot out of it because he met with an attorney who was in his peer group," the mother said. "I don't think he would have responded if he had gone before a

judge. I've been living with the kid for the past 10 days, and it's been a pleasure."

Thirty-one youth court grants were awarded throughout the state, with the Riverhead program getting $26,500, Brookhaven $24,000 and Southampton $26,500. But for now, the Riverhead program is the only one on Long Island to have tried a case.

State Assemblywoman Patricia Acampora, a Republican from Mattituck, helped procure funding for the Riverhead Youth Court and said she would like to see the teen-agers get more cases. According to her, there has been some resistance from the family court system because of a lack of state legislation that would establish clearer lines of accountability in case something went wrong with a youth court case. The supervising judge of the Suffolk County Family court, David Freundlich, declined to comment.

Although she can understand the concern and is in the process of researching the possibility of a future bill, Ms. Acampora believes that going through a lengthy legislative process would be difficult. "Let's not make it more complicated," she said, citing youth courts that have been operating successfully in other parts of the state.

Preventing Crime, Saving Children:
Sticking To The Basics

BY JOHN J. DiIULO, JR.

"Post-Crack," Not Post-Problem

Like media coverage of most complicated social problems, press attention to the problems of youth crime and substance abuse ebbs and flows. But make no mistake: the passing of the much publicized inner-city crack-cocaine-and-crime epidemic of the late 1980s and early 1990s is *not* synonymous with the passing of the challenges of youth crime and substance abuse, least of all in urban America. The news spotlight on juvenile crime and delinquency flickers, but the practical and moral challenges posed by millions of juveniles who murder, rape, rob, assault, burglarize, vandalize, join street gangs, deal illegal drugs or consume illegal drugs does not thereby fade.

To the contrary, an intellectually and ideologically diverse range of expert voices has been proclaiming that the challenges of youth crime and substance abuse are more pressing today than they were at the height of the crack plague. Consider, for example, reports released over the last several years by the National Research Council, the International Association of Chiefs of Police, and the Council on Crime in America.

A few years ago, the National Research Council's Panel on High-Risk Youth reported that at least seven million young Americans—roughly a quarter of adolescents aged 10 to 170—are at risk of failing to achieve productive adult lives.[1] The United States, the panel warned, is in danger of "losing generations" of low-income children who abuse illegal drugs, engage in unprotected premarital sex, drop out of school, prove unable to get and keep jobs, succumb to the blandishments of illegal drugs, commit serious crimes or become victims of serious crimes.

In 1996, the International Association of Chiefs of Police (IACP) held a major summit on youth violence. The IACP noted that the number of juvenile offenders had risen rapidly in recent years, and warned that juvenile crime "will get considerably worse as a big new group of youngsters reach their teenage years." Looking over the horizon of the next few years, the IACP envisioned more kids, more drugs, more guns and more murders.[2] According to the IACP, in 1996 crack cocaine use was down, but crack was hardly invisible on East Coast inner-city streets, heroin was making a roaring comeback (especially on the West Coast), and LSD, amphetamine, stimulant and inhalant use was rising among teenagers nationwide. Thus, in several big cities, the percentage of juveniles in custody who tested positive for illegal drug use has more than tripled since 1990.

In 1997, the bipartisan Council on crime in America stated flatly that "America's crime prevention challenge—at core a challenge of at-risk youth in need of adults—must be met, and soon." According to the Council, in 1994 there were over 2.7 million arrests of persons under age 18 (a third of them under age 15), up from 1.7 million juvenile arrests in 1991. Some 150,000 of these 2.7 million arrests were for violent crimes. In all, juveniles were responsible for an estimated 14 percent of all violent crimes and a quarter of all property crimes known to the police. Nationally, juveniles perpetrated 137,000 more violent crimes in 1994 than in 1985, and were responsible for 26 percent of the growth in violent crime over that period, including 50 percent of the increase in robberies, 48 percent of the increase in rapes, and 35 percent of the increase in murders. Juvenile violent crime arrest rates rose 5.2 percent in 1987–88 , 18.8 percent in 1988–89, 12.1 percent in 1989–90, 7.6 percent in 1990–91 , and by at least 4.4 percent in every year thereafter until 1994–95, when arrests for violent crime among juveniles aged 10 to 17 fell by 2.9 percent. While such recent drops in juvenile arrest rates are obviously welcome, the Council urged all Americans to place them against the backdrop of a decade's worth of steep annual increases in youth crime and violence.

Moreover, the Council warned, America is now home to about 57 million children

From *Perspectives*, Spring 1998, pp. 24-29. © 1998 by The Council of State Governments. Reprinted by permission of the American Probation and Parole Association.

under age 15, some 20 million of them aged four to eight. The teenage population will top 30 million by the year 2006, the highest number since 1975. Thus, "no one," the Council concluded, "should feel certain that recent declines in crime will continue into the next century."

Indeed, the nation's two most widely respected criminologists, Professor James Q. Wilson of UCLA and Professor Marvin E. Wolfgang of the University of Pennsylvania, have both expressed deep concerns about present and impending youth crime and delinquency patterns and trends. According to Wilson, average Americans of every race, creed and region are right to "believe that something fundamental has changed in our patterns of crime," namely, the tangible threat of unprecedented levels of youth crime and substance abuse, including acts of violence committed by youngsters who "afterwards show us the blank, unremorseful stare of a feral, pre-social being."[4] Likewise, Wolfgang has observed that today's juvenile offenders probably do about three times as much serious crime as did the crime-prone boys born in the 1940s and 1950s, and could represent a new and especially challenging "subculture of violence."[5]

The expert understandings, statistics and warnings about youth crime and substance abuse seem broadly consistent with the well-founded worries of young Americans themselves. Any juvenile between ages 12 and 17 is more likely to be the victim of violent crime than are persons past their mid-twenties, and about half of all crimes of violence committed by juveniles are committed against juveniles.[6] A 1994 survey asked teenagers "How much of the time do you worry about being the victim of a crime?" In response, about 36 percent of white teenagers and 54 percent of black teenagers said "A lot of some or some of the time."[7] Apparently, the number of youngsters who are growing up scared in America—scared of other juveniles, that is—has been increasing for some time now. A 1995 Gallup Youth Survey found that between 1977 and 1994 the fraction of teenagers who regularly fear for their physical safety at school increased by 38 percent to one in four. And one teen in four said there was at least one time in the past year when they feared for their physical safety while in school classrooms or hallways, on playgrounds, or walking to and from school.[8]

Sticking to the Basics, Acting Now

The good news is that we do know a lot about youth crime and substance abuse that is relevant to saving at-risk youth— and acting now. Strategically, the key to preventing youth crime and substance abuse among our country's expanding juvenile population is to improve the real, live, day-to-day connections between responsible adults and young people—period. Whether it emanates from the juvenile justice system or from the community, from government agencies or from civil institutions, from faith-based programs or secular ones, from nonprofits or for-profits or public/private partnerships, from structural theorists or cultural theorists, from veteran probation officers or applied econometricians, no policy, program or intervention that fails to build meaningful connections between responsible adults and at-risk young people has worked, or can.

> *Of all the factors we have found as contributing to delinquency, the clearest and most exhaustive evidence concerns the adequacy of parenting. Parents who are incompetent, abusive, or rejecting parents who fail to maintain adequate supervision over their children, and parents who, indeed, are little more than children themselves, have direct effects on anti-social behavior of their children.*

It is all well and good to acknowledge both the multivariate character of social problems, and the myriad legal, political, administrative, financial and other difficulties of replicating what works. But it is also all too easy to let such intellectually de rigeur acknowledgments of social complexity become convenient covers for academic excuse-mongering, inaction and, of course, calls for more grants for more basic research, more research symposia, more conferences—more of everything save more human and financial support of people and existing programs that actually put responsible adults into the daily lives of the at-risk kids of inner-city Detroit, Philadelphia, and other major metropolitan regions.

James Q. Wilson has argued that uncovering "the subtle interaction between individual characteristics and social circumstances requires policy-related research of a sort and on a scale that has not been attempted before."[9] I agree. But there is already a voluminous private foundation-funded literature on understanding and reducing violence.[10] There is also a huge and still-growing government-funded literature on the literally dozens of "contexts and factors" that determine crime patterns.[11]

Besides, easily the most persistent, policy-relevant and common-sensical finding of the literature is that most disadvantaged youth who commit crimes and abuse drugs begin as neglected or maltreated children in need of responsible adults. In the words of a 1996 draft report of an American Society of Criminology task force on juvenile delinquency:

Of all the factors we have found as contributing to delinquency, the clearest and most exhaustive evidence concerns the adequacy of parenting. Parents who are incompetent, abusive, or rejecting, parents who fail to maintain adequate supervision over their children, and parents who, indeed, are little more than children themselves, have direct effects on anti-social behavior of their children. Inadequacy of parenting cannot be viewed in isolation as the sole cause of delinquency. However, its association with other factors is critical in predicting future delinquency.[12]

Likewise, in a magisterial, still unsurpassed and only slightly dated 500-plus-page summary of the scientific literatures on criminal behavior, Wilson and the late Richard J. Hernstein concluded that "after all is said and done, the most serious offenders are boys who begin their careers at a very early age."[13] Numerous empirical studies have indeed found that most juveniles who engage "in frequent criminal acts against persons and property . . . come from family settings characterized by high levels of violence, chaos, and dysfunction."[14] For example, a study that compared the family experiences of more violent and less violent incarcerated juveniles found that 75 percent of the former group had suffered serious abuse by a family member, while "only" 33 percent of the latter group had been so abused; and 78 percent of the more violent group had been witnesses to extreme violence, while 20 percent of the less violent group had been witnesses.[15]

Similarly, a recent ethnography of nearly 200 young West Coast street gangsters and felons found that, almost without exception, the kids' families "were a social fabric of fragile and undependable social ties that weakly bound children to their parents and other socializers." Nearly all parents abused alcohol and illegal drugs or both. Most young street criminals and drug abusers had no father in the home; many had fathers who were in prison or jail. Parents who were present in the home often "beat their sons and daughters—whipped them with belts, punched them with fists, slapped them, and kicked them."[16] Much the same was found in a 1996 study that reconstructed the entire juvenile and adult criminal histories of a randomly selected sample of 170 Wisconsin prisoners from Milwaukee: "Most inmates were raised in dysfunctional families.... Drug and alcohol abuse was common among inmates, their parents, and siblings."[17]

Of course, today's at-risk child in need of meaningful connections with responsible adults is also tomorrow's young adult in need of a meaningful, living-wage job. At least with respect to the crime- and drug-abuse-reduction value of legitimate work opportunities, "liberal and conservative criminologists do not differ all that much about the causes of street crime."[18] There is almost universal agreement among crime analysts that "jobs matter," and that in the big-city neighborhoods that so many at-risk youth and the adults in their lives call home, jobs have virtually disappeared.[19] And there is also almost complete agreement among employment and training experts that, regardless of how bright or bleak general economic conditions may be, the most effective way—and perhaps the only way—to help no- and low-skill urban youth get and keep jobs is to "stick to basics: adult caring and guidance, plenty of legitimate things to do in a youth's spare time, and real help in connecting to employers. This is the stuff of successful human, citizen and worker development."[20]

Unfortunately, on youth crime, substance abuse and related social problems, sticking to the basics is anything but common, and anything but easy. The very conceptual and moral simplicity of the hard work that needs to be done—that is, the hard person-, place-, and institution-specific work of building meaningful connections between responsible adults and at-risk young people—makes getting it done very hard indeed. One little-acknowledged reason is that in the elite social policy, foundation and research communities, most financial, reputational and other rewards have been, and continue to be, skewed in favor of peddling "original" and esoteric (if often emptily erudite) ideas and "comprehensive" (if hardly feasible) top-down program strategies and designs.

But if we really care about getting a handle on our present and impending youth

crime and substance abuse problems, then the time has come to proceed inductively, building meaningful connections between at-risk youth and responsible adults via existing community-based programs; focusing on the highly particular and often banal barriers to helping at-risk youth in particular places with particular people at particular times; having the money to fix a broken pipe that flooded the inner-city church basement where a "latch-key" ministry operates; finding a way to transport a young job-seeker from a public housing site to a private job site; getting police and probation officers in a particular neighborhood to work together on a daily basis; funding an incremental expansion of a well-established national or local mentoring program; and so on.

In fact, the youth crime and delinquency problem is highly concentrated where America's most severely at-risk youth are concentrated, namely, on the predominantly minority inner-city streets of places like Newark, New Jersey, not on the predominantly white tree-lined streets of places like Princeton, New Jersey. This is hardly a new social fact. For example, in 1969, a presidential commission on violent crime broadcast it far and wide.[21] Still, the concentration of at-risk youth and associated social ills in America's big cities easily ranks among the most often ignored, distorted or forgotten of all policy-relevant social realities.

The concentration of crime and delinquency among low-income urban minority youth is especially striking for crimes of violence, including murder. In 1995, a nationwide total of 21,597 murders were reported to police, a total 7 percent lower than the 1994 total, and representing a national murder rate of 8 per 100,000 inhabitants. But 77 percent of murder victims in 1995 were males, 48 percent were black, and 12 percent were under age 18. Moreover, recent studies find that males ages 14 to 24 are roughly 8 percent of the country's total population, but they constitute over a quarter of all homicide victims and nearly half of all murderers. Between 1985 and 1992, for example, black males ages 14–24 remained just above 1 percent of the population but increased from 9 to 17 percent of the murder victims and from 17 to 30 percent of the assailants.[22]

One thing is tragically clear: "Homicide for young black males is very concentrated geographically," and remained so throughout the epidemic increases of the last decade.[23] As a 1994 study of youth violence concluded: "The violence now occurring within our cities is a national scourge. The fact that minority youth are disproportionately its victims makes it a tragedy as well as a disgrace."[24]

There is growing evidence of a substantial overlap between the highly concen-

trated populations of young crime victims and the highly concentrated populations of young offenders. For example, in an ongoing analysis of youth homicides in Boston, Professor Anne Morrison Piehl of Harvard University has found that about 75 percent of both offenders and victims of youth homicides (victim age 25 or younger) have criminal histories consisting of at least one arraignment. "In fact," Piehl observes, "among those with criminal histories, the victims and offenders were virtually indistinguishable in terms of criminal records. This finding suggests several things: the distribution of victimization may be even more concentrated than commonly believed, and strategic innovations based on law enforcement may be able to diffuse violent situations because there is leverage over both potential victims and potential offenders."[25]

Few "Guppies," Few "Great Whites"

But, as you well know, most juvenile offenders with whom the justice system deals are neither violent nor incorrigible.[26] Metaphorically speaking, today the system must handle relatively more young "Great White Sharks" (serious, violent, and predatory juvenile criminals) and relatively fewer "Guppies" (mere first-time midemeanants or delinquents) than it did in previous decades. Still, most juvenile offenders are neither Great Whites nor Guppies, and, for that reason, and even with the passage of so-called get-tough laws in many states, the system still rightly responds by putting the vast majority of juvenile offenders on probation, not behind bars.

For example, in 1993 public juvenile detention, correctional and shelter facilities held a total of over 60,000 juveniles (89 percent of them male, 43 percent of them black)—the largest number of juveniles in such public facilities on any given day since these data on juveniles in public facilities were first compiled in 1974. There were 1,025 facilities with a median population capacity of 24 and a mean capacity of 57—clearly not the huge, 500-plus bed juvenile reformatories of old. From 1991 to 1993, the one-day population of juveniles in publicly operated facilities increased by 5 percent. And note: the one-day population figures grossly minimize the actual amount of traffic in and out of these facilities each year. In 1993, for example, about 674,000 juveniles were admitted to these facilities, and 669,000 were released from their custody.[27]

Still, even today, it is probation authorities, not custodial institutions, that remain the true "workhorses" of the juvenile justice system. In 1993, 520,600 cases disposed by juvenile courts resulted in probation—a 21 percent increase over the 428,500 cases handled via probation in 1989. Probation has long been, and continues to be, the most severe disposition in over half (56 percent) of adjudicated delinquency cases. Between 1989 and 1993, the number of adjudicated juvenile cases placed on formal probation rose by 17 percent to 254,800. Over the same period, the number of juvenile probation cases involving a "person offense" such as homicide, rape, robbery, assault or kidnapping, soared by 45 percent to 53,900.[28]

As you also are well aware, alcohol, illegal drugs and substance abuse are clearly implicated in youth crime. The trouble almost always begins—both for the at-risk children and often for their parents as well—with child maltreatment in the home or a severe lack of positive adult-child relationships. Recently, a number of popular books have spoken to this harsh social reality in the vivid way that only first-rate journalism can.[29] In one such account, we are treated to the following summary of the research on at-risk youth, juvenile crime and related social ills:

Boiled down to its core (the research teaches) that most adolescents who become delinquent, and the overwhelming majority who commit violent crimes, started very young. . . . They were the impulsive, aggressive, irritable children. . . . If children know someone is watching them and that they may get caught, they are less likely to get into trouble.[30]

Even some older children who have gone badly astray and gotten "caught" (even incarcerated) can be saved if they are not only watched or monitored in the future, but mentored or ministered to as needed by responsible adults. Weigh the following synopses of a representative armful of relevant research monographs published over the last decade or so:

• Since 1986, the National Institute of Justice and the National Institute of Alcohol Abuse and Alcoholism have been conducting an ongoing examination of 1,575 child victims identified in court cases of abuse and neglect from 1967 to 1971. By 1994, almost half the victims (most of whom were then in their late twenties or early thirties) had been arrested for some type of nontraffic offense. About 18 percent had been arrested for a violent crime. Substance abuse rates were elevated, especially among women who were maltreated as children. Blacks who had been abused or neglected as children had higher crime rates than whites with the same background: 82 percent of black males had been arrested for some type of nontraffic offense; half of black males had at least one arrest for violence. For all child victims, in terms of future criminality, neglect appeared to be as damaging as physical abuse. The rate of

arrest for violent crimes of those who had been neglected as children was almost as high as the rate for those who had been physically abused. Overall, maltreatment of children increased their chances of delinquency and crime by about 40 percent.[31]

• A 1985 study based on a representative national sample of 7,514 adolescents aged 12 to 17 compared delinquency rates of children in single-parent (mother-only) households to rates of children in two-parent households. Delinquency was measured in terms of number of arrests, school disciplinary problems (truancy, for example), and similar indicators. By all measures, the children in single-parent households were more likely to be delinquent.[32]

• A major re-analysis of data from a classic study of crime and delinquency confirmed the primacy of family factors: "Despite controlling for these individual difference constructs, all family effects retained their significant predictive power. And once again mother's supervision had the largest of all effects on delinquency, whether official or unofficial. A major finding of our analysis is that the family process variables are strongly and directly related to delinquency . . . family processes of informal social control still explain the largest share of variance in adolescent delinquency."[33]

• A study of the relationship between adolescent motherhood and the criminality of her offspring revealed a birds-of-a-feather phenomenon. About "25 percent of boys with criminal fathers also have a criminal mother, compared to 4 percent in the case of non-criminal fathers. Similarly, 67 percent of boys with criminal mothers also have a criminal father, compared to just 19 percent when the mother is not convicted. . . . Our results suggest that the children latest in the birth order of women who begin childbearing early are at greatest risk of criminality. This finding appears to reflect the coming together of the deleterious impacts of poor parenting and role modeling and diminished resources per child."[34]

• A study of urban street criminals concluded: "An abundance of scholarly research shows that anti-social and delinquent tendencies emerge early in the lives of neglected, abused, and unloved youngsters, often by age nine. My ethnographic data support these findings and show that, once these youngsters leave home and go on the street, they are at best difficult to extricate from street culture. . . ."[35]

• A study of "resilient youth"—the half of all high-risk children who do not engage in delinquency or drug use—indicated that child "maltreatment itself has for a long time been associated with problematic outcomes for children. . . . Considerable research in both criminology and child

development suggests that family deviance, including criminality and substance abuse of family members, affects developing children because such parents are likely to tolerate and model deviance for children."[36]

Four decades ago, child psychologist Emmy Werner began studying the offspring of desperately poor, alcoholic and abusive Kauai, Hawaii parents. She was hoping to discover how these dysfunctions were passed from one generation to the next. Instead, she found that about a third of the children reached adulthood virtually unscathed—healthy, happy, employed, without substance abuse problems, and so on. So she shifted her attention to these abuse-and-neglect survivors, hoping to discover what made them so resilient and capable of beating the social odds. In 1992, a major storm flattened Kauai, leaving over 15 percent of its residents homeless and many others scrambling to find money for repairs, avoid bankruptcy, and fend off deep depression. But most of the study's resilient youth, then in their thirties, were not among the homeless, the foreclosed, or the depressed. They had heeded storm warnings, prepared their properties, saved for a stormy day, and bought insurance. For them, successfully riding out the storm was, as it were, an old habit. During the social hurricanes of their early lives, Kauai's resilient youth had responsible nonparental adults enter their lives, and through relationships with these adults the children had developed not only a sense of self-worth and respect for others, but, in Werner's words, personalities as "planners and problem solvers and picker-uppers." As she argued in her book, the crux of the Kauai story is consistent with the bottom line of the basic research on resilient youth: caring adults are the bedrock of a young person's behavior toward self and others, as well as the primary avenue for securing those skills, services, and opportunities (such as jobs) that are key to a civil and self-sufficient life.[37]

Thus, our brisk walk through the literatures on the concentrations and causes of youth crime and substance abuse returns us to the core strategic principle: no approach that does not build connections between responsible adults and at-risk youth has worked, or should rationally be expected to work. Again, no one can reasonably deny that, whatever the state of adult-child relationships, growing up in neighborhoods with few opportunities for healthy play and employment is a breeding ground for youth crime and substance abuse. But improving those opportunities, without first ensuring that there is adequate parental or nonparental adult caring, supervision, guidance and support, is unlikely to prevent or reduce youth crime and substance abuse, and hence unlikely to forestall the adult dysfunctions and criminal activities that fuel the "cycle of violence."

The single most consistent and powerful finding in the evaluation literature on youth development interventions is that positive effects accrue while at-risk children are in the programs, and sometimes for a few years thereafter, but diminish or dwindle to nothing by the time the child reaches adulthood. Many have met this finding as a counsel of despair. Logically, however, all the finding says is that the young generally do better when they are being helped by adults than when that help has stopped—better with and while in Head Start than without and after it; better when they stay in structured drug treatment than when they drop out of it; better during a summer education and training program than two summers later when they are older, more challenged, and unhelped by responsible adults; and so on. Many social programs do not so much "fail" as "stop." The obvious need, therefore, is to translate a series of short-term, non-stop positive adult-child connections into that long-term developmental success known as responsible, self-sufficient adulthood. To employ a football metaphor, winning at at-risk youth development is impossible when your most ill-equipped players have coaches or quarterbacks but only on alternate game days, are only occasionally given playbooks or schedules, and, should they even bother to keep playing, get invited to take the field as a team only during the first and third quarters of a four-quarter game. Or, shift the context from at-risk youth in need of responsible adults to children living with both parents in the best of all possible emotional, material and cognitive early life circumstances. Even for well-loved, advantaged children in their teens, we know that when their circumstances change for the worse—when, for example, their family breaks up or falls suddenly on economic hard times—the youth are more likely to experience a wide variety of life troubles than are comparable youth who remained, as it were, in the 'advantaged childrens' program. In short, the plural of short-term is long-term.

Likewise, many well-intentioned persons have concluded that unless interventions into the lives of at-risk youth are quite early, intensive and expensive, not much good can come of them. To some, "early" means while still in dirty diapers, and certainly no later than ages seven or eight. This perspective is, to be sure, a useful corrective to unfettered optimism about social programs, especially, perhaps, where our country's most severely at-risk youth are concerned. But there are, alas, few unfettered optimists still walking the social planet, and the "dirty diapers or doom" perspective is grossly inconsistent with recent findings on the efficacy of mentoring

programs like Big Brothers Big Sisters. Moreover, it is largely beside the point: whether or not we think we can help at-risk youth who are out of dirty diapers, the fact is that there are millions of them out there and on the way. In particular, intellectual confidence that these children are beyond help, even if it were justified (and I think it is most certainly not justified), would constitute no real answer to challenges posed by youth criminals and substance abusers—our youngest, most needy, and potentially our most dangerous fellow citizens.

The 3 M's of Youth Crime and Substance Abuse Prevention

The nation's at-risk youth population, including the segment of it that is involved in illegal activities, is not an undifferentiated mass. The best way, I believe, to think about and relate to present and potential juvenile offenders is with respect to their varying needs for adult supervision and guidance.

Specifically, I believe that some at-risk juveniles—for example, truants, petty thieves or kids who have had non-violent run-ins with their peers, neighbors and the law—need little more than a dedicated probation officer or a caring adult volunteer looking over their shoulder. They need monitoring. Other at-risk juveniles need responsible adults in their lives on a deeper, more intensive level, helping them with their personal problems, offering a sympathetic ear and a guiding hand. They need mentoring. Still other juveniles are among the nation's most severely at-risk children—abused and neglected as infants and toddlers, exploited for sex, drugs and money as adolescents, and already involved in (or quite likely to become involved in) serious, organized or predatory street crime as teenagers and young adults. Their badly broken lives and spirits cry out for a type and a degree of adult help that is holistic, personal and challenging. They need some type of ministering.

Over the last two years, I have spent most of my time working on the "3rd M"—ministering. I believe that local churches represent the single best hope for reaching some of our most severely at-risk youth, and I have witnessed, if you will, the capacity of "super-preachers" to stop potential "super-predators" before it's too late. But preachers and church volunteers need the support of prosecutors, probation and police to succeed.

In conclusion, a recent report from the Bureau of Justice Statistics indicates that, at present, the lifetime risks of a black male going to prison or jail in America are 1 in 3 versus 1 in 20 for the population as a

whole.[38] Strategies that put responsible adults into the lives of at-risk youth can change both odds for the better. But how much have monitoring, mentoring and ministering-type efforts proliferated to date? These programs are far from being taken to scale and need lots of human and financial help if they are to make a real difference. Precious little is now being done by private foundations to bolster this strategic, street-level approach to youth crime and substance abuse.

Endnotes

1. National Research Council, Panel on High-Risk Youth, Losing Generations (National Academy Press, 1993).

2. Youth Violence in America: Recommendations from the IACP Summit (International Association of Chiefs of Police, 1996), section III, tables 11 and 12.

3. Council on Crime in America, Preventing Crime, Saving Children (Center for Civic Innovation, Manhattan Institute, 1997), pp. 1–3.

4. James Q. Wilson, "Crime and Public Policy," in Wilson and Joan R. Pertersilia, Crime (Institute for Contemporary Studies, 1995), p. 20.

5. Marvin E. Wolfgang, "From Boy to Man, From Delinquency to Crime," University of Pennsylvania, Wharton School, Public Policy and Management Crime Policy Seminar Series, October 17, 1996, and personal correspondence of February 11, 1997; also see Wolfgang and Franco Ferracuti, The Subculture of Violence (Tavistock, 1967), esp. pp. 158–161.

6. Juvenile Offenders and Victims (U.S. Office of Juvenile Justice and Delinquency Prevention, June 1996), pp. 20, 47. Note: These estimates of youth crime and youth victimization in America are based on data gathered via the U.S. Bureau of Justice Statistics (BJS) and the National Crime Victimization Survey (NCVS). Unfortunately, the NCVS undercounts youth crime and youth victimization because it does not survey persons age 12 or younger; see John J. DiIulio, Jr. and Anne Morrison Piehl, "What the Crime Statistics Don't Tell You," Wall Street Journal, January 8, 1997, p. A22. Experts disagree about how severe the NCVS undercount is, but for some crimes it is clearly substantial. For example, other BJS data indicate that as many as 1 in 6 rape victims are age 12 or younger, but the NCVS does not capture these rapes; see Child Rape Victims 1992 (Bureau of Justice Statistics), June 1994. Likewise, it has been estimated that the NCVS undercounts the number of gun-shot victims by a factor of three; see Philip J. Cook, "The Case of the Missing Victims," Journal of Quantitative Criminology, 1985, pp. 91–102.

7. New York Times/CBS News Poll, as reported in The New York Times, July 10, 1994, p. 16.

8. George H. Gallup with Wendy Plump, Growing Up Scared in America (George H. Gallup International Institute, 1995), p. 2.

9. James Q. Wilson, On Character (American Enterprise Institute), p. 179; also see Wilson et al., Understanding and Controlling Crime (Springer-Verlag, 1986), and Wilson and Joan R. Petersilia, eds., Crime, op. cit.

10. For example, see 1993 Report of the Harry Frank Guggenheim Foundation: Research for Understanding and Reducing Violence, Aggression and Dominance (The Harry Frank Guggenheim Foundation, 1993).

11. For example, see "Understanding the Roots of Crime," National Institute of Justice Journal (National Institute of Justice, November 1994), p. 14.

12. "Critical Criminal Justice Issues," Task Force Reports from the American Society of Criminology, compiled by National Institute of Justice, draft, 1996, p. 2. I am grateful to Ross D. London for supplying a copy of this draft document.

13. James Q. Wilson and Richard J. Hernstein, Crime and Human Nature (Simon and Shuster, 1985), p. 509.

14. David M. Altschuler and Troy L. Armstrong, "Intensive Aftercare," in Armstrong, ed., Intensive Interventions with High-Risk Youths (Criminal Justice Press, 1991), p. 48.

15. Ellen Schall, "Principles for Juvenile Detention," in Francis X. Hartmann, ed., From Children to Citizens, vol. 2 (Springer-Verlag, 1987), p. 350.

16. Mark S. Fleisher, Beggars and Thieves (University of Wisconsin Press, 1995).

17. John J. DiIulio, Jr. and George Mitchell, Who Really Goes to Prison in Wisconsin? (Wisconsin Policy Research Institute, April 1996), pp. 2, 3.

18. Jerome H. Skolnick, "Passions of Crime," The American Prospect, March–April 1996, p. 92.

19. For example, see the following: Richard Freeman, "Crime and the Economic Status of Disadvantaged Young Men," in George Peterson and Wayne Vroman, eds., Urban Labor Markets and Job Opportunity (Urban Institute Press, 1992); Freeman, "Why Do So Many Young Men Commit Crimes and What Might We Do About It?," Journal of Economic Perspectives, Winter 1996, pp. 25–42; Jeffrey Grogger, "The Effect of Arrests on Employment and Earnings of Young Men," Quarterly Journal of Economics, February 1995, pp. 51–71; Joel Waldfogel, "The Effect of Criminal Conviction on Income and the Trust 'Reposed in the Workmen'," Journal of Human Resources,

1994, pp. 62–81; William Julius Wilson, When Work Disappears (Knopf, 1996).

20. Gary Walker, "Back to Basics: A New/Old Direction for Youth Policy," Public/Private Ventures News, Spring 1996, p. 3; and Gary Walker, testimony before the U.S. Subcommittee on Employment and Training, March 11, 1997.

21. Violent Crime: The Challenge to Our Cities (George Braziller, 1969). The commission's central findings were reinforced a few years later by the results of a major longitudinal study; see Marvin E. Wolfgang et al., Delinquency in a Birth Cohort (University of Chicago, 1972).

22. Trends in Juvenile Violence (Bureau of Justice Statistics, March 1996), p. 2.

23. Ibid, p. 30.

24. Violence in America: Mobilizing a Response (National Academy Press, 1994), p. ix.

25. Anne Morrison Piehl, personal correspondence of March 1997; also see Piehl et al., "Youth Gun Violence in Boston," in Law and Contemporary Problems, forthcoming 1997. I am grateful to Professor Piehl for supplying us with a copy of this draft essay, and for her additional insights.

26. For example, see James Alan Fox, "The Calm Before the Juvenile Crime Storm?," Population Today, September 1996, pp. 4, 5, and "Yes, the Federal Government Should Have a Major Role in Reducing Juvenile Crime," Congressional Digest, August–September 1996, pp. 206, 208, 210, and 212; and see DiIulio, "Our Children and Crime," Keynote Address, International Association of Chiefs of Police, April 25, 1996; testimony before the U.S. Senate Subcommittee on Children and Families, "Juvenile Crime: An Alarming Indicator of America's Moral Poverty," July 18, 1996; and "Stop Crime Before It Starts," The New York Times, July 25, 1996.

27. Juveniles in Public Facilities, 1993 (Office of Juvenile Justice and Delinquency Prevention, May 1995), p. 1, and Juveniles in Public Facilities, 1991 (Office of Juvenile Justice and Delinquency Prevention, September 1993), p. 1.

28. Juvenile Probation: Workhorse of the Juvenile Justice System (Office of Juvenile Justice and Delinquency Prevention, March 1996).

29. For example, see Fox Butterfield, All God's Children (Knopf, 1995), and Leon Dash, Rosa Lee: A Mother and Her Family In Urban America (Basic Books, 1996).

30. Butterfield, ibid., p. 327–328.

31. The cycle of Violence (National Institute of Justice, 1992), and The Cycle of Violence Revisited (National Institute of Justice, 1996).

32. Sanford M. Dornbusch et al., "Single Parents, Extended Households, and the Control of Adolescents," Child Development, 1985, pp.326-341. Also see the following: Anthony Pillay, "Psychological Disturbances in Children of Single Parents," Psychological Reports, 1987, pp. 803–806; Laurence Steinberg, "Single Parents, Stepparents, and Susceptibility of Adolescents to Antisocial Peer Pressure," Child Development, 1987, pp. 269-275 and Brigitte Mednick et al., "Patterns of Family Instability and Crime," Journal of Youth and Adolescence, 1990, pp. 201-220. I am grateful to Boston probation officer Milton Britton for directing our attention to these additional studies.

33. Robert J. Sampson and John H. Laub, Crime in the Making (Harvard University Press, 1993), pp.95-96.

34. Daniel S. Nagin et al., "Adolescent Mothers and the Criminal Justice System," unpublished paper, Carnegie Mellon University, December 15, 1995, pp. 28, 30.

35. Fleisher, Beggars and Thieves, op. cit., pp. 262–263.

36. Carolyn Smith et al., "Resilient Youth: Identifying Factors That Prevent High-Risk Youth from Engaging in Delinquency and Drug Use," Current Perspectives on Aging and the Life Cycle, 1995, p. 221.

37. Emmy Werner and Ruth Smith, Overcoming the Odds: High-Risk Children from Birth to Adulthood (Cornell University Press, 1992), and Joseph P. Shapiro, "Invincible Kids," U.S. News & World Report, November 11, 1996.

38. I am grateful to Dr. Allen Beck of the Bureau for supplying a draft copy of this document.

This article was based on an address given to the National District Attorneys Association on July 14, 1997.

John J. DiIulio, Jr. is a Professor of Politics and Public Affairs at Princeton University and a Douglas Dillon Senior Fellow at the Brookings Institute.

Pairing Juvenile Offenders with Volunteer Advocates

BY KIM G. FRENTZ

Mr. Kim G. Frentz is the program director for Partners Against Crime. The Partners Against Crime (PAC) program was established in 1991 by Volunteers in Prevention, Probation and Prison, Inc. (VIP³). VIP³ encourages and supports a nationwide network of community-based volunteer programs operating within the criminal justice system. In addition to providing service to the court and the citizens of Detroit, operating a volunteer program enables VIP³ to remain closely aligned with the programs and the needs of volunteer programs it seeks to foster and support. PAC and VIP³ share administrative offices in Detroit. For more information, contact: Partners Against Crime, 163 Madison Ave., Suite 120, Detroit, MI 48226, (313) 964–1110

Two hundred twenty cases, sixteen crowded Detroit courtrooms—it's a normal day at Wayne County Probate Court Juvenile Division. The halls of this Center for Juvenile Justice are filled with juvenile respondents, their families and defense attorneys. Had all the 10 to 17 year olds that were summoned this day shown up, the courthouse might well be filled beyond capacity. Some of the youth here will be adjudicated today; others will be back another day for their trial or disposition. All are missing another day from school, yet they do not really seem to mind. It is not surprising; most are doing poorly in school anyway. It would appear that poor school performance goes hand in hand with juvenile delinquency.

Twelve-year-old John is one whose destiny will be determined today. His appearance in court was guaranteed. He has been locked up in a county detention facility

since his arrest 17 days ago. He has formally been accused of a number of offenses, including motor vehicle felony, unlawful driving away, school truancy and incorrigibility. John is escorted into the courtroom by a deputy sheriff. He wears a deceptive mask of confident indifference as he takes a seat to the left of his court-appointed defense attorney. His mother, with a look of hopelessness, makes her way from a seat in the back of the courtroom to sit to the right of her son's attorney.

There is no acknowledgement of presence between John and his mother. The lack of eye contact is immediately obvious. One can only guess at the magnitude of the difficulties that have resulted from the charges against him. Regardless of this hearing's outcome, the problems facing John and his family will not likely be resolved today by the court.

Five minutes earlier John met his lawyer for the first time. She advised him to accept the prosecutor's plea offer; admitting guilt to the offense of unlawful driving away in exchange for dropping the other charges and a recommendation of a sentence to probation. John and his mother agree. The attorney communicates to the referee presiding over this pretrial hearing that John will accept the plea offer.

The referee now delivers a rather long discourse on defendant rights. John states for the record that he understands, though his comprehension seems feigned. His demeanor reveals he really has little or no clue to what is occurring. John is sworn in and takes the witness stand. He is instructed to give his explanation of stealing the car. After John's guilt has been established for the record, the referee allows him to resume sitting with his attorney.

Appropriately, the referee admonishes John for his admitted offense, scolds him

for not going to school and explains to him the definition of "incorrigible," telling John to stay out of further trouble. To reinforce his admonition, the referee renders the customary sentence of probation for a term to be determined by his probation officer (usually about six months). Statistics support the probability that this will not be John's last visit to juvenile court.

To this point, John's story is similar to many repeated daily in Detroit's juvenile court, and the proceedings in this court are replicated in such courts in hundreds of major cities nationwide. However, because John has been selected by this referee as one of the kids who might benefit from a mentoring experience, he is given the additional probation condition of participation in Detroit's Partners Against Crime (PAC) one-to-one mentoring program. With this seemingly small addition to the court order, John's life direction may have been altered. Through compliance, John has a good chance to lead a life devoid of repeated trips into the labyrinth constituting the juvenile and criminal justice systems.

PAC's mentoring concept is one solution to the huge problem of repeat juvenile crime that plagues urban centers across our nation. The PAC program takes an adjudicated young offender and matches him/her with a community volunteer who has been screened and trained. The PAC volunteer mentors a youth a minimum of one hour per week. The mentor's role is to support the youth in his/her various endeavors, not to try explicitly to change the youth's behavior or character. Over a period of time and with persistence, a close friendship emerges based on mutual esteem. Herein lies the key to the program's success, as it is through this friendship that desired attitudinal changes can occur.

Young offenders sentenced to participate are first affected by the program through efforts of a PAC courtroom volunteer. These volunteers are specially trained to meet with the parent and child at the time of sentencing. In John's case, the volunteer has been an observer in the courtroom in which John was sentenced. It is now this person's responsibility to help John and his mother begin the PAC journey. Initially, uncertainty and suspicion on the parent's part can sometimes lead to the child's failure to participate. Therefore, the PAC volunteer's goal is to approach the parent and child immediately after the hearing to help them formulate a positive opinion of PAC.

Like most direct service agencies, PAC enrollment includes completing paperwork, usually done during intake. For the program to be successful, it is essential that a distinction be made at intake between the generally negative court experience and the upcoming mentoring experience. Today the volunteer explains the program and overcomes initial resistance.

A little over a week later, John, his mother and four younger siblings arrive at the PAC office; they are over two hours late. They are greeted cheerfully, and the necessary paperwork is completed in an empathetic, conversational manner. Forty-five minutes later, any concern John's mother had relating to his involvement in the program has been dispelled, and John actually seems eager to get on with what he has conjured to be "meeting his mentor."

Fletcher, John's selected mentor, has been chosen primarily because his residence is near John's home. Even though Fletcher is experiencing normal mentor pre-match anxiety, he exhibits a confidence that is a byproduct of thorough training. After reviewing the PAC court file, he is now ready to be introduced to John and his mother. It has been a week and a day since John was adjudicated, and he is still weeks away from direct court supervision via a meeting [with] his probation officer. Today's introduction to Fletcher is going to stand out as the most significant in John's juvenile justice system experience and perhaps his life.

Fletcher's training has taught him to immediately establish an alliance with the parent. PAC experience has shown that many of the PAC mentor relationships that fail do so in part because the parent chooses to make the child unavailable. In fact, most of this first meeting will focus not on John, but on his family. Fletcher further shifts focus away from the court encounter while making it clear that John should be at home and ready for their scheduled meeting.

Fletcher is a member of a PAC chapter that was established at his church—a sat-

> *The mentor's role is to support the youth in his/her various endeavors, not to try explicitly to change the youth's behavior or character.*

ellite PAC program. Though the chapter operates under PAC guidelines, it remains autonomous, with unique methods of supporting PAC-trained mentors and their matches. Some of the ongoing meetings between the mentors and mentees will blend into activities already existing within the chapter. Fletcher and other mentors within this chapter have undergone thorough screening, which includes a criminal history check and completion of PAC's training series for justice system mentors.

All PAC volunteers inherently possess the number one PAC mentor requirement, the ability to become a friend. It is, however, through PAC training that the volunteers become well versed in the five characteristics PAC has determined to be pillars to successful justice system mentors. The degree to which mentors possess or learn these characteristics and successfully implement them relates directly to their degree of mentoring proficiency.

The central and keystone pillar is friendship. Volunteer mentors build friendships during the weekly meetings. Often just sitting and talking with a juvenile for a long period of time is difficult. Building a friendship with a young person almost always needs to include an activity: visiting each other at a PAC chapter; going for a walk; attending movies or sports events; window-shopping; playing a game; or having a soft drink and a hamburger. When mentors show that they care, that they are willing to give freely of their experience and that they accept their mentees "as they are," friendship is inevitable.

The second pillar is that successful mentors meet regularly with their mentee. It has been said that good intentions are no substitute for good results. All volunteers enter PAC with expectations of good things that will come out of their match to a juvenile offender, but without the one-to-one contact, there will be little or no effect. Through necessity, most people rely heavily on the phone to communicate, even with close friends and family. It is doubtful, though, that close personal mentoring friendships have ever resulted from any-

thing other than meeting face-to-face with consistency and continuity.

The third pillar is to listen. Listen attentively, indefinitely, and then listen some more is a reasonable approach for PAC mentors. The most frequent need among young people today is for someone willing to listen to them. Each mentee needs to know that someone outside of his/her own immediate family or peer group really cares. PAC volunteers begin establishing helping friendships by being good listeners.

The fourth pillar is tapping resources. The ability of juvenile offenders to fit into normal community life and to grow and mature into productive citizens is often due to mentors that help smooth the way into a complex society for the juvenile and their families. Volunteers often possess experience and knowledge of networks that they appropriately make available to their mentees. Once needs are identified, volunteers look into all possible areas that might benefit clients by meeting those needs. Volunteers often meet very basic needs, such as providing food for mentees and their families. Finding resources can mean getting a child involved in a recreation program, making arrangements for a tutor or helping them advance through the maze of applying for college financial aid. Persistent mentors almost always find a way of filling mentees' needs through personal or community resources.

The last pillar is reporting. Certainly one of the least popular tasks among PAC volunteers is that of reporting. Often volunteers perceive no relation between paperwork and successful mentoring. Unquestionably, the object of mentoring is time spent directly with the mentee; listening, becoming a friend, helping them solve problems and finding resources when needed. So why is it important to complete a written report each month? The reports are essential to relieving each mentee of their most compelling problem—being under court jurisdiction. Volunteers can accurately report to the supervising probation officer, the referee or the judge that the probationer is in fact complying with the court's condition related to PAC. Without such accountability, the court has no official way of verifying each match's compliance. To be truly successful, PAC volunteers must spend the time required each month to complete reports.

After six weeks of meetings, Fletcher is finally able to initiate discussion with John about his school attendance and performance. At first it is evident that John does not want to communicate on the subject, but Fletcher gently presses. What he finds out is that some other kids, his mother and evidently John, too, think that John is a "dumb kid." Fletcher knows this is not true.

Five Pillars of Mentoring

1. Developing a Friendship

2. Meeting Regularly

3. Listening

4. Tapping Resources

5. Reporting

Knowing that the mother's interest has been virtually nonexistent, Fletcher writes a personal letter to each of John's teachers. In the letters he explains that he is a court-appointed mentor who is going to take a personal interest in John's future scholastic achievements. He includes a copy of the authorization to release information form, signed by John's mother at the PAC intake.

At their next meeting, John is beaming. He announces with some pride that each of his teachers has mentioned receiving a letter from his friend Fletcher. In subsequent contact with the teachers and the school, Fletcher finds that John's attendance had improved dramatically. Although his academic performance still has ample room for improvement, John has begun to exhibit interest in his schoolwork. Fletcher's sincere display of attention, and John's perception of that interest has resulted in a huge boost in John's self esteem. The friendship between Fletcher and John has fortuitously strengthened their bond. Perhaps John won't be going back to juvenile court after all.

Mentoring is being touted as one of the most cost effective solutions to juvenile crime and recidivism. In 1995, Wayne State University conducted an impact evaluation of the Partners Against Crime program. The evaluation findings indicate that re-cidivism was 38 percent lower for PAC clients compared to the control group and more than 50 percent lower for PAC clients than for probationers who refused to participate in PAC.[1]

The results of the PAC program for Detroit continue to be impressive. Young boys and girls who might otherwise only see a probation officer once or twice during their probation now see a mentor an average of fifty hours during the same time period. Kids that appeared to be caught in the justice system downward spiral have new hope. They are improving in school, they are better able to cope with their family situations, and they are staying out of trouble. Individuals from the community taking time to demonstrate that they truly care make the difference.

Endnotes

1. Martin, D., A. Kusow and A. Thomson. "Impact Evaluation of Partners Against Crime (PAC) in Detroit, Michigan." Detroit: Wayne State University, Center for Urban Studies, College of Urban, Labor and Metropolitan Affairs (1995): 21.

Unit Selections

30. **Probation in the United States: Practices and Challenges,** Joan Petersilia
31. **Probation and Parole Supervision: Time for a New Narrative,** Edward E. Rhine
32. **Education as Crime Prevention: Providing Education to Prisoners,** Research Brief (The Center on Crime, Communities & Culture)
33. **Ethical Considerations in Probation Practice,** Marylouise E. Jones and Arthur J. Lurigio
34. **The Other Women of Bedford Hills,** Stephanie Gertler
35. **Prison Population Growing although Crime Rate Drops,** Fox Butterfield
36. **The Color of Justice,** John H. Trumbo
37. **Restorative Justice and Offender Rehabilitation: A Meeting of the Minds,** Ann H. Crowe
38. **Death County,** Arlene Levinson
39. **U.S. Prisons: Gulags or Country Clubs?** Alfred N. Himelson

Key Points to Consider

❖ What issues and trends are most likely to be faced by corrections administrators at the close of this century?

❖ What are some of the reasons for overcrowding in our nation's prisons?

❖ Why have prisons become so violent and difficult to manage in recent years?

❖ Discuss reasons for favoring and for opposing the death penalty.

 **Links** | **www.dushkin.com/online/**

28. **American Probation and Parole Association**
   http://www.csg.org/appa/
29. **The Corrections Connection**
   http://www.corrections.com
30. **Critical Criminology Division of the ASC**
   http://sun.soci.niu.edu/~critcrim/
31. **David Willshire's Forensic Psychology & Psychiatry Links**
   http://www.ozemail.com.au/~dwillsh/
32. **Oregon Department of Corrections**
   http://www.doc.state.or.us/links/welcome.htm
33. **Prison Law Page**
   http://www.wco.com/~aerick/prison.htm
34. **Stop Prisoner Rape, Inc.**
   http://www.spr.org/spr.html

These sites are annotated on pages 4 and 5.

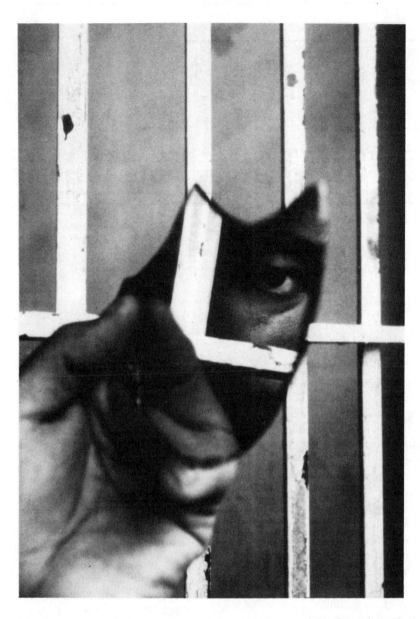

In the American system of criminal justice, the term "corrections" has a special meaning. It designates programs and agencies that have legal authority over the custody or supervision of persons who have been convicted of a criminal act by the courts. The correctional process begins with the sentencing of the convicted offender. The predominant sentencing pattern in the United States encourages maximum judicial discretion and offers a range of alternatives from probation (supervised, conditional freedom within the community), through imprisonment, to the death penalty.

Selections in this unit focus on the current condition of the U.S. penal system and the effects that sentencing, probation, imprisonment, and parole have on the rehabilitation of criminals.

In the lead essay, Joan Petersilia, asserting that many are calling for reform in probation, offers her recommendations in "Probation in the United States." Current probation and parole supervision tends to favor surveillance-oriented, control strategies,

according to Edward Rhine, in "Probation and Parole Supervision: Time for a New Narrative." He contends that this thrust is quite different from former approaches. Does education offered to inmates help steer them away from a criminal lifestyle? Should college courses be made available to qualified inmates? These are some questions that come to mind when reading "Education as Crime Prevention: Providing Education to Prisoners."

Probation officers frequently face decisions that place the needs of offenders in direct conflict with the welfare of society. "Ethical Considerations in Probation Practice" sheds light on this dilemma and asserts that probation officers can benefit from a firm foundation in ethics.

What is life on the inside like for women inmates at Bedford Hills (New York) Correctional Facility? Writer Stephanie Gertler describes her experience after visiting there in "The Other Women of Bedford Hills." Fox Butterworth asserts that the imprisonment boom continues unabated in spite of the decrease in the crime rate. This over-reliance on imprisonment is discussed in "Prison Population Growing although Crime Rate Drops."

In the article that follows, "The Color of Justice," John Trumbo points out that there are more nonwhite men on death row than there are Caucasian counterparts, according to the numbers. Is the disparity due to racial discrimination or to some other not-so-black-and-white issues? Ann Crowe, in her essay "Restorative Justice and Offender Rehabilitation: A Meeting of the Minds" contends that justice may be more effectively achieved by integrating and implementing both restorative justice and offender rehabilitation perspectives. She examines the potential for doing this.

Why is a county in Texas leading states in executions? Arlene Levinson examines this question and reports her findings in "Death County."

The unit closes with "U.S. Prisons: Gulags or Country Clubs?" which asks whether prison life should be made easier or harder, a question that is political and philosophical, based on our notions of retribution and justice.

PROBATION
in the UNITED STATES

Practices and Challenges

by Joan Petersilia

Joan Petersilia is Professor of Criminology, Law, and Society at the School of Social Ecology at the University of California, Irvine.

Adult probationers in the United States surged to nearly 3.2 million at the end of 1996, up from almost 2 million in 1985 and 1.1 million in 1980.[1] Today they comprise about 58 percent of all adults under correctional supervision.[2]

To cope with their workload, probation agencies—often the target of intense criticism—receive less than 10 percent of State and local government corrections funding.[3] Probation's funding shortfall often results in lax supervision of serious felons, thereby encouraging offender recidivism and reinforcing the public's soft-on-crime image of probation as permissive, uncaring about crime victims, and committed to a rehabilitative ideal that ignores the reality of violent, predatory criminals. This poor public image leaves probation agencies unable to compete effectively for scarce public funds.

Although current programs are often seen as inadequate, the *concept* of probation—begun in 1841 (see "Origin and Evolution of Probation")—has great appeal and much un-

realized potential. As one judge noted, "Nothing is wrong with probation. It is the *execution* of probation that is wrong."[4]

Exactly *how* would one go about reforming probation? Many judges are monitoring probationers more closely, while others are imposing more punitive and meaningful probation sentences. Some jurisdictions have implemented policies and programs designed to overcome the difficult problem of finding jail and prison capacity to punish probation violators.

Unfortunately, debating the merits of those and other probation-reform strategies is severely limited because so little is known about current probation practices. Assembling what is known about U.S. probation practices so public policy can be better informed is the main purpose of this article—along with offering suggestions on meeting the challenges facing probation agencies.

Probation and modern sentencing practice

Probation departments are more extensively involved with offenders and their cases—often starting at arrest—than any other justice agency. Many who are arrested and all who are convicted come into contact with the pro-

bation department. Probation officers interact with many criminal justice agencies and significantly affect a wide spectrum of justice processing decisions, including these:

- Probation officers, in addition to pretrial service agencies, usually perform personal investigations to determine whether defendants will be released on their own recognizance or bail.

- They prepare reports that courts use as the primary source of information to determine whether to divert defendants from formal prosecution. Probation officers supervise diverted offenders and inform courts about whether the diversionary sentence was successfully complied with, thereby influencing the court's decision to proceed or not with formal prosecution.

- They prepare presentence reports containing pertinent information about convicted defendants and their crimes. The information is critically important, for research repeatedly indicates that (1) the judge's knowledge of the defendant is usually limited to what is contained in the presentence report, and (2) the probation offi-

From *National Institute of Justice Journal*, September 1997, pp. 2-8. Adapted from the author's essay in Volume 22 of "Crime and Justice," edited by Michael Tonry. © 1997 by the University of Chicago Press. Reprinted by permission.

cer's recommendation for or against prison correlates strongly with the judge's sentence of probation, prison, or a combination thereof.

• They supervise offenders sentenced to probation, determine which court-ordered probation conditions[5] to enforce and monitor most closely, decide which violations of conditions to bring to the court's attention, and recommend sanctions.

• They affect, through presentence reports, the initial security classification (and eligibility for parole) of offenders sentenced to prison.

More than 2,000 probation agencies in the United States[6] carry out those and other responsibilities. The agencies differ in terms of whether they reside within the executive or judicial branch of government, how they fund services, and whether those services are primarily a State or local function.

According to one study, 52 percent of staff in the typical probation department are line officers; 48 percent are clerical, support staff, and management.[7] Of line probation officers, only about 17 percent supervise adult felons. The remaining line officers supervise juveniles (half of adult probation agencies have that responsibility) or misdemeanant probationers or prepare presentence reports.

Given an estimated 50,000 probation employees in 1994,[8] and given that 23 percent of them (11,500 officers) were supervising about 2.9 million adult probationers, the average caseload that year was 258 adult offenders per line officer. This contrasts with what many believe to be the ideal caseload of 30 adult probationers per line officer.

Of course, offenders are not supervised on "average" caseloads. Rather, probation staffs use a variety of risk and needs classification instruments to identify offenders needing more intensive supervision or services. Although risk instruments can identify offenders who are more likely to reoffend, funds are usually insufficient to implement the levels of supervision pre-

dicted by classification instruments.[9] Research findings indicate that, across all sites and felony crimes studied, about 20 percent of adult felony probationers were assigned to caseloads requiring no personal contact.[10]

Probation funding has long been recognized as woefully inadequate. From the beginning, probation has continually been asked to take on greater numbers of probationers and conduct a greater number of presentence investigations despite stable or declining funding. "Apparently, community supervision has been seen as a kind of elastic resource that could handle whatever numbers of offenders the system required it to."[11] (See "Who Is on Probation?")

Does probation work?

The most common question asked about probation is, "Does it work?" By "work," most mean whether the person granted probation has refrained from further crime or reduced his or her recidivism—that is, the number of rearrests. Recidivism is currently the primary outcome measure for probation, as it is for all corrections programs.

Probationer recidivism. Summaries of probation effectiveness usually report the recidivism rates of *felons* as if they represented the total adult probation population, instead of 55 percent[12] of it. Failure to make this distinction between felons and misdemeanants is why profoundly different assessments have been offered as to whether probation "works."

In reality, there are two stories about probationer recidivism rates. Recidivism rates are low for adults on probation for *misdemeanors*—data suggest that three-quarters successfully complete their supervision. However, recidivism rates are high for *felony* probationers, particularly in jurisdictions that use probation extensively, where offenders are

ORIGIN AND EVOLUTION OF PROBATION

Probation: "A court-ordered disposition alternative through which an adjudicated offender is placed under the control, supervision, and care of a probation field staff member in lieu of imprisonment, so long as the probationer meets certain standards of conduct."—American Correctional Association, *Probation and Parole Directory,* 1995–1997.

Probation in the United States began in 1841 with the innovative work of John Augustus, a Boston bootmaker, who was the first to post bail for a man charged with being a common drunk. Thanks to Augustus's persistence, a Boston court gradually accepted the notion that not all offenders required incarceration.

Virtually every basic practice of probation was conceived by Augustus. He developed the ideas of presentence investigation, supervision conditions, social casework, reports to the court, and revocation of probation.

By 1956, all States had adopted adult and juvenile probation laws. Between the 1950s and the 1970s, U.S. probation evolved in relative obscurity. But a number of reports issued in the 1970s brought national attention to the inadequacy of probation services and their organization.

In recent years, probation agencies have struggled—with continued meager resources—to upgrade services and supervision. Important developments have included the widespread adoption of case classification systems and various types of intermediate sanctions (e.g., electronic monitoring and intensive supervision). Those programs have had varied success in reducing recidivism, but evaluations of them have been instructive in terms of future program design.

serious to begin with, and where supervision is minimal.[13]

Recidivism rates vary greatly from place to place, depending on the seriousness of the underlying population characteristics, length of followup, and surveillance provided. A summary of 17 followup studies of adult felony probationers found that felony rearrest rates ranges from 12 to 65 percent.[14] Such wide variation in recidivism is not unexpected, given the wide variability in granting probation and monitoring court-ordered conditions. Despite the desirability of predicting offender recidivism, available data and statistical methods are insufficient to do so very accurately at this time.

Other probation outcomes. Another way to examine probation effectiveness is to look at the contribution of those on probation to the overall crime problem. Of all persons arrested and charged with felonies in 1992, 17 percent of them were on probation at the time of their arrest.[15]

Practitioners have expressed concern about the use of recidivism as the primary, if not sole, measure of probation's success.[16] The American Probation and Parole Association (APPA), representing U.S. probation officers nationwide, argues that recidivism rates measure just one probation task while ignoring others.[17] APPA has urged its member agencies to collect data on alternative outcomes, such as amount of restitution collected, number of offenders employed, amount of fines/fees collected, hours of community service, number of treatment sessions, percentage of financial obligations collected, enrollment in school, days employed, educational attainment, and number of days drug free.

Some probation departments have begun to report such alternative outcome measures to their constituencies and believe this practice is having a positive impact on staff morale, public image, and funding.[18]

How can probation be revived?

The public has come to understand that not all criminals can be locked up, and so renewed attention is being focused on probation. Policymakers are asking whether probation departments can implement credible and effective community-based sentencing options. No one advocates the abolition of probation, but many call for its reform. But how should that be done?

Implement quality programs for appropriate probation target groups. Probation needs first to regain the public's trust as a meaningful, credible sanction. During the past decade, many jurisdictions developed "intermediate sanctions," such as house arrest, electronic monitoring, and intensive supervision, as a response to prison crowding. These programs were designed to be community-based sanctions that were tougher than regular probation but less stringent and expensive than prison.[19]

The program models were plausible and could have worked, except for one critical factor: They were usually implemented without creating organizational capacity to ensure compliance with court-ordered conditions. When courts ordered offenders to participate in drug treatment, for example, many probation officers could not ensure compliance because local treatment programs were unavailable.[20]

Over time, what was intended as tougher community corrections in

---

WHO IS ON PROBATION?

According to a Bureau of Justice Statistics study of correctional populations in the United States in 1996:[1]

- About 55 percent of all offenders on probation had been convicted of a felony, 26 percent of a misdemeanor. About 17 percent had been convicted of driving while intoxicated, which can be considered either a felony or misdemeanor, and 2 percent for other offenses.
- Women comprised 21 percent of the Nation's probationers.
- About 64 percent of adult probationers were white, 35 percent black. Hispanics, who may be of any race, comprised 15 percent of the probation population.
- Southern States generally had the highest per capita ratio of adult probationers. Texas had the largest probation population, followed by California.

Data from one study suggest that many offenders who are granted felony probation are indistinguishable in terms of their crimes or criminal record from those who are imprisoned (or vice versa).[2]

Another analysis found that 50 percent of probationers did not comply with court-ordered terms of their probation; 50 percent of known violators went to jail or prison for their noncompliance.[3] A more recent analysis indicates that 33 percent of those exiting probation failed to successfully meet the conditions of their supervision.[4] A study of a national sample of felons placed on probation found that, on any given day, about 10 to 20 percent of probationers were on abscond status, their whereabouts unknown; no agency actively invested time finding those offenders.[5]

Notes

Bureau of Justice Statistics, *Nation's Probation and Parole Population Reached Almost 3.9 Million Last Year,* Press Release, Washington, D.C.: U.S. Department of Justice, Bureau of Justice Statistics, August 14, 1997.

Petersilia, Joan, and Susan Turner, *Prison versus Probation in California: Implications for Crime and Offender Recidivism,* Santa Monica, California, RAND Corporation, 1986.

Langan, Patrick, "Between Prison and Probation: Intermediate Sanctions," *Science,* 1994, 264:791–793.

Bureau of Justice Statistics, *Nation's Probation and Parole Population Reached Almost 3.9 Million Last Year.*

Taxman, Faye S., and James Byrne, "Locating Absconders: Results from a Randomized Field Experiment," *Federal Probation,* 1994, 58(1):13–23.

[T]he *concept* of probation … has great appeal and much unrealized potential. As one judge noted, "Nothing is wrong with probation. It is the *execution* of probation that is wrong.

most jurisdictions did not materialize, thereby further tarnishing probation's image. Although most judges still report a willingness to use tougher, community-based programs as alternatives to routine probation or prison, most are skeptical that the programs promised "on paper" will be delivered in practice.[21] As a result, some intermediate sanction programs are beginning to fall into disuse.[22]

However, some communities invested adequate resources in intermediate sanctions and made the necessary treatment and work programs available to offenders.[23] In programs where offenders received *both* surveillance (e.g., drug tests) and participated in relevant treatment, recidivism declined 20 to 30 percent.[24]

Solid empirical evidence shows that recidivism is reduced by ordering offenders into treatment and requiring them to participate.[25] So, the first order of business must be to allocate sufficient resources so that the designed programs (incorporating both surveillance and treatment) can be implemented. The resources will be forthcoming only if the public believes that the programs are both effective and punitive.

Public opinion is often cited by officials as a reason for supporting expanded prison policies. According to officials, the public's "get tough on crime" demands are synonymous with sending more offenders to prison for longer terms.[26] Recent evidence must be publicized showing that many offenders—whose opinions on such matters are critical for deterrence—judge some intermediate sanctions as *more* punishing than prison.[27]

When, for example, nonviolent offenders in Marion County, Oregon, were given the choice of serving a prison term or returning to the community to participate in intensive supervision probation (ISP) programs—which imposed drug testing, mandatory community services, and frequent visits with the probation officer—about one-third chose prison over ISP.[28]

Why should anyone prefer imprisonment to remaining in the community, no matter what the conditions? Some have suggested that prison has lost some of its punitive sting and, hence, its ability to scare and deter. One study found that for drug dealers in California, imprisonment confers a certain elevated "homeboy" status, especially for gang members for whom prison and prison gangs can be an alternative site of loyalty.[29] According to the California Youth Authority, inmates steal State-issued prison clothing for the same reason. Wearing it when they return to the community lets everyone know they have done "hard time."[30]

It is important to publicize these results, particularly to policymakers who say they are imprisoning such a large number of offenders because of the public's desire to get tough on crime. But it is no longer necessary to equate criminal punishment solely with prison. The balance of sanctions between probation and prison can be shifted, and at some level of intensity and length, intermediate punishments can be the more dreaded penalty.

Once probation's political support and organizational capacity are in place, offender groups need to be targeted on the basis of what is known about the effectiveness of various programs. Targeting drug offenders makes the most sense for a number of reasons. Large-scale imprisonment of drug offenders has only recently taken place, and new evidence suggests that the public seems ready to accept different punishment strategies for low-level drug offenders.

Over time, probation will demonstrate its effectiveness, in terms of both reducing the human toll that imprisonment exacts on those incarcerated and reserving scarce resources to ensure that truly violent offenders remain in prison.

The public appears to want tougher sentences for drug traffickers and more treatment for addicts—what legislators have instead given them are long sentences for everyone. Public receptiveness to treatment for addicts is important, because those familiar with delivering treatment say that is where treatment can make the biggest impact. A report by the Institute of Medicine (IOM) of the National Academy of Sciences notes that about one-fifth of the estimated population needing treatment—and two-fifths of those clearly needing it—are under the supervision of the justice system as parolees or probationers.

Because the largest single group of serious drug users in any locality comes through the justice system every day, IOM concludes that the justice system is one of the most important gateways to treatment delivery and should be used more effectively. Research has shown that those under corrections supervision stay in treatment longer, thereby increasing positive treatment outcomes.[31]

On the one hand, good-quality treatment is not cheap. On the other hand, it is an investment that pays for itself immediately in terms of crime and health costs averted. Researchers in California[32] concluded that treatment was very cost beneficial: For every dollar spent on drug and alcohol treatment, California saved $7 in reduced crime and health care costs.

The study found that each day of treatment *paid for itself on the day treatment was received,* primarily through an avoidance of crime. The level of criminal activity declined by two-thirds from before treatment to after treatment. The greater the length of time spent in treatment, the greater the reduction in crime.

Of course, there is much more to reforming the probation system than simply targeting low-level drug offenders for effective treatment, but this would be a start. There also needs to be serious reconsideration of probation's underlying mission, administrative structure, and funding base.

And a program of basic research to address some of probation's most pressing problems should be funded.

Make probation a priority research topic. Noted below are a few of the questions that would be highly useful for probation research to address.

What purpose is served by monitoring and revoking probation for persons committing technical violations, and is the benefit worth the cost? If technical violations identify offenders who are "going bad" and likely to commit crime, time could be well spent uncovering such violations and incarcerating those persons. But if technical violators are simply troublesome, but not criminally dangerous, devoting scarce prison resources to this population may not be warranted.

Despite the policy significance of technical violations, little serious research has focused on this issue. As the cost of monitoring and incarcerating technical violators increases, research must examine its crime control significance.

Who is in prison, and is there a group of prisoners who, based on crime and prior criminal records, could safely be supervised in the community? Some contend that many, if not most, prisoners are minor property offenders, low-level drug dealers, or technical violators—ideal candidates for community-based alternatives. Others cite data showing that most prisoners are violent recidivists with few prospects for reform.

Research examining the characteristics of inmates in different States (by age, criminal record, and substance-abuse history) is necessary to clarify this important debate. Also critical are better followup studies (ideally, using experimental designs) of offenders who have been sentenced to prison as opposed to various forms of community supervision. By tracking similarly-situated offenders who are sentenced differently, researchers will be able to refine recidivism prediction models and begin to estimate more accurately the crime and cost implications of different sentencing models.

How do probation departments and other justice agencies influence one another and, together, influence crime? Decisions made in one justice agency have dramatic workload and cost implications for other agencies and for later decisions (such as probation policy on technical violations). To date, these systemic effects have not been well studied but research examining how various policy initiatives affect criminal justice agencies, individually and collectively, is likely to generate many benefits.

Conclusion

Several steps may be taken to achieve greater crime control over probationers:

- Provide adequate financial resources to deliver treatment programs that have been shown to work.
- Combine *both* treatment and surveillance in probation programs and focus them on appropriate offender sub-groups. Current evidence suggests that low-level drug offenders are prime candidates for enhanced probation programs.
- Work to garner more public support by convincing citizens that probation sanctions are punitive and in the long run cost-effective.
- Convince the judiciary that offenders will be held accountable for their behavior.
- Give priority to research addressing probation's most pressing problems.

Over time, probation will demonstrate its effectiveness, in terms of both reducing the human toll that imprisonment exacts on those incarcerated and reserving scarce resources to ensure that truly violent offenders remain in prison.

This article is adapted from Professor Petersilia's essay in volume 22 of Crime and Justice, *edited by Michael Tonry (University of Chicago Press, 1997).*

Notes

1. Bureau of Justice Statistics, *Probation and Parole Population Reached Almost 3.9 Million Last Year,* Press Release, Washington, D.C.: U.S. Department of Justice, Bureau of Justice Statistics, August 14, 1997. See also Bureau of Justice Statistics, *Correction Populations in the United States, 1995,* Washington, D.C.: U.S. Department of Justice, Bureau of Justice Statistics, May 1997.
2. Ibid.
3. Petersilia, Joan, "A Crime Control Rationale for Reinvesting in Community Corrections," *Prison Journal,* 1995, 75(4):479–496.
4. Judge Burton Roberts, administrative judge of the Bronx Supreme and Criminal Courts. Cited in Klein, Andrew R., *Alternative Sentencing, Intermediate Sanctions, and Probation,* Cincinnati, Ohio: Anderson, 1997:72.
5. The judge's (and probation officer's) required conditions can include standard conditions (reporting to the probation officer and the like), punitive conditions (house arrest, for example) that reflect the seriousness of the crime and increase the burden of probation, and treatment conditions (such as for substance abuse).
6. Abadinsky, Howard, *Probation and Parole: Theory and Practice,* Englewood Cliffs, New Jersey: Prentice-Hall, 1997.
7. Cunniff, Mark, and Ilene R. Bergsmann, *Managing Felons in the Community: An Administrative Profile of Probation,* Washington, D.C.: National Association of Criminal Justice Planners, 1990.
8. Camp, George M. and Camille Camp, *The Corrections Yearbook 1995: Probation and Parole,* South Salem, New York: Criminal Justice Institute, 1995.
9. Jones, Peter R., "Risk Prediction in Criminal Justice," in *Choosing Correctional Options That Work: Defining the Demand and Evaluating the Supply,* ed. Alan Harland, Thousand Oaks, California: Sage Publications, Inc., 1996.
10. Langan, Patrick A., and Mark A. Cunniff, *Recidivism of Felons on Probation, 1986–89,* Washington, D.C.: U.S. Department of Justice, Bureau of Justice Statistics, 1992.
11. Clear, Todd, and Anthony A. Braga, "Community Corrections," in *Crime,* ed. James Q. Wilson and Joan Petersilia, San Francisco, California: Institute for Contemporary Studies, 1995:423.

12. Bureau of Justice Statistics, *Nation's Probation and Parole Population Reached Almost 3.9 Million Last Year.*

13. Petersilia, Joan, Susan Turner, James Kahan, and Joyce Peterson, *Granting Felons Probation: Public Risks and Alternatives,* Santa Monica, California: RAND Corporation, R-3186-NIJ, 1985.

14. Geerken, Michael, and Hennessey D. Hayes, "Probation and Parole: Public Risk and the Future of Incarceration Alternatives," *Criminology,* 1993, 31(4):549–564.

15. Reaves, Brian A., and Pheny Z. Smith, *Felony Defendants in Large Urban Counties, 1992,* Washington, D.C.: U.S. Department of Justice, Bureau of Justice Statistics, 1995.

16. Boone, Harry N., and Betsy A. Fulton, *Results-Driven Management: Implementing Performance-Based Measures in Community Corrections,* Lexington, Kentucky: American Probation and Parole Association, 1995.

17. Ibid.

18. Griffin, Margaret, "Hunt County, Texas, Puts Performance-Based Measured to Work," *Perspectives,* 1996:9–11.

19. Tonry, Michael, and Mary Lynch, "Intermediate Sanctions," in *Crime and Justice: A Review of Research,* vol. 20, ed. Michael Tonry, Chicago, Illinois, University of Chicago Press, 1996.

20. Petersilia, Joan, and Susan Turner, "Intensive Probation and Parole," in *Crime and Justice: A Review of Research,* vol. 17, ed. Michael Tonry, Chicago, Illinois: University of Chicago Press, 1993.

21. Sigler, Robert, and David Lamb, "Community-Based Alternatives to Prison: How the Public and Court Personnel View Them," *Federal Probation,* 1994, 59(2):3–9.

22. Petersilia, "A Crime Control Rationale for Reinvesting in Community Corrections."

23. Klein, *Alternative Sentencing, Intermediate Sanctions, and Probation.*

24. Petersilia and Turner, "Intensive Probation and Parole."

25. Gendreau, Paul, "The Principles of Effective Intervention with Offenders," in *Choosing Correctional Options That Work: Defining the Demand and Evaluating the Supply,* ed. Alan Harland, Thousand Oaks, California: Sage Publications, Inc., 1996.

26. Bell, Griffin B., and William J. Bennett, *The State of Violent Crime in America,* Washington, D.C.: Council on Crime in America, 1996.

27. Crouch, Ben, "Is Incarceration Really Worse? Analysis of Offenders' Preferences for Prisons over Probation," *Justice Quarterly,* 1993, 10:67–88; Petersilia, Joan, and Elizabeth Piper Deschenes, "Perceptions of Punishment: Inmates and Staff Rank the Severity of Prison versus Intermediate Sanctions," *Prison Journal,* 1994, 74:306–328; Spelman, William, "The Severity of Intermediate Sanctions," *Journal of Research in Crime and Delinquency,* 1995, 32:107–135; and Wood, Peter B., and Harold G. Grasmick, "Inmates Rank the Severity of Ten Intermediate Sanctions Compared to Prison," *Journal of the Oklahoma Criminal Justice Research Consortium,* 1995, 2:30–42.

28. Petersilia and Deschenes, "Perceptions of Punishment: Inmates and Staff Rank the Severity of Prison versus Intermediate Sanctions."

29. Skolnick, Jerome, "Gangs and Crime Old as Time: But Drugs Change Gang Culture," *Crime and Delinquency in California, 1989,* Sacramento, California: California Department of Justice, Bureau of Criminal Statistics, 1990.

30. Petersilia, Joan, "California's Prison Policy: Causes, Costs, and Consequences," *Prison Journal,* 1992, 72(1):8–36.

31. Institute of Medicine, Committee for Substance Abuse Coverage Study, "A Study of the Evolution, Effectiveness, and Financing of Public and Private Drug Treatment Systems," in *Treating Drug Problems,* vol. 1, ed. D. R. Gerstein and H. J. Harwood, Washington, D.C.: National Academy Press, 1990.

32. Gerstein, Dean, R. A. Johnson, H. J. Harwood, D. Fountain, N. Suter, and K. Malloy, *Evaluating Recovery Services: The California Drug and Alcohol Treatment Assessment,* Sacramento, California: State of California, Department of Alcohol and Drug Programs, 1994. The researchers studied a sample of 1,900 treatment participants, followed them up for as long as 2 years of treatment, and studied participants from all four major treatment modalities (therapeutic communities, social models, outpatient drug-free, and methadone maintenance).

PROBATION AND PAROLE SUPERVISION:

TIME FOR A NEW NARRATIVE

BY EDWARD E. RHINE

The criminal justice system is experiencing a crisis of legitimacy. For the past several decades public and political discourse have expressed a heightened anxiety about crime. These discourses have been rooted in fear, moralism and a belief in the need to restore retribution as the centerpiece of crime control policy. In response, legislative changes have been enacted that reflect an increasingly harsh and conservative philosophy in addressing the problem of crime. The most notable of these changes includes a massive expansion of prison capacity at the state and federal level and criminal code revisions emphasizing mandatory minimum terms and a commitment to "truth-in-sentencing." The conclusion has been drawn by legislators and opinion makers alike that punishment and incapacitation are the only appropriate goals in a system that seems unable to change offenders' criminality (Zimring and Hawkins 1995).

This represents a dramatic turn of events. Until as recently as the early 1970s, the system of criminal justice could finesse its failures; those driving the system could point to a future in which acknowledged shortcomings in dealing with criminal offenders would be overcome and meaningful changes effected. The strategies and practices adopted by professionals within the system for addressing criminal behavior offered a certain amount of reassurance to the public, political leaders and others that something of value was being done to combat criminality. There was a shared conviction on the part of many that—whatever the deficiencies—continued reform of the system would have a positive impact on reducing crime.

The current crisis in criminal justice is fueled by the growing conviction that the system itself no longer represents a credible response to the problem of crime. In a relatively short span of time, the optimism of earlier eras about the rationality and efficacy of the system of criminal sanctioning has now given way to a striking and corrosive skepticism about its very value (Garland 1990). In essence, the practice and discourse of criminal justice no longer succeed in providing the public with a convincing narrative of the goals being pursued or how it conducts its business.[1]

Though all components of criminal justice have been affected by this development, its impact has been especially noticeable in the area of probation and parole. Despite their importance to public safety the past twenty years have witnessed a marked devaluation of traditional probation and parole supervision. Acknowledging this trend, there has been a concerted effort on the part of many administrators in the field to adopt a set of practices and a discourse that represents a discernible shift toward risk management and surveillance. This shift in the mission and conduct of supervision represents a new narrative, the plausibility of which has yet to be established. What follows addresses these developments within the current crisis of criminal justice.

The Devaluing of Traditional Probation and Parole Supervision[2]

During the past several decades the prison population has grown more rapidly than at any other period of time since the founding of the penitentiary in the early 1800s (Blumstein 1988). In 1995 the total number of inmates in state and federal prisons exceeded more than 1,000,000 (Bureau of Justice Statistics 1995). The growth continues unabated. The historically unprecedented increases and the problems this has created for prison administrators are well understood. What is not so well understood or even acknowledged is the urgent problem of probation and parole population growth and the public safety issues associated with crowded supervision caseloads.

Reflecting the reality that the criminal justice system is primarily a system of community-based sanctioning, at the end of 1995 approximately 3.8 million offenders were on probation or parole. (Tonry 1996). Despite the commitment to incapacitation as the paramount goal of sentencing, these figures clearly illustrate that the vast majority of offenders are serving their time under supervision in the community. Even

> In essence, the primary focus of supervision has become almost exclusively that of crime control through more contacts, more enforcement, and more sanctioning of noncompliance.

though prison population growth has been dramatic, the increase in probation and parole populations has been equally as pro-

From *Perspectives*, Winter 1998, pp. 26-28. © 1998 by The Council of State Governments. Reprinted by permission of the American Probation and Parole Association.

nounced. At present, nearly three quarters of all criminal offenders are supervised in some manner by probation and parole officers.

The increased reliance on incarceration fueled by the crisis in criminal justice has been accompanied by ever greater expenditures for institutional corrections. Many states have engaged in massive prison construction programs to deal with the increased numbers of offenders sentenced to a term of confinement. The same is not so for probation and parole. Even though these components have experienced unprecedented growth in the offender populations over which they have jurisdiction, probation and parole budgets have not kept pace. In fact, since 1977 spending for probation and parole in proportion to institutional corrections has shown a steady decline (Ringle et al. 1994).

The inadequacy of funding is especially troublesome when it is placed beside the average supervision caseloads for probation and parole officers and the growing seriousness of the offenders they supervise. Numerous reports have long recommended that supervision caseloads be limited to an average of thirty-five cases or less (e.g., the President's Commission on Law Enforcement and Administration of Justice 1967). Petersilia (1995) reports that probation caseloads at the national level reflect a ratio of 150:1, while those in parole equal 80:1. Though research suggests there is no ideal caseload size (Byrne et al. 1989), it is also evident that caseloads this large (and larger) make it difficult to maintain anything but superficial and infrequent contacts with offenders under supervision. Public safety is compromised under such circumstances, a problem compounded by the fact that probationers and parolees seem increasingly to present more serious types of offenses and levels of risk than in years past (Petersilia 1995).

The Shifting Focus in Community Supervision

The gradual devaluing of traditional probation and parole supervision in concert with the crisis of confidence in criminal justice has sparked a profound change in the mission and strategies embraced by probation and parole administrators. In a number of states, especially since the mid-1980s, they have moved toward surveillance-oriented, control-based strategies of supervision. They have adopted a formal system for the classification and management of offender risk. This system self-consciously allocates limited resources to the management of probationers and parolees based on their formal identification and classification as high risk offenders. It places an emphasis on monitoring and enforcing compliance with the rules of probation or parole, and the detection of violations leading to revocation and return to custody. In essence, the primary focus of supervision has become almost exclusively that of crime control through more contacts, more enforcement, and more sanctioning of noncompliance.

The widespread adoption and continued use of formal risk assessment tools by probation and parole agencies represent one indicator of this shift. Other indicators include the rapid movement toward intensive supervision programs, the increasing use of electronic monitoring, home confinement, frequent drug testing of offenders, and the growing reliance on community service. Many of these indicators fall under the category of "intermediate sanctions" (Morris and Tonry 1990; Tonry and Lynch 1996).

The growing prominence of such sanctions in both discourse and practice on the part of probation and parole administrators reflects an effort to market a more credible approach to supervision, one that is viewed as tough-minded and uncompromising in relation to offender accountability. If success is measured by the number of probationers and parolees who are revoked, it is an approach that has been rather successful. According to a report by the National Council on Crime and Delinquency, in 1987 there were 62,729 prison admissions in California (Austin 1989). Of this number, 31,581 (or 50.3 percent) were parole violators. In 1991 probation and parole violators represented roughly 45 percent of the state prison population. The comparable figure for 1974 was 17 percent (Cohen 1995).

As probation and parole administrators move toward the twenty-first century, they find themselves in the position of having adopted ever more aggressive supervision strategies that focus almost singularly upon the management and control of criminal offenders (Simon 1993). These strategies do not make any assumptions about restoring or reintegrating offenders back into the community. Left on their own, the narratives these administrators have constructed face an intractable dilemma: as the perception of offender risk continues to escalate, politicians and the public alike become ever more convinced that the system of supervision is unable to manage such risk in a credible fashion. For evidence, they point to the very indicators that the surveillance-based, control-oriented model of supervision relies on as a benchmark of success: the swift revocation and return to custody of growing numbers of probation and parole violators.

The "New Penology" and Community Supervision

The current discourse and practice of probation and parole supervision reflect the imprint of what has been referred to recently as the "new penology" (Feeley and Simon 1992; Simon and Feeley 1995). The language of the new penology focuses on risk management, the allocation of resources and the management of internal system processes. Within this perspective, crime is viewed as a systemic phenomenon. Offenders are addressed not as individuals but as aggregate populations. The traditional correctional objectives of rehabilitation and the reduction of offender recidivism give way to the rational and efficient deployment of control strategies for managing (and confining) high risk criminal populations. Though the new penology refers to any agency within the criminal justice system that has the power to punish, the framework it provides has significant analytic value to probation and parole administrators.

The supervision of offenders in the community has shown notable change due to the impact of the Model Probation/Parole Classification and Case Management Project in the 1980s (Burke et al. 1990). The project then and now enabled probation and parole agencies to respond effectively to escalating caseload growth, dwindling resources and the need for greater accountability in the conduct of supervision. However, as noted above, there has been a steady devaluation of traditional probation and parole. Though the systems language

To some extent, the movement toward a surveillance-based, control oriented model of supervision represents an extension of traditional probation and parole, albeit with a greater emphasis on risk management, and the expanded use of intermediate sanctions.

> This modern day narrative must account for what is now known about how to achieve reductions in offender recidivism by wedding effective correctional programming with sound strategies for supervision.

of the new penology is clearly expressed in the supervision practices of probation and parole agencies across the country (Burke 1990), traditional supervision strategies do not offer a persuasive narrative for handling criminal offenders in the community.

To some extent, the movement toward a surveillance-based, control oriented model of supervision represents an extension of traditional probation and parole, albeit with a greater emphasis on risk management, and the expanded use of intermediate sanctions. There is, however, a significant difference. The recent shift in probation and parole strategies is premised on a deep cynicism about the capacity of any model or technique to change offender behavior. The paramount goal is not to curb criminality per se, but to manage its inevitability in the community through systemic coordination of limited resources and policies that selectively target high risk, felony offenders. This goal, firmly embedded within the framework of the new penology, does not (and will not in the future) provide a sufficiently compelling narrative that something meaningful is being done about the problem of crime (Simon and Feeley 1995).

The Need for a New Supervision Narrative

What the above analysis suggests is that the most pressing (and vexing) problem facing probation and parole administrators today is the need to develop a plausible

narrative of community-based supervision. This narrative must convey in both discourse and practice how the risk offenders present can be addressed in a credible fashion outside prison walls. According to Simon (1993:9), for such a narrative to be successful three elements must be addressed in a manner that conveys coherence and plausibility. These elements include the need for a theory of criminogenesis, a measurement of its degree and a set of practices that appear capable of controlling it. A sound narrative in probation and parole must provide a persuasive accounting of the problem of crime, its extent, and what can be done to address it. In addition, it must recognize and be responsive to the "rationality demands" that are placed on the system. That is, it must articulate the legitimate ends or goals that the system is pursuing and defend its practices and strategies as viable means of accomplishing these ends (Simon 1993:8).[3]

The legitimate or overriding goal for probation and parole may be found by revisiting an earlier era. From the Progressive Era of criminal justice in the 1920s–1930s through the 1960s, probation and parole supervision relied on a philosophy and a set of practices designed to restore offenders to the community. Despite the continuous tension between "conscience" and "convenience," there was a commitment to transforming the offender (Rothman 1980). In dramatic contrast to the new penology, the discourse of probation and parole must emphasize a return to the historic commitment of the field to offender reintegration. This modern day narrative must account for what is now known about how to achieve reductions in offender recidivism by wedding effective correctional programming with sound strategies for supervision.

The new narrative for probation and parole supervision must draw on the current state of knowledge regarding offender criminality, and in so doing, offer a theory of criminogenesis. It must then show how this knowledge may be applied to the reduction of criminal behavior. Fortunately, an extraordinary knowledge base has been accumulating since the early 1980s on offender rehabilitation and the principles that govern effective correctional intervention (Gendreau and Ross 1987; Andrews and Bonta 1994). In meta-analyses extending over hundreds of studies, the research has shown that "something works"; certain types of programs offer a promising vehicle for reducing the level of recidivism for some offenders. Of perhaps greater importance, the research has also identified those principles that drive effective correctional intervention. The evidence indicates that well designed and properly implemented programs incorporating these principles re-

sult in significant reductions in recidivism. Those programs that are most successful include a strong behavioral and cognitive skills development component (Porporino 1996; Rhine 1996).

In terms of the strategies adopted for supervision, this research suggests that probation and parole officers should target the criminogenic needs of high risk offenders. It also suggests that supervision should be delivered in an intensive manner and in combination with programming occupy a majority of offenders' everyday activities. The integration of programming with intensive supervision will be most effective if it is demanding on offenders' time and thinking and if it disrupts their criminal network by placing them in situations where prosocial activities predominate. In essence, the supervision of high risk probationers and parolees must be structured, intensive, maintain firm accountability for program participation and connect the offender with prosocial networks and activities.

The above is barely suggestive of what might constitute the beginnings of a new narrative of probation and parole supervision. It does not provide a fully developed narrative inclusive of the elements described by Simon (1993). It acknowledges, however, Simon and Feeley's argument that the discourse and practice of probation and parole does not provide a satisfying account to the public, political leaders and others that significant steps are being taken to effectively address the problem of crime and criminality (1995). The challenge for probation and parole administrators is to develop such a narrative and thereby create strategies and practices that have recognizable public value (Moore 1995).

Endnotes

1. This article draws on the recent writings of Feeley and Simon (1992), Garland (1990; 1995), Simon (1993) and Simon and Feeley (1995). These authors present contrasting arguments regarding the nature and form of modern penal practices.
2. Joan Petersilia's 1995 article provides a more in depth analysis of the trends discussed in this section. This section briefly highlights some of the more significant trends addressed in that article.
3. Simon's argument is developed in an incisive study of parole supervision. Nonetheless, his analysis may be extended to contemporary probation supervision.

Edward E. Rhine is the Deputy Director of the Parole, Courts & Community Services at the Department of Youth Services in Columbus, OH.

Education as Crime Prevention

Providing education to prisoners

This research brief presents the most recent data on the impact of education on crime and crime prevention, and examines the debate on providing higher education to inmates.

"WE MUST ACCEPT THE REALITY THAT TO CONFINE OFFENDERS BEHIND WALLS WITHOUT TRYING TO CHANGE THEM IS AN EXPENSIVE FOLLY WITH SHORT-TERM BENE-FITS— WINNING BATTLES WHILE LOSING THE WAR."—FORMER U.S. SUPREME COURT CHIEF JUSTICE WARREN BURGER[1]

In response to the American public's growing fear of crime and the call for more punitive measures to combat such fear, many legislators and policy-makers have promoted building more prisons, enacting harsher sentencing legislation, and eliminating various programs inside prisons and jails.

With re-arrest rates averaging around 60%, it is clear that incarceration alone is not working. In fact, the drive to incarcerate, punish, and limit the activities of prisoners has often resulted in the elimination of strategies and programs that seek to prevent or reduce crime.

For instance, research shows that quality education[2] is one of the most effective forms of crime prevention. Educational skills can help deter young people from committing criminal acts and can greatly decrease the likelihood that people will return to crime after release from prison. Despite this evidence, educational programs in correctional facilities, where they have proven to be extraordinarily effective, have in many cases been completely eliminated.

Over 1.6 million individuals are housed in adult correctional facilities in the United States,[3] and at least 99,682 juveniles are in custody.[4] The majority of these individuals will be released into the community unskilled, undereducated, and highly likely to be-come re-invovled in criminal activity. With so many ex-offenders returning to prison, it is clear that the punitive, incarceration-based approach to crime prevention is not working. We need to promote policies and procedures that are successful. Education, particularly at the college level, can afford individuals with the opportunities to achieve and maintain productive and crime-free lives, and help to create safer communities for all.

THE EDUCATIONAL LEVEL OF OFFENDERS IS LOW

Most individuals involved in the criminal justice system come from low-income, urban communities, which are also the most likely to be under-served in terms of educational support programs. Not surprisingly, a disproportionate number of the incarcerated are undereducated. To a great extent, the inadequate education of juvenile and adult offenders reflects the failures and inadequacies of public inner-city education.

Juvenile Offenders

While illiteracy and poor academic performance are not direct causes of criminal behavior, young people who have received inadequate education or who exhibit poor literacy skills are disproportionately found within the criminal justice system.

• According to a study conducted by Project READ, a national program designed to improve reading skills, youth that are confined to correctional facilities at the median age of 15.5 years and in the ninth grade read, on average, at the fourth-grade level.[5] More than one-third of all juvenile offenders of this age group read below the fourth-grade level.[6]
• Ninety percent of teachers providing reading instruction in juvenile correctional facilities reported that they had "students who [could not] read material composed of words from their own oral vocabularies."[7]
• Approximately 40% of youth held in detention facilities may have some form of learning disability.[8]

With such high rates of learning disabilities and poor educational skills, juvenile offenders are desperately in need of quality education, yet are likely to be denied it. For example, juvenile offenders in adult prisons can be prevented from participating in GED programs because of their age, and those requiring special education services are, in some facilities, no longer eligible to receive such education upon incarceration.[9]

In most cases, once juveniles are incarcerated, even for a short time, their line to education is forever broken. Most juvenile offenders aged 16 and older do not return to school upon release or graduate from high school.[10]

There is a strong link between low levels of education and high rates of criminal activity, and one of the best predictors of adult criminal behavior is involvement with the criminal justice system as a juvenile. With so few resources devoted to the education of juvenile offenders, it is not surprising that so many remain invovled in the criminal justice system well into their adult lives.

Adult Offenders

Like their juvenile counterparts, adults involved in the criminal justice system are severely undereducated. Nineteen percent of adult inmates are completely illiterate, and 40% are "functionally il-

From *The Center on Crime, Communities & Culture, Research Brief*, September 1997. © 1997 by the Open Society Institute, New York. Reprinted by permission.

THE HISTORY OF HIGHER EDUCATION IN PRISON

In 1965, Congress passed Title IV of the Higher Education Act, which explicitly permitted inmates to apply for financial aid in the form of Pell Grants to attend college. The passage of Title IV allowed for the expansion of what had been a smattering of higher education programs in correctional facilities. The number of programs peaked in 1982 at over 350 available in 90% of the states.[41]

In the 1970s, studies[42] were conducted to determine the achievements of correctional higher education. Success was measured by the rate of re-arrest and the offender's ability to obtain and maintain employment upon release. The results were overwhelmingly positive, indicating that higher education was responsible for reducing an individual's chances of returning to crime, which in turn resulted in savings by reducing the costs of incarceration and victimization, and by providing skilled workers to the economy.

In the early 1990s, elected officials began introducing legislation to prohibit federal tuition assistance to inmates. A counter-effort, started by educators, correctional officials, prison advocates, and prisoners themselves managed to stave off the legislation until 1994, when the Violent Crime Control and Law Enforcement Act effectively dismantled correctional higher education.

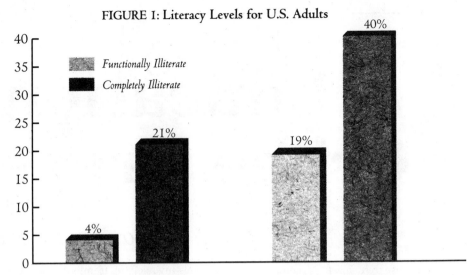

FIGURE I: Literacy Levels for U.S. Adults

literate," which means, for example, that they would be unable to write a letter explaining a billing error.[11] Comparatively, the national illiteracy rate for adult Americans stands at 4% with 21% functionally illiterate (see figure I).[12]

The rate of learning disabilities in adult correctional facilities runs high, at 11%, compared to 3% in the general population.[13] Low literacy levels and high rates of learning disabilities within this population have contributed to high dropout rates. Nationwide, over 70% of all people entering state correctional facilities have not completed high school, with 46% having had some high school education and 16.4% having had no high school education at all.[14]

EDUCATION LOWERS RECIDIVISM MORE EFFECTIVELY THAN CURRENTLY SUPPORTED PROGRAMS

Nationally, reported rates of recidivism for adult offenders in the United States are extraordinarily high, ranging from 41%[15] to 60%.[16] The difficulty in pinpointing specific rates of recidivism is often due to a confusion of terms. The national re-arrest rate, around 63%, is different from the re-imprisonment rate, which averages around 41%.[17] Programmatic efforts to reduce recidivism have ranged from boot camps and shock incarceration facilities to prison-based education efforts. The effectiveness of these programs varies, but research shows that prison-based education and literacy programs are much more effective at lowering recidivism rates than either boot camps or shock incarceration. For example, in a recent report on crime prevention programs conducted

at the request of the U.S. Justice Department,[18] researchers at the University of Maryland found that teaching reading skills to juveniles worked significantly better to reduce crime than boot camp programs.[19]

> "CORRECTIONAL EDUCATION APPEARS TO BE THE NUMBER ONE FACTOR IN REDUCING RECIDIVISM RATES NATIONWIDE."—ALABAMA STATE BOARD OF EDUCATION.[20]

According to the Federal Bureau of Prisons, there is an inverse relationship between recidivism rates and education. The more education received, the less likely an individual is to be re-arrested or re-imprisoned.[21]

• A report issued by the Congressional Subcommittee to Investigate Juvenile Delinquency estimates that the national recidivism rate for juvenile offenders is between 60% and 84%.[22] For juveniles involved in quality reading-instruction programs, the recidivism rate can be reduced by 20% or more.[23]

• A five-year follow-up study conducted by the Arizona Department of Adult Probation concluded that probationers who received literacy training had a significantly lower re-arrest rate (35%) than the control group (46%), and those who received GED education had a re-arrest rate of 24%, compared to the control group's rate of 46%.[24]

• Inmates with at least two years of college education have a 10% re-arrest rate, compared to a national re-arrest rate of approximately 60%.[25]

• Research studies conducted in Indiana, Maryland, Massachusetts, New York, and other states have all reported significantly low recidivism rates for inmate participants in correctional higher-education programs, ranging from 1% to 15.5%.[26,27]

As with all research on prisons and jails, data on correctional education tends to focus on specific localities or states. Texas is one jurisdiction which has done extensive research on the success of correctional higher education.

The overall recidivism rate for degree holders leaving the Texas Department of Criminal Justice between September 1990 and August 1991, was 15%, four times lower than the general recidivism rate of 60%. A two-year follow-up report found that the higher level of degree awarded was inversely related to the level of recidivism—individuals with associate's degrees had a recidivism rate of 13.7%, those with bachelor's degrees had a rate of 5.6%, and those with master's degrees had a rate of zero (see figure 2).[28]

CORRECTIONS OFFICIALS SUPPORT CORRECTIONAL EDUCATION

The vast majority of corrections officials believe that educational programs not only benefit inmates, but also the facility's administration and staff. Inmate students are better behaved, less likely to engage in violence, and more likely to have a positive effect on the general prison population.[29] Educated inmates can be a "stabilizing influence in an often chaotic environment, enhancing the safety and security of all who live and work in the correctional facility."[30] Indeed, 93% of prison wardens surveyed in a 1993 study conducted by the Senate Judiciary Committee of the United States Senate strongly supported educational and vocational programming in adult correctional facilities.[31]

CORRECTIONAL HIGHER EDUCATION IS A BARGAIN

The expense of providing higher education to inmates is minimal when considering the impact upon rates of recidivism and the future savings of preventing re-arrest and re-imprisonment.

New York State estimates that it costs $2,500 per year, per individual to provide higher education in a correctional facility. In contrast, the average cost of incarcerating an adult inmate per year is $25,000 (see figure 3).[32] Why are correctional education programs so inexpensive? For the most part, higher education in correctional facilities is provided by community colleges and universities that offer moderately priced tuition.

> "SOCIETY SHOULD RECOGNIZE THAT THE COST OF COLLEGE IS REALLY VERY INSIGNIFICANT WHEN YOU COMPARE THE COST OF THE DAMAGE DONE BY CRIME."—J. MICHAEL QUINLIN, FORMER DIRECTOR OF THE FEDERAL BUREAU OF PRISONS][33]

A combination of funding sources support an inmate's education, including in-kind donations from universities and colleges, outside support (foundations, community-based organizations, private donations), and individual contributions from inmates themselves, garnered while working at prison-based jobs. Until 1994, federal support in the form of Pell Grants did provide a substantial amount of tuition funding (see sidebar on next page).

THE SAVINGS OF PROVIDING CORRECTIONAL HIGHER EDUCATION ARE SIGNIFICANT

Even in a hypothetical situation with a comparatively expensive correctional higher-education program ($2,500 per year, per inmate in New York State) and one of the highest recorded rates of recidivism upon completion of such a program (15%), the savings of providing higher education are still substantial:

The cost of incarcerating 100 individuals over 4 years is approximately $10 million. For an additional $\frac{1}{10}$ of that cost, or $1 million, those same individuals could be given a full, four-year college education while incarcerated. Assuming a recidivism rate of 15% (as opposed to the general rate of 40–60%), 85 of those initial 100 individuals will not return to prison, saving U.S. taxpayers millions of dollars each year.

In addition to the millions saved by preventing an individual's return to incarceration and dependence on the criminal justice system, providing higher education to prisoners can save money in other ways. The prevention of crime helps to eliminate costs to crime victims and the courts, lost wages of the inmate while incarcerated, or costs to the inmate's family.

WHY SHOULD PRISONERS RECEIVE HIGHER EDUCATION?

The available statistical evidence overwhelmingly demonstrates the positive impact of higher education opportuni-

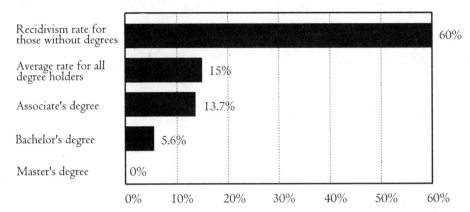

FIGURE 2: Recidivism Rates for Degree Holders Leaving the Texas Department of Criminal Justice, 1990–1991

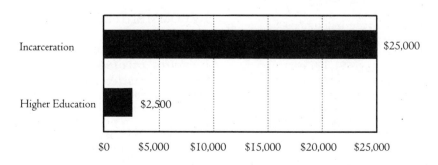

FIGURE 3: Cost of Incarceration vs. Higher Education in Correctional Facilities, per Year, per Inmate

THE ELIMINATION OF FEDERAL SUPPORT FOR CORRECTIONAL HIGHER EDUCATION

Despite tremendous evidence supporting the connection between higher education and lowered levels of recidivism, the U.S. Congress included a provision in the Violent Crime Control and Law Enforcement Act of 1994 which denied all prisoners access to federal Pell Grants. The provision was initiated to appeal to the notion that prisons have become places of leisure, and that inmates were given access to higher education at the expense of law-abiding taxpayers.

Yet prisoners who were eligible for federal tuition assistance never received support for college tuition at the expense of those in the free world. Pell Grants are non-competitive, need-based federal funds available to any and all qualifying low-income individuals who wish to attend college degree programs. The pool of money available for Pell Grants is not limited, and is only dictated by the number of individuals who apply and qualify. Whether in or out of prison, an individual must meet the exact same criteria to be awarded a Pell Grant.

For qualifying individuals in correctional facilities, the average Pell Grant award was less than $1,300 per year.[43] The total percentage of the Pell Grants' annual budget that was spent on inmate higher education was 1⁄10 of 1%.[44]

ties on the prison population. Some of the resulting benefits are as follows:

• An estimated 97% of adult felony inmates are eventually discharged from confinement and released into the community.[34]

• Studies have shown that individuals who receive higher education while incarcerated have a significantly better rate of employment (60–75%) than those who do not participate in college programs (40%).[35]

• The financial and societal savings of providing an inmate higher education are enormous. Upon an inmate's release, the cost-benefit of reducing recidivism will begin to be realized immediately. If we consider the additional benefit of this individual obtaining work, paying taxes, and contributing to the general economy, and the prevention of costs to victims of crime and the criminal justice system, the benefits are significantly greater.

• The RAND Corporation, a public policy think tank based in California, recently released a study showing that crime prevention is more cost-effective than building prisons. Of all crime prevention methods, education is the most cost-effective.[36]

• Higher education has a stabilizing influence on the correctional environment and can help a facility to run more smoothly and less violently than correctional institutions without educational programs.

• The educational level of a parent is a clear predictor of both the educational achievements of a child and the level of parental involvement in a child's education.[37,38] As the majority of prisoners are parents,[39] the education of adults in prison can have a positive and long-lasting impact upon the lives of their children.

• Well-run, high-quality higher education programs in correctional facilities can inspire correctional officers to pursue additional education, and in some instances scholarship moneys can be made available to those who work inside the facilities. The positive impact of education in prisons should inspire better public education for all citizens, both in and out of our prisons and jails.

RECOMMENDATIONS

Ensure quality education for juveniles involved in the criminal justice system.

A child's involvement in the criminal justice system, can be a critical intervention point to prevent future criminal activity. Because we do know that education can be a catalyst for change,

it is essential to provide appropriate programs, including special education, to juvenile offenders. Particular attention must be paid to juveniles housed in adult correctional facilities, and programs designed to assist juveniles in their transition from incarceration into the community must be supported and evaluated to ensure the best possible opportunities for successful reintegration upon release.

"MY INVOLVEMENT WITH COLLEGE . . . HAS OPENED MY EYES TO ALL OF THE THINGS THAT WERE WRONG IN MY LIFE. NOW I HAVE A SENSE OF PRIORITY, A SENSE OF ACCOUNTABILITY, AND HAVE MADE A LEGITIMATE PREMISE FOR MYSELF ON WHICH TO BUILD. . . . MY NEEDS ARE STILL IMPORTANT, BUT NOT AT SOMEONE ELSE'S EXPENSE."—STATEMENT BY AN INMATE STUDENT.[40]

Garner financial support for correctional education programs from various sources.

With all of the evidence available supporting the positive impact of correctional higher education, it is critical that programs be fully maintained to allow for the maximum number of qualified participants. The reinstatement of federal financial assistance in the form of Pell Grants to inmates is crucial. Alternative and varied sources of funding must also be considered. For example, in New York state, a variety of sources, including university assistance, private and in-kind donations, and the individual financial contributions of inmates and their families, have combined to provide the financial support for correctional higher-education programs.

Implement and fund post-release supportive services.

The benefit of higher education is clearly an incentive to maintain a crime-free life. However, because of the dearth of supportive services, many individuals may find themselves released without access to employment opportunities and/or additional training and education programs. As the first few months after release are critical, it is imperative that supportive services are in place and that ex-offenders are provided with access to them.

Fund evaluation of educational programs.

While it is clear that there is a strong link between quality education and

As a relatively small percentage of inmates attended higher education programs and actually received federal tuition assistance, Pell Grant support directly affected only a small part of the prison population.[45] Still, this support had a large and lasting impact on entire correctional systems.

• Educated prisoners often serve as teachers and tutors for other inmates, and often as examples and role models.

• Educational programs help to provide structure and lessen the need for supervision, and in the words of one federal prison warden, "help to keep the prison running smoothly."[46]

As the impact of federal higher-education tuition support was felt beyond the lives of individual recipients, the denial of financial assistance to inmates has also reverberated.

• At least 25 states have cut back on vocational and technical training programs since the Pell Grants were cut.[47] In 1990, there were 350 higher education programs for inmates. In 1997, there are 8.[48]

• 25,168 college students in correctional facilities were recipients of Pell Grants for the school year 1993–1994, the last year federal tuition support was available to them.[49] While no follow-up study has been done to track these individual students, it is highly likely that the majority of them were unable to continue their college education.

lowered levels of recidivism, there are difficulties in determining exactly which types of educational programs are most effective. Public and private funders should support evaluation of correctional education programs, which would include long-term follow-up to determine the impact of programs upon employment and the chance of re-involvement in the criminal justice system for both female and male ex-offenders and their children.

If we are serious about preventing and reducing crime, it is critical to adopt the most effective, humane, and cost-efficient means of doing so. As a reasonably priced, highly efficient, and continually beneficial method of crime prevention, education is clearly one of the most successful means we have.

REFERENCES

1. Taylor, J. M. (1993, January 25). Pell Grants for prisoners. *The Nation.* p. 90.

2. The use of the term 'quality education' is meant here to distinguish between programs implemented to fulfill federal and/or state guidelines requiring the education of both adult and juvenile offenders but which are rarely tested or evaluated for effectiveness, and educational programs that have a documented success rate at both providing education that meets community standards and reducing recidivism.

3. Gilliard, D. K. and Beck, A. J. (1997). *Prison and jail inmates at midyear 1996.* (NCJ Publication No. 162843). Washington, DC: U.S. Department of Justice, Bureau of Justice Statistics, p. 1.

4. Juvenile is defined as an individual under the age of 18. It is difficult to collect data on juvenile offenders. This total does not include the number of juveniles in police lock-ups, and only reflects the results of a 1-day census count at private and public juvenile facilities, adult jails, and state and federal correctional facilities. See: DeComo, R., Tunis, S., Krisberg, B., Herrera, N. C., Rudenstine, S., and Del Rosario, D. (1995). *Juveniles taken into custody: Fiscal year 1992 report.* (NCJ Publication No. 153851). Washington, DC: Office of Juvenile Justice and Delinquency Prevention, p. 28.

5. Project READ. (1978). *To make a difference.* Silver Spring, MD: READ, Inc. p. 27. In Brunner, M. S. (1993). *Reduced recidivism and increased employment opportunity through research-based reading instruction.* (NCJ Publication No. 141324). Washington, DC: Office of Juvenile Justice and Delinquency Prevention, p. 5.

6. Project READ. (1978). *To make a difference.* Silver Spring, MD: READ, Inc. p. 27. In Brunner, M. S. (1993). *Reduced recidivism and increased employment opportunity through research-based reading instruction.* (NCJ Publication No. 141324). Washington, DC: Office of Juvenile Justice and Delinquency Prevention, p. 5.

7. Brunner, M. S. (1993). *National survey of reading programs for incarcerated juvenile offenders.* (NCJ Publication No. 144017). Washington, DC: Office of Juvenile Justice and Delinquency Prevention. p. 29.

8. Gemignani, R. J. (1994). *Juvenile correctional education: A time for change.* (NCJ Publication No. 150309). Washington, DC: Office of Juvenile Justice and Delinquency Prevention, p. 2.

9. Juvenile Law Center. (1996, December). *1996 Annual Report.* Philadelphia, PA: Juvenile Law Center. pp. 8–9.

10. Gemignani, R. J. (1994). *Juvenile correctional education: A time for change.* (NCJ Publication No. 150309). Washington, DC: Office of Juvenile Justice and Delinquency Prevention. p. 3.

11. There is not a statistically significant difference between the literacy rates of male and female offenders. See: Haigler, K. O., Harlow, C., O'Conner, P., and Campbell, A. (1994). *Literacy behind prison walls: Profiles of the prison population from the national adult literacy survey.* (NCES Publication No. 94-102). Washington, DC: U.S. Department of Education, National Center for Education Statistics, p. 124.

12. U.S. Department of Education, National Center for Education Statistics. (1992). *1992 national adult literacy survey.* Washington, DC: National Center for Education Statistics. [On-line]. Available: http://www.ed.gov/NCES/nadlits/overview.html.

13. Haigler, K. O., Harlow, C., O'Conner, P., and Campbell, A. (1994). *Literacy behind prison walls: Profiles of the prison population from the national adult literacy survey.* (NCES Publication No. 94-102). Washington, DC: U.S. Department of Education, National Center for Education Statistics, p. xxiii.

14. Maguire, K. and Pastore, A. L. (1996). *Sourcebook of criminal justice statistics—1995* (NCJ Publication No. 158900). Washington, DC: U.S. Department of Justice, Bureau of Justice Statistics. p. 567.

15. Harer, M. D. (1994). *Recidivism among federal prison releases in 1987: A preliminary report.* Washington, DC: Federal Bureau of Prisons, Office of Research and Evaluation. p. 2.

16. News and views: A possible reprieve for prisoner higher education. (1995, December 31). *The Journal of Blacks in Higher Education.* paragraph 5.

17. Bureau of Justice Statistics. (1997). *Criminal offender statistics.* [On-line]. Available: http://www.ojp.usdoj.gov/bjs/crimoff.htm.

18. Sherman, L. W., Gottfredson, D., MacKenzie, D. L., Eck, J., Reuter, P. and Bushway, S. *Preventing crime: What works, what doesn't, what's promising.* (NCJ Publication No. 165366). Washington, DC: National Institute of Justice.

19. Sherman, L. W. (1997, August 6). Crime prevention's bottom line. *The Wall Street Journal.* p. A15.

20. Mosso, G. E. (1997, Winter). The truth about prison education. *Prison Connections.* Volume 1, Number 3. [On-line] Available: http://persephone.hampshire.edu/wmpig/VIN3/prisoned.html. paragraph 2.

21. Harer, M. D. (1994). *Recidivism among federal prison releases in 1987: A preliminary report.* Washington, DC: Federal Bureau of Prisons, Office of Research and Evaluation. p. 4.

22. Brunner, M. S. (1993). *Reduced recidivism and increased employment opportunity through research-based reading instruction.* (NCJ Publication No. 141324). Washington, DC: Office of Juvenile Justice and Delinquency Prevention. p. 1.

23. Brunner, M. S. (1993). *Reduced recidivism and increased employment opportunity through re-*

search-based reading instruction. (NCJ Publication No. 141324). Washington, DC: Office of Juvenile Justice and Delinquency Prevention. p. 6.

24. Siegel, G. R. (1997). *A research study to determine the effect of literacy and general educational development programs on adult offenders on probation.* Tucson, AZ: Adult Probation Department of the Superior Court in Pima County.

25. Marks, A. (1997, March 20). One inmate's push to restore education funds for prisoners. *The Christian Science Monitor,* paragraph 14.

26. Bettendorf, E. (1996, October 25). Prisoner poets. *The State-Journal Register.* paragraph 52.

27. Tracy, C. and Johnson, C. (1994). *Review of various outcome studies relating prison education to reduced recidivism.* Windham School System: Huntsville, TX. pp. 6–7.

28. Data is averaged and does not add up to 100 percent. Tracy, C. and Johnson, C. (1994). *Review of various outcome studies relating prison education to reduced recidivism.* Windham School System; Huntsville, TX. p. 7.

29. Taylor, J. M. (1993, January 25). Pell Grants for prisoners. *The Nation.* p. 88.

30. Consortium of the Niagara Frontier. (no date). *The benefits to New York state of higher education programs for inmates.* [pamphlet]. Amherst, NY: Consortium of the Niagara Frontier. paragraph 4.

31. Elikann, P. T. (1996). *The Tough-on-Crime Myth: Real Solutions to Cut Crime.* New York, NY: Insight Books. p. 151.

32. Taylor, J. M. (1993, January 25). Pell Grants for prisoners. *The Nation.* p. 88.

33. Marks, A. (1997, March 20). One inmate's push to restore education funds for prisoners. *The Christian Science Monitor.* paragraph 13.

34. Boyce, C. J. (1994, July 15). For those behind bars, education is rehabilitation. *Minneapolis Star Tribune.* paragraph 12.

35. Taylor, J. M. (1993, January 25). Pell Grants for prisoners. *The Nation.* p. 88.

36. Greenwood, P. W., Model, K. E., Rydell, C. P. and Chiesa, J. (1996). *Diverting children from a life of crime: Measuring costs and benefits.* Santa Monica, CA: Rand.

37. Brown, P. C. (1989). *Involving parents in the education of their children.* Urbana, IL: ERIC Clearinghouse on Elementary and Early Childhood Education. [On-line]. Available: http://www.ed.gov/databases/ERIC_Digests/ed30 8988.html.

38. U.S. Department of Education. (1996). *The digest of education statistics 1996.* Washington, DC: National Center for Education Statistics. [On-line]. Available: http://www.ed.gov/NCES/pubs/D96/d96t024.html.

39. Over 75% of female inmates and 64% of males have children. See: Snell, T. L. and Morton, D. C. (1994, March). *Women in prison.* (NCJ Publication No. 145321). Washington, DC: U.S. Department of Justice, Bureau of Justice Statistics, pp. 6–7.

40. Consortium of the Niagara Frontier. (no date). *Prison higher education programs: Statements by inmate students and graduates.* [pamphlet]. Amherst, NY: Consortium of the Niagara Frontier. paragraph 6.

41. Taylor, J. M. (1993, January 25). Pell Grants for prisoners. *The Nation.* p. 88.

42. Taylor, J. M. (1993, January 25). Pell Grants for prisoners. *The Nation.* p. 88.

43. U.S. Department of Education, Office of Correctional Education. (1995). *Pell Grants and the incarcerated.* [pamphlet]. Washington, DC: U.S. Department of Education.

44. U.S. Department of Education, Office of Correctional Education. (1995). *Pell Grants and the incarcerated.* [pamphlet]. Washington, DC: U.S. Department of Education.

45. Less than 1% of inmates received federal Pell Grants in their final year of availability. See: U.S. Department of Education, Office of Correctional Education. (1995). *Pell Grants and the incarcerated.* [pamphlet]. Washington, DC: U.S. Department of Education.

46. Worth, R. (1995, November). A model prison. *The Atlantic Monthly.* paragraph 7.

47. Worth, R. (1995, November). A model prison. *The Atlantic Monthly.* paragraph 12.

48. Bettendorf, E. (1996, October 25). Prisoners poets. *The State-Journal Register.* paragraph 50.

49. Office of Correctional Education. (1995). *Pell Grants and the incarcerated.* [pamphlet]. Washington, DC: U.S. Department of Education.

The Center wishes to thank Michelle Fine, Ph.D., Professor of Psychology at The Graduate Center, CUNY, and Paula H. Mayhew, Ph.D., Dean of the Faculty at Marymount Manhattan College, for their comments on a draft of this research brief.

Ethical Considerations in Probation Practice

by Marylouise E. Jones, Department of Psychology, Research Unit and Arthur J. Lurigio, Department of Criminal Justice, Research Unit, Loyola University Chicago (IL)

Editor's Note: Portions of this paper were presented at APPA's 21st Annual Training Institute, July 1996, Chicago, Illinois.

Probation officers frequently face decisions that place the needs of offenders in direct conflict with the welfare of society. In making such decisions, they can benefit from a firm foundation in ethics. Recent books have highlighted the importance of ethics for criminal justice professionals (Braswell, McCarthy, & McCarthy, 1991; Pollock-Byrne, 1994; Souryal, 1992). For example, Pollock-Byrne (1994) notes that within the criminal justice system, there is a variety of moral dilemmas, including "questions of responsibility and excuse, the limits of the state's right to control the individual, the ethical use of force, and the appropriate use of discretion" (p. 200). Ethical issues in probation practice, however, have been largely ignored (Brown, 1989).

Criminal justice is a young discipline, far more concerned with crime control than with philosophy. Most probation practitioners have not been exposed adequately to the philosophy of justice or to any serious or formal study of ethics. Courses in ethics and justice usually are not required for criminal justice degrees—the most common degree among probation officers—or included in probation officers' training curricula. Nonetheless, ethical issues in community corrections are significant and complex. These issues are common to other professions. But criminal justice agents, including probation officers, can be distinguished from other professionals in terms of the broad ethical nature and ramifications of their decisions.

Criminal justice professionals often render decisions on behalf of society as a whole. These judgments entail a far greater responsibility than the decisions of many other professionals and are not just inci-dentally, but are primarily, moral decisions (Sherman, 1992). For example, when a police officer decides to arrest a person or when a judge decides to release a person on bail, the decision has significant ethical and moral implications.

Upholding the social order is a fundamental obligation of the criminal justice system (Souryal, 1992). Social order focuses on the rights and welfare of individuals and of society at large. Laws and sanctions are designed to ensure that everyone has the freedom to pursue their interests and activities without undue fear or threat of victimization. Difficulties arise when the needs of individuals conflict with those of the broader community. For example, locking up someone who is a neighborhood nuisance may alleviate the misery of a few persons while infringing on an individual's freedoms and fundamental rights. Balancing individual rights with society's well-being begs the question of how much social control (i.e., laws and punishments) is needed to maintain an orderly society. Striking such a balance forces criminal justice practitioners to reconcile the welfare of their clients with the welfare of society.

Ethics and Probation Officer Discretion

Community corrections practitioners experience ethical challenges because of the formidable task of weighing an offender's welfare against the welfare of society. The basic rationale of probation is that society is willing to take a chance on offenders who are able to conform to its rules. Probationers are allowed to remain in the community as long as they adhere to the court-ordered conditions of release. If they violate the conditions of release, which constitutes their contract with society, probation may be revoked and they may be subsequently incarcerated.

When probation began, and throughout most of its early history, its purposes were primarily altruistic, as probation caseloads comprised mostly lower-risk property and first-time offenders. There were fewer offenders with developmental disabilities, psychological disturbances or drug addictions, and fewer offenders convicted of violent crimes and other felonies. With changes in the size and seriousness of probation caseloads, balancing offenders' welfare with the safety and protection of the community has now become the ethical imperative of probation.

Ethical decisions in probation are made within less rigidly defined contexts than are found in other criminal justice domains. Probation officers exercise considerable discretion in handling their caseloads. They typically have a lot of flexibility with regard to scheduling their time and structuring their activities. Probation officer discretion is an important aspect of supervision. Many probation officers do not automatically submit violation petitions after they discover offenders' infractions. In fact, some may give offenders second and third chances before initiating the revocation process. Probation officer discretion also plays a critical role in determining the nature of these officers' reports to judges (Souryal, 1992). Probation officers can sway judicial decisions by portraying probationers in different lights. Probation officers' judgments are especially influential in presentence investigations. Because probation officers' recommendations in presentence investigations often are adopted by judges (Abadinsky, 1996), ethical decisions affecting the way they present information are significant and can have serious consequences for offenders.

Offenders' performance on probation is affected by officers' ability to broker suitable employment or treatment services. Outcomes also are affected by officers' handling of probation infractions and their interest in clients' rehabilitation and reintegration. However, probation officers' success with clients may be hampered for

that the morality of an action is judged in terms of its consequences. A moral action produces good results, that is, it increases pleasure and decreases pain; an immoral action produces bad or harmful results, that is, it decreases pleasure and increases pain. Simply put, cheating, stealing and murder are all wrong because of their bad

the pleasure of one. The greatest good for the greatest number creates the context for community. The proportionality of pain and pleasure must be judged in this context.

Utilitarianism calculus is illustrated by the following example. A probationer misses a report date in order to take care of his children. Adhering to a zero tolerance policy for nonreporting, his probation officer files a petition to have him violated. The probationer then is convicted of a violation and is sentenced to jail. Consequently, the probationer cannot provide for his family while he is incarcerated and his relationship with his officer is strained. Should the probation officer have filed a petition to violate him? Following the principles of utilitarianism, the officer should have weighed the possible pain of the probationer against the possible pain inflicted on the community if the probationer does not follow rules. If the probationer presented little threat to society, a utilitarian would maintain that the probation officer was wrong to violate him.

Moral principals have lost their distinctiveness. For modern man, absolute right and absolute wrong are a matter of what the majority is doing. Right and wrong are relative to likes and dislikes and the customs of a particular community. We have unconsciously applied Einstein's theory of relativity, which properly described the physical universe, to the moral and ethical realm."

—Martin Luther King Jr.

Deontological Ethics

Immanuel Kant, a proponent of deontological ethics, believed that by focusing solely on consequences, utilitarianism misses something even more basic to morality, namely, goodwill or the intention to do what is right. For Kant, the key to morality is human intention, not consequences. An act is right if it is motivated by the goodwill or intentions of an actor regardless of whether the action achieves positive consequences. Right actions arise from virtues such as honesty, loyalty and respect for the law (Dewey & Hurlbutt, 1977). Wrong actions arise out of selfish or malicious motives.

Consider the following scenario involving two probation officers working in the same department: One probation officer files a violation of probation petition against a probationer who missed last month's payment of restitution. He does so to teach the probationer the importance of obeying the rules of the court and to deter future rule breaking. The other violates a probationer who missed his last payment of restitution because the probationer belongs to a racial group that the probation officer is prejudiced against.

Kant would have argued that there is a fundamental moral difference between the first and the second probation officers' actions, despite the fact that the consequences of the two cases are identical. In the utilitarian view, because the ends of both officers' actions are the same, they have the same moral value. Nonetheless, from Kant's perspective, there is still a moral difference. The first probation officer acted morally in order to instruct the pro-

a number of reasons over which they have little control. High caseloads, long work hours, lack of training and the absence of clear goals can all interfere with the quality of services (Whitehead, 1996). Furthermore, probation officers cannot always depend on the public support or resources that they need to do their jobs effectively (Wehmhoefer, 1993). The constant interplay of intra- and extra-agency factors that influence officers' effectiveness and the fact that probation officers are often the final arbiters for many caseload decisions require their judgments and activities to be grounded firmly in basic ethical principles.

Foundation of Ethics

Normative ethics is the study of right and wrong. In particular, normative ethics tries to discover the fundamental aspects of all ethical judgments. For example, lying, cheating, stealing, raping and killing generally are considered wrong. If so, what is the common characteristic of all these actions? One of the most preeminent figures in the history of Western philosophy, Socrates, searched for the universal principle that is common to all just or virtuous actions.

Utilitarianism

An ethical theory that attempts to describe universal moral principles is utilitarianism, developed by Jeremy Benthem and John Stuart Mill. Utilitarianism posits

or harmful consequences. According to Benthem, "An action . . . conforms to the principle of utility . . . when the tendency it has to augment the happiness of the community is greater that any it has to diminish it" (Dewey & Hurlbutt, 1977, p. 227). Charity and benevolence are moral actions because they produce beneficial consequences. Thus, Benthem contended that all human actions are motivated by the desire to increase pleasure or decrease pain. He argued that a person's motivation does not determine the rightness or wrongness of given action. Even if the motivation for an action is to increase pleasure (which is good), the result of that action may inflict pain on a large number of people. Such an action must be regarded as bad because of its outcomes, not because of the original intentions of the actor.

A central question when weighing the correctness or goodness of actions in utilitarianism is, "Whose happiness or pleasure is paramount?" According to utilitarianism, all parties affected by an action should be considered. Therefore, both the happiness of the individual and that of the community should be calculated in determining the goodness of a particular action. The morally correct action is the one that produces the greatest good for the greatest number of people. Presumably, the pleasure of one individual does not outweigh the pleasure of an entire community. For example, stealing makes a thief feel good. But the thief's victims may suffer sadness, anger, fear and physical and emotional distress as a result of the thief's actions. In this instance, the pain of many outweighs bationer and to help him to avoid future difficulties. In contrast, the second probation officer was motivated by prejudice. For Kant, although the second probation officer engaged in the same action as his colleague, he filed the petition for the wrong reason so his action has no moral worth. In short, he did the right thing for the wrong reason.

Kant's principle of morality contains a categorical imperative: People have the unconditional duty to behave morally. Kant's belief is that people should do only what they would permit others to do. In our example, the categorical imperative is that a probation officer who chooses a particular response to deal with a probationer's rule breaking must believe that the response would be the same one chosen by other probation officers and that it would apply to all probationers in the same situation.

Another formulation of Kant's categorical imperative focuses on the belief that human beings have intrinsic value and that they ought to be treated with respect. Within this formulation, probationers should never be regarded as objects, that is, used to prove that one is "tough on crime" or to demonstrate the punitiveness of a particular sanction. Because probation officers constantly must weigh the needs of individual offenders against those of society, they may have difficulty satisfying the moral imperative.

Problems with both utilitarianism and deontological ethics complicate moral decisions. Utilitarianism has trouble dealing with situations involving the maximum pleasure for the majority at the expense of the minority. For example, a large group enslaves a small group so that the large group can gain certain comforts and benefits from the servitude of a few. Utilitarianism holds that the suffering of a few is outweighed by the pleasure of the many. Nonetheless, regardless of the pleasurable consequences for some, slavery and oppression are patently wrong, just as hurting or exploiting others is inherently unjust.

Similarly, Kant's moral theory has no way to deal with conflicting motives. For example, a probation officer is required to keep probationers' records confidential. But when a probationer with a prior conviction for a sexual offense applies for a job as a janitor in a school, the probation officer may fear for the safety of students and school staff. Does the probation officer reveal confidential information to the potential employer or protect the confidentiality of the probationer? Kantian theory offers no solution to this predicament. The utilitarian would weigh the harm done by revealing the information against the potential harm that may arise from not doing so. Much more harm could result from failing to warn an employer of possible dangers.

Common Ethical Dilemmas of Probation Officers

In the moral dilemmas facing probation officers, it is not always clear what effects an officer's actions may have for offenders or society. The probation officer who does not violate probationers for failing drug tests may be either facilitating their success or enabling their addictive behaviors. Probation officers may promise services to clients without any guarantee that these services will ever be offered. Promising probationers possible employment may be helpful in motivating them to fulfill probation requirements but may demoralize them when jobs never become available.

Probation officers also may be forced to weigh the needs of particular clients against those of other probationers. Because of severely limited treatment resources, such as for substance abuse, the probation officer who enrolls a probationer in a program may prevent another person—perhaps one more likely to succeed in the program—from getting treatment (Duffee & Carlson, 1996; Silverman, 1993). Similarly, a probation officer may interact with agencies that might be reluctant to accept other clients from the officer's caseload if particular clients fail in their programs.

Besides balancing societal and offender needs, probation officers also belong to the wider criminal justice system, which imposes expectations that affect ethical decision making (Silverman, 1993). These demands may come in the forms of sentencing requirements, administrative exigencies or peer pressures. Whistle blowing against the probation administration may be another area of ethical concern for officers if they perceive that their agencies' practices are interfering with the rights and well-being of their clients (Rosecrance, 1988). Administrators may be more willing to cover up inadequacies rather than to allow the undesirable practices of their departments to come to light. Officers must weigh loyalty to their profession and colleagues against the harm that may ensue if they permit unethical practices to continue. As Pollock-Byrne (1994) noted, "All criminal justice professionals are more likely to operate in an ethical manner when they believe in the validity and justness of the system that employs them."

As discussed earlier in the context of Kant's theory, probation officers can be confronted with ethical dilemmas relating to confidentiality. For example, an offender enters into a romantic relationship with a person who is not aware of his previous convictions for domestic violence. Is it the duty of the officer to keep this information confidential or to inform the offender's partner out of concern for her safety? Confidentiality issues become even more difficult with juvenile probationers (Goldsmith, 1988).

Confidentiality issues also arise when probation officers come in contact with offenders' families. With more severe programs, for example, home confinement and intensive probation supervision, offenders' punishments spill onto the lives of others. Von Hirsch (1990) suggested that concern for the rights of others has been overlooked in community corrections. For example, he pointed out that home visits may shame or demean offenders because of the presence of unconvicted third-party witnesses whose sense of privacy is diminished. Confidentiality issues can arise yet again when probation officers are concerned with the well-being of crime victims (Whitehead, 1996). Issues concerning the confidentiality of an offender's whereabouts vs. informing a victim who might be at risk again from that offender are often under probation officer discretion.

> ## "Integrity without knowledge is weak and useless, and knowledge without integrity is dangerous and dreadful."
>
> —Samuel Johnson

Other circumstances may place professional ethics in conflict with personal ethics. For example, probation officers may not agree with their clients' choices (e.g., the decision to have an abortion) or they may condone—either explicitly or implicitly—illegal behaviors (e.g., recreational drug use) (Pollock-Byrne, 1994).

Most probation sentences require offenders to report to a probation site, but there may be instances when doing so is not in probationers' best interests (Close & Meier, 1995). Such cases include probationers who may be too ill or physically handicapped to travel. In addition, probationers in gangs may be placed at risk if they have to travel through rivals' neighborhoods to report to their officers.

Finally, ethical issues may arise out of the unequal relationship between probation officers and their clients. Probation officers may misuse their power (Pollock-Byrne, 1994). Concerns with the misuse of force come into play even more so when probation officers carry weapons and work in stricter surveillance programs. According to Sherman (1992), "Force is the essence of criminal justice. . . . The decisions of whether to use force, how much to use and under what conditions are confronted by police officers, juries, judges, prison officials and probation and parole officers" (p. 17).

Typology of Probation Officers

What are probation officers supposed to do when faced with the kinds of dilemmas described here? Whom should they be serving? How can they maximize benefits for offenders and minimize harm to society? A well-known typology of probation officers helps to illuminate the ethical postures that officers may assume (e.g., Klockars, 1972; Souryal, 1992). Each of these probation officer types acts out of a particular ethical principle or a set of principles. Not every officer fits into one type. Rather, most officers represent a combination of types, and those within a type may not always behave the same way. In addition, no type is considered completely ethical or unethical. Such determinations require knowledge of the context in which actions take place (Souryal, 1992).

Punitive Officers

The first type of officer is the punitive or law enforcement practitioner who always places society's interests above clients' interests. "This type underscores a dogmatic, utilitarianism view that seeks to maximize goodness through serving the largest number of beneficiaries—community members" (Souryal, 1992, p. 366). Controlling offenders and enforcing the conditions of probation are the main goals of these officers. They file petitions to violate probationers no matter what the circumstances in order to uphold all the rules and regulations of probation.

The relationship between probation officers and offenders is distant and built on only the conditions of the sentence. Their interactions are frequent, formal and brief. Punitive officers are detached from offenders and depersonalize them. They have little concern for probationers or their families. Whether probationers complete their sentences successfully is of minor importance to punitive or law enforcement practitioners. As Souryal (1992) notes, "In this model, recognition of the true purpose of supervision, of the obligation to assist a fellow human being in distress, or of fidelity to the ethics of treatment is all but ignored" (p. 366).

The punitive officer is concerned with preserving community safety by controlling probationers. Probation is viewed as a privilege, not as a right. Probationers are perceived as criminals who should be closely supervised, a danger from whom society must be protected. The punitive officer frequently reminds offenders that probation will be revoked, without exception, if conditions are violated. This style of supervision emphasizes firmness, legal authority and rule abidance. Interaction between the rule enforcer and probationers tends to be formal, official and largely a manifestation of "one upmanship" on the part of the officer. Punitive officers uphold the law for its own sake, irrespective of whether the best interests of probationers have been satisfied.

Punitive officers attempt to protect society by monitoring offenders and making sure that they adhere to the conditions of release. By ignoring probationers' needs, however, such officers may bring more harm to the community. Although offenders may comply with the conditions of probation, they may not be able to reintegrate successfully into society because they lack the services or skills to do so. Society may be harmed by these probationers in the future.

Welfare Officers

The welfare/therapeutic practitioner or social worker is the second type. Probation officers in this category focus on offender treatment and rehabilitation. Even if clients violate the conditions of probation, their welfare outweighs the possible harm to the larger community. Probation officers concentrate their energies on "advocating, brokering, educating, enabling, and mediating" for their clients (Souryal, 1992, pp. 366–367). Offenders' needs are crucial. Officers of this type attempt to broker services such as employment, housing and psychological counseling for their clients. They treat clients with care and respect.

Welfare/therapeutic officers attempt to rehabilitate offenders and reintegrate them into the community, and they view the conditions of probation as ways to facilitate offenders' progress. Probation is a time for problem solving. Social-work oriented offi-

---

Table 1

American Probation and Parole Association's Code of Ethics

1. I will render professional service to the justice system and the community at large in effecting the social adjustment of the offender.

2. I will uphold the law with dignity, displaying an awareness of my responsibility to offenders while recognizing the right of the public to be safe-guarded from criminal activity.

3. I will strive to be objective in the performance of my duties, recognizing the inalienable right of all persons, appreciating the inherent worth of the individual, and respecting those confidences which can be reposed in me.

4. I will conduct my personal life with decorum, neither accepting nor granting favors in connection with my office.

5. I will cooperate with my co-workers and related agencies and will continually strive to improve my professional competence through the seeking and sharing of knowledge and understanding.

6. I will distinguish clearly, in public, between my statements and actions as an individual and as a representative of my profession.

7. I will encourage policy, procedures and personnel practices which will enable others to conduct themselves in accordance with the values, goals and objectives of the American Probation and Parole Association.

8. I recognize my office as a symbol of public faith and I accept it as a public trust to be held as long as I am true to the ethics of the American Probation and Parole Association.

9. I will constantly strive to achieve these objectives and ideals, dedicating myself to my chosen profession.

cers cultivate close relationships with offenders in order to formulate a suitable treatment plan that will assist offenders in avoiding future crimes and in making their lives more productive. Officers in this category assume that individuals are fundamentally good and will choose noncriminal behaviors and life styles once they are

> *"The ethic of care recognizes individuals' basic rights and values but it does not elevate them above society's.*

helped to understand themselves. This self-knowledge will promote personal growth and unnecessary prosocial attitudes. Within this framework, offenders are seen as emotionally disturbed, victims of circumstances or socially disadvantaged.

Welfare/therapeutic officers' actions are noble from the viewpoint of Kant's model because of the sincere and benevolent motivations behind their actions. However, these officers may be inclined to "rescue" clients by finding resources for them without allowing clients to make mistakes and learn how to acquire necessary services. "Finally, there is a danger of becoming too personally involved with clients, a situation that may lead to considerable disappointment and frustration for the practitioner" (Souryal, 1992, p. 367).

Passive Officers

The third type of officer, the passive time saver or civil servant, cares about neither clients' needs nor the welfare of the community. The only persons these probation officers care about are themselves. Practitioners of this type see the greatest good in inactivity and avoidance of work. They merely manage their caseloads, viewing their work as meaningless. They may be employees who do not define themselves as service providers or professionals. Or they may have once belonged to one of the aforementioned probation officer types but have become burned-out and are waiting for promotion or retirement. Or they may simply be amoral.

Probation officers who adopt the role of civil servant invest in their jobs a modicum of effort and personal commitment. Civil servants concentrate on maintaining or advancing their positions within the agency and find no law enforcing or casework vo-

cation in probation. Instead, this type of officer works within the probation bureaucracy and concentrates on retirement, pension or entry into another field such as law or police work. Consistent work attendance, proper and prompt completion of paperwork, and the kind of self-enhancement that results in salary increases are characteristic of the time saver. Their job performance contributes to the smooth flow of office functioning; however, all responsibilities are met minimally and mechanically. Although contact with offenders is regular, civil servants attempt to minimize personal interactions with them. Civil servants' duties, as they perceive them, are advising probationers about their failure to obey rules, apprising the court of offenders' criminal behaviors and observing probationer progress as opposed to initiating client changes.

Synthetic Officers

The final type of role identification of probation officers incorporates both the treatment and control components of probation. Synthetic or combined officers' supervisory styles reflect the desire to satisfy the basic orientations of the rule enforcer

and social worker. In doing so, these officers are, perhaps unknowingly, coming to grips with the probation officer's fundamental quandary: reconciling the conflicting tensions arising from the legal and social services dimensions of probation work. Synthetic officers integrate monitoring and rehabilitation by evaluating each case to determine which particular strategy will best protect community safety and meet the offender's needs. This type of officer is most likely to develop working relationships with community resource agencies and local police departments. They understand the complexity of probationers' difficulties and acknowledge the inherent limitations in working through these problems.

In the combined type, practitioners see the highest good in the middle ground between the welfare of their clients and the protection of the community. Although offender control is important, these probation officers also try hard to obtain client services. Practitioners of this type are both humanitarian and justice-oriented. Their decisions are based on the view that offenders' interests are critical. As we noted earlier, their decisions are made on a case-by-case basis; sometimes, the welfare of the individual is secondary to the com-

---

Table 2

Federal Probation Officers' Association Code of Ethics

As a Federal Probation Officer, I am dedicated to rendering professional service to the courts, the parole authorities, and the community at large in effecting the social adjustment of the offender.

I will conduct my personal life with decorum, will neither accept nor grant favors in connection with my office, and will put loyalty to moral principles above personal consideration.

I will uphold the law with dignity and with complete awareness of the prestige and stature of the judicial system of which I am a part. I will be ever cognizant of my responsibility to the community which I serve.

I will strive to be objective in the performance of my duties; respect the inalienable rights of all persons; appreciate the inherent worth of the individual; and hold inviolate those confidences which can be reposed in me.

I will cooperate with my fellow workers and related agencies and will continually attempt to improve my professional standards through seeking of knowledge and understanding.

I recognize my office as a symbol of public faith and I accept it as a public trust to be held as long as I am true to the ethics of the Federal Probation Service. I will constantly strive to achieve these objectives and ideals, dedicating myself to my chosen profession.

Source: Close and Meier (1995)

munity's and vice versa. Because of this, such probation officers must be attuned closely to the basic ethical principles underpinning their actions. In practice, they are probably the most ethical of all the probation officer types.

What about probation officers who are inclined to act according to a certain type but are prevented by their current work environments from doing so? For example, officers may be inclined toward the welfare/therapeutic model. However, because of the constraints of large caseloads, lack of resources and agency expectations, they are prevented from being more social work-oriented with their clients. Similarly, punitive officers may want to impose harsh penalties on probationers to keep them in line but are prevented from doing so because of judges' decisions. Hence, probation officers also are influenced by the contexts in which they work. The greater the degree of discontinuity between officer type and department culture, the more likely it is that officers will become frustrated, cynical and at risk of becoming passive time savers. The best situation is one in which officer type and department culture are congruent.

Conclusions

Probation officers should be aware of basic ethical principles (Braswell, 1996). Specifically they should be guided by the ethic of care, the central goal of which is to reintegrate individuals into the community (Pollock-Bryne, 1994). Such a posture embodies the belief that probationers are human beings no matter what types of crimes they have committed. The ethic of care recognizes individuals' basic rights and values but it does not elevate them above society's. Within all relationships, a continual re-evaluation of needs, responsibilities

and rights must occur to insure that the well-being of all parties is promoted. Therefore, ethical probation officers must be ready to override the needs of offenders who pose a serious threat to the welfare of the community.

Probation officers will be able to make competent moral decisions better by examining the values and motivations underlying their actions. They must work out of a combined model of enforcement and treatment. Such a challenge can be met by adhering to basic ethical principles. In making ethical decisions, probation officers can receive guidance from the American Probation and Parole Association's and the Federal Probation Officers' Association's codes of ethics (see Tables 1 and 2). In addition, officers can enroll in recently developed training sessions on professional ethics (Wehmhoefer, 1993). The wider network of staff within probation departments, including fellow officers, supervisors and chiefs, also can encourage and support officers' ethical decisions and give them a forum to air ethical concerns and problems. The continually changing nature of probation supervision will create new ethical questions for practitioners (Silverman, 1993). A basic grounding in ethics is necessary in fulfilling probation's goal of serving both offenders and the community.

References

Abadinsky, H., Probation and Parole: *Theory and Practice*. Englewood Cliffs, NJ: Prentice-Hall, 1996.

Braswell, M. C., *Criminal Justice: An Ethic for the Future*. In M. C. Braswell, B. R. McCarthy, and B. J. McCarthy eds., *Justice, Crime and Ethics*, pp. 399–411. Cincinnati,OH: Anderson Publishing Company, 1996.

Braswell, M. C.; McCarthy, B. R; and McCarthy, B. J. eds. *Justice, Crime and Ethics*. Cincinnati, OH: Anderson Publishing Company, 1994.

Brown, P. W., Ethics: Right or Wrong [Book Review]. Federal Probation, 53, 82(1989).

Camp, C. G., and Camp, G. M.. *Corrections Year 1994: Probation and Parole*. South Salem, NY: Criminal Justice Institute, 1994.

Close, D., & Meier, N., *Morality in Criminal Justice: An Introduction to Ethics*. Belmont, CA: Wadsworth Publishing Company, 1995.

Dewey, R. E., and Hurlbutt, R. H., eds., *An Introduction to Ethics*. New York: Macmillan, 1977.

Duffee, D. E., and Carlson, B. E., "Competing Value Premises for the Provision of Drug Treatment to Probationers," *Crime and Delinquency*, 42(1977):574.

Goldsmith, H. R., "The Role of the Juvenile Probation Officer Regarding the Adolescent Sex Offender and Related Issues," *Journal of Offender Counseling, Services & Rehabilitation*, 12(1988):115–122.

Klockars, J. P, *The Reality of the Probation Officers' Dilemma*. Federal Probation, 36(1972)18–29.

Pollock, J. M., *Ethics in Crime and Justice: Dilemmas and Decisions*, 2nd ed. Belmont, CA: Wadsworth Publishing Company, 1994.

Rosecrance, J., "Maintaining the Myth of Individualized Justice: Probation Presentence Reports," *Justice Quarterly*, 5 (1988):235–256.

Sherman, L., "Learning Police Ethics," *Criminal Justice Ethics*, 1(1992):10–19.

Silverman, M., "Ethical Issues in the Field of Probation," *International Journal of Offender Therapy and Comparative Criminology*, 37(1993):85–94.

Souryal, S. S., *Ethics in Criminal Justice: In Search of the Truth*. Cincinnati, OH: Anderson Publishing Co., 1992.

Von Hirsh, A., "The Ethics of Community-Based Sanctions," *Crime and Delinquency*, 36(1990):162–173.

Whemhoefer, R. A., "Ethics in the Probation and Parole Profession: A Vision for the Future," *Perspectives*, 17(1993):8–9.

Whitehead, J. T., *Ethical Issues in Probation and Parole*. In M. C. Braswell, B. R. McCarthy, and B. J. McCarthy, eds. *Justice, Crime and Ethics*, pp. 243–260. Cincinnati, OH: Anderson Publishing Company 1996.

the other WOMEN of bedford hills

Some women in this affluent Westchester community live behind white picket fences and sprawling estates. Others live behind barbed wire. Writer **Stephanie Gertler** enters Bedford Hills Correctional Facility to learn about life on the inside.

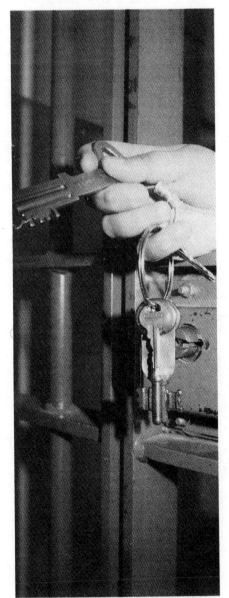

The drive through the rural streets is misleading. A country road winds past small clapboard houses and down a steep hill. Suddenly, in the midst of suburban homes there appear swirls of razor wire and an imposing guard tower. Distinguished by a small wood sign that might mark a playground or school is the Bedford Hills Correctional Facility: a maximum security prison for women and the clearinghouse for all women who receive sentences in New York State.

Bedford Hills has often made its way into headlines with its high-profile residents: Jean Harris, Pam Smart, Amy Fisher. Most of its inmates, however, never make it onto the nightly news. Nevertheless, according to a report by the Justice Department's Bureau of Justice Statistics (BJC), the number of female prisoners nationwide grew 9.1 percent in 1996, almost double the 4.7 percent increase in male inmates. At the end of the year, 6.3 percent (74,730 inmates) were women. Notoriety, however, is more often than not desperate or simply lonely. The prisoners at Bedford are women first, then inmates.

---

* All names except for Mary Riechers have been changed to protect the identities of those interviewed.

Alex, our photographer, meets me in the visitors parking lot. Prison officials requested we bring only what was stated in our clearance letter. Once inside the visitors reception area, a sign warns us not to place anything on the table until we are told. We empty our belongings into a bin. Another sign states regulations for visitors with children: three diapers per baby, one diaper bag with wipes and ointment. No powder. Plastic baby bottles only.

Once our things are checked against our lists, we are electronically frisked, arms out to the side. Turn back, turn front, turn sideways. After passing through a metal detector, our guide meets us on the other side and walks us through yet another checkpoint even more forbidding: a door made of heavy glass lined with steel bars. Our hands are stamped, IDs checked again.

The door slams forcefully behind us, confirming that we are now "inside," where getting out isn't an option. We walk through the "yard": a large, open area lined with eclectic buildings, some left over from the early 1990s when the prison was a reform school called Westfield Farms. Steam pours out from the industrial laundry building. Quite surrealistically, a Häagen-Dazs truck rolls by. All is lifeless and still.

A pretty woman with short hair stops our guide to ask a question. She is serving 75 years for an armed robbery during which two guards were killed. Another

From *Spotlight,* April 1998, pp. 40-43, 117. © 1998 by Stephanie Gertler. Reprinted by permission.

woman stops and hugs our guide and asks if she can have an adjustment on her medication. She's in for 25 to life, accessory to murder.

We wait inside the building where we are to meet with five inmates, stepping back against the wall to make room for a woman in prison garb mopping the linoleum floor.

"You're like us now," says the woman. "Just waiting."

The inmates meet us in a room where a sign on the door reads *No Más Abuso* (no more abuse)—the counseling center for family violence. The women enter, dressed in drab military green. They cannot wear black, gray, orange and blue, colors found in the officers' uniforms; this ensures that nothing will be "reconstructed" to resemble official garb. Even in the nursery unit, if yarn in any of these colors is donated for mothers to knit blankets or buntings, the contribution is rejected.

"I wish I could wear black," one of the inmates sighs, eyeing my black t-shirt and black jeans.

Charlene, Sybil, Hope, Mo and Melissa* sit on worn sofas, slouching sideways, wary of my tape recorder. They shield their faces from the lens of Alex's camera, clearly uncomfortable. Apparently, so am I.

"Are you always this nervous when you interview someone?" Charlene asks provocatively.

"Always," I say. "Until I get to know my subject better."

She laughs. After an hour or so, the women move in closer, still blocking their faces from the prying camera lens. Charlene, 33, wears a bright yellow shirt under the prison jacket stenciled with her name and number; her nails are manicured and polished bright red. She carries a mesh bag with a journal and some photographs.

"I'm here for murder," she states, slurring the word murder. "But I didn't murder no one. It was an accident. I was actually doing a burglary and the lady whose house we was robbing died of a heart attack. It happened in 1980, I was 15 years old and tried as a juvenile."

Charlene, the fifth of six children, grew up in a typical two-parent home: Her mother was a registered nurse, her father managed a grocery store. With the exception, perhaps, of Charlene, it was a regular home. "They had money, but not for the things I wanted," she admits. "I wanted furs and diamonds and leather. My parents said I didn't need those material things. Looking back, I guess I didn't. It wasn't worth *this*."

Charlene has been incarcerated almost six years—this time. Before that, she was busted with four and a half ounces of

> **I'm here for murder. But I didn't murder no one. It was an accident. I was actually doing a burglary and the lady whose house we was robbing died of a heart attack.**
>
> **—CHARLENE**

cocaine and violated her parole after four years in prison. When they fingerprinted her for parole violation, the prints matched the ones she left at the 1980 robbery. There was also a lot of what Charlene calls "in

between"—in between the times she was in and she was out. She got involved with a guy and was sent back to prison for three and a half years for attempted robbery. Then, she was let out again.

"I have spent the last . . . oh . . . 15 years incarcerated—in and out. My mother and stepfather live in Virginia now," explains Charlene, who is among the 28 percent of repeat offenders at Bedford. "My mother comes to see me during the holidays. She never says anything about any of this. When I try to tell her what happened, she won't let me."

The basic bond between mother and child persists, despite the otherworldliness of life behind bars and the sense of separation from the outside. For some, like Charlene, mothers are among their only visitors. For others, who are mothers themselves, the slamming of the prison gates doesn't sever emotional ties and responsibility for childcare. More than three-quarters of all women in state prisons have children. Among those with kids under age 18, only 25 percent of women—as opposed to 90 percent of men—report that their children are living with the other parent. Grandparents are the most common caregivers.

Nationally, some 6 percent of women who enter prison are pregnant. Melissa, sentenced for robbery during her teens, is now 20 years old, the unwed mother of an infant girl who was born during her stay in the Westchester facility.

Although she had the option to stay with the baby in Bedford's nursery for a year, her daughter, born in a nearby hospi-

tal, is cared for by Melissa's boyfriend and her mother. The nursery is, with a total of 30 women and 28 babies (including a couple of pregnant women and some twins), an outstanding feature at the prison.

"Sometimes everyone gets along very well and sometimes they don't. It fluctuates," says Nursery Supervisor Mary Riechers. "We stress that we all have to get along for the welfare of the babies. There are a lot of different personalities and so many things going on with these women. We resolve difficulties through unit meetings, community meetings and individual meetings."

The unit is a privilege for Bedford's women, who apply for nursery residency and hope their request is approved by the administration. Escorted under guard, the inmates deliver their babies either at Westchester County Medical Center or Northern Westchester Hospital so that the birth certificates indicate either Valhalla or Mount Kisco as place of birth rather than Bedford Hills Correctional Facility.

About 80 percent of the women get to go home with their infants. Inmates with lengthy sentences, particularly the lifers, usually don't spend time in the prison nursery. "We structure it that way. They are required to give us a placement plan regarding what they will do when they leave the facility. . . . We try not to accept women who have long sentences where we know the baby will go out into the system or be adopted, preferring that the baby bond with the person who will raise it," explains Riechers. "Those babies are taken from the mother at the hospital." The system aims to avoid the development of maternal ties to babies that will ultimately be taken away.

But for most inmates who had children before Bedford, maternal ties were secured long ago. It's these women, separated from their children by barbed wire, who sadden

> **I was afraid. I didn't have a job. I didn't know how I would raise those children by myself. Relatives ask me why I never said anything to them. I asked them why they didn't ask me how I got the black eye.**
>
> **—SYBIL**

Riechers most. Apparently, she has reason to worry. Studies show that maternal imprisonment affects future generations because children's psychological health and sense of family are severely damaged by being torn away from their mothers.

Sybil is one of the those women who aches for her kids. The 40-year-old received 25 years to life for "acting in concert" with her husband in the murder of their 4-year-old daughter. Her husband tied the child to a chair and beat her to death while Sybil stood by helplessly; with every attempt at intervention, she says she was beaten as well. He is serving a life term elsewhere; they are no longer in contact. A large, attractive woman with rheumy eyes that gaze down a great deal, she has four remaining children—11, 10, 9 and 6—who stay with a distant aunt in Brooklyn.

The district attorney asked her why she didn't just pick up her children and leave.

"Why?" asks Sybil, who had her debutante coming-out party at The Waldorf-Astoria and went to CCNY until she met her husband at 19. "I was afraid. I didn't have a job. I didn't know how I would raise those children by myself. Relatives ask me why I never said anything to them. I asked them why they didn't ask me how I got the black eye. I was so ashamed."

Sybil says she never hurt her children short of spanking their bottom if they ran into the street. But, she says, she never was able to help them either. "I will bear that responsibility the rest of my life. Knowing that and having them away from me, well, this just hurts so much."

Sybil's pain is palpable. It's hard to see her as merely the number printed on her uniform jacket. She says her 11-year-old just got her first bra and wrote her a letter asking how old she was when she got hers. Her son talks about the problems he has in school with other kids who ask him where his parents are. Although Sybil is a statistic within the system, she is decidedly a mother within the prison compound. Only recently has she been able to utter the name of the child who died.

One common denominator that connects the inmates is fear. This isn't especially surprising considering BJS findings that more than 4 in every 10 imprisoned women reported physical or sexual abuse at least once prior to incarceration. Ironically, for some, Bedford is the only safe haven they have ever known.

Prison is the greatest independence Sybil has experienced in the last 20 years. Her husband wouldn't allow her to have friends; now she has some she says are like sisters. "It's a funny thing, isn't it? I mean, being in jail and all. But for the first time in years I am not afraid of a husband, of having to screen everything I say. I was always scared for myself and my babies. In many ways this place is less of a prison

183

A woman came over and my mother showed her the food in the kitchen and asked the woman whether she thought I looked abused. No, I didn't look abused because you don't *see* emotional abuse.

—HOPE

than my home was. But believe me, I want to go home."

"I'm afraid of being out there alone," says Hope, now so accustomed to living within Bedford's gates. "I can function in here. I'm not a violent person anymore. Things are guaranteed for me here."

Hope, 23, has been in Bedford for five and a half years. When she was 16, she accompanied her boyfriend and two of his friends to her older sister's house, where they beat up and killed her sister's boyfriend, Luke. (He had hit her with a hot chicken rotisserie when she rejected his advances.) "I was numb. I kept thinking, 'This is my boyfriend and he's doing this for me.'" Hope was arrested a week later on a kidnapping technicality, having moved Luke's body from the bathroom to the living room.

Like the 47 percent of women in state prison who have had at least one member

of their immediate family incarcerated, Hope's older siblings were also in and out of jail. The five kids in her family were from three different fathers—none of which were around—and her mother, a single parent, worked in a barber shop in Harlem. "Emotionally," she says, "I had nobody."

Hope was 15 when her mother moved out with yet another boyfriend, leaving her daughter alone in the apartment they once shared. The teen was so furious that she called the Department of Social Services. "A woman came over and my mother showed her the food in the kitchen and asked the woman whether she thought I looked abused. No, I didn't look abused because you don't *see* emotional abuse."

But even physical abuse, which may seem apparent to an outsider hearing stories of fury and violence, isn't always evident to its victim. The first thing Mo, 56, did when she got to prison was enter ther-

apy to figure out if she was crazy. "I didn't realize that I had been abused," she says. The first time her lesbian lover threw a plate of spaghetti, Mo chalked it up to a tantrum. When she flew into jealous rages, Mo admits she was almost flattered. "When incidents began to escalate, I began to realize that something was very wrong."

When she told her lover it was time to part ways, her lover held her at gunpoint for seven hours. Mo ultimately got the gun and turned it on her captor, and was convicted of murder in the second degree in 1984. "I never understood at the time why I did what I did," says the former owner of a dog grooming and training business. "I had a nervous breakdown afterward. I was in total denial; I kept thinking I couldn't have done it, yet I knew I did because my friends and family told me so."

Once upon a time, Mo says she considered herself politically conservative. When she heard stories about inmates and their crimes, she always thought, "My God, how could they?" Now it never enters her mind as to why someone is here. "Today I look at the way people treat me and who and how they are." Mo is coming to terms with the grim reality that she may not ever get

doned. The official line from the prison is that "it doesn't happen." According to the inmates, they happen more often than not.

"If they're caught," says Jamie, a former prison employee who spoke anonymously. "They are given what's called a DG ticket—DG for degenerate. There is a misbehavior report given for a degenerate act. They are fined five dollars." With hourly prison wages averaging less than 75 cents, the punishment for sexual relationships is steep.

"Within the confines of the women's prison system, women have not made strides the way they have on the outside," maintains Chris, who formerly worked on the inside. "The prison is representative of the paucity of women's rights in general. It becomes exaggerated within the confines of the system."

Alex and I leave the prison silently. Once outside the razor wire, we take deep breaths and look at the sky. We stop to take some telephoto pictures from the road outside the compound. Once back at the visitors lot, a guard with his hand on his hip holster approaches us, asking who we are and what we are doing. We explain and gaze up as he waves an "okay" to the guard tower.

We have only spent a few hours in Bedford. It is more than enough.

A freelance writer living in Scarsdale, New York, Stephanie Gertler writes a weekly column, "These Days," which appears every Thursday in The Hour, The Norwalk Weekly Life and Times *and* The Wilton Villager.

out. When she arrived 13 years go, she was eligible for work release. State government has since taken away that option for people who commit violent crimes.

"When it begins to sink in that you're here, you have to figure out what to do with your time," says Mo. "Women tend to look for direction. Although we never plan to stay here, we look for a little bit of happiness."

In some cases, the search for happiness includes building relationships with other prisoners, friendships sometimes so close that they border on surrogate families. Very often, inmates even call one another "ma" or "sis." Lesbian relationships are not uncommon although sexuality appears in many cases to be an outgrowth of the need for nurturing and comfort. But homosexual encounters are neither allowed nor con-

Prison Population Growing Although Crime Rate Drops

Sentencing Is One Factor, Justice Dept. Says

By FOX BUTTERFIELD

The nation's prison population grew by 5.2 percent in 1997, according to the Justice Department, even though crime has been declining for six straight years, suggesting that the imprisonment boom has developed a built-in growth dynamic independent of the crime rate, experts say.

In a new report, the Justice Department said the number of Americans in local jails and in state and Federal prisons rose to 1,725,842 in 1997, up from 1.1 million in 1990. During that period, the incarceration rate in state and Federal prisons rose to 445 per 100,000 Americans in 1997, up from 292 per 100,000 in 1990.

As for why the number of prisoners continues to grow while crime drops, Martin Horn, Pennsylvania's Secretary of Corrections, said: "You have to understand that as incarcerating more people has helped reduce crime, the number of people we sent to prison in previous years is tending to build up, creating a delayed effect. So you've built in this escalating growth."

In the short term, Mr. Horn said, "most people who work in the prison business don't look for drops in crime to lead to drops in the prison population; the two lines are somewhat independent." But, he added: "If crime stayed down for the long term, then the incarceration rate might fall. But crime never does stay down for long."

Among the specific reasons for the continued growth in the prison population, Mr. Horn and other experts said, are longer sentences, reduced use of parole, increased arrests of parole violators, sending them back to prison, and improved efficiency by the police in solving crimes as there are fewer crimes to solve.

The report, by the Bureau of Justice Statistics, the statistical branch of the Justice Department, found that violent offenses accounted for the largest source of growth among male prisoners in 1997, 52 percent of their total increase. But drug crimes constituted the

biggest source of growth for female inmates, 45 percent of their total.

Using new methods to analyze the race of state and Federal prisoners, the report found that the incarceration rate for black men in 1996 was 3,096 per 100,000, eight times the rate for white men, 370 per 100,000, and more than double the rate for Hispanic men, 1,276 per 100,000. The figures provided one of the most powerful illustrations of racial disparity in the nation's prisons.

A CLOSER LOOK

Regional Disparity

States with the highest and lowest rates of Federal and state prisoners in 1997.

HIGHEST	PRISONERS	PER 100,000 PEOPLE
Texas	140,729	717
Louisiana	29,265	672
Oklahoma	20,542	617
South Carolina	21,173	536
Mississippi	15,447	531
Nevada	9,024	518
Alabama	22,290	500
Arizona	23,484	484
California	157,547	475
Georgia	36,450	472
Connecticut	18,521	397
New York	70,026	386
New Jersey	28,361	351
LOWEST		
North Dakota	797	112
Minnesota	5,326	113
Maine	1,620	124
Vermont	1,270	140
West Virginia	3,172	174
New Hampshire	2,164	184
Nebraska	3,402	200
Utah	4,284	205
Rhode Island	3,371	213
Oregon	7,999	232

Source: Bureau of Justice Statistics

At the end of 1996, the report also said, there were more black men in prison than whites, 526,200 to 510,900. The racial disparities were particularly striking among young men, the report found, with 8.3 percent of black men age 25 to 29 in prison in 1996, compared with 2.6 percent of Hispanic men in the same age group and 0.8 percent of white men of those ages.

There are also sharp regional differences in incarceration rates, according to the report, with 7 of the 10 states with the highest rates being in the South, led by Texas with a rate of 717 prisoners per 100,000 and Louisiana with 672 per 100,000. The states with the lowest rates were North Dakota, 112 prisoners per 100,000; Minnesota, 113 per 100,000; Maine, 124 per 100,000; and Vermont, 140 per 100,000.

Over all, the South had the highest incarceration rate, with 506 prisoners per 100,000, while the Northeast had the lowest rate, 317 per 100,000. The South has long had the highest crime rates of any region, but the report did not try to analyze whether the South's high incarceration rate was a result of its high crime rate or a matter of public policy favoring tough sentencing laws.

Allen J. Beck, one of the authors of the report, said that to understand how the number of prisoners nationwide could continue to grow while crime fell, it was important to remember that "the sources of growth are independent, to a certain extent, of crime."

Many states, for example, have adopted tougher sentencing laws, with mandatory minimum sentences, and this is helping increase the amount of time prisoners serve, which in turn increases the prison population. In addition, some states have abolished parole, and in many other states parole boards have much less discretion than they used to, Mr. Beck said, changes that also lengthen the amount of time prisoners serve. In 1990, decisions by parole boards accounted for 39.4 percent of all prisoners released, a sharp drop from 55 percent in 1980.

Still another reason for the growth, while crime drops, is that an increasing number of prisoners are being incarcerated for parole violations, about 30 percent today compared with 15 percent in 1980, Mr. Beck said. That means that the larger the number of prisoners, the bigger the number of people who will someday be released, and then, either because of their own criminal propensities or their experience behind bars, will be likely to commit some new violation and be rearrested.

THE COLOR OF JUSTICE

When the question of equal treatment for people of all colors is discussed, it makes some capital punishment scholars see red.

JOHN H. TRUMBO

John H. Trumbo is a reporter and columnist for the daily Auburn Journal in Placer County, Calif. He covers primarily law enforcement and courts.

The fact that there are more non-white men on death row than their Caucasian counterparts is a fact supported by the numbers. The real question is that: Is the disparity due to racial discrimination or some other not-so-black-and-white issues?

It appears that a defendant who has enough money to hire a high-priced lawyer has better odds of beating the death row rap.

If black men who are accused of killing white victims are prime candidates for death row, then why isn't O. J. Simpson facing the ultimate punishment?

And why aren't there more women on death row? It's discrimination, but a closer look at the numbers will show it has nothing to do with color.

Racial discrimination on death row has become a familiar refrain among public defenders and nonprofit organizations dedicated to protecting the rights of condemned men and women.

But there may be bigger, less well-defined factors that determine who gets a cell on death row and who doesn't.

Organizations whose focus includes death row issues have sprung up from San Francisco to Washington, D.C., ever since civil

rights became a national outcry three decades ago. Not surprisingly, many southern states are home to the most active of these organizations.

"Everyone would concede there is racial discrimination," says Clive Stafford Smith of the Louisiana Crisis Assistance Center in New Orleans. "Debate is absurd. Who could pretend it doesn't have an impact?" he said.

A look at the statistics seems to support Smith's contention.

The Death Penalty Information Center in Washington, D.C., reports that 65 blacks have been executed for murders of whites since 1976, compared to one white person executed for the death of a black victim. However, a look at the race of victims for capital cases shows whites are way ahead of blacks—85 percent to 11 percent. Hispanic victims make up 2 percent and Asians represent 1 percent.

When you remove the racial aspects, the statistical portrait shifts dramatically. From 1976 to 1991, there were 157 executions in the United States. Ninety-four of them were Caucasians and 63 were African-Americans. That is 59.9 percent white and 40.1 percent black, which is almost a perfect match to the ratio of white and black people who occupy the nearly 2,500 death row cells in this country.

If we are to assume that Smith is correct and racial discrimination is significant, then who is to blame?

Americans can blame the decision-makers, says Smith. Like many death penalty defense lawyers, Smith believes that racial bias occurs at every step in the criminal justice process—from the time the officer flicks on the red light for a traffic stop to that moment when the jury foreperson declares that the maximum penalty should be imposed.

Justice Comes With a Price

The first problem, says Smith, is for a death row candidate to get an adequate defense.

"Often, you have a bunch of town drunks representing people who don't have a lot of money," Smith said. In 10 years of wrangling with death penalty cases at the Louisiana Crisis Assistance Center, Smith says death penalty case defendants almost never have hired attorneys to represent them. He can recall only two cases out of 200 in the past decade where the hapless defendants have had hired attorneys.

"And those," he says wryly, "were $5,000 lawyers here in Louisiana who were no better than public defenders."

It appears, then, that a defendant who has enough money to hire a high-priced lawyer has better odds of beating the death row rap.

For example, Smith was not surprised when the Los Angeles District Attorney's Office chose not to pursue the death penalty with O. J. Simpson.

Even though he is black, Simpson is also rich—and that is a different kind of color issue. Some would call it green.

It's simple, Smith says. Prosecutors are less inclined to press for capital punishment when the defense is well-financed. "They (Simpson's prosecutors) aren't charging the death penalty because they won't get it. His defense is too well equipped," Smith said.

Prosecutor Bill Murray, who is black and number two in the San Joaquin County District Attorney's Office in Stockton, Calif., doesn't buy into the poverty factor in death row cases.

"That's not accurate in this country," Murray said. "We don't spare the expense for court-appointed or public defenders." He says even the middle-class defendants who can afford their own attorneys by mortgaging everything they own still end up on death row if they deserve it.

Murray believes Simpson escaped the death penalty phase for the simple reason that there is too much positive history with the defendant. "That case is not strong factually, and there are too many mitigating circumstances on the positive things he's done in his life. They would have been crazy to seek the death penalty on Simpson because the jury may not return that verdict," Murray said.

That argument flies in the face of a quote from U.S. Supreme Court Justice William O. Douglas, who in 1972, observed there were no examples of the wealthy on death row in America.

"One searches our chronicles in vain for the execution of any member of the affluent strata of this society," Justice Douglas wrote.

More recently, Associated Press Writer Bob Egelko reported that there appears to be a direct relationship between dollars and death row.

According to his September 1994 report, every one of the 384 men and four women awaiting execution as of July 1, 1994, was poor enough to qualify for a lawyer at state expense.

Atlanta lawyer Stephen Bright concurs.

"The death penalty is for poor people," said Bright, who serves as the director of the Southern Center for Human Rights in Atlanta and has handled capital cases for 15 years.

"Unlike most of my clients, whose IQs are in the high 60s or low 70s, you're talking about people (rich defendants) who have their lives together, who have the ability to make money. . . . You would think those would be the cold, calculated murderers most fit for the death penalty. But the death penalty is for poor people," Bright told the Associated Press.

The Gender Debate

Actually, statistics show that death row is for men who, for the most part, are poor, have never married and didn't complete high school. As of 1994, 98.5 percent of death row inmates in this country were men.

This in itself indicates discrimination, albeit in favor of women, says Smith. Since society still sees women as fairer and less violent than men, women who are accused of murders where there are special circumstances that could lead to the death penalty often obtain an escape route that is not available to them.

A typical, little-known case in nearly all-white, upper-middle class Placer County, Calif., illustrates the point.

Aaron S. Harper, 25, was found guilty of a first-degree, lying-in-wait murder of a white man in July 1994. Harper, who is black, faced the death penalty but ended up with life in prison without the possibility of parole.

Trial testimony showed that Harper agreed to do the February 1993 murder as a favor for a white woman, Trina Werly. She wanted revenge on her former boyfriend, whom she believed had molested their young daughter.

Werly was tried for murder and found guilty of a lesser charge of voluntary manslaughter. She was the mastermind of the crime—a capital offense that warrants the death penalty—but expects to serve only 12 years in prison. Harper, who was the only defendant who faced the death penalty, got life in prison.

"It's sexist, and women are the beneficiaries of discrimination, but I don't think we should start executing more women just to be fair," Smith said.

Racial Bias Seen at Every Level

Although Bright observes that in Georgia, 65 percent of all murder victims are black and most perpetrators are black, discrimination enters when there is a white victim. And, he says, there are at least three opportunities for racial discrimination that play a role in bringing about the death penalty: the race of the victim, the skin color of the prosecutor and racial makeup of the jury.

First, police investigators tend to invest "huge responses of resources and effort when white victims are involved,"

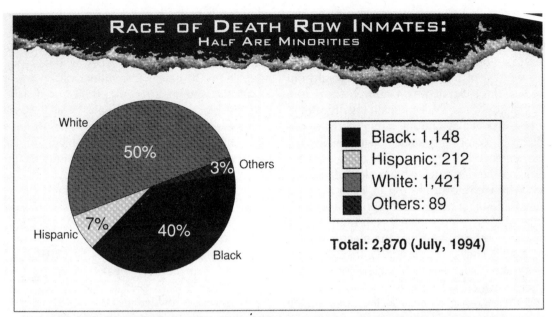

RACE OF DEATH ROW INMATES:
HALF ARE MINORITIES

Black: 1,148
Hispanic: 212
White: 1,421
Others: 89

Total: 2,870 (July, 1994)

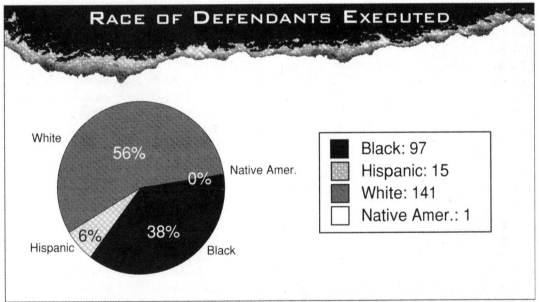

RACE OF DEFENDANTS EXECUTED

Black: 97
Hispanic: 15
White: 141
Native Amer.: 1

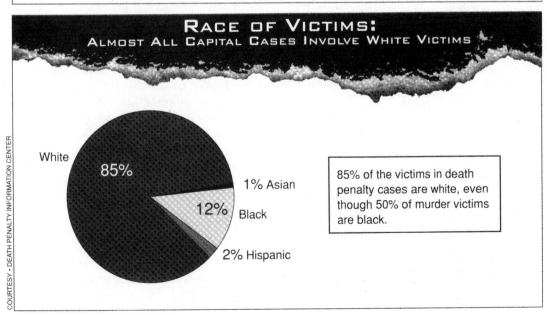

RACE OF VICTIMS:
ALMOST ALL CAPITAL CASES INVOLVE WHITE VICTIMS

85% of the victims in death penalty cases are white, even though 50% of murder victims are black.

COURTESY • DEATH PENALTY INFORMATION CENTER

Bright said. He added that Georgia prosecutors go for the death penalty in 70 percent of interracial crime. "It becomes an issue of who you kill," Bright noted.

Take the example of Jerry Walker, who made the mistake of killing the son of a white brigadier general from Fort Benning, Ga., in 1991. It was a convenience store robbery, and the jury gave Walker death, partly, Bright believes, because the victim and his family had the politically-correct skin color and social status. However, Walker was re-sentenced to life in 1993.

Or, consider the murder case of black defendant John Michael Davis who went to death row in 1985 after the district attorney in Georgia's Muscogee County asked the stepfather of the young, white female victim if he wanted Davis to be imprisoned for life or get the electric chair.

Three years after the conviction, the grateful stepfather contributed $5,000 to the district attorney's judgeship campaign.

A second factor which can lead to discrimination on the way to death row, Bright notes, is the color of the prosecutor.

"In a lot of places in the country, a white person is the one who is making the decision to pursue the death penalty," he said.

That's not the case in Stockton, Calif., where the number two prosecutor Murray is African-American and has the responsibility to make final calls on death penalty cases. "As long as I've been here, race has not been an issue," said Murray, who came to California after being a prosecutor in New York.

Typically, any case which has death penalty potential goes through a two-tier process. There is a general discussion on the merits among staff, then one person—in Stockton it is Murray—makes the decision on whether or not to seek capital punishment.

But Murray acknowledges that biases may exist in other parts of the country.

"The southern states have a different situation which they haven't quite shaken," he said.

Even though racial discrimination doesn't appear to be an issue in his San Joaquin County now, they do have three cases pending in federal courts in which the black defendants are appealing based on racial discrimination, Murray said. All three were handled prior to his arrival, he noted.

The third factor—the color of the jury—can also make a difference, said Bright.

William Henry Hance, a black man who was executed in Georgia in March 1994, was given the death penalty by a jury composed of one African-American and 11 Caucasians.

Ensuring there is a racially color-blind jury isn't that easy. Often in predominantly black Atlanta, said Bright, the black defendants are accused of killing white victims in predominately white neighborhoods. Consequently, the trials are in those mostly white counties, and the jury pools contain few non-whites.

In such situations, it becomes relatively easy for a prosecutor to excuse a black juror without cause. And even when good cause is required, Bright said, any attorney "with brains can come up with another reason that isn't race-related."

Bright likes to make an example of Ocmulgee County (Ga.) District Attorney Joe Briley, who has sought the death penalty in 30 cases. Twenty-four of those were black defendants, and in 20 cases, Briley used 169 jury strikes against black citizens and only 19 against white citizens.

In cases where victims were white, Briley exercised 94 percent of his jury strikes against black jurors, Bright said.

There are other examples from Bright's files, including a district attorney in Hinds County, Miss., whose public policy is to "get rid of as many" black jurors as possible. And there's documented evidence in Chambers County, Ala., that a prosecutor there ranked prospective jurors as "strong," "medium," "weak," and "black."

Murray acknowledges the problem with trying to obtain an unbiased jury.

"Selecting jurors is not a perfect process. You just can't control them," he said.

Even with all the opportunities for racial bias to occur, Murray has noticed a safety net that exists on death penalty issues because of human nature.

"People just aren't all that anxious to render death verdicts," he said. "If anything, in this state jurors are going the other way," Murray said.

An Act of Racial Justice

The Racial Justice Act, which proponents tried to include in President Clinton's Crime Bill, would have been a small step toward bringing accountability for racial disparity, Bright said.

"It was a very watered-down remedy and would not have been that effective. It would have just forced the prosecutors to come up with other reasons to put non-whites on death row," he said, even though he was one of its early supporters.

Watered-down or not, Stockton prosecutor Murray is relieved that the Racial Justice Act was rejected.

"It would have been a nightmare for district attorneys," he said, noting that a quota or statistical basis for determining death row cases would be impossible because the Supreme Court has already decided pure statistics are not enough to prove racial bias.

The case that triggered the Supreme Court decision involved Warren McCleskey of Georgia, who was executed September 1991 for shooting a white police officer. His

> Since 1977, only two California death row inmates have seen the inside of th[e] gas chamber at San Quentin State Prison. There are 397 California inmates still awaiting execution—149 of whom are black.

EXECUTIONS BY RACE — BY STATE
(1977-1994)

STATE	B	H	I	W	Count
AL	7	0	0	3	10
AR	2	0	0	7	9
AZ	0	0	0	3	3
CA	0	0	0	2	2
DE	2	0	1	1	4
FL	11	0	0	22	33
GA	12	0	0	6	18
ID	0	0	0	1	1
IL	0	0	0	2	2
IN	1	0	0	2	3
LA	9	0	0	12	21
MD	0	0	0	1	1
MO	5	0	0	6	11
MS	3	0	0	1	4
NC	0	0	0	6	6
NE	1	0	0	0	1
NV	0	0	0	5	5
OK	1	0	0	2	3
SC	0	0	0	4	4
TX	29	15	0	41	85
UT	2	0	0	2	4
VA	14	0	0	10	24
WA	0	0	0	2	2
WY	0	0	0	1	1
Count:	**99**	**15**	**1**	**142**	**257**

K. WILLIAM HAYES/CAPITAL PUNISHMENT STUDY

> "The system is nothing to write home about, especially when it deals with the question of who should live and who should die."
>
> —Stephen Bright, Director, Southern Center for Human Rights

defense referred to a study, conducted by the National Association for the Advancement of Colored People (NAACP), which indicated that blacks who killed whites were more likely to receive the death penalty than whites who killed whites. A review of the NAACP study by an expert methodologist showed that black-on-white murders—including the McCleskey case—often involved other aggravating elements like armed robbery.

The 1987 Supreme Court decision followed the logic represented with Georgia's homicide statistics, which showed that 67 percent of black-on-white killings involved armed robbery, compared with 7 percent of black-on-black killings.

Rep. Don Edwards, D-Calif., told the Wall Street Journal in July 1994 that the Racial Justice Act was an attempt to root out bias among decision-makers on death sentencing.

"Decision-makers in death sentencing—like those in other endeavors, such as voting, employment or jury selection—rarely, if ever, admit that they are racially biased," said Edwards, who at the time, was chairman of the House Civil and Constitutional Rights Committee.

According to the National Center for Policy Analysis in Dallas, the racial makeup of murderers indicates no great disparity nationally for the percentage of blacks on death row (42 percent) and the percentage charged with homicide (48 percent).

In July 1991, Bright testified before the House Subcommittee on Civil and Constitutional Rights. "We make significant public policy decisions based upon a finding that a smoker is 1.7 times more likely to die of heart disease than a nonsmoker," he said, "but we ignore the fact that in Georgia, a person accused of murdering a white person is 4.3 times more likely to be sentenced to death than a person accused of murdering a black (person)."

Bright noted that prosecutors' decisions on who will face the death penalty are highly subjective, and there are no statewide standards that govern when the death penalty is sought.

Mississippi, for example, can impose the death penalty for forcible rape of a person under 14 years old. And in Montana, a state prison inmate who has a prior homicide conviction, or been previously declared a persistent felony offender, can be executed for a deliberate attempted homicide, aggravated assault or aggravated kidnapping.

"The system is nothing to write home about, especially when it deals with the question of who should live and who should die," Bright said.

Restorative Justice and Offender Rehabilitation: A Meeting of the Minds

BY ANN H. CROWE

Ann Crowe is a research associate with the American Probation and Parole Association in Lexington, Kentucky.

Two Parables of Justice

Parable One

Once upon a time (and very far away), a man stole a wagon load of hay from his neighbor. The neighbor was very upset, because he needed the hay to feed his cow during the cold winter months. He needed the cow's milk to nourish his children, and he feared that, without the hay, the cow would starve to death and so would his children. He also planned to trade some of the hay for necessities he could not grow or make. He would not be able to barter for new shingles for the roof of his cottage, and his family would suffer with the cold and damp winter weather, perhaps becoming ill.

The victim of this theft was named Jacob. Now Jacob started going to each of the families in his village and asking if they knew what happened to his hay. None of them knew, but they told Jacob how sorry they were about his loss. They assured him they would help him if they could. Some of them offered to share small amounts of their hay with him to see him through the winter. Two of his friends joined him as he went from house to house asking about his hay. Many of the villagers returned to their fields to gather their own hay as quickly as possible and store it securely. They posted watches over their invaluable hay, lest they

should experience the same fate as their neighbor, Jacob. There was a feeling of uneasiness among the villagers.

Jacob and his friends continued their search for the missing hay. They came to the home of Bartholomew and asked his wife if they might speak with him. She said he was not at home. They told her why they had come, and she promised to give Bartholomew their message. Bartholomew's wife seemed uncomfortable and eager for them to leave. This being the last house in the village, Jacob and his friends turned to go home. They passed Bartholomew's field and saw that his cow looked fat and healthy. They went to his shed and found a lot of fresh hay.

Jacob and his friends waited for Bartholomew to return. When he did, they asked him where he got the hay, for they knew he had not grown it himself. Bartholomew reluctantly confessed to taking Jacob's hay, He said his cow was hungry because his crop of hay had failed. He knew his children would be malnourished without the cow's milk. He said he did not want to steal Jacob's hay, but he had no money to buy hay and he saw no other way to resolve his problem.

Jacob and the elders of the village called a meeting. Bartholomew was questioned about his theft of the hay. He explained how he had been able to take the hay without being caught by Jacob. Jacob told him what the loss of the hay meant to him. He said his cow and his children would go hungry, and he felt betrayed and violated by his neighbor, Bartholomew. Other villagers also spoke to Bartholomew. They said that once they had felt their property was safe, but now they were afraid and had started hiding their pos-

sessions. Bartholomew said he was very sorry for what he had done and the suffering he had caused.

The group then discussed how Bartholomew could amend his wrong. He was to return the unused hay to Jacob, and he promised to help Jacob plant his new crop of hay in the Spring to repay the hay he had already fed to his cow. Jacob said he felt that would repair the harm that had been done. The villagers then turned to the question of Bartholomew's family and their need. If Bartholomew's cow was hungry and his children didn't have enough to eat, they would not be able to learn at school or work effectively. Some of the villagers were afraid that Bartholomew's children would begin stealing food from other children. The villagers decided to start a hay bank. Each person would donate any extra hay they could spare, and it would be given to Bartholomew and his family to see them through the winter. Several of the farmers also offered to show Bartholomew how to plant his hay crop next year so it would be more likely to survive. In return, they asked Bartholomew, who was good at woodworking, to carve an ornament for the town's place of religious worship. Many years later, villagers referred to Bartholomew's sculpture as the "Work of Justice."

Parable Two

In a more recent time (and not so far away), a teenager named Tiffany stole some jewelry from a store. She traded the stolen items for alcohol. She and her friends went to a vacant building and got drunk. They became boisterous and broke all the windows in the building.

The next day, police investigated the two crimes. They took a report from Mr. Miller, the storekeeper where the shoplifting occurred, and they spoke with Mrs. Stevens, the woman living next to the vacant building. Mrs. Stevens told the police the group of youth had vandalized the building the night before. She said she thought she recognized one of the girls who lived in her neighborhood, but she did not want to identify the suspect. She said she feared that if the youth thought she had reported them, they might damage her property or even hurt her for revenge. She also expressed her concern that, now that the building was in disrepair, it would attract other groups of trouble-making youths.

The police advised her to stay in her house and keep all the doors locked. They suggested she also warn her neighbors to do the same. They assured her they would investigate the incident and, if they could find the perpetrators, they would be brought to justice.

The police used their excellent investigative skills to find and arrest the youth involved in the incident. They filed a report with the prosecutor who felt they had enough evidence to try the case.

A defense lawyer was appointed for Tiffany, the teenager who had shoplifted. Her attorney negotiated a plea bargain with the District Attorney. As a result, Tiffany was sentenced to a year of supervised probation, 200 hours of community service, and treatment for her alcohol abuse. She completed all of the requirements for her probation, including her community service work picking up trash along the highways on the outskirts of town, and was discharged a year later.

Meanwhile, one year after the incident, Mr. Miller, the store owner, and Mrs. Stevens, the neighbor, did not know what had happened. Tiffany had "paid her debt to society" through her community service work. She had achieved sobriety because of her substance abuse treatment program. She was even doing well in school and looked forward to a future as a law abiding citizen. Mr. Miller had reported the theft of merchandise on his business income tax return, and therefore, he contributed slightly less in taxes to state and federal governments. However, because he feared ongoing shoplifting, Mr. Miller had gone to the additional expense of installing sophisticated detection equipment in his store. All totaled, the theft cost him more than $5,000.

The vacant building next to Mrs. Stevens' house still has broken windows, and there have been reports of drug deals and drug use occurring there. Mrs. Stevens and many of her neighbors are very frightened of all teenagers in their neighborhood. Some members of the neighborhood have moved away, saying they want to live in safer areas of the city. Others have made fortresses out of their homes and seldom interact with their neighbors now. The crime rate in the neighborhood has increased markedly during the past year.

The Legacy of Criminal "Justice"

Billions of dollars are spent annually in the United States, its territories, and Canada to arrest, prosecute, and punish law violators. However, our ancestors and some present-day indigenous people may have found more effective ways to achieve justice. Synonyms of justice include fairness, equity, fair play, and impartiality. However, contemplation of these terms begs the question of justice for whom and fairness to whom.

Among the earliest written codes of law is the code of Hammurabi. During the rule of King Hammurabi of Babylon (1792 to 1750 B.C.), an extensive written code of laws was engraved in stone. It consisted of a collection of 282 judgments used in actual cases that subsequently became the jurisprudence of the land. These applied to situations that would be defined today as both criminal and civil law matters. Principles undergirding this code included "the strong should not injure the weak and . . . punishment should fit the crime." Laws often prescribed "an eye for an eye, a tooth for a tooth" (*New Grolier Multimedia Encyclopedia,* 1993). Based on these case laws, if someone wronged another, repayment (often with interest) or a punishment in kind was required (Klein, 1996).

On the way to their current status, United States and Canadian laws were influenced by many legal perspectives, primarily Roman Law, religious canons, and English common law. King William I, who conquered England in 1066, imposed royal authority on the courts to ensure the supremacy of the king. He decreed that crimes were a disruption "of the King's peace."

Therefore, offenders were held accountable to the King's Courts rather than their victims and communities. This system secured the king's power over his subjects and increased his wealth through the collection of fines paid to the court rather than restitution being paid to victims (Quinn, 1996).

American jurisprudence has evolved to a system that is controlled by the state and focused on the offender. This perspective has resulted in a burgeoning criminal justice system that each year processes millions of cases and increasingly incarcerates, supervises, and "treats" larger numbers of offenders. The victims' rights movement, begun in the 1970s, has slowly focused attention on the missing pieces of the system—the wronged victim and the community (Klein, 1996).

Presently, the criminal justice system finds itself being redefined and reshaped by several perspectives that often are competing for prominence, but are not necessarily mutually exclusive. Deterrence, retribution and incapacitation are employed to punish offenders, thus theoretically meeting the needs of the State and assuaging citizens' fears of crime. Rehabilitation of offenders is intended to reduce recidivism and prevent future criminal acts. Clearly in third place at present is the restoration of victims and communities and reparation of the harm caused by the offense. However, this perspective is gaining acceptance as an overarching principle for the implementation of a justice system, returning us full circle to our earliest roots, and perhaps the truest meaning of justice.

Restorative Justice/Offender Rehabilitation: Opening Discussions

Two seemingly discrepant approaches to the problem of criminal behavior may be more compatible than previously thought. That was the conclusion of a panel of criminal justice researchers, academicians, community advocates and restorative justice adherents who came together to explore theories, practices, and evaluations of restorative justice and offender rehabilitation at a one and one-half day meeting held in Lexington, Kentucky in July 1997.

Sponsored by the National Institute of Corrections, in conjunction with the American Probation and Parole Association and the Council of State Government, the goal of the meeting was to examine these two perspectives to determine the potential for their integration and practical implementation.

The impetus for this gathering was concerns recently expressed by advocates of both restorative justice and offender rehabilitation theories and practices. Some researchers in the area of offender rehabilitation questioned whether or not restorative justice principles adequately incorporated the research-supported principles of offender rehabilitation. Conversely, advocates of restorative justice voiced concerns that assertions made by researchers regarding offender rehabilitation programs did not adequately consider the needs of victims of crime and the community. The meeting's purpose was to examine the principles, values, and goals driving each of these movements within corrections and to discern commonalities upon which agreement and mutual benefit could be based.

While proponents of each ideological position defended their particular perspective, they also listened to, questioned, and ultimately valued the viewpoints and positions of others. (Please see the sidebar on page 203 for a list of the participants attending the meeting on restorative justice and offender rehabilitation.)

This article provides a summary of the discussion and conclusions reached during this meeting. After synthesizing the group's deliberations, as well as literature reviews of the restorative justice and offender rehabilitation perspectives, the potential linkages and congruent implementation of these approaches will be explored as discussed by the group.

A Comparison of Justice Paradigms
Traditional Approaches

Increasing professionalization and depersonalization of the modern American justice system (especially as it evolved during the 1970s and 1980s) has been disquieting for both practitioners and observers. Offenders, victims, or litigants often come in contact with justice system professionals who earn their income and career advancements based on their ability to sort out facts and people. Moving "cases" through the justice system often outweighs responding to the needs of individual victims and offenders. Once offenders are fit into similar groupings, sanctions are provided according to pre-determined ranges for the category. Offenders who commit certain crimes are eligible for probation, while those who commit different offenses face incarceration. Equity takes precedence over individualization. To enhance equity, individual differences and circumstances are ignored.

The system increasingly focuses on the crime and the offender. Punishment, both to hold the offender accountable and to deter others from wrong-doing, is the primary concern. Less attention is paid to victim and community concerns. Victims often are left to bear the cost of the crime, both economically and emotionally, and their needs and concerns seldom are addressed.

American jurisprudence of recent vintage, drawing on English Common Law, primarily viewed crimes as offenses against the State. Therefore, the State was responsible for arresting the offender, investigating the crime, prosecuting the case, and punishing the offender. Offender rehabilitation also must be included in the State's

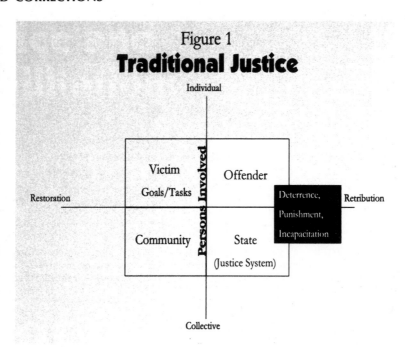

Figure 1
Traditional Justice

response for the purpose of reducing the probability that a particular offender would continue to engage in criminal conduct. Despite their rather complex and costly system that increasingly relies on sophisticated technology, the offender population continues to grow.

Traditional justice system responses to crime provide very little for victims and the communities in which crimes occurred. Restitution of victim's losses often are not ordered, and if ordered, frequently are not collected from offenders and disbursed to victims. Without any direct involvement, victims often have no sense of whether or not an offender feels remorse for his or her behavior, nor does the offender have the opportunity to appreciate the consequences of his/her actions. While offenders may receive help with employment, schooling, substance abuse, and other issues, victims are often left on their own to pay for any losses suffered, including needed medical or mental health treatment.

Figure 1 graphically depicts the focus of the traditional justice system. The possible participants are located in the center of the graphic, including victims, offenders, the community and the State, whose interests are served by the justice system. The perpendicular axis represents the persons involved, moving from individuals to collectives. The horizontal axis depicts the goals and tasks of justice, ranging from restoration to retribution. In the Traditional Justice system, both offenders and the State (Justice System) are actively involved, while victims and the community have minimal to no involvement. The primary goals and tasks of the traditional justice approach involve attempts to deter crime and punish or incapacitate offenders.

Offender Rehabilitation

Offender rehabilitation subscribes to a concept that providing a balance of supervision, sanctions and treatment to offenders will lead to safer communities by encouraging prosocial lifestyles and reduced recidivism. It has evolved out of the traditional justice system and incorporates both the concept of punishing offenders (i.e., holding them accountable for their actions) and protecting the public by engaging in risk management activities. This approach relies heavily on assessment of offender risk and providing a range of interventions appropriate to the individual offender. These interventions include sanctioning or punishing the offender to ensure accountability, and they symbolically demonstrate societal disapproval of wrongful acts. The punishment rendered is commensurate with the severity of the act. For example, with a relatively minor law violation, and where the risk of continued criminality is also relatively low, the intervention may simply be restitution, community service, a fine, etc., and no more. However, for more serious acts, and where risk is higher, the type and intrusiveness of the interventions increase. This would include appropriate and empirically validated treatment services designed to enhance the offender's own ability to control his/her behavior and thereby reduce the risk of future criminal acts (D. Dillingham, personal communication, January 26, 1998).

For more serious and higher risk offenders, offender rehabilitation and its risk management stance also provides external controls through criminal justice interventions such as surveillance, monitoring, and incapacitation. Again, the issue is public protection. However, simultaneously, the offender is learning internal, personal control through the rehabilitation process (D. Dillingham, personal communication, January 26, 1998). When this occurs, potential victims benefit from the offender's diversion from future criminality. Similarly, communities are enhanced by reduced criminal behavior and increased productivity and participation by former offenders. The State (justice system) is involved in the process of supervision, sanctioning, and treatment, but other agencies and professionals often are drawn into the provision of services offenders need. Services often furnished to offenders include alcohol and other drug treatment, education, employment training and referral, and cognitive behavior therapies. Clients are matched with appropriate services based on their assessed needs (Lattin, 1993).

The offender rehabilitation approach recognizes that fear of punishment is a weak deterrent to criminal behavior. Rather, general socialization practices and the community's stance toward crime are more powerful. Without a moral relationship to the community, offenders are minimally affected by the sanctions placed on them by the State (Andrews, 1996). This change in their thinking about their behavior and their relationship and responsibility to others is fostered through the treatment process.

The primary target of offender rehabilitation strategies is the offender. However, the foremost goal of intervention is public protection. Rehabilitation of the offender is "an intermediate step necessary to achieve the end goal of reduced recidivism, lower crime, and a better community in which to live." Offender accountability is a central tenet of this approach. Punishment is directed toward moral accountability for wrongdoing, while service interventions attempt to change higher-risk offenders as a means for promoting public safety, decreased victimization, and community well-being (D. Dillingham, personal communication, January 26, 1998).

Figure 2 pictures the locus of intervention and primary objectives of Offender Rehabilitation. The offender is the immediate target for services. Both the State and professionals in the community are involved in providing the services. The purpose of the intervention is not just true retribution (i.e., holding the offender accountable), but also the reduction of recidivism and, there-

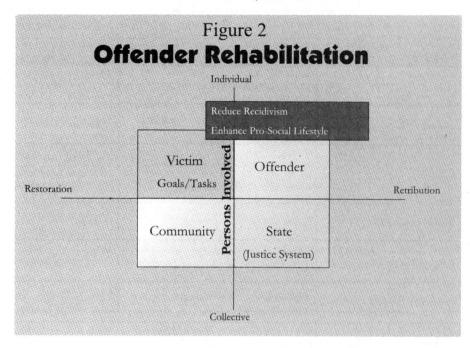

Figure 2
Offender Rehabilitation

fore, making potential victims and the community safer. Supervision, sanctions and treatment are combined in helping the offender develop a prosocial lifestyle.

Restorative Justice

As in the first parable, restorative justice would redefine the criminal justice system in very fundamental ways. While the victim, offender, and the community are all involved, the focus is on resolving the problem and restoring the harm done. Emphasis shifts from the offender to the victim and the State gives up its central role in dispensing justice. It assumes the function of facilitating reparation of the harm done to the victim and the community. The harm

caused the victim and community is assessed by the parties involved, and the offender is accountable for restoring the victim and community, as much as possible, to their pre-offense condition.

The participants in the meeting discussed the following three fundamental concepts that define the essence of a restorative justice approach (these concepts are discussed in greater detail later):

- Victims
- community residents and
- the offender should be involved in resolving the problem.

It is focused on the harm done by the offender's criminal behavior. Offenders incur an obligation to repair the damages caused and are held accountable for doing so.

Figure 3 illustrates restorative justice concepts. It focuses greater attention on victims and the entire community. The goals and tasks depicted in the outer perimeter include restoration of victims, reparation of the community and improved quality of life for all citizens.

Comparison of Approaches to Achieve "Justice"

Throughout the process of the meeting on restorative justice and offender rehabilitation, participants compared and contrasted the two models with each other and with our present criminal justice system. Table 1 captures some of the readily apparent differences between the three paradigms.

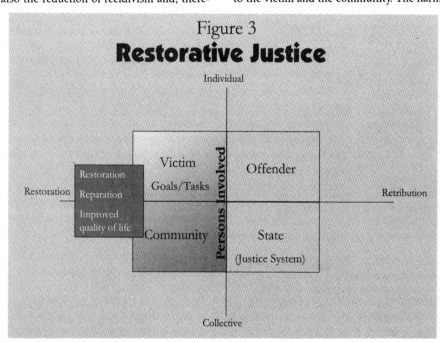

Figure 3
Restorative Justice

Table 1: Comparison of Restorative Justice, Offender Rehabilitation, and Criminal Justice Models

Criteria	Restorative Justice	Offender Rehabilitation	Criminal Justice System
Primary Focus of Attention	Victims and Community	Higher-risk Offenders	The criminal offense
Goals	Safe communities with improved quality of life for all citizens, Restoration of Victims and Community; reparation of harm	Safe communities with improved quality of life for all citizens, Rehabilitate offenders and reduce probability of re-offending	Safe communities with improved quality of life for all citizens, deterrence, retribution and incapacitation
Role of Government	Limited	Moderate	Extensive
Principal Methods used	Personal Interactions	Cognitive/Behavioral interventions	Surveillance and isolation of offenders from community
Community members involved	Victim, offender, community members, community agencies	Primarily offenders, criminal justice agencies, and select community agencies	Offenders and criminal justice agencies and personnel
Flow of resources	From offenders to victims and community	From offenders, victims and community to treatment programs	From victims and community to criminal justice services

Implementation Offender
Rehabilitation—"What Works"

"What Works" in offender rehabilitation is so named because it espouses several principles and practices for intervening with offenders based on research findings that, in general, studies have shown are effective and can be replicated in other settings to achieve similar results with different offenders. Related to the general goals of public safety and improved quality of life shown in Table 1 above, the more immediate goal of offender rehabilitation is to reduce the probability that an individual will re-offend. It focuses on diminishing the possibility of future victimization of individuals and communities. To oversimplify, one measure of the effectiveness of offender rehabilitation is recidivism rates.

A meta-analysis conducted on a large sample of research studies of juvenile and adult corrections yielded findings that led the researchers to formulate three principles of effective offender rehabilitation (Andrews et al., 1990):

1. Offender services should target higher risk offenders;
2. Rehabilitation services should be directed toward changing offenders' criminogenic needs; and
3. Offenders should be matched with programs in which the treatment mode, structure, and staff are appropriate for the needs of a given offender.

Risk Level of Offenders

Research makes it possible to determine those factors most likely to predict an individual's risk of reoffending. These factors include (Andrews et al., 1990; Huizinga, Loeber, & Thornberry, 1992; as cited by Wicklund, 1995):

- Antisocial/delinquent associations without sufficient influence from others who are not engaged in criminal behaviors;
- Antisocial/anti-authority/procriminal attitudes, values and beliefs;
- Termperament and personality factors conducive to criminal activity (e.g., weak socialization, impulsivity, egocentricity, below average verbal IQ, proclivity to engage in risky activities, poor problem solving and self regulation skills, lack of empathy);
- History of antisocial behavior from an early age;
- Family factors including criminality, mental health problems, substance abuse, lack of parental affection, poor supervision by parents, absent or harsh parental discipline, family reliance on welfare, poor work habits and history;
- Difficulties in relationships with others;
- Preference for unsupervised leisure and recreational activities; and
- Being male.

While some of these characteristics are not inherently negative, the compilation of multiple factors increases the level of risk.

Measuring risk improves the accuracy of proving the appropriate interventions for each offender, thus reducing reoffending. The intensity of treatment services should increase in conjunction with risking levels of risk. Treatment effectiveness is greater when services are provided higher risk cases. Conversely, it is a waste of resources to focus on lower risk cases where the likelihood of committing new offenses is already relatively low, and it is dangerous to rely on treatment where the risk is very high. For a very small number of offenders, risk is so great, and our present knowledge of effective interventions so limited, that public protection demands physical incapacitation.

Criminogenic Needs

Some risk factors discussed in the previous section are static, that is, they are impossible or extremely difficult to change (e.g., being male, I.Q., previous criminal behavior, some family characteristics, and some personality factors). On the other hand, some risk factors are dynamic, or amenable to change (e.g., criminal attitudes, beliefs and values; attitudes toward authority figures; antisocial peers; substance abuse). It is the latter set of factors, described as criminogenic needs, that should be targeted for intervention by the criminal justice system (Fulton, Stone, & Gendreau, 1994).

Participants in the Restorative Justice and Offender Rehabilitation meeting stressed that risks and needs should not be collapsed into one description of the offender, thus losing sight of the difference between factors that are likely to increase one's risk for criminal conduct and those that should be targeted for intervention and change. The former are valuable for case classification, but the latter are essential for developing an effective case plan. Similarly, participants stressed the need for using research-based risk and needs assessment instruments to obtain the most accurate predictions of continued criminal involvement and to target those characteristics or deficits most closely linked to criminal behavior and that will change with appropriate intervention.

Matching Offenders with Treatment Programs

To be effective, programs must be capable of intervening with the specific criminogenic needs presented by a given offender, and these interventions must be conducted in a way that is compatible with the offender's learning style. Social and behavioral learning experiences can be used to influence offenders' skills, cognitions and interpersonal relationships. Program staff, structure, and treatment modalities must be appropriate for individual clients (Andrews et al., 1990).

When working with offenders, cognitive behavioral social learning models are most effective when targeting criminogenic needs. Programs should model and reinforce prosocial attitudes and behaviors, and provide concrete problem solving and social skills training. Staff should be firm but fair, and capable of relating to offenders in a warm, flexible, and enthusiastic manner (Andrews et al., 1990). Where feasible, treatment programs should be provided for offenders in the community. Community intervention provides opportunities for learning different attitudes and skills through instruction, role playing and other activities in a treatment setting and a "real life" laboratory for immediately applying these in day-to-day situations. Community members can play a vital role by providing effective feedback to offenders as they implement new learning in their jobs and other settings.

Restorative Justice

Several important principles, including the following ones, underlie the restorative justice perspective.

Engage Victims, Community and Offender

The hallmark of restorative justice is its inclusiveness and approaches that involve interactions among victims, communities and offenders. Those most directly affected by a crime are involved in responding to it. It does not imply that justice system professionals have better solutions to crimes than victims and communities. This approach is apparent when a specific victim is injured, suffers economic or property losses, or experiences emotional trauma because of a crime. In such cases, a restorative justice response proposes the victim will have the option of being included in determining how the criminal behavior is addressed. This does not, as some might fear, give *carte blanche* to a victim to decide on a course of retribution for the offender without protection of the offender's due process rights. It does mean that victims play an active role, if they choose to, from the beginning to the conclusion of the process. Victim impact statements and victim-offender mediation approaches are examples of including victims in a restorative justice system.

Justice system professionals who have engaged victims with trepidation have been pleasantly surprised and relieved to find they usually are quite reasonable with their requests. They typically do not exaggerate their trauma or losses, and many are quite genuinely concerned about the well-being and rehabilitation of the offender. When given the opportunity to participate in the process, victims feel validated and can turn their energies toward constructive resolutions of problems.

Crime goes beyond a specific offense committed against a known victim. It is also "a rupture in society . . . [and] is better conceived as a crisis, pointing to a three-fold breakdown: in an individuals' self control, in the community's ability to maintain healthy behavior standards, and in society's obligation to provide its inhabitants avenues for meeting their physical, psychological and social needs" (Chupp, 1997, p. 2). Some crimes may be considered "victimless" if specific individuals cannot be identified as those who are harmed by the offense. Air and water pollution and drug trafficking are two examples of such "victimless crimes." Nevertheless, there are victims of such crimes. When an entire community suffers the consequences of a crime, the community-at-large becomes the victim. Unsafe conditions that decrease the overall quality of life for the community are true detriments to everyone living there. If a large plant discharges pollutants, it affects the air and/or water quality for all citizens; if drug dealers wield terror in the community, fear affects everyone. Thus, in such cases, "victim impact statements" and "victim-offender mediation" may include many people from the community interacting with the offender and the justice system to identify the aftermath of the crime and search for acceptable ways of addressing it.

Communities play another valuable role in restorative justice. Indeed, some proponents of restorative justice refer to the community as "the ultimate customer of the system" (Barajas, 1996). Bazemore and Day (1996) assert that the justice system should be restructured "to make it community-focused rather than bureaucracy-driven" (p. 10). In the first parable, community members coalesced to support the victim of the crime. However, they also came together to discuss possible solutions and hold the offender accountable. Not only were they involved to see that justice was done regarding a specific crime, they also recognized a problem in the community (Bartholomew's lack of hay) and took steps to resolve it (creating a hay bank and teaching him to grow a better crop of hay).

In a truly restorative justice context, communities would provide leadership to the entire process. However, involving communities in restorative justice strategies is very difficult, in part because this practice has not been undertaken routinely in the recent past. Community members often express strong sentiments about crime and justice, but they have typically had few roles in the criminal justice process. Crime represents both financial and social costs to communities which often leads to disorganization, distrust between community members and an inability for the community to ensure public safety. Although challenges facing communities have never been greater, members often have inadequate skills and resources to address these (Full Circle, 1997).

Restorative justice approaches seek to involve community and neighborhood residents more directly in addressing issues related to crime. The participants in the Restorative Justice and Offender Rehabilitation meeting grappled with the concepts of neighborhood and community without fully resolving them. The *New Webster's Dictionary* defines community as "a body of people living near one another and in social relationship." "Common ownership" and "sharing" also are meanings of the term (p. 198). The dictionary definition of neighborhood is "a district . . . , the people in a district . . . , an area of a town planned as a unit with its own shops, services and amenities . . ." (p. 670). Meeting participants discussed the difficulty in modern society of identifying and uniting "communities" to address problems of crime. People tend to define neighborhoods by smaller and smaller areas. One's primary community is not necessarily a geographic area. Allegiances and obligations may be felt more readily to diverse areas than to one's own immediate neighborhood. While some people live and work in the same geographic area, others live, work, and socialize in multiple communities. Chupp (1997, p. 2) characterizes this complexity by saying, "Community is more than a place . . . [but] restorative justice ultimately means a recognition of the importance of place, community as diverse people in interdependent relationship linked by geography, if by little else."

Because of these realities, there tends to be less cohesion and more disorganization at neighborhood and community levels. However, the extent of criminal activity in a location affects the quality of life for all residents. Overcoming the apathy and disaffection of neighborhood and community residents becomes a particular challenge for implementing a restorative justice framework. Nonetheless, involving citizens in creative problem-solving and resource development is a vital part of a restorative justice approach.

Focus on Harm

By shifting all responsibility for crime to the State, the harm caused victims often is overlooked. Focusing on the harm caused by offenses to victims and communities necessitates a shift in the response to crime. Instead of committing resources solely to punishment and rehabilitation of the offender, emphasis is placed on natural and logical consequences of his or her criminal behavior. If the victim was injured, an offender might have to pay for medical costs or do tasks the victim cannot perform while healing from the injuries. If the offender stole from or damaged property of the victim, the consequence might be repaying the cost of items or repairing damages. If victims suffer emotional trauma from the criminal incident, the offender may have to apologize and pay for the victim's counseling services needed to restore him or her to more productive functioning.

Offender Obligation, Accountability, Reintegration

Active, rather than passive, participation of offenders in the justice process also is a feature of restorative justice. Typically, offenders are treated as objects of the traditional justice process, being acted upon in response to their offenses. They often are stripped of the opportunity to make choices or have a voice in criminal justice proceedings. They also often are deprived of human dignity. However, restorative justice approaches involve the offender in active encounters with victims and community members. Offenders must hear about the consequences of their behavior from their victims and they must respond to victims' and community members' questions about the cause of the behavior. They also are engaged in designing appropriate ways of restoring victims and the community, as much as possible, to their condition before the crime occurred.

The concept of restorative justice encompasses an obligation on the part of the offender to repair the harm caused and restore victims and the community, as nearly as possible, to their condition before the crime occurred. The specific requirements of this obligation may be reached through a consensus process engaged in by the victim, community, and offender, as discussed in the two previous sections. Accountability, therefore, must be viewed differently than it is presently. From a restorative justice perspective, accountability is not synonymous with punishment. Accountability literally means to answer to, explain something, or to give an account. The offender, then, has responsibility for reaching a conclusion about what the harm is, owning it, and taking action to repair it. Accountability is victim-focused rather than offender-focused. It involves the development of empathy for victims and an understanding of the harm done. The primary obligation is to restore the victim, not change the offender. Often, through both restorative justice and offender rehabilitation methods, offenders do grow, learn, and renounce their criminal behavior, but that

is not the chief reason for offender accountability in a restorative justice context.

Many people who work with offenders recognize that they (the offenders) often are victims too. A person who grows up in a violent home, subsists in poverty, experiences discrimination and harassment, is addicted to alcohol or other drugs, or generally has been victimized and experienced harm in the past, may engage in criminal behavior for a variety of reasons related to his or her own victimization. However, it should be recognized that the majority of such victims do not participate in a criminal lifestyle, and such victimization cannot become an excuse to relieve offenders of their obligations and accountability. In restorative justice, the instant offense is the focus of the justice process. The previous experiences are checked at the door to be dealt with in other contexts.

However, the two issues—the offender's victimization of others and his or her previous experiences of victimization—are not as incongruous as they might seem. Through restorative justice approaches that include offenders in associations with victims and community members, relationships sometimes are formed, skills are learned, and offenders may experience reparation as well.

Reintegration of the offender is an objective of offender rehabilitation and often is an outcome of the restorative justice process, although it is not the primary intent of restorative justice. Rather than seeking to exclude offenders from society, both approaches strive to include reintegration of offenders as productive, law-abiding citizens. By assuming and carrying out tasks to restore victims and the community, offenders may learn valuable skills and form supportive associations that will lead to more prosocial lifestyles. Anecdotal accounts of victims and community members providing mentoring and other benefits to offenders after participating in this process are found in the growing literature on restorative justice.

Role of the Justice System

Adoption of a restorative justice framework requires a shifting role for the State and the present justice system. The role of justice professionals becomes somewhat diminished. They become advocates, coaches, and protectors of due process and human rights principles. One would expect to see a reduction of government involvement with a commensurate increase in the community's role. Restorative justice approaches do not require standardized responses to various situations. Fairness is an important issue, but different perspectives and diversity in problem resolutions can be tolerated. In restorative justice, the interests of those directly involved are central. Oversight of the

process would be a legitimate role for government to ensure that victims, communities, and offenders view it as fair, not necessarily to provide "equal" responses to every participant. In reality, with present systems of plea bargaining and differences in sentencing practices and sanctions, defendants who commit the same offense do not necessarily receive the same consequences or services.

Restorative justice advocates do not envision the complete demise of the justice system as it is now known. There are some offenders who are too violent or otherwise antisocial to remain in the community. Some victims are too frightened to encounter their offenders. Some communities are unable to provide needed services and treatment for offender rehabilitation. There likely will always be a role for supervision and treatment of many offenders and incapacitation of some offenders. But proponents of restorative justice do believe that roles and responsibilities should shift, the balance of power should be re-distributed, and priorities should change for many criminal cases, especially those that are less serious in nature.

Exhibit 1 on page 200, is a summary of fundamental concepts of restorative justice as outlined by Zehr and Mika (1997). Beginning on page 10, examples of programs based on restorative justice goals are provided.

Integration of Restorative Justice and Offender Rehabilitation Practices

Throughout the meeting, participants acknowledged that, while differences between restorative justice and offender rehabilitation are inherent, the two models share common ground, and in practice, bridges should be built to link the two more closely. Such a relationship would necessitate a fundamental restructuring of our present justice system and the priorities to which it subscribes. As shown in Figure 4, the current criminal justice system is top heavy, with the majority of attention and resources being directed to programs of incapacitation, moderate focus and funding allotted to offender rehabilitation, and minimal consideration paid to prevention or victims' and communities' needs in a restorative justice context.

Figure 5, on the other hand, depicts the priorities and resource allocations for a system that is undergirded by a philosophy of prevention and restorative justice. Prevention provides the largest building block because it theoretically affects the largest portion of the population. Through effective crime prevention, capital currently being used for criminal justice interventions would go toward the greater good of the

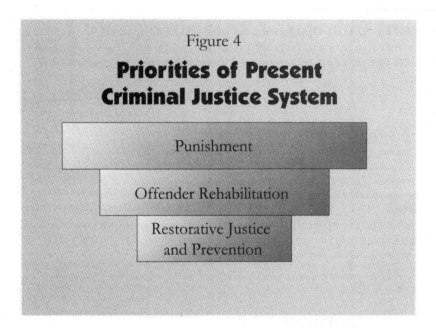

Figure 4

Priorities of Present Criminal Justice System

Punishment

Offender Rehabilitation

Restorative Justice and Prevention

general community and thus avert crime from occurring in the first place. At the next level, if crime does occur, resources and attention would be directed toward the implementation of restorative justice principles, engaging the next largest portion of the population. Restorative justice promotes community responsibility for public safety and focuses first on the needs of victims and the community. However, it also incorporates obligation, accountability, and reintegration of offenders. As illustrated in Figure 5, offender rehabilitation activities are undertaken concurrently within a restorative justice strategy, as these ultimately increase public safety and address offenders' accountability to victims when their criminogenic needs are addressed. Finally, for the few intractable cases that were not averted or resolved through the earlier steps, typical criminal justice services would be applied. This approach would focus traditional criminal justice services on violent and persistent criminals who must be removed from the community for the safety of other citizens.

Common Ground

The foregoing parts of this paper primarily emphasized the differences between restorative justice and offender rehabilitation, rather than their commonalities. However, as the meeting progressed and participants examined the principles of each paradigm, clarified underlying values and discussed differences, it became apparent that there were ample points upon which there was congruity. At the most visionary level, both approaches seek to improve the quality of life within a community by promoting public safety, albeit using somewhat different strategies. In practice, both approaches advocate victims'

rights and both are concerned about the reintegration of offenders as productive members of the community. Both approaches also recognize that some offenders cannot remain in the community and must be incarcerated for the protection of the public, but both also agree that lower risk offenders can be managed in the community and held accountable through appropriate means.

In reality, it appears that there is much overlap between restorative justice and offender rehabilitation. The two perspectives might appropriately be viewed on a justice continuum ranging from victim restoration at one end to offender interventions at the other. However, between the two extremes are shared goals and practices, including promotion of public safety, prevention of future crime, and reintegration of marginalized individuals.

A program example that illustrates a beginning in co-mingling of the two approaches is the Youthful Offender Pre-Trial Intervention Program in Polk County, Iowa. It is for youth who commit felony crimes for which they may be waived to adult court. Youthful offenders must plead guilty to a non-felony charge, usually receiving a deferred judgment and then are released on pre-trial status to complete the program requirements. Approximately 75 percent of the program participants complete the program and than are placed on formal probation. First-time youthful offenders are provided with services that are unavailable in the adult corrections system. These include substance abuse evaluation and treatment, educational assessment and opportunity to earn a GED, courses in lifestyle changes, street law, and pre-employment skills as well as curfew restrictions and random drug testing. In addition, there are victim-offender meetings to discuss the

impact of the crime on the victim and to reach a restitution agreement plus community work service and mentoring (Gay, 1997).

While Figure 5 showed the relative weight and position of different components of a restorative justice system, Figure 6 illustrates the integration of Offender Rehabilitation within a Restorative Justice Framework. Within the broader socio-political system, restorative justice and prevention frameworks form the backdrop for all activities within the community and the criminal justice system. A given community becomes the focal point of that system, and within each community, there are victims, offenders, and other community members. Restorative justice activities involving victims, offenders, and the community are at the forefront of a community justice model. These activities include victim-offender mediation, victim restitution, and many other activities focused on repairing the harm caused by criminal behavior, where possible. The offender remains in the community and receives rehabilitative services with a goal of reintegration and return to full acceptance and productivity within the community. The justice system in this model assumes a supportive role to victims, offenders, and the community. One of its primary, State-delegated tasks would be insuring fairness to all involved. Only if crimes are so violent as to jeopardize community safety, or if repeated attempts at restorative justice and offender rehabilitative activities fail, would the justice system become more prominent by causing an offender to be incapacitated within the community or excluded from the community. Community members and victims drive this system rather than criminal justice professionals.

Meeting participants agreed that attention to victims and the community should be a part of a risk management and offender rehabilitation strategies and offender rehabilitation was an important element that should operate within a restorative justice framework. Priority within this conceptual frame is ultimately a safe community where all citizens are valued and enjoy a positive quality of life. In practice, restoration of victims and the community would become a central focus, with rehabilitation of offenders also contributing to the primary goals by preventing further criminality and victimization.

Additionally, the participants felt that restorative justice and offender rehabilitation concepts needed to infuse other social systems so that all citizens become familiar with these approaches and are able to participate knowledgeably in these processes. As an example, blending these concepts and practices into the education system was discussed. Table 2 summarizes these ideas.

Exhibit 1: Fundamental Concepts of Restorative Justice

1.0 *Crime Is Fundamentally A Violation Of People And Interpersonal Relationships.*

1.1 Victims and the community have been harmed and are in need of restoration.

    1.1.1 The primary victims are those most directly affected by the offense but others, such as family members of victims and offenders, witnesses and members of the affected community, are also victims.

    1.1.2 The relationships affected (and reflected) by crime must be addressed.

    1.1.3 Restoration is a continuum of responses to the range of needs and harms experienced by victims, offenders, and the community.

1.2 Victims, offenders and the affected communities are the key stake-holders in justice.

    1.2.1 A restorative justice process maximizes the input and participation of these parties—but especially primary victims as well as offenders—in the search for restoration, healing, responsibility and prevention.

    1.2.2 The roles of these parties will vary according to the nature of the offense as well as the capacities and preferences of the parties.

    1.2.3 The state has circumscribed roles, such as investigating facts, facilitating processes and ensuring safety, but the state is not a primary victim.

2.0 *Violations Create Obligations And Liabilities.*

2.1 Offenders' obligations are to make things right as much as possible.

    2.1.1 Since the primary obligation is to victims, a restorative justice process empowers victims to effectively participate in defining obligations.

    2.1.2 Offenders are provided opportunities and encouragement to understand the harm they have caused to victims and the community and to develop plans for taking appropriate responsibility.

    2.1.3 Voluntary participation by offenders is maximized; coercion and exclusion are minimized. However, offenders may be required to accept their obligations if they do not do so voluntarily.

    2.1.4 Obligations that follow from the harm inflicted by crime should be related to making things right.

    2.1.5 Obligations may be experienced as difficult, even painful, but are not intended as pain, vengeance or revenge.

    2.1.6 Obligations to victims such as restitution take priority over other sanctions and obligations to the state such as fines.

    2.1.7 Offenders have an obligation to be active participants in addressing their own needs.

2.2 The community's obligations are to victims and to offenders and for the general welfare of its members.

    2.2.1 The community has a responsibility to support and help victims of crime to meet their needs.

    2.2.2 The community bears a responsibility for the welfare of its members and the social conditions and relationships which promote both crime and community peace.

    2.2.3 The community has responsibilities to support efforts to integrate offenders into the community, to be actively involved in the definitions of offender obligations and to ensure opportunities for offenders to make amends.

3.0 *Restorative Justice Seeks To Heal And Put Right The Wrongs*

3.1 The needs of victims for information, validation, vindication, restitution, testimony, safety and support are the starting points of justice.

    3.1.1 The safety of victims is an immediate priority.

    3.1.2 The justice process provides a framework that promotes the work of recovery and healing that is ultimately the domain of the individual victim.

    3.1.3 Victims are empowered by maximizing their input and participation in determining needs and outcomes.

    3.1.4 Offenders are involved in repair of the harm insofar as possible.

3.2 The process of justice maximizes opportunities for exchange of information, participation, dialogue and mutual consent between victim and offender.

    3.2.1 Face-to-face encounters are appropriate in some instances while alternative forms of exchange are more appropriate in others.

    3.2.2 Victims have the principal role in defining and directing the terms and conditions of the exchange.

    3.2.3 Mutual agreement takes precedence over imposed outcomes.

    3.2.4 Opportunities are provided for remorse, forgiveness and reconciliation.

3.3 Offenders' needs and competencies are addressed.

    3.3.1 Recognizing that offenders themselves have often been harmed, healing and integration of offenders into the community are emphasized.

    3.3.2 Offenders are supported and treated respectfully in the justice process.

    3.3.3 Removal from the community and severe restriction of offenders is limited to the minimum necessary.

    3.3.4 Justice values personal change above compliant behavior.

3.4 The justice process belongs to the community.

    3.4.1 Community members are actively involved in doing justice.

    3.4.2 The justice process draws from community resources and, in turn, contributes to the building and strengthening of community.

    3.4.3 The justice process attempts to promote changes in the community to both prevent similar harms from happening to others, and to foster early intervention to address the needs of victims and the accountability of offenders.

3.5 Justice is mindful of the outcomes, intended and unintended, of its responses to crime and victimization.

    3.5.1 Justice monitors and encourages follow-through since healing, recovery, accountability and change are maximized when agreements are kept.

    3.5.2 Fairness is assured, not by uniformity of outcomes, but through provision of necessary support and opportunities to all parties and avoidance of discrimination based on ethnicity, class and sex.

    3.5.3 Outcomes which are predominantly deterrent or incapacitative should be implemented as a last resort, involving the least restrictive intervention while seeking restoration of the parties involved.

    3.5.4 Unintended consequences such as the co-optation of restorative processes for coercive or punitive ends, undue offender orientation, or the expansion of social control, are resisted.

Excerpted from Howard Zehr and Harry Mika (1998), "*Fundamental Concepts of Restorative Justice,*" **Contemporary Justice Review**, 1 (1), 47–55.

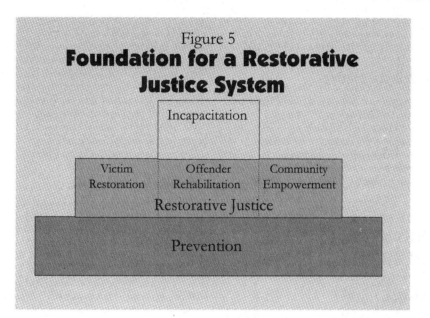

Figure 5
Foundation for a Restorative Justice System

Incapacitation

| Victim Restoration | Offender Rehabilitation | Community Empowerment |

Restorative Justice

Prevention

Family and Community Involvement

Many Native American and other indigenous people around the globe have forums such as family gatherings and talking circles, presided over by family elders or community leaders. Interpersonal issues are usually the focus of these encounters, and traditional tribal laws and practices are followed (Melton, 1996).

The Honorable Robert Yazzie (1997) describes the Navajo response to crime as one that includes a "peacemaker," the victim and his or her family, and friends, neighbors, and anyone else who is involved in the matter or affected by it. These persons are engaged in a "talking out" process that includes a traditional opening prayer, venting, and discussion to reach a consensus about what should be done. The goal of this process is not punishment or correction of a person; rather, the aim is correction of the action and remedy of the harm caused by the offender's conduct. Families of both the offenders and victims are involved to help speak for them and to take responsibility for their relatives.

New Zealand has developed a system of family group conferences for juvenile justice cases based on a Maori tradition. The victim and offender and both of their families come together for a conference facilitated by a social service worker. This approach involves a discussion of the impact of the crime on the victim and the community and public shaming of the deed (not the offender). The offender earns his or her way back into the community's favor. This program has been evaluated and shown to be effective in diverting cases from prosecution and reducing commitments to youth correctional facilities (Quinn, 1996).

Practitioners who use restorative justice principles have developed creative approaches to answer the questions:
- Who has been harmed?
- What can be done to make things right?

Treatment providers who work in the area of offender rehabilitation similarly have developed skills for effectively helping offenders change attitudes and behaviors toward more prosocial and productive lifestyles.

The challenge, however, remains in changing social attitudes and political priorities so that these principles become more generally accepted and receive the needed resources for full implementation. As allies, the supporters of restorative justice and offender rehabilitation present a more convincing case and can better support each others' efforts than each can do separately. The participants in this meeting left with a conviction to continue the dialogue, explore further the compatibility of the two perspectives, and to attempt to advance practice and demonstrate effective implementation of these two responses to criminal conduct.

Examples of Restorative Justice Programs and Strategies

Although the following examples are presented in a context of restorative justice, many of them also contain instances of offender-focused rehabilitative strategies and illustrate the compatibility of the two approaches.

Involvement of Other Community Systems and Professionals

The justice system cannot single-handedly mediate all law violation and civil disagreements. Conversely, educational systems, child welfare programs, mental health providers and other community resources should be enlisted to share in the mission and delivery of restorative justice. For example, schools can incorporate conflict resolution skills, peer mediation, and other skill development into the curriculum. Schools can be peace sites and use appropriate and constructive disciplinary approaches (Anderson, 1996).

Victim-Offender Reconciliation and Mediation Programs

These programs involve face-to-face meetings between victims and offenders. Both tell their account of the incident, and a trained mediator helps them discuss the harm and negotiate an agreement (Gehm,

Figure 6
Community Justice Model

Socio-Political Environment

Community

Victims and Offenders

Victim Restoration
Victim Restitution
Victim Offender Mediation

Offender Rehabilitation and Reintegration in Community

Due Process

Justice System

Incapacitation of Violent Offenders

Restorative Justice Framework   Prevention

1995). Victim-Offender Reconciliation and Mediation Programs vary widely. They may be situated in court, State, or community agencies. Some are related to religious and other nonprofit and volunteer organizations. The origin of referrals may vary among police, prosecutors, judges, probation officers, victims' advocates, and others. The occurrence of victim-offender meetings ranges from pre-adjudication to post-incarceration. Types of crimes and offenders for whom victim-offender reconciliation or mediation programs are used is also diverse. Age, type of crime and emotional state are some of the factors used to determine eligibility (Fahey, 1997).

Community Policing

Community policing departs from traditional law enforcement strategies by developing partnerships with the community and empowering community members to make their neighborhoods safer. It is decentralized and personalized and involves community-based problem-solving approaches within a results-oriented system (Bucqueroux, 1996).

An example of restorative justice/community policing strategies is the beat meetings held in Chicago. Residents and law enforcement officers come together in small groups around the city to discuss community problems. In turn, police work with other community resources to address identified problems and promote residents' feelings of security (Skogan, 1996).

Community Prosecution

Burgeoning caseloads, crowded prisons, and overburdened community corrections programs are among the realities with which prosecutors must contend when making charging decisions, pre-trial detention, and sentencing recommendations. In Polk County, Iowa, the County Attorney's Office uses trained mediators to resolve disputes that otherwise might be prosecuted through the courts (Gay, 1997).

In Dakota County, Minnesota, the County Attorney diverts many first-time juvenile offenders from the court process. This is done with the condition that they pay victim restitution and perform 15 to 35 hours of community work service. The diverted juveniles and their parents also are required to attend educational classes related to restoration of community values, respect for others, and healthy decision making (Rubin, 1997).

Community Courts

Judicial leaders also can implement restorative justice programs such as the ones in Dakota County, Minnesota. Dispositions of juvenile cases often include orders to pay victim restitution, perform community work service and write letters of apology to victims. Juvenile offenders may be given the option of performing community work service or making a cash donation to a victim restitution fund (Rubin, 1997).

Community Corrections

There are many examples of ways restorative justice principles can be implemented in community corrections agencies to make communities safer and strengthen the community's ability to address its own needs. Placing probation offices in neighborhoods from which offenders come, and assigning probation officers to particular geographic areas facilitates communication with victims and community members and problem-solving work within the neighborhood (Dickey, 1996).

Vermont has developed the reparative probation program consisting of five or six trained community volunteers who form a citizen reparative board. The program diverts many cases from traditional probation services, allowing more resources to be allocated toward the most serious offenders.

Table 2: Restorative Justice and Offender Rehabilitation Principles in Educational Settings

Restorative Justice

- All school curricula should include conflict resolution, and teachers should be trained in conflict resolution.
- Curricula should focus on the harm of wrong-doing and should make students aware of victimization.
- Students and staff should be trained in mediation.
- Family conferencing techniques should be employed.
- Family involvement in schooling should be stressed, and competency development in family life should be a goal of education.
- Students should be involved as the community in addressing harmful behaviors that occur in the school.
- Problems should be viewed as learning opportunities and restorative justice principles should be used to process incidents. They should be accepted, and creative solutions should be sought.
- Schools should use peer development, support, and problem-solving strategies rather than always imposing adult standards and discipline.
- Restorative justice strategies should be used rather than suspensions and expulsions.
- Students should be required to participate in community projects, and community services should be brought into the school.
- Mutual respect, relationships and rituals that affirm people should be instilled.

Offender Rehabilitation

- Students should be prepared to succeed in the larger society through educational achievement and attachment to work.
- School culture, atmosphere, and activities that promote prosocial attitudes, values and beliefs should be encouraged.
- Healthy, prosocial, inclusive relationships should be developed.
- There should be a sufficient variety of appropriate activities to appeal to all students.
- The school curriculum and instruction should be sensitive to different learning styles.
- Good assessment strategies should be routine and identify risks and needs and respond appropriately to them.
- Cognitive skills and conflict resolution should be an integral part of the curriculum.
- Schools should be open to the community after hours; they should be responsible and responsive to community needs.
- Schools should be sensitive to children who are victims.
- School should be connected to other social and justice systems in the community.

Judges may place offenders in a reparative program if they admit their guilt, are deemed willing to avoid further offenses, and agree to complete the conditions imposed by the community reparative board. Examples of offenses that might qualify an offender for the program include possession of stolen property, retail theft, bad checks, use of forged credit cards, and similar nonviolent crimes. The offender comes before the community reparative board and the offense and its effect on victims are discussed. Victims are invited, but not required, to participate. The board considers and concurs upon a restorative agreement and then discusses it with the offender. Sanctions are explained and all parties sign an agreement stating what the offender must do. Four goals are considered for offenders: 1) restore victims; 2) make amends to the community; 3) learn how their crime impacts victims and the community; and 4) learn ways to avoid re-offending (Dooley, 1996, pp, 32–33). Expectations of offenders might include written apologies, victim restitution, community service, participation in skill development courses, victim-offender mediation, and family group conferences. Compliance with these conditions is monitored by the community reparative board. This process shifts responsibility away from the corrections department and toward the community, families, and offenders (Dooley, 1996; Sinkinson & Broderick, 1997).

The Deschutes County, Oregon Probation Department developed a Restorative Justice Corps that provides community work service opportunities for offenders. Offenders have built a seventy-bed shelter for the homeless, stocked firewood for poor elderly residents, and accomplished other services for the community (Klein, 1996).

Dakota County, Minnesota has developed a Crime Repair Crew for both juvenile and adult probationers. The purpose of the program is to repair property that has been damaged by criminal activity. Victims are informed of the availability of the service by law enforcement officers when they answer complaints. The victim then may contact the program to schedule the needed repairs. These crews can perform tasks such as replacing broken windows, removing graffiti, and repairing damages caused by vandalism. In addition to restoring the damages inflicted on victims and learning valuable skills, offenders also are exposed to the offensive destruction caused by other offenders (Rubin, 1997).

Institutional Corrections

Restorative justice does not have to be a foreign concept even in incarceration facilities. Although the concept of restorative justice would place only the most violent or persistent offenders away from the community in jails and prisons, it is still pos-

sible to provide opportunities for them to experience the benefits of giving back something to the community. Lund (1997) describes her encounters with restorative justice concepts in the Minnesota Correctional Facility—Shakopee. She participated in a speakers' bureau through which she gave talks to teenagers in area high schools about her personal story and attempted to reach at-risk youths with a message of avoiding criminal behavior. She also raised a small puppy that was later turned over for specialized training to assist an impaired person. Finally, she took part in a project sponsored by the prison that allowed inmates to assist a local elementary school through fund-raising, cleaning the school and grounds, and making and donating needed items such as banners, costumes for the children, and benches and boxes. Lund says these opportunities allow incarcerated women to learn to care for others. She says, "They get a chance to make a difference and they are learning that it feels really good to affect someone's life in a positive way. Restorative Justice is more than it appears on the surface because the more you do it the more you learn about and care for yourself, others, and the world around you" (p. 55).

Participants

Meeting on Restorative Justice and Offender Rehabilitation
Lexington, Kentucky, July 28–29, 1997

Dr. Don Andrews
Carleton University
Ottawa, Ontario, Canada

Dr. Gordon Bazemore
Florida Atlantic University
Ft. Lauderdale, Florida

Mark Carey
Dakota Co. Community Corrections
Hastings, Minnesota

Vern Fogg
Colorado Judicial Department
Denver, Colorado

John Larivee
Crime and Justice Foundation
Boston, Massachusetts

Susan Laurence
Office for Victims of Crime
Washington, DC

Tom Quinn
Wilmington, Delaware

David D. Dillingham
National Institute of Corrections
Washington, DC

Mike Dooley
National Institute of Corrections
Longmont, Colorado

Don Evans
Toronto, Canada

Greg Richardson
Restorative Justice Institute
Washington, DC

Dr. Marilyn Van Dieten
Ottawa, Ontario, Canada

Carl Wicklund
APPA
Lexington, Kentucky

Howard Zehr
Eastern Mennonite University
Harrisonburg, Virginia

References

Anderson, C. (1996, April). *Restorative measures fit state DCFL plan*. Restorative Justice Newsletter. St. Paul, MN: Minnesota Department of Corrections.

Andrews, D. A. (1996). *Why correctional interventions?* Paper prepared for The National Institute of Corrections.

Andrews, D. A., Zinger, I., Hoge, R. D., Bonta, J., Gendreau, P., & Cullen, F. T. (1990). *Does correctional treatment work? A clinically relevant and psychologically informed meta-analysis*. Criminology, 28 (3), 369–397.

Barajas, E. (1996). *Moving toward community justice*. In *Community justice: Striving for safe, secure, and just communities*. Washington, DC: National Institute of Corrections, U.S. Department of Justice.

Bazemore, G., & Day, S. E. (1996). *Restoring the balance: Juvenile and community justice*. Juvenile Justice, 3 (1), 3–13.

Bucqueroux, B. (1996). *Community criminal justice: Building on the lessons that community policing teaches*. In *Community justice: Striving for safe, secure, and just communities*. Washington, DC: National Institute of Corrections, U.S. Department of Justice.

Chupp, M. (1997). *Restorative justice as community building*. Full Circle (Newsletter of the Restorative Justice Institute), 1 (4), 2–3.

Dickey, W. J. (1996). *Why neighborhood supervision?* In *Community justice: Striving for safe, secure, and just communities.* Washington, DC: National Institute of Corrections, U.S. Department of Justice.

Dooley, M. (1996). *Restorative justice in Vermont: A work in progress.* In *Community justice: Striving for safe, secure, and just communities.* Washington, DC: National Institute of Corrections, U.S. Department of Justice.

Fahey, J. G. (1997, May/June). *The use of mediation in criminal justice—Part I.* Community Corrections Report, 51, 61–62.

Full Circle (1997) (Newsletter of the Restorative Justice Institute), Vol. 1 No. 4.

Fulton, B. A., Stone, S. B., & Gendreau, P. (1994). *Restructuring intensive supervision programs: Applying "what works."* Lexington, KY: American Probation and Parole Association.

Gay, F. (1997). *Restorative justice and the prosecutor.* The ICCA Journal on Community Corrections, 8 (1), 30–33.

Gehm, J. (1995, September). *Victim and offender face to face.* Federal Probation, 59, 94.

Huizinga, D., Loeber, R., & Thornberry, T. (1992, May 15), *New findings on delinquency and substance abuse in urban areas* (Congressional briefing). Washington, DC: United States Congress.

Klein, A. (1996). *Community probation: Acknowledging probation's multiple clients.* In *Community justice: Striving for safe, secure, and just communities.* Washington, DC: National Institute of Corrections, U.S. Department of Justice.

Lattin, D. (1993). *What works? A review of the corrections literature on program effectiveness.* Eugene, OR: Lane County Community Corrections.

Lund, L. (1997). *Restorative justice from prison.* The ICCA Journal on Community Corrections, 8 (1), 50–51, 55.

Melton, A. P. (1996, April). *Indigenous ways are restorative justice models.* Restorative Justice Newsletter. St. Paul, MN: Minnesota Department of Corrections.

New Grolier Multimedia Encyclopedia (1993). Grolier, Inc.

New Webster's dictionary and thesaurus of the English language. (1993). Danbury, CT: Lexicon Publications, Inc.

Quinn, T. J. (1996). *Corrections and restorative justice.* In *Community justice: Striving for safe, secure, and just communities.* Washington, DC: National Institute of Corrections, U.S. Department of Justice.

Rubin, H. T. (1997, August/September). *Dakota County, Minnesota: Repairing harm and holding juveniles accountable.* Juvenile Justice Update, 3–4, 10–11.

Sinkinson, H. D., & Broderick, J. J. (1997, August). *Restorative justice in Vermont—Citizen's reparative boards.* Overcrowded Times, 8 (4), 1, 12–13, 20.

Skogan, W. G. (1996). *The community's role in community policing.* National Institute of Justice Journal.

Wicklund, C. (1995). *Research/literature review of effective programming options.* Unpublished Paper.

Yazzie, R. (1997, November 2–3). *The Navajo response to crime* (Paper prepared for the National Symposium on Sentencing: The Judicial Response to Crime). San Diego, CA; The American Judicature Society.

Zehr, H. and Mika, H. (1998), "Fundamental Concepts of Restorative Justice," Contemporary Justice Review, 1 (1) 47–55.

DEATH COUNTY

One Texas county leads other *states* in executions

By Arlene Levinson
Associated Press

HOUSTON—Toward the end of June in a dimly lit county courtroom, Arthur Lee Burton was fighting for his life. He was accused of strangling a jogger with her own shoelaces. He didn't do it, he insisted.

In another courtroom around that time, Coy Wayne Wesbrook took the stand in a rumpled suit and ashen face. He massacred five people, among them his ex-wife. Wesbrook claimed he never meant to.

Both men wept. But no tears or pleas could stop the mighty force that is the death penalty in Harris County, Texas. Juries decided they were guilty and deserved to die.

At a time when the death penalty is on the rise again, endorsed by most Americans, this place does it best.

Since capital punishment was reinstated in Texas in 1976, Harris County convictions have led to 53 of the state's 155 executions. In the same period, the county has killed as many killers as Virginia, which has more than twice the population. And Virginia's is the busiest death chamber after Texas'.

Among the reasons are a hawkish district attorney, his army of prosecutors, a weak system of court-appointed defense lawyers, state law that bars juries from learning a life sentence really means decades in Texas—plus lots of practice.

This is where pickax murderer Karla Faye Tucker was sentenced to die. On Feb. 3 she became the first woman executed in Texas since the Civil War.

Executions, which peaked nationwide at 199 in 1935, had become rare by 1972, when the U.S. Supreme Court abolished the death penalty as "cruel and unusual punishment" because states used it in arbitrary and capricious ways. Executions were allowed again in 1976 when the high court approved new, narrower laws in Texas, Florida and Georgia, paving the way for reinstatement nationwide. At the same time, Texas was among the first to trade its electric chair for the cleaner and quieter lethal injection.

Today, 38 states, the federal government and military have the death penalty. The overall death row population is approaching 3,500. Of these, Texas had 452 inmates in August, second only to California's 510.

But Texas, the second most populous state, leads them all in executions. It sends so many people to its death house in Huntsville, 80 miles north of Houston, that the customary hour of executions was rolled back from midnight to the more convenient 6 p.m.

Even for Texas, Harris County sets an awesome pace. A pulsing urban giant with Houston at its hub, this county the size of Delaware has 3.1 million people—one-sixth of Texas' population. But it accounts for one-third of the executions, and nearly one-third of death row.

The murder rate—last year it was 10.4 per 100,000 population—is lower than comparable urban counties'.

The county's ethnic mix with 54 percent Anglo, 22 percent Hispanic and 18 percent black is typical for a lot of urban America. Here, immigrants and cross-country transplants jostle with the heirs of founding wildcatters for their piece of the Texas dream. And there is plenty to

> **"We're good at it because we never let up on the pressure. [An overturned conviction is] like eating leftovers that haven't been refrigerated. So our effort is push, push, push. And it's not because we're bloodthirsty. . . .**
>
> **John B. Holmes Jr.,**
> **district attorney of Harris County, Texas"**

share where shipping, high-tech industries and huge gas refineries have squeezed the rice farms and ranches to the rural fringe.

Few in the county call the death penalty a deterrent. It's more a matter of being fed up with violent crime, according to Tanya Linn, an alternate juror in Wesbrook's trial. It's "the eye-for-an-eye, tooth-for-tooth thing," she said.

Four years ago, the Scripps Howard Texas Poll found 83 percent in this part of the state favored the death penalty. In June that number was 71 percent. The results are in line with similar national polls.

At the wrong end of downtown Houston, long steamy blocks from glittering office towers and amid an asphalt sea of parking lots, stands the Harris County Court House. Behind tan brick walls, its eight floors swarm with tense jurors, sweating defendants, furious victims and opposing hordes of lawyers. They lean against grimy walls murmuring confidences and crowd wooden benches that line the narrow corridors.

This is where Burton, a 28-year-old cement finisher with four children, was tried for last year's slaying of Nancy Adleman, a 48-year-old mother of three.

Burton said his interrogators slapped and browbeat him into making a false confession.

Wesbrook, a onetime security guard, was tried in the same week in the same place. The defendant, who is 40 and has a daughter, admitted the crime. He said he had gone to patch things up with Gloria Jean Coons, his 32-year-old former wife, and found her giving a party where she had sex with two guests. He went to his truck intending to leave, he said, but someone took his keys so he returned with a high-powered rifle.

"He didn't mean to kill anybody," Robert Loper, one of two defense attorneys, told the jury.

"This is evidence of cold-blooded murder," countered prosecutor Hans Nielsen, lifting the killer's gun above his head. "He knew exactly what he was doing, and he did it."

Burton's fate was decided in seven days, Wesbrook's in 11.

Both requested new trials, a routine move before appeals begin. Wesbrook's bid was denied. A Sept. 9 hearing was set for Burton.

People ascribe Harris County's extraordinary numbers to District Attorney John B. Holmes Jr. Named 19 years ago to fill his boss's unexpired term, Holmes has won every election since. Voters evidently like the way he runs his team of 200-plus prosecutors.

The blunt-talking 57-year-old Republican, a familiar face in Texas with his handlebar mustache, is acutely aware of being a media attraction and declined a face-to-face interview, agreeing only to talk by telephone.

He's never seen an execution and doesn't want to, he said, although "there are some I would be tickled to death to do myself."

But seeking the death penalty is nothing personal, he said. "I'm a lawyer, I follow the law."

"We're good at it because we never let up on the pressure," Holmes said. He is proud of his staff and what he's built, including an entire division devoted to post-conviction appeals. If a case is overturned, he said, "that's like eating leftovers that haven't been refrigerated. So our effort is push, push, push. And it's not because we're bloodthirsty. . . ."

He complains that critics depict him as a "death penalty guru" with a "notch-in-your-belt mentality." He gets hate mail, and worse. ("You probably never had people lined up outside your office, wearing T-shirts with your picture with a slash across it.")

He couldn't succeed without agreeable juries, he says. "You've got to have the support of the people who are really doing it—and that's those 12 people in that box."

Prosecutors in Harris County have won more than twice as many death sentences as those in Dallas County, the next biggest urban county in Texas, since the 1970s.

"Our standards may be different," said Norman Kinne, Dallas first assistant district attorney. "I know Mr. Holmes runs a very efficient office. I have admiration. I'm not saying we're better or worse. It's a matter of philosophy."

One critic is Richard Burr, a defense attorney in Houston. "The DA's office in Harris County is answerable to no one," he said. "It has no check on its own power."

"We're spending millions of dollars killing people," said another critic, Harris County District Judge Douglas Shaver. He supports the death penalty but feels it's pursued too often in his county and courtroom—"to the extent of being abusive."

Another complaint is that the odds are unfairly stacked against murder suspects.

For one thing, Harris County has no public defender agency, so trial judges must find defense attorneys willing to work cheap. The county pays a lead attorney $20,000 at most per case, an assistant $15,000.

Wilford Anderson, a prosecutor-turned-criminal defense lawyer, was tapped to represent Arthur Burton. He takes maybe two capital murders a year, he said, and sometimes digs into his own pocket for the defense. "The time that's involved, the preparation, the actual trial itself. It can be substantial," Anderson said.

Because of stories of incompetent defense lawyers, the county now requires attorneys appointed for death penalty cases to pass a special exam.

Better lawyers might save some people from conviction, but they also give the condemned fewer grounds on which to make their appeals.

Until 1995, Texas appellants had no automatic right to a lawyer. Now they do, and the state provides money, but not much: $15,000 for the lawyer and about $5,500 for an investigator and expert witnesses. Appeals to federal courts pay better, up to $125 an hour for the lawyer and no cap. But by then it's usually too late.

Texas capital murder trials come in two parts. If the jury finds the defendant guilty, a second trial is held to choose between death and life imprisonment.

Critics object that juries go for the death penalty because state law forbids judges to tell them that a life sentence means at least 40 years in prison.

"The Texas rule unquestionably tips the scales in favor of a death sentence that a fully informed jury might not impose," four U.S. Supreme Court justices wrote in an opinion last year, even as the full court let a Texas death sentence stand. Harris County judges are taking note, and legislators may change the law.

At the same time, the high court is getting tougher on appeals, as is Congress, Texas and other states where new laws seek to shorten the time between sentence and death. In Texas the average time on death row currently approaches 10 years. New limits on Texas appeals should cut that lag by two or three years.

Race is also presumed by some to figure in Harris County's high death row count. Blacks, Hispanics and other minorities are 46 percent of the population. But they make up 75 percent of Harris County convicts now on death row.

Is that because they commit more murders, or because they are more likely to be targeted for a capital trial? "I think . . . if you're a defendant of color, that you're more likely to be tried in a capital case," said Anderson, Burton's attorney.

While no known research on this has been done in Harris County, a recent study of black inmates in Philadelphia found they were nearly four times as likely to get a death sentence as others convicted of similar crimes.

Holmes, who is white, insists justice in his office is colorblind. "I have a rule here," he said. "When prosecutors come in here to talk to me about whether there should be death . . . I don't want to know the color of anybody. If I don't know, there's no way I can be accused of being racially biased."

Wesbrook, his attorneys and prosecutors are white. Anderson and Burton are black, as is the prosecutor who won Burton's conviction.

As other states move to exercise and broaden capital punishment, Texas and Harris County could lose their lead.

Last year, Texas executed half the 74 people put to death nationwide. Of 42 men and women executed through Aug. 24 this year, just 11 were in Texas—two of them Harris County convicts.

In this decade, Kansas and New York reinstated the death penalty and Delaware added "hate crime" to its capital offenses. In Florida, the death penalty now applies in murders of abused children under 12 and against drug traffickers whose trade could cause death.

Connecticut's capital crimes now include murder of a prison worker. In Tennessee, death penalty cases go to the head of the court docket. The federal Anti-terrorism and Effective Death Penalty Act of 1996 cut both the time and grounds for appeal in federal courts.

Still, executions could slow again, according to Richard Dieter of the Death Penalty Information Center, a Washington-based group critical of how capital punishment is applied.

That's because most death penalty states have added the option of life without parole, he said. And even in Texas some lawmakers are considering such a change.

"Juries are squeamish about the death penalty," Dieter said, "and when they're told this person will never get out, that seems to make a difference."

U.S. Prisons: Gulags or Country Clubs?

by Alfred N. Himelson

By the sheer number of people incarcerated in this country today we have created an American gulag every bit as soul-incinerating as the Soviet penal system—or so some claim.

Others, however, contend that our prisons more resemble country clubs and resorts, with their individual TVs, swimming pools, and tennis courts. According to this view, prisoners do not suffer for their crimes, do not fear imprisonment, and therefore are not deterred from committing serious criminal acts after their release.

The Bureau of Criminal Justice of the U.S. Department of Justice said that on December 31, 1996, there were 1,182,169 inmates in federal and state prisons. About 100,000 of them were in federal confinement. Another 500,000 or so were being held in local jails, awaiting trial or serving sentence.

How do these prisoners live, in reality, and how does U.S. prison life today compare with that in the jails of other countries, in particular Japan?

U.S. PRISON CONDITIONS

Recent developments in American prisons include the following:

• There are many more TVs in today's prisons than in previous years. In some institutions, inmates are allowed to have individual TVs in their cells.

• Weight rooms are available for bodybuilding.

• Court mandates and other pressures have required prisons to maintain law libraries for inmate use.

• Liberal conjugal visits help reduce sexual frustration.

• The inmates' use of the telephone to contact people on the outside would have been unimaginable in an earlier period.

Robert Johnson in *Hard Times* asserts that there is no official prison policy to physically or psychologically abuse inmates. It is only the special high-security institutions such as Pelican Bay in the California system or the Marion, Illinois, lockup operated by the Federal Bureau of Prisons that have generated controversy over their use of isolation and physical restraint.

On the surface, life appears to be more comfortable for inmates today than it would have been if they were serving time 40 years ago. Then, material conditions were often worse. The amenities available in most institutions today were absent from their lives. The correctional staffs of the 1997 prisons are on the whole far more professional than those of earlier periods.

Forty years ago, many prison systems—though by no means all—were subject to rule by politically appointed staff at all levels, from wardens to guards, and often provided a substandard physical environment, meager resources, and few programs for prisoners. But this is much less likely to be true today.

Given all this improvement, can it be said that inmates are being pampered?

To really understand the situation of inmates in the contemporary era, it is necessary to look at the world of the prisoner.

THE NEW, SINISTER INMATE SOCIETY

The kinds of inmates in contemporary prisons are quite different from those described in earlier periods. According to penologists, a far larger proportion of today's inmate body is likely to be violent and predatory.

This has created a much different inmate society from those of past decades. The picture of inmate life described by Donald Clemmer in his 1940 book *The Prison Community* is of a society oriented around a set of informal, prisoner-initiated rules of acceptable behavior.

Foremost among those rules was solidarity with other inmates in their antagonism toward prison staff. Almost as important was their endeavor to make prison life less burdensome. Inmates talked about how to "do time" and "hold their mud." They tried to create a society that made life more predictable and therefore usually more secure.

This article originally appeared in *The World & I,* October 1997, pp. 60-65. Reprinted by permission from *The World & I,* a publication of the Washington Times Corporation. © 1997.

Life in the Lockup

➡ U.S. prisons have become far more "luxurious" in recent years. TVs, weight rooms, and law libraries have proliferated, and inmates have liberal access to telephones and conjugal visits.

➡ But violence, brutality, and an atmosphere of fear have swelled as the inmate population has come to hail more from mean inner cities, broken families, and drug-using communities.

➡ Compared to amenities in Japanese prisons, U.S. lockups provide inmates with a "country club" life.

➡ But in terms of physical security and predictability, it is the American prisons that some charge are gulags.

A somewhat similar environment is described by sociologist Gresham Sykes in his 1958 book *Society of Captives*, an investigation of inmate culture in a New Jersey prison.

Sociologist Donald Wieder's interviews with men on parole who had served time in California prisons indicated the importance of the inmate code in prison life even into the 1960s.

PRISONS BECOME POWDER KEGS

The social turmoil of the 1960s resulted in major changes in the nature of inmate society.

Ethnic identity now assumed a greater importance. Violent revolutionary groups arose in many institutions. The ascent of rival prison gangs mirrored to some degree the operation of organized crime and street gangs.

Another factor was the influx of a significant number of prisoners who were involved with illegal drug use. Most were not part of the traditional criminal subculture that supported the old, rule-based way of convict life.

Many of the new prisoners were members of the recently developing underclass of the inner cities or came from other locales of disintegrating family life. With the mass entry of these people into the convict world, the prison became for both inmates and staff an even more dangerous and unpredictable setting. John Irwin titles his book about this period *The Prison in Turmoil*.

The characteristics of today's prison inmates still resemble in many ways those of the years of turmoil in the nation's penal institutions—the one major exception being the absence of any important political revolutionary organizations. The prison gangs remain and are a source of trouble for other inmates and staff. Their numbers have proliferated. And attempts at suppression have often allowed newer gangs to emerge.

Many systems today contain a high percentage of inmates serving sentences for drug-related offenses. And probably a larger proportion of prisoners comes from an underclass that values individual toughness and the use of violence to attain ambitions and settle conflicts.

Can better material conditions overcome the negatives of a more dangerous inmate body? Not very well. Prisoners respond to the atmosphere of anomie and fear by attempting physical and psychological isolation from other prisoners.

Richard McKorkle, a sociologist at the University of Nevada at Las Vegas, studied inmates in a maximum-security prison in Tennessee and reported that 77 percent of the convicts he interviewed withdrew as much as possible from the general prison scene. Forty percent avoided such mess halls and recreation areas other than their own.

For prisons that don't have much to offer in the way of programs for inmates, the use of television serves the same function it does in many retirement homes for the aged—as a soporific. Johnson describes these inmates as "most commonly slouching semicomatose before incessantly blaring TVs, which have become the baby-sitter of choice in many prisons."

But the presence of TVs and other shared material items can also set off power struggles among inmates over who controls them. For example, some institutions have been plagued by miniriots resulting from arguments over who selects the TV programs.

NEW DEVELOPMENTS IN PRISON AFFAIRS

In a country as large and diverse as the United States, where each state has its own correctional system and there is a separate federal system, there is no uniform direction of change.

Each state has had to deal with the problems created by a rapid increase in the number of violent offenders being incarcerated, longer sentences, and the overcrowding that follows the greater use of the prison option. But states vary in the scope of the problems they face, their previous penal traditions, the resources they have available, and the attitudes of their politicians and citizens.

Two developments illustrate different modes of change that are taking place.

The "no-frills" prisons. To have inmates serve "hard time," some state correctional systems and the Federal Bureau of Prisons have established or are moving in the direction of creating prisons in which amenities—and even some necessities—are withheld. The items typically removed or withheld are weight-lifting equipment, in-cell TVs, coffeepots and hot plates, pornographic materials, electronic instruments, computers, and personal clothing.

There is now staff monitoring of inmate phone calls. And, as a way to reduce prison expenses, inmates may be required to make copayments for their medical treatment—the money coming from their prison earnings, their trust fund, or other sources.

There is no uniform conception of how the no-frills idea should operate. In some systems, the motivation for the program stemmed from a view of the prison as a "country club"—or at least as a not very difficult experience. Therefore, corrections officials reasoned, to ensure that prisoners did "hard time," many of the pleasures and conveniences that were added to prison life in the last 30 years should be removed.

That there might be a reduction in prison expenses was seen as a bonus.

Kansas operates its no-frills program in a different way. According to Peter Finn, of the research firm Abt Associates, newly arrived inmates are not allowed to have key amenities and privileges. If, after a defined period, they meet the standards of behavior set by prison authorities, they are appropriately rewarded.

The underlying theory here is a form of behavior modification. The immediate benefit to the Kansas system will probably be quieter and more manageable institutions.

What can we expect from no-frills corrections? Will it affect recidivism? Probably not. In the past, a compari-

---

> Even in countries with traditionally liberal outlooks, prison authorities are becoming less informal in their dealing with inmates and are exercising tighter disciplinary power.

---

son of inmates with similar personality profiles, criminal records, and sentences who were released from different forms of prison showed similar rates of reoffending. My prediction is that the no-frills program will have a negligible influence on recidivism rates.

The Oklahoma plan. Other states have reacted differently to prison overcrowding and public attitudes. Oklahoma is undertaking a major transformation of its penal system: As of July 1, 1998, all nonviolent offenders will be sentenced only to community programs. These could include treatment programs for alcohol or drug abuse, the performance of community service, job training, and restitution. Noncompliance can lead a judge to order local jail time.

As of July 1, 1998, violent felons will be sent to state prison, where they must serve 85 percent of their sentence before parole consideration. Nonviolent offenders already serving prison time must complete 75 percent of their time before coming before the parole board.

What happens when Oklahoma's prison population is made up mostly of violent offenders should be of special interest to penologists and correctional administrators.

OTHER COUNTRIES

Changes in the prisons of some other countries loosely parallel what has happened in the United States.

The Prison Service of England and Wales reported a rise in the prison population from approxi-

mately 40,000 at the beginning of 1993 to almost 52,000 in April 1995. In 1995, it projected a prison population of 56,000 by the year 2002.

The reality is that, by April 1997, the number of prisoners in England and Wales passed 60,000. The incarceration rate is now 116 per 100,000, still far less than that of the United States (at 615 per 100,000) but one of the highest in Europe.

But it wasn't just the rising number of inmates that was noteworthy. There were changes in who was being incarcerated. According to the prison service, the convict population is becoming younger, more violent, and more volatile. A higher percentage of inmates are serving longer time—often life sentences for violent or drug-related crimes.

To deal with this new situation, the government has reorganized the prison service, given it a separate identity, and undertaken a major prison-building and renovation program. In addition, there is an expansion in the use of private-enterprise prisons and ancillary services.

Outside of Britain, even in countries with traditionally liberal outlooks, the prison administrations are becoming less informal in their dealing with inmates and are exercising tighter disciplinary power.

In the Netherlands, this trend has been ascribed to the need to manage an increasing number of drug-dependent and aggressive prisoners who have received longer sentences. Many are of non-Dutch origin. The prison population of the Netherlands rose from 5,002 in 1987 to 10,329 in 1995.

Japan's prison system is a far cry from America's. It contained 37,000 sentenced inmates as of 1994, almost all of whom are required to perform productive work like dressmaking, assembling consumer goods, woodworking, printing, cooking, and laundry tasks.

According to Human Rights Watch, Japanese prison life is stringent. The prison rules regulate almost every

Prison Labor in America

The growing prison budgets, the hardening of public attitudes about the amenities convicts get, and the desire to prepare inmates for life on the outside have been factors in increasing the use of prison labor. As of 1994, 80,000 of the nation's 1.1 million convicts worked in prison industries.

The value of the products produced by inmates runs into the billions of dollars. An astonishing range of products and services are the product of work in prisons. Meatpacking, handling airline reservations, and manufacturing of furniture, toys, and garments are just a few of them.

Prisoners work within one of two major types of organizations.

Most states have their own, government-run prison industries. The largest state, California, operates 31 enterprises employing 7,000 of its 131,000 inmates. According to the California Legislative Analysts, sales exceeded $152 million.

The federal system's UNICOR organization provides a wide variety of products and services for sale to government agencies and outside buyers.

Inmates may also work for private industry. The work is usually done within the confines of the prison. The companies supervise the work environment, but the correctional setting requires the close collaboration of the prison staff to deal with the special problems that may arise.

The use of prison labor is not without controversy. Manufacturers and labor unions have claimed that goods and services produced by prison labor constitute unfair competition. They assert that inmates are paid less than outside laborers (although some companies pay inmates a form of prevailing wage).

Critics also charge that both government-run prison industries and free-venture enterprises are subsidized by the government in various ways.

—A.N.H.

aspect of prisoners' daily life. They cover where to put every object in the cell and how to put it in its place.

Cell inspections occur every day, and during them inmates are required to have their clothing properly arranged and to sit quietly in a kneeling position facing the door. Until all the cells have been inspected and the order to relax is given, prisoners may not talk, get up, or read. At night, once the lights are out, they must immediately recline.

Inmates are allowed no access to telephones. Visitors have to speak to prisoners through partitions, and the conversations are monitored by a prison officer who takes notes. All letters in and out are read by staff members.

According to researchers Yuichi Kaido and Katsuhiko Iguchi, the daily routine in most prisons is as follows. 6:45 A.M., wake up; 7:00, roll call and breakfast; 8:00, start work; 9:45–10:00, break; noon, lunch; 12:40 P.M., start work again; 2:30–2:45,

break; 4:40, work ends; 5:00, roll call and dinner; 6:00, free time; 9:00, sleep. Prisoners don't have to work on Saturday, Sunday, and national holidays.

As inmates move from cell to work in the morning and from work to cell in the afternoon, they are subjected to strip searches down to their underwear.

As they work, prisoners are required to maintain complete silence. Making eye contact with other inmates or guards is strictly prohibited.

All revenues from the prison industry go to the national treasury. Prisoners receive no wages for their work but get a nominal stipend of about $35 a month.

The Japanese prison style, however, would probably not be implementable in America, for it is uniquely tailored to the regimented Japanese culture.

Still, American prisons today are not "country clubs." The atmosphere of fear, the unpredictability of inmate life, and the institutions' monotony belie such a conception.

Whether to make U.S. prison life harder or softer, although having ramifications for how smoothly our prisons operate, is basically a political and philosophical question regarding notions of retribution and justice.

Alfred N. Himelson, professor of sociology emeritus at California State University at Northridge, is a former senior research analyst for the California Department of Corrections.

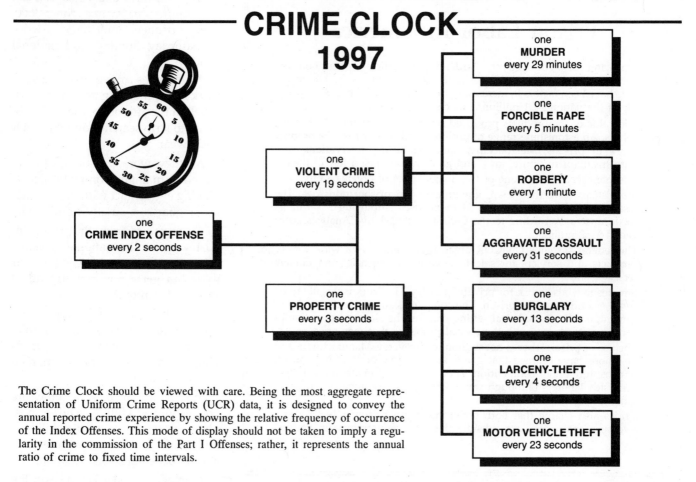

CRIME CLOCK 1997

one
CRIME INDEX OFFENSE
every 2 seconds

one
VIOLENT CRIME
every 19 seconds

one
PROPERTY CRIME
every 3 seconds

one
MURDER
every 29 minutes

one
FORCIBLE RAPE
every 5 minutes

one
ROBBERY
every 1 minute

one
AGGRAVATED ASSAULT
every 31 seconds

one
BURGLARY
every 13 seconds

one
LARCENY-THEFT
every 4 seconds

one
MOTOR VEHICLE THEFT
every 23 seconds

The Crime Clock should be viewed with care. Being the most aggregate representation of Uniform Crime Reports (UCR) data, it is designed to convey the annual reported crime experience by showing the relative frequency of occurrence of the Index Offenses. This mode of display should not be taken to imply a regularity in the commission of the Part I Offenses; rather, it represents the annual ratio of crime to fixed time intervals.

Crime in the United States, 1997

In 1997, the Crime Index total, estimated at approximately 13.2 million offenses, dropped 2 percent from the 1996 total. This decline represented the lowest annual serious crime count since 1985 and the sixth consecutive annual decline. The Nation's cities reported a decline of 3 percent collectively. Those cities with populations of 250,000 to 999,999 reported the greatest decrease, 6 percent. A 3-percent decrease was reported in the suburban counties, while the rural counties showed an increase of 1 percent.

Five- and 10-year percent changes showed the 1997 national total was 7 percent lower than the 1993 level and 5 percent lower than the 1988 total.

Geographically, the most populous Southern States accounted for 40 percent of the total volume of Crime Index offenses. Following were the Western States, 24 percent; the Midwestern States, 22 percent; and the Northeastern States, 15 percent. Compared to 1996, in 1997 the Northeastern States showed a Crime Index decrease of 5 percent. The Southern and Western States each showed a 2-percent decrease, and the Midwestern States showed a 1-percent decrease.

July was the month in which the most Crime Index offenses occurred, and February was the month in which the least occurred.

Rate

Crime rates relate the incidence of crime to population. In 1997, there were an estimated 4,923 Crime Index offenses for each 100,000 in United States population, the lowest rate since 1984. The Crime Index rate was highest in the Nation's metropolitan areas and lowest in the rural counties. The national 1997 Crime Index rate fell 3 percent from the 1996 rate, 10 percent from the 1993 level, and 13 percent from the 1988 rate.

Regionally, the Crime Index rates ranged from 5,547 in the South to 3,734 in the Northeast. Rates in all four regions declined from 1996 to 1997.

Nature

The Crime Index is composed of violent and property crime categories, and in 1997, 12 percent of the Index offenses reported to law enforcement were violent crimes and 88 percent, property crimes. Larceny-theft was the offense with the highest volume, while murder accounted for the fewest offenses.

Property estimated in value at $15.6 billion was stolen in connection with all Crime Index offenses, with the greatest losses due to thefts of motor vehicles followed by jewelry and precious metals; televisions, radios, stereos, etc; and currency, notes, etc.

Table 1.—Index of Crime, United States, 1987–1996

Population[1]	Crime Index total[2]	Modified Crime Index total[3]	Violent crime[4]	Property crime[4]	Murder and non-negligent man-slaughter	Forcible rape	Robbery	Aggravated assault	Burglary	Larceny-theft	Motor vehicle theft	Arson[3]
	Number of Offenses											
Population by year:												
1988—245,807,000	13,923,100		1,566,220	12,356,900	20,100	92,490	542,970	910,090	3,218,100	7,705,900	1,432,900	
1989—248,239,000	14,251,400		1,646,040	12,605,400	21,500	94,500	578,330	951,710	3,168,200	7,872,400	1,564,800	
1990—248,709,873	14,475,600		1,820,130	12,655,500	23,440	102,560	639,270	1,054,860	3,073,900	7,945,700	1,635,900	
1991—252,177,000	14,872,900		1,911,770	12,961,100	24,700	106,590	687,730	1,092,740	3,157,200	8,142,200	1,661,700	
1992—255,082,000	14,438,200		1,932,270	12,505,900	23,760	109,060	672,480	1,126,970	2,979,900	7,915,200	1,610,800	
1993—257,908,000	14,144,800		1,926,020	12,218,800	24,530	106,010	659,870	1,135,610	2,834,800	7,820,900	1,563,100	
1994—260,341,000	13,898,500		1,857,670	12,131,900	23,330	102,220	618,950	1,113,180	2,712,800	7,879,800	1,539,300	
1995—262,755,000[5]	13,862,700		1,798,790	12,063,900	21,610	97,470	580,510	1,099,210	2,593,800	7,997,700	1,472,400	
1996—265,284,000	13,473,600		1,682,280	11,791,300	19,650	95,770	537,050	1,029,810	2,501,500	7,894,600	1,395,200	
1997—267,637,000	13,175,100		1,634,770	11,540,300	18,210	96,120	497,950	1,022,490	2,461,100	7,725,500	1,353,700	
Percent change: number of offenses:												
1997/1996	−2.4		−3.2	−2.2	−7.3	−.1	−7.0	−1.4	−1.8	−2.3	−2.9	
1997/1993	−6.9		−15.1	−5.6	−25.8	−9.3	−24.5	−10.0	−13.2	−1.2	−13.4	
1997/1988	−5.4		+4.4	−6.6	−11.9	+3.9	−8.3	+12.4	−23.5	+.3	−5.5	
	Rate per 100,000 Inhabitants											
Year:												
1988	5,664.2		637.2	5,027.1	8.4	37.6	220.9	370.2	1,309.2	3,134.9	582.9	
1989	5,741.0		663.1	5,077.9	8.7	38.1	233.0	383.4	1,276.3	3,171.3	630.4	
1990	5,820.3		731.8	5,088.5	9.4	41.2	257.0	424.1	1,235.9	3,194.8	657.8	
1991	5,897.8		758.1	5,139.7	9.8	42.3	272.7	433.3	1,252.0	3,228.8	659.0	
1992	5,660.2		757.5	4,902.7	9.3	42.8	263.6	441.8	1,168.2	3,103.0	631.5	
1993	5,484.4		746.8	4,737.6	9.5	41.1	255.9	440.3	1,099.2	3,032.4	606.1	
1994	5,373.5		713.6	4,660.0	9.0	39.3	237.7	427.6	1,042.0	3,026.7	591.3	
1995[5]	5,275.9		684.6	4,591.3	8.2	37.1	220.9	418.3	987.1	3,043.8	560.4	
1996	5,078.9		634.1	4,444.8	7.4	36.1	202.4	388.2	943.0	2,975.9	525.9	
1997	4,922.7		610.8	4,311.9	6.8	35.9	186.1	382.0	919.6	2,886.5	505.8	
Percent change: rate per 100,000 inhabitants:												
1997/1996	−3.2		−4.0	−3.1	−8.1	−1.1	−7.8	−2.3	−2.7	−3.1	−3.8	
1997/1993	−10.2		−18.2	−9.0	−28.4	−12.7	−27.3	−13.2	−16.3	−4.8	−16.5	
1997/1988	−13.1		−4.1	−14.2	−19.0	−4.5	−15.8	+3.2	−29.8	−7.9	−13.2	

[1]Populations are Bureau of the Census provisional estimates as of July 1, except 1990 which [is] the decennial census count.
[2]Because of rounding, the offenses may not add to totals.
[3]Although arson data are included in the trend and clearance tables, sufficient data are not available to estimate totals for this offense.
[4]Violent crimes are offenses of murder, forcible rape, robbery, and aggravated assault. Property crimes are offenses of burglary, larceny-theft, and motor vehicle theft. Data are not included for the property crime of arson.
[5]The 1996 figures have been adjusted.

Complete data were not available for the states of Illinois, Kansas, Kentucky, Montana, New Hampshire, and Vermont; therefore, it was necessary that their crime counts be estimated.

All rates were calculated on the offenses before rounding.

Nationwide, law enforcement agencies recorded a 37-percent recovery rate for dollar losses in connection with stolen property. The highest recovery percentages were for stolen motor vehicles, consumable goods, livestock, clothing and furs, and firearms.

Law Enforcement Response

In 1997, law enforcement agencies nationwide recorded a 22-percent clearance rate for the collective Crime Index offenses and made an estimated 2.7 million arrests for Index crimes. Crimes can be cleared by arrest or by exceptional means when some element beyond law enforcement control precludes the placing of formal charges against the offender. The arrest of one person may clear several crimes, or several persons may be arrested in connection with the clearance of one offense.

The Index clearance rate has remained relatively stable throughout the past 10-year period. In both 1993 and 1988, the clearance rates were 21 percent.

The 1997 total Crime Index arrests dropped 3 percent from 1996. Juvenile arrests for Index crimes decreased 6 percent. By gender, arrests of males decreased 4 percent, and arrests of females showed virtually no change.

Between 1997 and 1996, declines in the number of persons arrested were recorded for all but one of the individual offenses composing the Index. Decreases ranged from 8 percent for motor vehicle theft to 3 percent for aggravated assault.

As in the past years, arrests for larceny-theft, estimated at nearly 1.5 million in 1997, accounted for the highest volume of Crime Index arrests.

CRIME INDEX OFFENSES REPORTED

MURDER AND NONNEGLIGENT MANSLAUGHTER

DEFINITION
Murder and nonnegligent manslaughter, as defined in the Uniform Crime Reporting Program, is the willful (nonnegligent) killing of one human being by another.

TREND

Year	Number of offenses	Rate per 100,000 inhabitants
1996	19,645	7.4
1997	18,209	6.8
Percent change	−7.3	−8.1

Volume

The number of persons murdered in the United States in 1997 was estimated at 18,209, representing a 7-percent decline from the 1996 estimate, the 1997 figure was down 26-percent from the 1993 total, and 12-percent from the 1988 estimate.

When compared to 1996 figures, 1997 murder volumes in the Nation's cities dropped 9 percent. Decreases ranged from 14 percent in cities with populations of 250,000 to 499,999 to 5 percent in cities with populations of 10,000 to 49,999. Declines of 7 and 2 percent were reported in suburban and rural counties, respectively.

Regarding the four regions of the Nation, the most populous region, the Southern States, accounted for 43 percent of murders. The Western and Midwestern States accounted for 22 and 21 percent, respectively; and the Northeastern States accounted for 13 percent. From 1996 to 1997 all regions showed declines in the number of murders. The Northeastern States, reporting 12 percent, and the Western States, reporting 11 percent, experienced the greatest declines. Decreases were also recorded in the South, 6 percent, and in the Midwest, 3 percent.

Monthly figures show that in 1997 most murders occurred in July and the fewest were committed in February.

Rate

Down 8 percent from the 1996 rate, the national murder rate in 1997 was 7 per 100,000 inhabitants, the lowest since 1967.

Murder by Month, 1993–1997
[Percent distribution]

Months	1993	1994	1995	1996	1997
January	8.3	8.2	8.3	8.7	8.5
February	6.9	7.5	6.8	7.8	7.3
March	7.8	8.8	7.6	7.5	8.4
April	7.8	8.1	8.4	7.5	7.7
May	8.0	8.2	7.9	8.3	8.1
June	8.6	8.3	8.2	8.8	8.7
July	9.4	9.0	8.9	8.8	9.0
August	9.3	9.1	9.9	9.1	8.8
September	8.4	8.2	8.6	8.1	8.3
October	8.4	8.4	8.8	8.5	8.7
November	8.3	7.8	8.0	8.0	8.1
December	8.8	8.4	8.6	8.9	8.5

Five- and 10-year trends show the 1997 rate was 28 percent lower than in 1993 and 19 percent below the 1988 rate.

On a regional basis, the South averaged 8 murders per 100,000 people; the West 7 per 100,000; the Midwest, 6 per 100,000, and the Northeast, 5 per 100,000. Compared to 1996 rates, murder rates in 1997 declined in all of the four geographic regions, with the West experiencing the greatest change, a 12-percent decrease, and the Midwest, the smallest, a 5-percent drop.

The Nation's metropolitan areas reported a 1997 murder rate of 7 victims per 100,000 inhabitants. Rural counties reported a murder rate of 5 per 100,000, and in cities outside metropolitan areas, the rate was 4 per 100,000.

Nature

Supplemental data were provided by contributing agencies for 15,289 of the estimated 18,209 murders in 1997. Submitted monthly, the data consist of the age, sex, and race of both victims and offenders; the types of weapons used; the relationships of victims to the offenders; and the circumstances surrounding the murders.

Based on this information, 77 percent of the murder victims in 1997 were males; and 88 percent were persons 18 years of age or older. Forty-five percent were ages 20 through 34. The percent of whites murdered was 48 and of blacks murdered were 49 percent, and other races accounted for the remaining 3 percent.

Supplemental data were also reported for 17,272 murder offenders in 1997. Of those for whom sex and age were re-

Murder Victims by Race and Sex, 1997

Race of Victim	Sex of Victims			
	Total	Male	Female	Unknown
Total White Victims	7,261	5,325	1,935	1
Total Black Victims	7,394	6,037	1,357	—
Total Other Race Victims	453	328	125	—
Total Unknown Race	181	109	49	23
Total Victims[1]	15,289	11,799	3,466	24

[1]Total murder victims for whom supplemental data were received.

ported, 90 percent of the offenders were males, and 87 percent were persons 18 years of age or older. Seventy percent were ages 17 through 34. Of offenders for whom race was known, 53 percent were black, 45 percent were white, and the remainder were persons of other races.

Murder is most often intraracial among victims and offenders. In 1997, data based on incidents involving one victim and one offender show that 94 percent of the black murder victims were slain by black offenders, and 85 percent of the white murder victims were killed by white offenders. Likewise, males were most often slain by males (88 percent in single victim/single offender situations). These same data show, however, that 9 of every 10 female victims were murdered by males.

FORCIBLE RAPE

DEFINITION

Forcible rape, as defined in the Program, is the carnal knowledge of a female forcibly and against her will. Assaults or attempts to commit rape by force or threat of force are also included; however, statutory rape (without force) and other sex offenses are excluded.

Year	TREND Number of offenses	Rate per 100,000 inhabitants
1996	96,252	36.3
1997	96,122	35.9
Percent change	−.1	−1.1

Volume

The 96,122 forcible rapes reported to law enforcement agencies across the Nation during 1997 represented the fifth consecutive annual decrease. The 1997 count was about the same as 1996, and 9 percent below the 1993 level, but 4 percent higher than the 1988 volume.

Geographically, 40 percent of the forcible rape total in 1997 was accounted for by the most populous Southern States, 25 percent by the Midwestern States, 23 percent by the Western States, and 13 percent by the Northeastern States. Two-year

trends show that forcible rapes declined 2 percent in the Midwest, and 1 percent in the Northeast. The South and the West showed a 6 percent increase from the 1996 level.

Monthly totals show the lowest volume occurred in December, while the largest number of forcible rapes was reported during the month of July.

Forcible Rape by Month, 1993–1997
[Percent distribution]

Months	1993	1994	1995	1996	1997
January	7.7	7.5	7.7	7.9	7.9
February	6.9	7.3	7.1	7.9	7.0
March	8.5	8.3	8.5	8.1	8.0
April	8.2	8.4	8.0	8.1	8.3
May	8.9	8.9	8.9	9.0	9.1
June	9.2	9.2	8.5	8.8	9.5
July	9.7	9.7	9.4	9.5	9.7
August	9.3	9.6	9.9	9.1	9.4
September	8.3	8.7	8.8	8.8	8.8
October	8.1	8.5	8.7	8.5	8.3
November	7.5	7.3	7.8	7.4	7.4
December	7.7	6.5	6.9	6.9	6.6

Rate

By Uniform Crime Reporting definition, the victims of forcible rape are always female, and in 1997, an estimated 70 of every 100,000 females in the country were reported rape victims. The 1997 female forcible rape rate was 1 percent lower than the 1996 rate and 13 percent lower than the 1993 rate.

The Nation's metropolitan areas recorded the highest forcible rape rate in 1997, 74 victims per 100,000 females. In cities outside metropolitan areas, the rate was 70 per 100,000 females, and in rural counties, it was 48 per 100,000 females. Although metropolitan areas record the highest rape rates, they have shown the only rate decline over the past 10 years (1988–1997), 11 percent. During this same period, the rate increased in cities outside metropolitan areas by 43 percent and in rural counties by 33 percent.

By region in 1997, the highest female rape rate was in the Southern States, which recorded 79 victims per 100,000 females. Following were the Midwestern States with a rate of 74; the Western States with a rate of 72 and the Northeastern States with a rate of 48. Since 1996, forcible rape rates declined 1 percent in the Midwest and the West, and 2 percent in the Northeast. The South's rate remained the same.

Over the last 10 years, female forcible rape rate decreases were recorded in three regions. Rates in the Northeast and West showed 16- and 11-percent decreases, respectively. The smallest decrease, 1 percent, was recorded in the Midwest. A 1-percent increase was shown in the Southern States.

Nature

Rapes by force constitute the greatest percentage of total forcible rapes, 88 percent of the 1997 incidents. The remaining 12 percent were attempts or assaults to commit forcible rape.

When compared to the 1996 volume, the number of rapes by force in 1997 showed virtually no change; a 5-percent decrease in attempts to rape was noted.

As with all other Crime Index offenses, complaints of forcible rape made to law enforcement agencies are sometimes found to be false or baseless. In such cases, law enforcement agencies "unfound" the offenses and exclude them from crime counts. The "unfounded" rate, or percentage of complaints determined through investigation to be false, is higher for forcible rape than for any other Index crime. Eight percent of forcible rape complaints in 1997 were "unfounded," while the average for all Index crimes was 2 percent.

Law Enforcement Response

In 1997, over half of the forcible rapes reported to law enforcement nationwide were cleared by arrest or exceptional means. Rural and suburban county law enforcement clearance rates, at 52 and 55 percent respectively, were slightly higher than the city law enforcement clearance rate at 50 percent.

By geographic region, forcible rape clearance rates in 1997 were 56 percent in the South, 50 percent in the Northeast, 48 percent in the Midwest, and 45 percent in the West.

Of the total clearances for forcible rape in the country as a whole, 11 percent involved only persons under 18 years of age. The percentage of juvenile involvement varied by community type, ranging from 11 percent in the Nation's cities to 13 percent in rural counties. Cities with populations under 10,000 had the greatest juvenile involvement, 15 percent.

Participating law enforcement agencies throughout the Nation made an estimated 32,060 arrests for forcible rape in 1997. Of the forcible rape arrestees, 44 percent were under age 25. Fifty-eight percent of those arrested were white.

The national arrest total for forcible rape fell 4 percent from 1996 to 1997. Arrests also declined 6 percent both in the Nation's cities and 3 percent in the suburban counties. In rural counties a 4-percent increase in arrests for forcible rape was recorded.

ROBBERY

DEFINITION
Robbery is the taking or attempting to take anything of value from the care, custody, or control of a person or persons by force or threat of force or violence and/or by putting the victim in fear.

Volume

Nationally, the 1997 estimated robbery total, 497,950, was the lowest since 1985. The robbery volume for 1997 was down 7 percent from the 1996 national total and showed an 8-percent decrease in cities. The largest decline—12 percent—was reported by cities with 500,000 to 999,999 inhabitants. During the same period, the robbery volume dropped 6 percent in suburban counties and increased by 11 percent in rural counties.

Regionally, the Southern States, the most populous area of the Nation, accounted for 36 percent of all reported robberies.

Year	TREND Number of offenses	Rate per 100,000 inhabitants
1996	535,594	201.9
1997	497,950	186.1
Percent change	–7.0	–7.8

The Western States followed with 23 percent, the Northeastern States with 21 percent, and the Midwestern States with 20 percent. Two-year trends show the number of robberies in 1997 was down in all regions as compared to 1996 figures. The Northeast and West marked 11- and 10-percent decreases, the Midwest a 2-percent drop, and the South a 5-percent decline.

In 1997, the number of robbery offenses was 25 percent lower than in 1993 and 8 percent lower than in 1988.

Monthly volume figures for 1997 show robberies occurred most frequently in January and least often in February and April.

Robbery by Month, 1993–1997
[Percent distribution]

Months	1993	1994	1995	1996	1997
January	8.9	8.6	8.6	9.2	9.2
February	7.2	7.7	7.3	8.0	7.6
March	8.2	8.6	8.0	8.1	7.9
April	7.5	8.0	7.5	7.5	7.6
May	7.6	8.0	7.8	7.9	8.3
June	8.0	8.0	8.0	7.9	8.0
July	8.8	8.5	8.5	8.5	8.6
August	8.9	8.8	8.9	8.6	8.8
September	8.5	8.3	8.5	8.2	8.5
October	9.0	8.7	9.3	8.6	8.7
November	8.5	8.1	8.7	8.4	8.3
December	9.0	8.8	8.9	9.1	8.5

Rate

The national robbery rate in 1997 was 186 per 100,000 people, 8 percent lower than in 1996. In metropolitan areas, the 1997 rate was 223; in cities outside metropolitan areas, it was 72; and in the rural areas, it was 18. With 578 robberies per 100,000 inhabitants, the highest rate was recorded in cities with populations 1 million and over.

Regionally, the robbery rate was 1993 per 100,000 population in the West, 203 in the Northeast, 192 in the South, and 157 in the Midwest. Compared to 1996 rates, 1997 robbery rates were down in all regions. The West marked a 12-percent decrease; the Northeast, a decline of 11 percent; the South, a 6-percent decrease; and the Midwest, a 3-percent decline.

Nature

During 1997, losses estimated at nearly $500 million were attributed to robberies. The value of property stolen averaged $995 per robbery, up from $921 in 1996. Average dollar losses in 1997 ranged from $576 taken during robberies of gas or service stations to $4,802 per bank robbery. The impact of this

Robbery, Percent Distribution, 1997

[By region]

	United States Total	North-eastern States	Mid-western States	South-ern States	Western States
Total[1]	100.0	100.0	100.0	100.0	100.0
Street/highway	50.0	60.2	57.6	44.5	46.0
Commercial house	13.8	9.3	11.4	14.6	17.0
Gas or service station	2.4	2.3	3.1	2.2	2.3
Convenience store	5.7	4.4	4.0	7.3	5.5
Residence	11.6	11.6	9.7	14.6	9.2
Bank	1.9	1.3	1.7	1.7	2.7
Miscellaneous	14.6	10.9	12.5	15.1	17.3

[1]Because of rounding, percentages may not add to totals.

violent crime on its victims cannot be measured in terms of monetary loss alone. While the object of a robbery is to obtain money or property, the crime always involves force or threat of force, and many victims suffer serious personal injury.

More than half (51 percent) of the offenses in this category during 1997 were robberies on streets or highways. Robberies of commercial and financial establishments accounted for 24 percent, and those occurring at residences, 12 percent. The remainder were miscellaneous types. All robbery types declined in 1997 as compared to 1996 totals. Decreases ranged from 13 percent for those committed on streets and highways to 5 percent for commercial house robberies.

AGGRAVATED ASSAULT

DEFINITION
Aggravated assault is an unlawful attack by one person upon another for the purpose of inflicting severe or aggravated bodily injury. This type of assault is usually accompanied by the use of a weapon or by means likely to produce death or great bodily harm.

Year	TREND Number of offenses	Rate per 100,000 inhabitants
1996	1,037,049	390.9
1997	1,022,492	382.0
Percent change	–1.4	–2.3

Volume

Aggravated assaults decreased in 1997, marking the fourth consecutive year of decline. Accounting for 63 percent of violent crimes in 1997, the total of 1,022,492 aggravated assaults represented a 1-percent drop for this offense.

Forty-one percent of the aggravated assault volume was accounted for by the Southern Region, the Nation's most popu-

lous area. Following were the Western Region with 24 percent, the Midwestern Region with 20 percent, and the Northeastern Region with 15 percent. All of the Nation's regions registered decreases in the number of reported aggravated assaults.

The 1997 monthly figures show that the greatest number of aggravated assaults was recorded during July while the lowest volume occurred during February.

The Nation's cities collectively experienced a decrease of 2 percent in the aggravated assault volume from 1996 to 1997. Among all city population groupings, decreases ranged from 4 percent in cities with populations from 10,000 to 24,999 to 1 percent in cities with 500,000 to 999,999 inhabitants. The number of aggravated assaults decreased 1 percent in suburban counties and increased by 2 percent in the rural counties during the same 2-year period.

Five- and 10-year trends for the country as a whole show aggravated assaults 10 percent lower than in 1993 and 12 percent above the 1988 figure.

Aggravated Assault by Month, 1993–1997

[Percent distribution]

Months	1993	1994	1995	1996	1997
January	7.6	7.2	7.6	7.8	7.5
February	6.6	6.9	7.0	7.4	7.0
March	8.1	8.2	8.1	8.0	8.3
April	8.5	8.5	8.3	8.1	8.2
May	9.1	8.7	8.8	8.9	9.3
June	9.1	8.9	8.8	9.1	9.1
July	9.7	9.4	9.4	9.4	9.5
August	9.3	9.3	9.4	9.3	9.4
September	8.5	8.8	8.9	8.6	8.7
October	8.6	8.7	8.7	8.5	8.3
November	7.5	7.6	7.5	7.4	7.5
December	7.3	7.7	7.4	7.6	7.2

Rate

In 1997, there were 382 reported victims of aggravated assault for every 100,000 people nationwide. The rate was 2 percent lower than in 1996 and 13 percent below the 1993 rate. The 1997 rate was, however, 3 percent higher than the 1988 rate.

Higher than the national average, the rate in metropolitan areas was 416 per 100,000 inhabitants in 1997. Cities outside metropolitan areas experienced a rate of 343 and rural counties, a rate of 183.

Compared to 1996 rates, 1997 aggravated assault rates were down in all regions. The aggravated assault rate was 441 per 100,000 people in the south, 415 in the West, 326 in the Midwest, and 304 in the Northeast. The South and West both decreased by 3 percent, the Midwest registered a 2-percent drop, and the Northeast marked a 1-percent decline.

Nature

In 1997, 35 percent of the aggravated assaults were committed with blunt objects or other dangerous weapons. Personal weapons such as hands, fists, and feet were used in 27

Aggravated Assault, Types of Weapons Used, 1997

[Percent distribution by region]

Region	Total all weapons[1]	Fire-arms	Knives or cutting instruments	Other weapons (clubs, blunt objects, etc.)	Personal weapons
Total	100.0	20.0	17.9	35.3	26.7
Northeastern States	100.0	10.0	19.6	41.1	29.3
Midwestern States	100.0	22.8	17.9	34.3	25.0
Southern States	100.0	23.4	19.7	36.2	20.7
Western States	100.0	18.3	14.2	31.3	36.2

[1]Because of rounding, percentages may not add to totals.

percent of the assaults; firearms in 20 percent; and knives or cutting instruments in 18 percent.

When broken down by weapon, aggravated assaults in three of four weapon categories decreased from the previous year's totals. Assault decreases were as follows: firearms, 9 percent; knives or other cutting instruments, 2 percent; and other dangerous weapons, 1 percent. Aggravated assaults with personal weapons (hands, fists, feet, etc.) increased 4 percent.

BURGLARY

DEFINITION
The Uniform Crime Reporting Program defines burglary as the unlawful entry of a structure to commit a felony or theft. The use of force to gain entry is not required to classify an offense as burglary.

	TREND	
Year	Number of offenses	Rate per 100,000 inhabitants
1996	2,506,400	944.8
1997	2,461,120	919.6
Percent change	−1.8	−2.7

Volume

The estimated 2.5 million burglaries in the United States in 1997 marked the sixth consecutive annual decline. Distribution figures for the regions showed that the highest burglary volume in 1996, 42 percent, occurred in the most populous Southern States. The Western States followed with 24 percent, the Midwestern States with 20 percent, and the Northeastern States with 14 percent.

In 1997, the greatest number of burglaries occurred during July while the lowest number took place in February.

The burglary volume dropped 2 percent nationwide during 1997 as compared to the 1996 total. By population group, the Nation's cities overall experienced a 3-percent decline; the largest decrease was in cities with populations of 1 million and over, which showed a 7-percent decline. Suburban counties recorded 1-percent decreases, while rural counties experienced a 1-percent increase.

All four regions of the United States reported decreases in burglary volumes in 1997 as compared to the previous year's figures. The Northeastern States registered a 7-percent decline; the Western States, a less than 1 percent decrease; and the Midwestern and Southern States recorded 1-percent decreases each in burglary volumes.

Long-term national trends show burglary down 13 percent from the 1993 level and down 24 percent compared to the 1988 volume.

Burglary by Month, 1993–1997
[Percent distribution]

Months	1993	1994	1995	1996	1997
January	8.4	7.9	8.4	8.3	8.4
February	7.0	7.1	7.2	7.6	7.2
March	8.2	8.2	8.2	7.8	7.8
April	7.8	7.9	7.7	7.8	7.8
May	8.1	8.4	8.4	8.3	8.3
June	8.5	8.3	8.3	8.1	8.2
July	9.1	9.1	9.0	9.1	9.1
August	9.2	9.3	9.2	8.9	9.0
September	8.7	8.6	8.5	8.6	8.7
October	8.5	8.5	8.8	8.8	8.8
November	8.2	8.3	8.3	8.0	8.2
December	8.4	8.5	8.1	8.6	8.5

Rate

The burglary rate in 1997, the lowest in more than two decades, was 920 per 100,000 inhabitants nationwide. The rate was 3 percent lower than in 1996, down 16 percent from the 1993 level, and 30 percent below the 1988 rate. In 1997, the burglary rate for every 100,000 in population was 963 in the metropolitan areas, 932 in the cities outside metropolitan areas, and 622 in the rural counties.

Looking at the Nation's regions, the burglary rate was 1,102 in the Southern States, 986 in the Western States, 804 in the Midwestern States, and 651 in the Northeastern States. A comparison of 1996 and 1997 rates showed a decline of 7 percent in the Northeast. The Midwestern, Southern, and Western regions each experienced a 2-percent decline.

Nature

Sixty-six percent of all burglaries involved forcible entry, 27 percent were unlawful entries (without force), and the remainder were forcible entry attempts in 1997. Offenses for which time of occurrence was reported showed that 52 percent of burglaries happened during daytime hours and 48 percent at night. Two of every 3 burglaries in 1997 were residential in nature. Sixty percent of residential burglaries occurred during the daytime, while 65 percent of nonresidential burglaries occurred during the nighttime.

Burglary victims experienced estimated losses of $3.3 billion in 1997. Overall, the average dollar loss per burglary was $1,334; for residential offenses, $1,305; and for nonresidential offenses, $1,391. The 1997 average loss for residential burglary decreased from the previous year's figures, and the average loss for nonresidential property increased.

Two-percent declines were observed in both residential and nonresidential burglary volumes from 1996 to 1997.

LARCENY-THEFT

DEFINITION
Larceny-theft is the unlawful taking, carrying, leading, or riding away of property from the possession or constructive possession of another. It includes crimes such as shoplifting, pocket-picking, purse-snatching, thefts from motor vehicles, thefts of motor vehicle parts and accessories, bicycle thefts, etc., in which no use of force, violence, or fraud occurs.

Year	TREND Number of offenses	Rate per 100,000 inhabitants
1996	7,904,685	2,979.7
1997	7,725,470	2,886.5
Percent change	–2.3	–3.1

Volume

Estimated at nearly 7.7 million offenses during 1997, larceny-theft comprised 59 percent of the Crime Index total and 67 percent of the property crimes. Continuing the pattern of recent years, larceny-thefts were recorded most often during July and least frequently in February.

The Nation's most populous region, the Southern States, recorded 40 percent of the larceny-theft total. Both the Western and Midwestern States recorded 23 percent, and the Northeastern States, 14 percent.

In 1997, the volume of larceny-thefts nationwide was 2 percent lower than the 1996 total. By community type, decreases of 3 percent were recorded both in cities collectively and suburban counties, while virtually no change was experienced in the rural counties.

All four geographic regions experienced decreases in incidents of larceny-theft from 1996 levels. The decreases were 3 percent in the West and the Northeast and 2 percent in the South and Midwest.

An examination of long-term national trends indicated larceny was down 1 percent when compared to the 1993 total. However, there was virtually no change when compared to the 1988 level.

Rate

During 1997, the larceny-theft rate was 2,887 per 100,000 inhabitants in the United States. Five- and 10-year trends show

Larceny-theft by Month, 1993–1997
[Percent distribution]

Months	1993	1994	1995	1996	1997
January	7.8	7.3	7.9	7.8	8.0
February	6.9	7.0	7.1	7.5	7.3
March	8.1	8.1	8.1	7.9	8.0
April	8.0	8.0	7.8	8.0	8.0
May	8.3	8.4	8.5	8.6	8.5
June	8.7	8.6	8.6	8.6	8.6
July	9.2	9.1	9.1	9.3	9.2
August	9.3	9.4	9.4	9.2	9.1
September	8.5	8.5	8.5	8.4	8.5
October	8.6	8.8	8.8	8.8	8.7
November	8.1	8.2	8.1	7.8	7.9
December	8.3	8.5	8.1	8.1	8.2

the rate was 5 percent below the 1996 rate and 8 percent below the 1988 rate. The 1997 rate was 3,087 per 100,000 inhabitants of metropolitan areas; 3,586 per 100,000 population in cities outside metropolitan areas; and 1,082 per 100,000 people in the rural counties.

The 1997 larceny-theft rate per 100,000 inhabitants declined across all regions of the Nation. The West recorded an 4-percent decline, the Northeast and the South each marked a 3-percent drop, and the Midwest a decrease of 2 percent. The regional rates ranged from 2,126 per 100,000 people in the Northeast to 3,259 per 100,000 population in the South.

Nature

During 1997, the average value of property stolen due to larceny-theft was $585, up from $547 in 1996. When the average value was applied to the estimated number of larceny-thefts, the loss to victims nationally was over $4.5 billion for the year. This estimated dollar loss is considered conservative since many offenses in the larceny category never come to law enforcement attention, particularly if the value of the stolen goods is small. Losses under $50 and those over $200 jointly accounted for 77 percent of the thefts reported to law enforcement. The remaining 23 percent involved losses ranging from $50 to $200.

Losses of goods and property reported stolen as a result of pocket-picking averaged $466; purse-snatching, $403; and shoplifting, $130. The average value loss due to thefts of motor vehicle accessories was $390 and for thefts of bicycles, $293. Thefts from buildings resulted in an average loss of $963; from motor vehicles, $584; and from coin-operated machines, $453.

Thefts of motor vehicle parts, accessories, and contents made up the largest portion of reported larcenies—36 percent. Also contributing to the high volume of thefts were shoplifting, accounting for 15 percent; thefts from buildings, 14 percent; and thefts of bicycles, 6 percent. The remainder was distributed among pocket-picking, purse-snatching, thefts from coin-operated machines, and all other types of larceny-thefts.

MOTOR VEHICLE THEFT

> ## DEFINITION
> Defined as the theft or attempted theft of a motor vehicle, this offense category includes the stealing of automobiles, trucks, buses, motorcycles, motorscooters, snowmobiles, etc.

Year	TREND Number of offenses	Rate per 100,000 inhabitants
1996	1,394,238	525.6
1997	1,353,707	505.8
Percent change	−2.9	−3.8

Volume

During 1997, there were nearly 1.4 million thefts of motor vehicles nationwide, marking the lowest total for that offense since 1987. The regional distribution of thefts in 1997 showed 35 percent of the volume was in the Southern States, 29 percent in the Western States, 20 percent in the Midwestern States, and 16 percent in the Northeastern States.

An examination of the monthly distribution of motor vehicle thefts reveals the highest percentage of vehicles was stolen during the month of January and the lowest percentage was stolen in February.

In the Nation as a whole, motor vehicle thefts declined 3 percent from 1996 to 1997 and 5 percent in cities. Among city population groupings, the decreases ranged from 8 percent in cities 500,000 to 999,999 in population to virtually no change in those with populations under 10,000. During the same 2-year period, a 1-percent decrease in the volume of motor vehicle thefts occurred in suburban counties, while rural counties registered a 5-percent increase.

Motor Vehicle Theft by Month, 1993–1997
[Percent distribution]

Months	1993	1994	1995	1996	1997
January	8.5	8.1	8.6	8.8	9.0
February	7.4	7.4	7.5	8.0	7.6
March	8.2	8.5	8.2	8.2	8.2
April	7.9	7.9	7.8	7.9	7.9
May	7.9	8.2	8.2	8.1	8.3
June	8.4	8.3	8.1	8.0	8.1
July	8.9	8.9	8.6	8.8	8.7
August	8.9	9.0	9.0	8.6	8.7
September	8.5	8.4	8.4	8.2	8.3
October	8.7	8.7	8.9	8.6	8.6
November	8.3	8.3	8.5	8.3	8.3
December	8.4	8.3	8.3	8.6	8.3

Geographically, decreases in motor vehicle thefts were recorded in the Northeast, with 10 percent; the South with a 3-percent decline; and the Midwest, with 1 percent. The Western states showed virtually no change. Motor vehicle thefts in 1997 declined 13 percent from the 1993 volume.

Rate

The 1997 national motor vehicle theft rate—506 per 100,000 inhabitants—was 4 percent lower than in 1996 and 17 percent below the 1993 rate. The 1997 rate was 13 percent below the 1988 rate.

For every 100,000 inhabitants living in metropolitan areas, there were 591 motor vehicle thefts reported in 1997. The rate in cities outside metropolitan areas was 234 and that in rural counties, 129. As in previous years, the highest rates were in the Nation's most heavily populated municipalities, indicating that this offense is primarily a large-city problem. For every 100,000 inhabitants in cities with populations over 250,000, the 1997 motor vehicle theft rate was 1,133. The Nation's smallest cities, those with fewer than 10,000 inhabitants, recorded a rate of 251 per 100,000.

Among all regions of the country, motor vehicle theft rates ranged from 656 per 100,000 inhabitants in the Western States to 436 in the Midwestern States. The Southern States' rate was 504, and the Northeastern States' rate was 421. All regions registered rate declines from 1996 to 1997. The Northeast reported the greatest rate decrease, 10 percent. The West and the Midwest, a decrease of 2 percent each; and the South, a decrease of 4 percent.

Motor Vehicle Theft, 1997
[Percent distribution by region]

Region	Total[1]	Autos	Trucks and buses	Other vehicles
Total	100.0	77.0	17.7	5.3
Northeastern States	100.0	91.3	4.8	3.9
Midwestern States	100.0	81.1	14.3	4.6
Southern States	100.0	74.0	19.7	6.3
Western States	100.0	71.2	23.5	5.2

[1]Because of rounding, percentages may not add to totals.

Nature

The estimated value of motor vehicles stolen nationwide in 1997 was more than $7 billion. At the time of theft, the average value per vehicle was $5,416. The recovery percentage for the value of vehicles stolen was higher than for any other property type. Relating the value of vehicles stolen to the value of those recovered resulted in a 67-percent recovery rate for 1997.

Seventy-seven percent of all motor vehicles reported stolen during the year were automobiles, 18 percent were trucks or buses, and the remainder were other types.

Abet: To encourage another to commit a crime.

Accessory: One who harbors, assists, or protects another person, although he or she knows that person has committed or will commit a crime.

Accomplice: One who knowingly and voluntarily aids another in committing a criminal offense.

Acquit: To free a person legally from an accusation of criminal guilt.

Adjudicatory hearing: The fact-finding process wherein the court determines whether or not there is sufficient evidence to sustain the allegations in a petition.

Admissible: Capable of being admitted; in a trial, such evidence as the judge allows to be introduced into the proceeding.

Affirmance: A pronouncement by a higher court that the case in question was rightly decided by the lower court from which the case was appealed.

Affirmation: Positive declaration or assertion that the witness will tell the truth; not made under oath.

Alias: Any name by which one is known other than his or her true name.

Alibi: A type of defense in a criminal prosecution that proves the accused could not have committed the crime with which he or she is charged, since evidence offered shows the accused was in another place at the time the crime was committed.

Allegation: An assertion of what a party to an action expects to prove.

American Bar Association (ABA): A professional association, comprising attorneys who have been admitted to the bar in any of the 50 states, and a registered lobby.

American Civil Liberties Union (ACLU): Founded in 1920 with the purpose of defending the individual's rights as guaranteed by the U.S. Constitution.

Amnesty: A class or group pardon.

Annulment: The act, by competent authority, of canceling, making void, or depriving of all force.

Appeal: A case carried to a higher court to ask that the decision of the lower court, in which the case originated, be altered or overruled completely.

Appellate court: A court that has jurisdiction to hear cases on appeal; not a trial court.

Arbitrator: The person chosen by parties in a controversy to settle their differences; private judges.

Arraignment: The appearance before the court of a person charged with a crime. He or she is advised of the charges, bail is set, and a plea of "guilty" or "not guilty" is entered.

Arrest: The legal detainment of a person to answer for criminal charges or civil demands.

Autopsy: A postmortem examination of a human body to determine the cause of death.

Bail: Property (usually money) deposited with a court in exchange for the release of a person in custody to ensure later appearance.

Bail bond: An obligation signed by the accused and his or her sureties that ensures his or her presence in court.

Bailiff: An officer of the court who is responsible for keeping order in the court and protecting the security of jury deliberations and court property.

Bench warrant: An order by the court for the apprehension and arrest of a defendant or other person who has failed to appear when so ordered.

Bill of Rights: The first 10 amendments to the U.S. Constitution that state certain fundamental rights and privileges that are guaranteed to the people against infringement by the government.

Biocriminology: A relatively new branch of criminology that attempts to explain criminal behavior by referring to biological factors which predispose some individuals to commit criminal acts. *See also* Criminal biology.

Blue laws: Laws in some jurisdictions prohibiting sales of merchandise, athletic contests, and the sale of alcoholic beverages on Sundays.

Booking: A law-enforcement or correctional process officially recording an entry-into-detention after arrest and identifying the person, place, time, reason for the arrest, and the arresting authority.

Breathalyzer: A commercial device to test the breath of a suspected drinker and to determine that person's blood-alcohol content.

Brief: A summary of the law relating to a case, prepared by the attorneys for both parties and given to the judge.

Bug: To plant a sound sensor or to tap a communication line for the purpose of surreptitious listening or audio monitoring.

Burden of proof: Duty of establishing the existence of fact in a trial.

Calendar: A list of cases to be heard in a trial court, on a specific day, and containing the title of the case, the lawyers involved, and the index number.

Capital crime: Any crime that may be punishable by death or imprisonment for life.

Career criminal: A person having a past record of multiple arrests or convictions for crimes of varying degrees of seriousness. Such criminals are often described as chronic, habitual, repeat, serious, high-rate, or professional offenders.

Case: At the level of police or prosecutorial investigation, a set of circumstances under investigation involving one or more persons.

Case law: Judicial precedent generated as a by-product of the decisions that courts have made to resolve unique disputes. Case law concerns concrete facts, as distinguished from statutes and constitutions, which are written in the abstract.

Change of venue: The removal of a trial from one jurisdiction to another in order to avoid local prejudice.

Charge: In criminal law, the accusation made against a person. It also refers to the judge's instruction to the jury on legal points.

Circumstantial evidence: Indirect evidence; evidence from which a fact can be reasonably inferred, although not directly proven.

Clemency: The doctrine under which executive or legislative action reduces the severity of or waives legal punishment of one or more individuals, or an individual exempted from prosecution for certain actions.

Code: A compilation, compendium, or revision of laws, arranged into chapters, having a table of contents and index, and promulgated by legislative authority. *See also* Penal code.

Coercion: The use of force to compel performance of an action; The application of sanctions or the use of force by government to compel observance of law or public policy.

Common law: Judge-made law to assist courts through decision making with traditions, customs, and usage of previous court decisions.

Commutation: A reduction of a sentence originally prescribed by a court.

Complainant: The victim of a crime who brings the facts to the attention of the authorities.

Complaint: Any accusation that a person committed a crime that has originated or been received by a law enforcement agency or court.

Confession: A statement by a person who admits violation of the law.

Confiscation: Government seizure of private property without compensation to the owner.

Conspiracy: An agreement between two or more persons to plan for the purpose of committing a crime or any unlawful act or a lawful act by unlawful or criminal means.

Contempt of court: Intentionally obstructing a court in the administration of justice, acting in a way calculated to lessen its authority or dignity, or failing to obey its lawful order.

Continuance: Postponement or adjournment of a trial granted by the judge, either to a later date or indefinitely.

Contraband: Goods, the possession of which is illegal.

Conviction: A finding by the jury (or by the trial judge in cases tried without a jury) that the accused is guilty of a crime.

Corporal punishment: Physical punishment.

Corpus delicti (Lat.): The objective proof that a crime has been committed as distinguished from an accidental death, injury, or loss.

Corrections: Area of criminal justice dealing with convicted offenders in jails, prisons, on probation, or parole.

Corroborating evidence: Supplementary evidence that tends to strengthen or confirm other evidence given previously.

Crime: An act injurious to the public, which is prohibited and punishable by law.

Crime Index: A set of numbers indicating the volume, fluctuation, and distribution of crimes reported to local law enforcement agencies for the United States as a whole.

Crime of passion: An unpremeditated murder or assault committed under circumstances of great anger, jealousy, or other emotional stress.

Criminal biology: The scientific study of the relation of hereditary physical traits to criminal character, that is, to innate tendencies to commit crime in general or crimes of any particular type. *See also* Biocriminology.

Criminal insanity: Lack of mental capacity to do or refrain from doing a criminal act; inability to distinguish right from wrong.

Criminal intent: The intent to commit and act, the results of which are a crime or violation of the law.

Criminalistics: Crime laboratory procedures.

Criminology: The scientific study of crime, criminals, corrections, and the operation of the system of criminal justice.

Cross examination: The questioning of a witness by the party who did not produce the witness.

Culpable: At fault or responsible, but not necessarily criminal.

Defamation: Intentional causing, or attempting to cause, damage to the reputation of another by communicating false or distorted information about his or her actions, motives, or character.

Defendant: The person who is being prosecuted.

Deliberation: The action of a jury to determine the guilt or innocence, or the sentence, of a defendant.

Demurrer: Plea for dismissal of a suit on the grounds that, even if true, the statements of the opposition are insufficient to sustain the claim.

Deposition: Sworn testimony obtained outside, rather than in, court.

Deterrence: A theory that swift and sure punishment will discourage others from similar illegal acts.

Dilatory: Law term that describes activity for the purpose of causing a delay or to gain time or postpone a decision.

Direct evidence: Testimony or other proof that expressly or straightforwardly proves the existence of fact.

Direct examination: The first questioning of witnesses by the party who calls them.

Directed verdict: An order or verdict pronounced by a judge during the trial of a criminal case in which the evidence presented by the prosecution clearly fails to show the guilt of the accused.

District attorney: A locally elected state official who represents the state in bringing indictments and prosecuting criminal cases.

Docket: The formal record of court proceedings.

Double jeopardy: To be prosecuted twice for the same offense.

Due process model: A philosophy of criminal justice based on the assumption that an individual is presumed innocent until proven guilty.

Due process of law: A clause in the Fifth and Fourteenth Amendments ensuring that laws are reasonable and that they are applied in a fair and equal manner.

Embracery: An attempt to influence a jury, or a member thereof, in their verdict by any improper means.

Entrapment: Inducing an individual to commit a crime he or she did not contemplate, for the sole purpose of instituting a criminal prosecution against the offender.

Evidence: All the means used to prove or disprove the fact at issue. *See also* Corpus delicti.

Ex post facto (Lat.): After the fact. An *ex post facto* law is a criminal law that makes an act unlawful although it was committed prior to the passage of that law. *See also* Grandfather clause.

Exception: A formal objection to the action of the court during a trial. The indication is that the excepting party will seek to reverse the court's actions at some future proceeding.

Exclusionary rule: Legal prohibitions against government prosecution using evidence illegally obtained.

Expert evidence: Testimony by one qualified to speak authoritatively on technical matters because of her or his special training or skill.

Extradition: The surrender by one state to another of an individual accused of a crime.

False arrest: Any unlawful physical restraint of another's freedom of movement; unlawful arrest.

Felony: A criminal offense punishable by death or imprisonment in a penitentiary.

Forensic: Relating to the court. Forensic medicine would refer to legal medicine that applies anatomy, pathology, toxicology, chemistry, and other fields of science in expert testimony in court cases or hearings.

Grand jury: A group of 12 to 23 citizens of a county who examine evidence against the person suspected of a crime and hand down an indictment if there is sufficient evidence. *See also* Petit jury.

Grandfather clause: A clause attempting to preserve the rights of firms in operation before enactment of a law by exempting these firms from certain provisions of that law. *See also* Ex post facto.

Habeas corpus (Lat.): A legal device to challenge the detention of a person taken into custody. An individual in custody may demand an evidentiary hearing before a judge to examine the legality of the detention.

Hearsay: Evidence that a witness has learned through others.

Homicide: The killing of a human being; may be murder, negligent or nonnegligent manslaughter, or excusable or justifiable homicide.

Hung jury: A jury which, after long deliberation, is so irreconcilably divided in opinion that it is unable to reach a unanimous verdict.

Impanel: The process of selecting the jury that is to try a case.

Imprisonment: A sentence imposed upon the conviction of a crime; the deprivation of liberty in a penal institution; incarceration.

In camera (Lat.): A case heard when the doors of the court are closed and only persons concerned in the case are admitted.

Indemnification: Compensation for loss or damage sustained because of improper or illegal action by a public authority.

Indictment: The document prepared by a prosecutor and approved by the grand jury that charges a certain person with a specific crime or crimes for which that person is later to be tried in court.

Injunction: An order by a court prohibiting a defendant from committing an act, or commanding an act be done.

Inquest: A legal inquiry to establish some question of fact; specifically, an inquiry by a coroner and jury into a person's death where accident, foul play, or violence is suspected as the cause.

Instanter: A subpoena issued for the appearance of a hostile witness or person who has failed to appear in answer to a previous subpoena and authorizing a law enforcement officer to bring that person to the court.

Interpol (International Criminal Police Commission): A clearing house for international exchanges of information, consisting of a consortium of 126 countries.

Jeopardy: The danger of conviction and punishment that a defendant faces in a criminal trial.

Judge: An officer who presides over and administers the law in a court of justice.

Judicial notice: The rule that a court will accept certain things as common knowledge without proof.

Judicial process: The procedures taken by a court in deciding cases or resolving legal controversies.

Jurisdiction: The territory, subject matter, or persons over which lawful authority may be exercised by a court or other justice agency, as determined by statute or constitution.

Jury: A certain number of persons who are sworn to examine the evidence and determine the truth on the basis of that evidence. *See also* Hung jury.

Justice of the peace: A subordinate magistrate, usually without formal legal training, empowered to try petty civil and criminal cases and, in some states, to conduct preliminary hearings for persons accused of a crime, and to fix bail for appearance in court.

Juvenile delinquent: A boy or girl who has not reached the age of criminal liability (varies from state to state) and who commits an act that would be a misdemeanor or felony if he or she were an adult. Delinquents are tried in Juvenile Court and confined to separate facilities.

Law Enforcement Agency: A federal, state, or local criminal justice agency or identifiable subunit whose principal functions are the prevention, detection, and investigation of crime and the apprehension of alleged offenders.

Libel and slander: Printed and spoken defamation of character, respectively, or a person or an institution. In a slander action, it is usually necessary to prove specific damages caused by spoken words, but in a case of libel, the damage is assumed to have occurred by publication.

Lie detector: An instrument that measures certain physiological reactions of the human body from which a trained operator may determine whether the subject is telling the truth or lying; polygraph; psychological stress evaluator.

Litigation: A judicial controversy; a contest in a court of justice for the purpose of enforcing a right; any controversy that must be decided upon evidence.

Mala fides (Lat.): Bad faith, as opposed to *bona fides*, or good faith.

Mala in se (Lat.): Evil in itself. Acts that are made crimes because they are, by their nature, evil and morally wrong.

Mala prohibita (Lat.): Evil because they are prohibited. Acts that are not wrong in themselves but which, to protect the general welfare, are made crimes by statute.

Malfeasance: The act of a public officer in committing a crime relating to his official duties or powers, such as accepting or demanding a bribe.

Malice: An evil intent to vex, annoy, or injure another; intentional evil.

Mandatory sentences: A statutory requirement that a certain penalty shall be set and carried out in all cases upon conviction for a specified offense or series of offenses.

Martial law: Refers to control of civilian populations by a military commander.

Mediation: Nonbinding third-party intervention in the collective bargaining process.

Mens rea (Lat.): Criminal intent.

Miranda rights: Set of rights that a person accused or suspected of having committed a specific offense has during interrogation and of which he or she must be informed prior to questioning, as stated by the Supreme Court in deciding *Miranda v. Arizona* in 1966 and related cases.

Misdemeanor: Any crime not a felony. Usually, a crime punishable by a fine or imprisonment in the county or other local jail.

Misprison: Failing to reveal a crime.

Mistrial: A trial discontinued before reaching a verdict because of some procedural defect or impediment.

Modus operandi: A characteristic pattern of behavior repeated in a series of offenses that coincides with the pattern evidenced by a particular person or group of persons.

Motion: An oral or written request made to a court at any time before, during, or after court proceedings, asking the court to make a specified finding, decision, or order.

Motive: The reason for committing a crime.

Municipal court: A minor court authorized by municipal charter or state law to enforce local ordinances and exercise the criminal and civil jurisdiction of the peace.

Narc: A widely used slang term for any local or federal law enforcement officer whose duties are focused on preventing or controlling traffic in and the use of illegal drugs.

Negligent: Culpably careless; acting without the due care required by the circumstances.

Neolombrosians: Criminologists who emphasize psychopathological states as causes of crime.

No bill: A phrase used by a grand jury when it fails to indict.

Nolle prosequi (Lat.): A prosecutor's decision not to initiate or continue prosecution.

Nolo contendre (Lat., lit.): A pleading, usually used by a defendant in a criminal case, that literally means "I will not contest."

Notary public: A public officer authorized to authenticate and certify documents such as deeds, contracts, and affidavits with his or her signature and seal.

Null: Of no legal or binding force.

Obiter dictum (Lat.): A belief or opinion included by a judge in his or her decision in a case.

Objection: The act of taking exception to some statement or procedure in a trial. Used to call the court's attention to some improper evidence or procedure.

Opinion evidence: A witness's belief or opinion about a fact in dispute, as distinguished from personal knowledge of the fact.

Ordinance: A law enacted by the city or municipal government.

Organized crime: An organized, continuing criminal conspiracy that engages in crime as a business (e.g., loan sharking, illegal gambling, prostitution, extortion, etc.).

Original jurisdiction: The authority of a court to hear and determine a lawsuit when it is initiated.

Overt act: An open or physical act done to further a plan, conspiracy, or intent, as opposed to a thought or mere intention.

Paralegals: Employees, also known as legal assistants, of law firms, who assist attorneys in the delivery of legal services.

Pardon: There are two kinds of pardons of offenses: (1) the absolute pardon, which fully restores to the individual all rights and privileges of a citizen, setting aside a conviction and penalty, and (2) the conditional pardon, which requires a condition to be met before the pardon is officially granted.

Parole: A conditional, supervised release from prison prior to expiration of sentence.

Penal code: Criminal codes, the purpose of which is to define what acts shall be punished as crimes.

Penology: The study of punishment and corrections.

Peremptory challenge: In the selection of jurors, challenges made by either side to certain jurors without assigning any reason, and which the court must allow.

Perjury: The legal offense of deliberately testifying falsely under oath about a material fact.

Perpetrator: The chief actor in the commission of a crime, that is, the person who directly commits the criminal act.

Petit jury: The ordinary jury composed of 12 persons who hear criminal cases and determines guilt or innocence of the accused. *See also* Grand jury.

Plaintiff: A person who initiates a court action.

Plea bargaining: A negotiation between the defense attorney and the prosecutor in which the defendant receives a reduced penalty in return for a plea of "guilty."

Police power: The authority to legislate for the protection of the health, morals, safety, and welfare of the people.

Postmortem: After death. Commonly applied to an examination of a dead body. *See also* Autopsy.

Precedent: Decision by a court that may serve as an example or authority for similar cases in the future.

Preliminary hearing: The proceeding in front of a lower court to determine if there is sufficient evidence for submitting a felony case to the grand jury.

Premeditation: A design to commit a crime or commit some other act before it is done.

Presumption of fact: An inference as to the truth or falsity of any proposition or fact, made in the absence of actual certainty of its truth or falsity or until such certainty can be attained.

Presumption of innocence: The defendant is presumed to be innocent and the burden is on the state to prove his or her guilt beyond a reasonable doubt.

Presumption of law: A rule of law that courts and judges must draw a particular inference from a particular fact or evidence, unless the inference can be disproved.

Probable cause: A set of facts and circumstances that would induce a reasonably intelligent and prudent person to believe that a particular person had committed a specific crime; reasonable grounds to make or believe an accusation.

Probation: A penalty placing a convicted person under the supervision of a probation officer for a stated time, instead of being confined.

Prosecutor: One who initiates a criminal prosecution against an accused. One who acts as a trial attorney for the government as the representative of the people.

Public defender: An attorney appointed by a court to represent individuals in criminal proceedings who do not have the resources to hire their own defense council.

Rap sheet: Popularized acronym for record of arrest and prosecution.

Reasonable doubt: That state of mind of jurors when they do not feel a moral certainty about the truth of the charge and when the evidence does not exclude every other reasonable hypothesis except that the defendant is guilty as charged.

Rebutting evidence: When the defense has produced new evidence that the prosecution has not dealt with, the court, at its discretion, may allow the prosecution to give evidence in reply to rebut or contradict it.

Recidivism: The repetition of criminal behavior.

Repeal: The abrogation of a law by the enacting body, either by express declaration or implication by the passage of a later act whose provisions contradict those of the earlier law.

Reprieve: The temporary postponement of the execution of a sentence.

Restitution: A court requirement that an alleged or convicted offender pay money or provide services to the victim of the crime or provide services to the community.

Restraining order: An order, issued by a court of competent jurisdiction, forbidding a named person, or a class of persons, from doing specified acts.

Retribution: A concept that implies that payment of a debt to society and thus the expiation of one's offense. It was codified in the biblical injunction, "an eye for an eye, a tooth for a tooth."

Sanction: A legal penalty assessed for the violation of law. The term also includes social methods of obtaining compliance, such as peer pressure and public opinion.

Search warrant: A written order, issued by judicial authority in the name of the state, directing a law enforcement officer to search for personal property and, if found, to bring it before the court.

Selective enforcement: The deploying of police personnel in ways to cope most effectively with existing or anticipated problems.

Self-incrimination: In constitutional terms, the process of becoming involved in or charged with a crime by one's own testimony.

Sentence: The penalty imposed by a court on a person convicted of a crime, the court judgment specifying the penalty, and any disposition of a defendant resulting from a conviction, including the court decision to suspend execution of a sentence.

Small claims court: A special court that provides expeditious, informal, and inexpensive adjudication of small contractual claims. In most jurisdictions, attorneys are not permitted for cases, and claims are limited to a specific amount.

Stare decisis (Lat.): To abide by decided cases. The doctrine that once a court has laid down a principle of laws as applicable to certain facts, it will apply it to all future cases when the facts are substantially the same.

State's attorney: An officer, usually locally elected within a county, who represents the state in securing indictments and in prosecuting criminal cases.

State's evidence: Testimony by a participant in the commission of a crime that incriminates others involved, given under the promise of immunity.

Status offense: An act that is declared by statute to be an offense, but only when committed or engaged in by a juvenile, and that can be adjudicated only by a juvenile court.

Statute: A law enacted by, or with the authority of, a legislature.

Statute of limitations: A term applied to numerous statutes that set limits on the length of time after which rights cannot be enforced in a legal action or offenses cannot be punished.

Stay: A halting of a judicial proceeding by a court order.

Sting operation: The typical sting involves using various undercover methods to control crime.

Subpoena: A court order requiring a witness to attend and testify as a witness in a court proceeding.

Subpoena *duces tecum*: A court order requiring a witness to bring all books, documents, and papers that might affect the outcome of the proceedings.

Summons: A written order issued by a judicial officer requiring a person accused of a criminal offense to appear in a designated court at a specified time to answer the charge(s).

Superior court: A court of record or general trial court, superior to a justice of the peace or magistrate's court. In some states, an intermediate court between the general trial court and the highest appellate court.

Supreme court, state: Usually the highest court in the state judicial system.

Supreme Court, U.S.: Heads the judicial branch of the American government and is the nation's highest law court.

Suspect: An adult or juvenile considered by a criminal agency to be one who may have committed a specific criminal offense but who has not yet been arrested or charged.

Testimony: Evidence given by a competent witness, under oath, as distinguished from evidence from writings and other sources.

Tort: A breach of a duty to an individual that results in damage to him or her, for which one may be sued in civil court for damages. Crime, in contrast, may be called a breach of duty to the public. Some actions may constitute both torts and crimes.

Uniform Crime Reports (U.C.R.): Annual statistical tabulation of "crimes known to the police" and "crimes cleared by arrest," published by the Federal Bureau of Investigation.

United States Claims Court: Established in 1982, it serves as the court of original and exclusive jurisdiction over claims brought against the federal government, except for tort claims, which are heard by district courts.

United States district courts: Trial courts with original jurisdiction over diversity-of-citizenship cases and cases arising under U.S. criminal, bankruptcy, admiralty, patent, copyright, and postal laws.

Venue: The locality in which a suit may be tried.

Verdict: The decision of a court.

Vice squad: A special detail of police agents, charged with raiding and closing houses of prostitution and gambling resorts.

Victim and Witness Protection Act of 1984: The federal VWP Act and state laws protect crime victims and witnesses against physical and verbal intimidation where such intimidation is designed to discourage reporting of crimes and participation in criminal trials.

Victimology: The study of the psychological and dynamic interrelationships between victims and offenders, with a view toward crime prevention.

Vigilante: An individual or member of a group who undertakes to enforce the law and/or maintain morals without legal authority.

Voir dire (Fr.): The examination or questioning of prospective jurors in order to determine his or her qualifications to serve as a juror.

Warrant: A court order directing a police officer to arrest a named person or search a specific premise.

White-collar crime: Nonviolent crime for financial gain committed by means of deception by persons who use their special occupational skills and opportunities.

Witness: Anyone called to testify by either side in a trial. More broadly, a witness is anyone who has observed an event.

Work release (furlough programs): Change in prisoners' status to minimum custody with permission to work outside prison.

World Court: Formally known as the International Court of Justice, it deals with disputes involving international law.

SOURCES

The Dictionary of Criminal Justice, Fourth Edition, © 1994 by George E. Rush. Published by Dushkin/McGraw-Hill, Guilford, CT 06437.

A

accountability, 117, 122–123, 126
actus reus, 129
Addams, Jane, 143
adversarial nature, of trial system, 96–103
affluence, 188
African Americans. *See* blacks
"AFTERBURN" training program, 79–81
Aid to Families with Dependent Children (AFDC), 22
Alcoholics Anonymous, 45
American Probation and Parole Association (APPA), 162
appeals, 110, 111
Aragon, Randall, interview with, 84–93
Arnold, Thurman, 96
attachment disorder, stalking and, 48
attorney statements, 99
attorneys, 96–103
Augustus, John, 161
Australia, 121

B

balanced and restorative justice (BRJ), 121, 122–128
Baltimore, Maryland, 24, 144
Batson v. Kentucky, 105
battered-person syndrome, 117
battered-woman syndrome, 116–117
battering. *See* domestic violence
Bazelton, David, 113
Bedford Hills Correctional Facility, 181–185
Bentham, Jeremy, 176
bilingual officers, 75
Bill of Rights, 110
Billy the Kid, 134–135
black(s), 187; in criminal justice system, 22–30; influence of slavery on homicide rate in South and, 35; substance abuse and delinquency in, males, 151, 152
bonding, 126
Bonney, William, 135
Boston, Massachusetts, 139
Brady, Sarah, 133–134
Brady Law, 133–134
Braithewaite, John, 121, 125
Bratton, William J., 133
"broken window" theory, 19, 21, 133
Brown, Raymond Maxwell, 134
Brownstein, Henry, 133, 134
Burton, Arthur Lee, 205, 206, 207

C

California, 140
Campaign To Prevent Handgun Violence Against Kids, 140
capital punishment. *See* death penalty
car chases, police brutality and, 69–70
central research and development model, 19

Certified Peer Advocate Program (CPAP), domestic abuse programs and, 73
cheating, 31–32
Cheney, Lynne, V., 32
Chicago, Illinois, 142, 143, 144
Child Development-Community Policing (CD-CP), 140
Chisholm, G. Brock, 113
citizen patrols, 77
citizen police academies, 76–77
citizen reparative boards, 202–203
Cleveland, Ohio, 26
coaching, of witnesses, 99
"cobras," domestic abusers as, 50–52
cocaine, crack, 145
Cochran, Johnnie, 97, 100
code of Hammurabi, 193
community justice system, for youthful offenders, 121–128
Community Mental Health Centers Act, 113
community policing, 75, 77, 133, 140, 202; marketing of, 82–83; in Whiteville, North Carolina, 84–93
community supervision, probation and parole and, 167–168
competency development, in balanced approach model, 122, 123, 126, 127
Concord, Massachusetts, domestic abuse program in, 71–74
Constitution, U.S., 101, 110, 117
continuous process improvement, TQM and, 85
corpus delecti, 129
Council for Court excellence, jury system and, 104–107
counselors, police as, 77
crack cocaine, 145
Crime and Human Nature (Herrnstein and Wilson), 29
crime rate, prison population and, 186
Critical Incident Stress Management (CISM), police families and, 81
cultural diversity training, for police officers, 76
curfews, 123, 145

D

Dakota County, Minnesota, 202, 203
Daley, Richard M., 145
date rape, 42
D. C. Jury Project, 104–107
death penalty: in Harris County, Texas, 205–207; racial discrimination in, 187–191
defense counsel, 142
delinquency, 144, 145
depositions, as aggressive weapon, in trial system, 97
depression, as learned helplessness, 116
deviants, 44, 46
Diagnostic and Statistical Manual for Mental Disorders (DSM) (American Psychiatric Association), 114

discovery tactics, 97
"dismissing" stalkers, 49
Disraeli, Benjamin, 96
disrespect, as catalyst for police brutality, 66–70
diversity, in police departments, 75–78
domestic violence, 40, 116–117; personality traits of men in, 50–52; program to prevent, 71–74
Domestic Violence Training and Resource Institute (DVTRI), 72–74
Dominguez, Edward, 69–70
double jeopardy, 110, 111
drug abuse. *See* substance abuse
Drug and Alcohol Resistance Education (D.A.R.E.), 75
drug use, sensor patch for, during parole, 93
drugs, psychiatry and, 114
dual sovereignty doctrine, 110
Durham v. United States, 113

E

education, as crime prevention, 169–174
empathy, loss of, in U.S., 32
empowerment, 85
equal protection clause, of Constitution, 120
ethics, in probation practice, 175–180
expert witnesses, 115–117

F

faith, loss of, in U.S., 33
family: loss of, in U.S., 32–33; restorative justice and, 201
"fearful" stalkers, 49
felonies, 175
feminism, 42, 44
Fernandez, Vincente, 69–70
fight theory, of trial system, 96, 97
Florida, 121, 124
force, use of deadly, 111, 117; criminal justice and, 177; ethical use of, 175
Frankel, Marvin, 96
fronting, 28
Fuchs, Ester, 19
Fukuyama, Francis, 32
Fulcrum, Robert, 125, 126
Fully Informed Jury Associations, 111
Future of Peremptory Challenges, The (Munsterman), 105

G

grand juries, 9
Great Britain, prisons in, 210
Greene, Graham, 29–30
gun control, 133–134
guns, juveniles and, 136–141
Georgia, 188, 190
Giuliani, Rudy, 133
Gottman, John, 50, 52

H

Harris, Taquana, 66
Harris County, Texas, death penalty in, 205–207
Hawaii Healthy Start, 59, 61–62
Head Start, 57, 58
hearsay, 103; rule of, 102
Herrnstein, Richard, 29, 150
Higher Education Act, Title IV of, 170
Hoffman, Morris, 105–106
Holmes, John B., Jr., 206, 207
home visitation programs, 55, 56–57
homicide rate, 33; U.S., and South, 34–37
honor, homicide rate in South and, 35, 37
Hyde, Samuel, Jr., 35, 37

I

incapacitation, 123
incarceration. *See* prisons
independence, loss of, in U.S., 32
informing, 27–28
insanity defenses, psychiatric testimony and, 112–114
intensive supervision probation (ISP) programs, 163
intergenerational crime, 28–29
intergenerational projects, for youthful offenders, 126
International Association of Chiefs of Police (IACP), 149
interventions, 55–58; adverse effects of, 29; by criminal justice system, 121; therapeutic, 53
"irresistible impulse" rule, 113

J

Jackson, Andrew, 35
Jacksonville, Florida, 24
Jacobson, Neil, 50, 51–52
Japan, prisons in, 210–211
judges, 98, 103, 142, 145; trial system and, 102
judicial instructions, 102, 110, 111
juries, 98–103, 111, 117, 190; African American, 109; unaccountability of, 111
jury consultants, 103
jury nullification, 108–111, 117
jury system, reform of, 104–107
juvenile courts, 120–128, 142–146; founding of, 142; origins of, in social welfare, 146; paternalism of, 129–130, 143; Riverhead Youth Court and, 147–148
juvenile offenders, 132–135; adult courts and, 129–131; education and, 169; guns and, 136–141; substance abuse and, 149–154; volunteer advocates and, 155–157
juvenile justice system, 12, 120–128, 142–146, 147–148

K

Kansas City (Missouri) Gun Experiment, 138
Kansas, prisons in, 210
Kant, Immanuel, 176
Kelling, George, 19
Kienlen, Kristine K., 48–49
King, Rodney, 103, 109, 110

L

Law Enforcement Explorer Program, 76, 77
leadership, 77–78
learned helplessness, 116
Levine, Daniel R., 31–32
Los Angeles, California, 23, 98
Los Angeles survey of jurors, 98, 99, 101
Louisiana, homicide rate in, 35, 37
Louisville, Kentucky, 144
lynching, 35

M

Maori, 201
marketing, of community policing, 82–83
Marshall, Thurgood, 105
Mead, George Herbert, 26, 29
media, 44–45
mediation, victim-offender, 126, 127, 201–202
memories, repression of, 42
mens rea, 129
mentoring: of juvenile offenders, 155–157; police officers and, 77; youth crime and substance abuse prevention and, 153
Mill, John Stuart, 176
ministering, youth crime and substance abuse prevention and, 153
monitoring, youth crime and substance abuse prevention and, 153
moral literacy, loss of, in U.S., 31–32
moral relativism, 20–21
Moral Sense, The (Wilson), 20–21
morality, state of, in U.S., 31–33
motherhood, women prisoners and, 182–183
Mugford, Stephen, 121, 125
multilingual officers, 97
Munsterman, G. Thomas, 105
murder rate. *See* homicide rate

N

National Association for the Advancement of Colored People (NAACP), 26–27, 190
National Institute of Alcohol Abuse and Alcoholism, 152
National Institute of Justice (NIJ), 138, 139, 140, 152
Native Americans, 201
Netherlands, prisons in, 210

New Haven, Connecticut, 140
New Orleans, Louisiana, 144
New York City, New York, 133; police brutality in, 66–70
New Zealand, 121, 123, 125, 201
Newton, Massachusetts, domestic abuse program in, 71–74
Nisbett, Richard, 35
"no duty to retreat," 134
"no-frills" prisons, 210
nolo contendere, 9
note taking, on juries, 101
nullification, jury, 108–111, 117
nurseries, for women prisoners, 182–183

O

Oakland, California, 144
offender obligation, 198
Office of Juvenile Justice and Delinquency Prevention (OJJDP), 138, 139, 140
Oklahoma, prisons in, 210
Oregon, 122
overcharging, of defendants, 23, 27

P

parens patriae, 129–130
parenting, juvenile crime and, 150
parole supervision, 166–168; sensor patch for drug use and, 93
participative management, TQM and, 85
Partners Against Crime (PAC) program, 155–157
Partnership To Reduce Juvenile Gun Violence, 139
patch, sensor, for parolees' drug use, 93
Pell Grants, education of prisoners and, 170, 172, 173
peremptory challenges, 98, 103; jury reform and, 105–106
Peremptory Challenges Should Be Abolished: A Trial Judge's Perspective (Hoffman), 105–106
Perry preschool project, 55, 57, 58
"pit bulls," domestic abusers as, 50–52
Pittsburgh, Pennsylvania, 121
plea bargaining, 23, 145
police academies, citizen, 76, 77
Police Athletic Leagues, 76, 77
police brutality, disrespect as catalyst for, 66–70
police cadet programs, 77
police families, stress and, 79–81
"political correctness," loss of values in U.S. and, 31
post-traumatic stress disorder (PTSD), police families and, 80–81
poverty, 116, 144, 188
prejudice, 110, 115, 176–177. *See also* racial discrimination
"preoccupied" stalkers, 49
President's Commission on Law Enforcement and Administration of Justice, looking back at, 14–18
pretrial-release decisions, 9

"primal honor," homicide rate in South and, 35
prison labor, 210–211
prison population, crime rate and, 186
prisons, 145; state of, in U.S., 208–211; for women, 181–185
probation, 10, 142, 145, 160–165, 166–168, 175–180
probation officers, 145, 160, 161–162, 175–180
"professional ex's," 44, 45, 46
prosecutors, 8–9, 102, 109, 110, 111, 142, 145, 190
psychiatric testimony, 112–114
public defenders, death penalty and, 206
public safety, 121, 122, 123, 126, 127
punishment, 121, 123

R

racial discrimination: in criminal justice system, 23–27; death penalty and, 187–191, 207; peremptory challenges and, 105–106
rape, date, 42
recidivism, 12, 126, 143; education and, 170–171; probation and, 161–162, 163
reciprocal discovery, in California, 97
recovery movement, 45
recruitment, of officers, 75
recruits, training of, 76
Rees, J. R., 113
rehabilitation, 142, 143, 178, 192–204
reintegration, 198
"resilient youth," 152
restitution, 10–11, 125, 126
restorative justice, 122–128, 192–204
"right-wrong" test, 113
risks of litigation, 109
ritual abuse, victims of, 40
Riverhead Youth Court, 147–148
role models, police as, 77

S

Sageman, Marc, 112
San Jose, California, 144
Sanctions, 9–11, 121, 122
Satanic ritual abuse, victims of, 40, 42, 43, 44, 45
self-defense, 111, 117

self-esteem: improved, 77; low, 116
self-help movement, 45
sensor patch, for parolees' drug use, 93
sentencing, 9–11
sexual abuse, 40, 42–43, 44
sexual harassment, 40, 43
Shapiro, Robert, 100
Simpson, O. J., trial of, 96, 97–98, 99, 100, 101, 109, 187
"situational crime prevention," 17
slavery, homicide rate in South and, 35
Snyder, Douglas, 68
social control, 46
social justice, criminal justice and, 14, 15, 17, 18
social order, 46, 175
South, homicide rate in, 34–37
special units, police, 75
Sperlich, Peter, 100
spousal abuse. See domestic violence
stalkers, 47–49
Stransky, Erwin, 113
Stuart, Barry, 121
substance abuse, 41; juvenile crime and, 149–154; probation and, 163
substations, police, 76
Supreme Court, U.S., 40, 96, 110, 111
Symbols of Government, The (Arnold), 96

T

"talking out" process, 201
teams, TQM and, 85, 86
"temporary insanity" plea, 113
theatrical performances, trials as, 99–100
"three strikes and you're out," 146
Tong, Nancy, 67–68
total quality management (TQM) movement, 125; community policing and, 85, 86, 92
trial by jury. See juries
trial system, 96–103; reform of, 102, 103
truancy, 143
trust, loss of, in U.S., 32
truth from fight assumption, of trial system, 96
truth, loss of, in U.S., 31
"Twinkie" defense, 112

U

UFO abductions, 40, 42, 43, 45
UNICOR, 211
Uniform Crime Reports (UCR), 23
utilitarianism, 176, 177

V

values, loss of, in U.S., 31
Vermont, 202–203
victim impact statements, 40
victim industry, 40–46
victimization, 40–46; ideology of, 40, 41–43, 44, 45, 46; interventions in child, 53–63; medicalization of, 44; psychological consequences of, 41
victimizers, 41–42, 44, 45, 46
victims' rights, 40, 41, 43–44, 122
Violent Crime Control and Law Enforcement Act of 1994, 172
virtue, 176
voir dire, 98
volunteer advocates, juvenile offenders and, 155–157

W

Washington, D. C., jury system in, 104–107
welfare reform, 29
Werner, Emmy, 152
Wesbrook, Coy Wayne, 205, 206, 207
Whiteville, North Carolina, community policing in, 84–93
Wilson, James Q., 19–21, 29, 150
witchhunts, 45–46
witness abuse, by attorneys, 99
"Wizard's hat" amendment, 112
Wolfgang, Marvin E., 150
women, in prisons, 181–185

Y

youth court, in Riverhead, New York, 147–48
youth programs, 76, 77
Youthful Offender Pre-Trial Intervention Program, 199

AE Article Review Form

We encourage you to photocopy and use this page as a tool to assess how the articles in **Annual Editions** expand on the information in your textbook. By reflecting on the articles you will gain enhanced text information. You can also access this useful form on a product's book support Web site at **http://www.dushkin.com/online/.**

NAME: _____ DATE: _____

TITLE AND NUMBER OF ARTICLE: _____

BRIEFLY STATE THE MAIN IDEA OF THIS ARTICLE: _____

LIST THREE IMPORTANT FACTS THAT THE AUTHOR USES TO SUPPORT THE MAIN IDEA:

_____

WHAT INFORMATION OR IDEAS DISCUSSED IN THIS ARTICLE ARE ALSO DISCUSSED IN YOUR TEXTBOOK OR OTHER READINGS THAT YOU HAVE DONE? LIST THE TEXTBOOK CHAPTERS AND PAGE NUMBERS:

_____

LIST ANY EXAMPLES OF BIAS OR FAULTY REASONING THAT YOU FOUND IN THE ARTICLE:

_____

LIST ANY NEW TERMS/CONCEPTS THAT WERE DISCUSSED IN THE ARTICLE, AND WRITE A SHORT DEFINITION:

_____

ANNUAL EDITIONS revisions depend on two major opinion sources: one is our Advisory Board, listed in the front of this volume, which works with us in scanning the thousands of articles published in the public press each year; the other is you—the person actually using the book. Please help us and the users of the next edition by completing the prepaid article rating form on this page and returning it to us. Thank you for your help!

ANNUAL EDITIONS: Criminal Justice 99/00

ARTICLE RATING FORM

Here is an opportunity for you to have direct input into the next revision of this volume. We would like you to rate each of the 39 articles listed below, using the following scale:

1. Excellent: should definitely be retained
2. Above average: should probably be retained
3. Below average: should probably be deleted
4. Poor: should definitely be deleted

Your ratings will play a vital part in the next revision.
So please mail this prepaid form to us just as soon as you complete it.
Thanks for your help!

RATING

ARTICLE

1. What Is the Sequence of Events in the Criminal Justice System?
2. Looking Backward to Look Forward: The 1967 Crime Commission Report in Retrospect
3. A Thinker Attuned to Doing: James Q. Wilson Has Insights, Like Those on Cutting Crime, That Tend to Prove Out
4. African American Males in the Criminal Justice System
5. Is the U.S. Morally in Trouble?
6. Why America's Murder Rate Is So High
7. Victimization and the Victim Industry
8. Researchers Unravel the Motives of Stalkers
9. Battered Women Face Pit Bulls and Cobras
10. Child Victims: In Search of Opportunities for Breaking the Cycle of Violence
11. Disrespect as Catalyst for Brutality
12. Advocacy and Law Enforcement: Partners against Domestic Violence
13. Incorporating Diversity: Police Response to Multicultural Changes in Their Communities
14. Afterburn: The Victimization of Police Families
15. Marketing Community Policing: What Can We Expect?
16. A LEN Interview with Police Chief Randall Aragon of Whiteville, N.C.
17. Adversarial Justice
18. How to Improve the Jury System
19. Jury Nullification: A Perversion of Justice?
20. Confronting the Breakdown of Law and Order

RATING

ARTICLE

21. A Little Learning
22. Restoring the Balance: Juvenile and Community Justice
23. Juvenile Offenders: Should They Be Tried in Adult Courts?
24. A Decline in Crime?
25. Kids and Guns: From Playgrounds to Battlegrounds
26. With Juvenile Courts in Chaos, Critics Propose Their Demise
27. Now, Justice Is Served by Youths, for Youths
28. Preventing Crime, Saving Children: Sticking to the Basics
29. Pairing Juvenile Offenders with Volunteer Advocates
30. Probation in the United States: Practices and Challenges
31. Probation and Parole Supervision: Time for a New Narrative
32. Education as Crime Prevention: Providing Education to Prisoners
33. Ethical Considerations in Probation Practice
34. The Other Women of Bedford Hills
35. Prison Population Growing although Crime Rate Drops
36. The Color of Justice
37. Restorative Justice and Offender Rehabilitation: A Meeting of the Minds
38. Death County
39. U.S. Prisons: Gulags or Country Clubs?

(Continued on next page)

We Want Your Advice

ANNUAL EDITIONS: CRIMINAL JUSTICE 99/00

BUSINESS REPLY MAIL
FIRST-CLASS MAIL PERMIT NO. 84 GUILFORD CT

POSTAGE WILL BE PAID BY ADDRESSEE

**Dushkin/McGraw-Hill
Sluice Dock
Guilford, CT 06437-9989**

ABOUT YOU

Name

Date

Are you a teacher? ☐ A student? ☐

Your school's name

Department

Address

City

State

Zip

School telephone #

YOUR COMMENTS ARE IMPORTANT TO US !

Please fill in the following information:
For which course did you use this book?

Did you use a text with this *ANNUAL EDITION*? ☐ yes ☐ no
What was the title of the text?

What are your general reactions to the *Annual Editions* concept?

Have you read any particular articles recently that you think should be included in the next edition?

Are there any articles you feel should be replaced in the next edition? Why?

Are there any World Wide Web sites you feel should be included in the next edition? Please annotate.

May we contact you for editorial input? ☐ yes ☐ no
May we quote your comments? ☐ yes ☐ no